Documents of International Organisations: a Bibliographic Handbook

covering the United Nations
and other
intergovernmental
organisations

Compiled and Edited by
TH. D. DIMITROV
CHIEF, PROCESSING SECTION
UNITED NATIONS LIBRARY
GENEVA

LONDON : 1973
INTERNATIONAL UNIVERSITY PUBLICATIONS
CHICAGO : 1973
AMERICAN LIBRARY ASSOCIATION

International University Publications Limited

EDUCATION · LEARNING · INFORMATION · KNOWLEDGE

Management House, Parker Street, London WC2B 5PT, England

Publisher: Martin J. McManus

ISBN 0 7040 0560 3

PUBLISHED SIMULTANEOUSLY IN THE UNITED STATES OF AMERICA BY

The American Library Association

50 East Huron Street, Chicago, Illinois 60611

ISBN 0 8389 0159 X

PRINTED AND BOUND IN GREAT BRITAIN AT
THE UNIVERSITY PRESS, GLASGOW,
BY ROBERT MACLEHOSE AND COMPANY LIMITED

TABLE OF CONTENTS

TABLE DES MATIERES

TABLA DE MATERIAS

СОДЕРЖАНИЕ

目次

PREFACE

THIS WORK is offered as a guide and a source of reference to international documentation. It developed from a working paper by the author presented to the International Symposium on the Documentation of the United Nations and other Intergovernmental Organisations which was convened in Geneva in August 1972.

I am indebted to the UN, the specialised agencies, and many other organisations for their invaluable co-operation. I also wish to express my gratitude to the numerous persons who were kind enough to advise and encourage me in preparing this work.

The future holds promise of supplementary material, and I would be pleased to receive any suggestions readers may have in this respect. Meanwhile, I sincerely trust that the book, in its present form, will prove of value.

THEODORE D. DIMITROV

INTRODUCTION

THE INTERNATIONAL INSTITUTE OF BIBLIOGRAPHY, founded at Brussels in 1895, was the first body to use the term "international documentation". The first international organisations, of course, appeared much earlier, particularly after the Congress of Vienna of 1815 (cf *Union of International Associations: Past, Present and Future*). Between 1815 and 1849 six international organisations were established and fourteen international congresses held. From 1850 to 1869 twenty-nine international organisations were created and there were twenty-two international congresses. By 1904 there were more than one hundred international congresses a year. In 1914 the number of international organisations had reached 500. At present there are more than 4,000, of which ten per cent are inter-governmental and over 5,000 international congresses are now held every year.

Historically, international documentation has been shaped by each new international organisation and linked to its new institutional structure. The documentation appeared as a distinct phenomenon after the First World War with the creation of the League of Nations, and has now become an enormous and highly complicated working tool of the United Nations, its specialised agencies and all other intergovernmental and non-govern-mental organisations. Today, in order to serve the constantly growing system of inter-national organisations, international documentation has proliferated at a staggering rate and has now reached figures of immense proportions. A glimpse into the future can be unnerving: It is forecast that by the year 2,000 there will be 13,000 international organisations and no less than 30,000 international congresses will be held annually.

International Documentation: Organisation & Management

The words "volume" and "value" are most often used to describe all the problems of organisation and management of international documents. The production of the documentation statistics are a clear indication of the volume and its critical proportions. The value question is not as easily defined and, indeed, is yet to be finally assessed. Those who have attempted to deal with this question have met difficulties in devising the necessary criteria and methodology. The two methods that have been applied (partial enquiries into the value of certain international documents and citation surveys) have their obvious limitations.

There were some results from an enquiry carried out among holders of large collections of United Nations documents made by the Joint Inspection Unit in 1971. 1,400 recipients of United Nations periodical publications and 75 subscribers expressed their views on the value of 84 of these. Citation surveys involve the counting of all bibliographical references to United Nations documents made in one or several documentary publications. The references are available by classifying them by subject, by main language, by form of the publications in which they appear, or by date. When applied to the subject of statistics, the citation survey method does, indeed, support the assertion that authors of govern-mental statistical publications cannot avoid referring to United Nations documents. The technical limitations of these methods require that the results gained must be evaluated within the confines of the individual inquiry and cannot really be used for comparative purposes.

Administrative approach. The problem of volume and cost is regularly characteristic of the administrative approach to international documents by the responsible bodies. The problem of their value is sometimes studied with inadequately defined criteria and usually on the assumption that there is a contradiction or conflict between their value and their volume. The same point is reflected in the difficulties met by delegations using this documentation who feel that its volume is excessive and thereby detracts from its value and usefulness. This is the thinking behind the General Assembly's attempt to define a policy for the control and limitation of documentation set forth in document A/INF/124 of March 1968, which emphasises (a) its high cost, (b) the difficulty which many governments find in studying and assimilating its information so as to prepare themselves to take part usefully in discussions at meetings, and (c) the Secretariat's inability to supply documents punctually in the necessary translations. This administrative analysis has resulted in useful directives concerning summary records of meetings, reports of meetings and annexes, and the difficulties raised by the documentation directly relevant to the life of the Organisation itself.

Library management approach. The library management approach is particularly interesting because it differs from the administrative approach to the value problem. The library is primarily concerned with the material's organisation, its acquisition, and the indexing, classification and reference work which make it usable. This approach, notwithstanding the difficulties of organisation caused by the excessive volume of documents, largely ignores the volume-value difficulty. Admittedly international and national libraries and documentation centres judge the value of documentation by different standards. If the library makes any value judgement, it is based more on documentation resulting from scientific research conducted by the organisations than on that resulting from meetings and conferences.

International documents, with the exception of working documents for the exclusive use of delegates, circulate mainly (90 per cent) among four groups of libraries: international, national, parliamentary, and research.

The responsibility to organise the use of international documentation has been one of the primary tasks of the international libraries. But there is no doubt that duplication of organisational effort, a general problem for all other publications as well, takes place for international documents. The many difficulties through which all libraries and documentation centres in the world passed during the last decade, has also seriously affected international libraries. As a result, existing catalogues and indexes, produced on an international level, are not sufficiently oriented to meet national information needs. In addition there has been no evaluation of those resolutions and recommendations passed since 1948, when the problem appeared with all its complications.

In any event implementation of such resolutions was accepted only in theory.

Duplication of effort could be diminished if a plan for organising this material were to be developed at the editorial level by the organisations. Brief mention should be made here of the present trend to formulate, within the international organisations, a scientific and technical information policy which has become an integral part of their general policy and that of their various organs. In recent years this information policy has taken definite shape: for example, in the establishment of the UNISIST (World Science Information System) by UNESCO, of ISIS (Integrated Set of Information Systems) by the International Labour Office, of CAIP (Computer Assisted Indexing Programme) by the Dag Hammarskjöld Library, New York, of INIS (International Nuclear Information System), by the IAEA, of the AGRIS (International Information System for the Agricultural Sciences and Technology), by FAO, Rome, of INDIS (Industrial Information System), by UNIDO, Vienna, of CLADES (Latin American Centre for Economic and Social Documentation), by ECLA, Santiago de Chile, etc.

These activities should not preclude librarians from contributing other ideas in the process of making the material available for use in their particular library to meet the needs of the users of that library. In this perspective, the librarian can choose between two alternative solutions depending on his purpose:

1. If the library intends to create a specialised collection of international publications, then a special procedure of specific treatment of the material is necessary.

2. If the library intends to integrate the international publications and major documents into the rest of its collections, the cataloguer should submit the material to the general treatment and to the principles governing the descriptive and subject cataloguing and the classification system established in this given library.

In the case of depository libraries, and parliamentary and research libraries, the international study centres, information centres of the United Nations, economic commissions, the specialised agencies, the non-governmental organisations and lastly those libraries and institutions having special arrangements for obtaining a complete series of international publications and documents, we can suppose that all these bodies which receive a complete distribution would be inclined to accept the first alternative, i.e. to create a special collection which involves organisational work.

The research approach: the experience of the Geneva Symposium. Lastly, there is the research approach to international documentation. The decision to convene the International Symposium on Documentation of the United Nations and other Intergovernmental Organisations in 1972 in Geneva, which was supported by the most competent institutions (Association of International Libraries, International Federation for Documentation, International Federation of Library Associations, and the United Nations Institute for Training and Research), inaugurated a major effort in this approach to international documentation.

It was noted that international organisations do not have consistent and/or effective information policies and systems. Co-ordination of existing systems and instruments of policy is a primary task to avoid overlapping in research and documentation. The many methods and techniques now being used emphasise the need to harmonise existing information systems. Recommendations were addressed to governments to seek their assistance and support in the formulation of a suitable information policy.

Measures that need to be taken to improve existing distribution systems ensuring the availability of documents in time, languages, and other factors were also discussed. As the content of documentation is closely linked to the destination of the documents, an attempt was made to establish a documentation typology and to consider the de-classification of confidential documents from the researcher's point of view. Another aspect of distribution is the study of the recipients, especially the conditions of use in societies with different political systems.

The creation of regional collections of international documents to act as clearing centres to ensure efficient use was also considered. The existing network of depository libraries should be radically rationalised at the national level with the co-operation and involving the responsibility of governmental authorities.

The awareness of the availability of documentation, the structure and operation of libraries and other centres for the accumulation and storage of the material were given particular attention. In order to facilitate processing work, it was recommended to adopt an authority list of intergovernmental corporate authors which will help in the establishment of authorship. The adoption of the international standard bibliographic description for international documents was also recommended. The International Standard Book Numbering, through Group 92, has been applied since the autumn of 1972 by a few intergovernmental organisations under the auspices of UNESCO.

In addition, each organisation remains free to maintain its existing symbol and sales numbering.

The Symposium was also concerned with the question of the volume of documents produced and whether this could be affected by improvement of their quality and use. All the organisations are reviewing their technical means of disseminating information in order to measure the productivity of information in terms of its social cost. The use of international documentation as an element of international life is now the subject of studies on the impact of international information on social change and on political and economic decisions.

The Symposium report contains 64 recommendations on international documents. On the national level there are a number of proposals to encourage national action on the Geneva recommendations. As a result of several suggestions, the International Documents Task Force of the American Library Associations Government Documents Round Table has extended a proposal to hold a national workshop/symposium on international documents in 1975. Recommendations from this action will be referred to as a proposed second international symposium. On the international level, a joint AIL/FID/IFLA/UIA/UNESCO/UNITAR advanced training course on international documentation is to be conducted on a regular basis in various continents for the degree of Master of International Documentation. Participants, upon their return to their countries, would then become organisers of, and trainers in, national courses. To sum up, current research is influencing the use of international documentation to the point where the subject is finally receiving the universal recognition it so justly deserves.

The Bibliography

The primary objective of the bibliography is to examine the cumulative experience of the use of international documentation in the dissemination of information.

All aspects of the subject including acquisitions, management and servicing are considered. It is hoped that bibliographic examination may provide a source of reference for the development of international collections in libraries and for study of the documentation itself. Of particular note, in this regard, is the section on specialised information for librarians and documentalists interested in international information systems.

The section on bibliographies and indexes, which illustrates the subject approach on a selective basis, and also the wide-ranging, multidisciplinary character of the informative function of international documentation, has been compiled as a contribution to general bibliographic control. Scholarly bibliographies listed in research projects are included because they are an additional source of general bibliographic control and are, therefore, also of interest to both scholars and students of world affairs.

Most of the material in the bibliography has originated from the international organisations and libraries. In the treatment of multi-lingual bibliographic material English is used as the working language. Cross-references in chapters and indexes refer the reader to the recognised form of entry. The titles included are filed according to the order of the English alphabet. Titles not in the Roman alphabet have been transliterated. The form of entries is decided in conformity with Anglo-American cataloguing rules (American Library Association 1967), the bibliographic description is according to these same rules supplemented by the International Standard Bibliographic Description (ISBD).

Current serials are left open in most cases. In some instances the last issue is indicated by the description of the contents. For works containing special bibliographies, the bibliography note is stressed by its position following the title statement.

Geneva *May 1973*   THEODORE D. DIMITROV

★

C'est après le Congrès de Vienne (1815) qu'apparaît le phénomène de la documentation internationale, avec la création des premières organisations internationales, et qui prendra ensuite une signification historique, surtout à partir de l'époque de la Société des nations. A l'heure actuelle il y a plus de 4,000 organisations internationales dont 10% intergouvernementales, et plus de 5,000 congrès ont lieu chaque année. Les perspectives des relations internationales donnent pour l'année 2000 environ 13,000 organisations et 30,000 congrès annuels. La documentation constitue un instrument de travail et une synthèse des résultats des recherches des organisations internationales. Le problème fondamental de cette documentation présente deux aspects: (a) volume, et (b) valeur. Lors des Journées d'études internationales sur la documentation des Nations Unies et d'autres organisations intergouvernementales, tenues à Genève en 1972, ce problème a été abordé sous trois points de vue : administratif, gestion bibliothéconomique, et recherches.

Le présent ouvrage se propose d'examiner les différentes étapes du contrôle bibliographique des documents internationaux : acquisitions, catalogage ou indexage, utilisation. L'anglais est employé comme langue de travail. Les entrées principales sont établies d'après les Règles de catalogage anglo-américaines. La description bibliographique suit les mêmes règles complétées par la Description bibliographique internationale normalisée.

★

Es después del Congreso de Vena (1815) que aparece el fenómeno de la documentación internacional, con la creación de las primeras organizaciones internacionales, y que tomará después una significación histórica, sobre todo a partir de la época de la Sociedad de naciones. A la hora actual existen más de 4000 organizaciones internacionales, de las cuales 10% interguvernamentales, y más de 5000 congresos tienen lugar cada año. Las perspectivas de las relaciones internacionales hacen pensar que en el año 2000 existirán cerca de 13.000 organizaciones y tendrán lugar alrededor de 30.000 congresos anuales. La documentación constituye un instrumento de trabajo y una síntesis de resultados de investigación de las organizaciones internacionales. El problema fundamental de la documenación presenta dos aspectos : (a) volumen, (b) valor. Durante las Jornadas de estudios internacionales sobre la documentación de las Naciones Unidas y de otras organizaciones interguvernamentales, tenidas en Ginebra en 1972, este problema ha sido examinado bajo tres puntos de vista : administrativo, gestión biblioeconómica, y investigación.

El presente trabajo se propone examinar las diferentes etapas del control bibliográfico de los documentos internacionales : adquisición, catalogación y utilización. El idioma inglés es empleado como lengua de trabajo. Las entradas principales son establecidas según las reglas del Código anglo-americano. La descripción bibliográfica sigue las mismas reglas que han sido complementadas por la Descripción bibliográfica internacional normalizada.

★

Международная документация стала реальным фактором общественной жизни после Венского конгресса (1815 г.) вместе с созданием первых международных организаций. Историческую значимость она начала приобретать главным образом в период существования Лиги наций. В мире сейчас насчитывается более 4.000 международных организаций, 10 % из них являются межправительственными, и ежегодно созывается более 5.000 международных конгрессов. Можно предположить, что к 2000 году будет существовать 13 тыс. международных организаций и созываться ежегодно около 30 тыс. международных конференций и съездов. Международная документация является инструментом работы и обобщением результатов исследований, проводимых международными организациями. Можно указать на два основных аспекта проблемы документации: ее объем и ее использование. Международный симпозиум по документации ООН и других межправительственных организаций, состоявшийся в Женеве в 1972 г., обсудил этот вопрос с точки зрения административной, библиотековедческой и научно-исследовательской.

Автор настоящего труда ставить своей целью рассмотреть разные этапы библиотечной деятельности: комплектование, каталогизация и индексация, использование документов международных организаций. Английский язык является рабочим. Авторское описание сделано по «Англо-американским правилам каталогизации». Библиографическое описание следует. тем же правилам, дополненным правилами «Международного стандартного библиографического описания».

I. GENERAL. DEFINITION OF PURPOSES AND FUNCTIONS

1. **Association of international libraries.** Newsletter. - no. 1-36;
    1963-1973. - Geneva, 1963-1973. - 1 v.

2. **El-Ayouty, Y.** The dissemination, use and impact of knowledge
    relevant to UNITAR - a program for research and action.
    - Social science information=Information sur les sciences sociales
    10: 55-72, October 1971.

3. **Bates, M. L.** International documentation: an introduction/ by
    Margaret L. Bates and Robert K. Turner. - International
    organization I: 607-618, 1947.

4. **Berry, J. N.** International by definition. - Library journal 89:
    4469-4472, 1964.

5. **Bourgeois, P.** Internationale Dokumentations- und Bibliotheks-
    fragen im Blickfeld der FID, der FIAB und der UNESCO.
    - Biblos 5: 1-16, Heft 1, 1956.

6. **Brekke, A.** FN-dokumenter og FN-publikasjoner. - Oslo, 1958.
    - p. 85-98.
    "Særtrykk av 'Bibliotek og forskning', 7 (1958)."
    Bibliography: p. 97-98.

7. **Breycha-Vauthier, A. C.** Documentación internacional. - Madrid,
    Escuela de funcionarios internationales, 1962. - 26 p.
    "Versión española de Vicente Ramírez Montesinos."

8. - - --- Sources of information: a handbook on the publications
    of the League of Nations. - New York, Columbia University
    Press, 1939. - 118 p.
    Contents:
    pt. 1. Publications of the League of nations.
    pt. 2. League of nations Library.
    pt. 3. Numbering and arrangement of publications.
       Annexes. Index.

9. **Carnegie endowment for international peace. European centre.**
    Les publications officielles et la documentation internationale:
    travaux de la conférence de documentation réunie à Paris
    le 29 janvier 1951. - Pub. sous la direction de Michel Roussier.
    - Paris, etc., 1952. - 81 p.

10. **Carroll, M. J.** League of Nations documents and publications
    comparable with or continued in United Nations publications.
    - College and research libraries 13:   44-52, 64; January 1952.

11. **Chaplin, A. H.** National and international library organizations:
    preliminary list. - London, The British Museum, 1971. - 18 p.
    At head of title: 1971 IFLA Council, Liverpool.

B

12. Cholganskaia, V. L. Publikaťsii Organizaťsii Ob"edinenykh Naťsiľ
     i ee speťsializirovannykh uchrezhdeniľ: obzor za 1945-1965 gg.
     - Moskva, 1968. - 399 p.

13. Comité consultatif international de la documentation des
     bibliothèques et des archives. 2nd, Paris, 1969. Rapport de
     la session. - Paris, 1969. - 1 v.
     At head of title: Organisation des Nations Unies pour l'éducation, la science et la
     culture.

14. Les communications mondiales à l'ère spatiale: vers une nouvelle
     UIT: rapport d'une conférence internationale réunie sous l'égide
     de la John and Mary R. Markle foundation et du Twentieth
     century fund. - New York, 1972. - xi, 27 p.
     Compte rendu de la conférence: introduction, fonctions de l'UIT, résumé des
     principales recommandations, universalité de l'UIT, élaboration d'une politique générale,
     planification et administration, règlement des conflits et différences, recherche dans le
     domaine des communications, assistance technique, le secrétariat de l'UIT, conclusions.

15. Conference on UN publications, Oslo, 1970. FN publikasjoner:
     kurs ved Nobelinstituttets bibliotek 8.-10. oktober 1970. - Referat
     ved Björg Löken og Elisabeth Mellbye. - Oslo, Norske forsknings-
     bibliotekarers forening, 1971. - 29, 24, 13 1.
     At head of title: Nordisk vitenskapelig bibliotekarforbund.

16. Conference on United Nations and specialized agency documentation,
     Paris, 1948. Report on conference held at the European center
     of the endowment in Paris. - New York, Carnegie endowment,
     1949. - 35 1.
     At head of title: Carnegie endowment for international peace.

17. Congrès mondial des associations internationales. 1st, Brussels, 1910.
     Actes: Documents préliminaires, rapports, procès-verbaux, code. -
     2ème éd. en complément à l'Annuaire de la vie internationale
     1910-1911. - Brussels, 1910. - ix, 1246 p. - (Office central des
     associations internationales. Publication no. 2a.)

18. -- 2nd, Brussels, 1913. - Actes: Première partie: Introduction -
     Documents préliminaires. - Liste des adhérents. - Rapports. Seconde
     partie: Procès-verbaux des séances. Troisième partie: Résolutions. -
     Réceptions et visites. - Tables. - Brussels, 1914. - clxxxx, 1264 p. -
     (Union des associations internationales. Publications no. 46.)

19. Conseil de l'Europe. Presse et information. 300 bibliothèques de
     recherche collaboreront dans le cadre du Conseil de l'Europe.
     - Strasbourg, 1971. - 2 p.

20. Dimitrov, T. D. International documentation as a source of informa-
     tion. - Geneva, 1971. - 14 p. - (Séminaire sur la documentation
     des organismes des Nations Unies, Geneva, 1971. Working paper.
     no. 3.)
     United Nations. Documents. UNITAR/EUR.3/3.

21. -- --- Mezhdunarodnaia dokumentaťsiia kak istochnik nauchnoľ
     informaťsii: ob izdaniiakh sistemy OON. - Mirovaia ekonomika i
     mezhdunarodnye otnosheniia: p. 143-145, no. 7, iiul' 1972.

2. **Dolo-André, E.** International periodicals. - Associations internationales =International associations 10: 704-710, no. 10, 1959.

3. **Encyclopedia** of library and information science. - v. 1-   . - New York, M. Dekker, 1968-   . -   v.
   Editor: v. 1-   . Allen Kent and Harold Lancour.
   Includes bibliographies. .
   Chapters and articles concerning definition of analysis of information, automatic data processing, documentation, etc.

4. **European parliament.** The European communities own resources and the budgetary powers of the European parliament: selected documents. - Luxembourg, 1972. - 287 p.
   Preface by Walter Behrendt.

5. **Evans, L. H.** Documents and publications of contemporary international governmental organizations. - Law library journal 64: 338-362, August 1971.

6. **Everyman's** United Nations: a complete handbook of the activities and evolution of the United Nations during its first twenty years, 1945-1965. - 8th ed. - New York, United Nations, Office of public information, 1968. - xii, 634 p. - (United Nations. Publications. Sales numbers. 1967.I.5.) E F
   A five year supplement 1966-1970: A summary of the activities of the United Nations: 1966-1970. (United Nations. Publications. Sales numbers. 1971.I.10.)

7. **Feis, H.** Research activities of the League of nations: a report made to the Committee on international relations of the Social science research council on the methods and progress of research in the League of nations and International labour organisation, June 1929.

8. **Frank, O.** Modern documentation and information practices: a basic manual/ edited by O. Frank. - The Hague, International federation for documentation, 1961. - x,225 p. - (Fédération internationale de documentation. Publications. 334.)
   Bibliography: p. 199-217.

9. **Handbook** of the United Nations and the specialized agencies. - New York, Department of public information, United Nations, 19   . - v. - (United Nations. Publications. Sales numbers.   .)
   This handbook of essential facts is designed to serve as a guide to the structure, the purposes and the functions of these organizations.

30. **L'informatique.** - no. 1-   ; 1971-   . - Paris, 1971-   . -   v.

31. **L'informatique,** la documentation et les sciences sociales. - Revue internationale des sciences sociales 23, no. 2, 1971.

32.   **Instituto per gli studi di politica internazionale.** Annuario di politica
      internazionale: 1967-1971. - Milano, Dedalo libri, 1972. - xx, 969 p.
      Contents:
      pt. 1. I grandi temi della politica mondiale. pt. 2. La politica estera italiana.
      pt. 3. Documentazione. pt. 4. Appendici: Struttura delle organizzazioni internazionali;
      i nuovi paesi del mondo; bibliografia generale; trattati e convenzioni: trattati e accordi
      firmati dall'Italia; la diplomazia italiana; corpo diplomatico a Roma; indice analitico.

33.   **International advisory committee on documentation, libraries and
      archives. 1st sess., Paris, 1967.** Final report. - Paris, 1968. - 10 p.
      - (United Nations educational, scientific and cultural organization.
      Documents. COM/CS/125/5.)

34.   **International labour office.**   L'œuvre scientifique du Bureau inter-
      national du travail. - Paris, Presses modernes, 1930. - 1 v.

35.   **International symposium on documentation of the United Nations
      and other intergovernmental organizations, Geneva, 1972.**
      Information note. - no. 1-4. - Geneva, 1971-1972. - 1v.
      (UNITAR/FUR/SEM.1/INF.1-4.)
      Organized by the United Nations institute for training and research (UNITAR), at
      the initiative and with the cooperation of the Association of international libraries
      (AIL), with the support of the International federation of library associations
      (IFLA) and the International federation for documentation (FID).
      G. Gribaudo: Secretary of the Symposium. O. Cerny: Treasurer.
      Opening ceremony under the chairmanship of Natalia Tyulina. Addresses by:
      George Palthey, Hernando Samper, José Leymarie, Pierre Piganiol, György Rózsa.

36.   -- ---- Reports of the Symposium.

      Judge, P. Report on the work of Panel I. (UNITAR/SEM.1/WP.I/IR.)
      Judge, A. J. N. Report on the work of Panel II. (UNITAR/EUR/SEM.1/WP.II/IR.)
      Goormaghtigh, J. Report on the work of Panel III. (UNITAR/EUR/SEM.1/WP.III/IR.)

      Casadio, F. A. Final report of the International symposium on documentation of
      the United Nations and other intergovernmental organizations. (UNITAR/EUR/SEM.1/REP.)

      Contents:
      p.t.1. Historical background. pt.2. Trends of thought and recommendations.
      Contains 64 recommendations of interest to governments and national administrations,
      intergovernmental organizations, Symposium organizers, libraries and documentation
      centres, users in general.

37.   -- Working documents.

      Panel I: Sources of international documentation.
      1. Arntz, H. The change in the production of scientific literature through new
          techniques. (UNITAR/EUR/SEM.1/WP.I/1.)
      2. Charlesworth, B. The need of modernization in production, editing and
          distribution of intergovernmental documentation. (UNITAR/EUR/SEM.1/WP.I/2.)
      3. Moss, A. G. A suggested change in the method of issuance and the storage and
          retrieval of United Nations documentation. (UNITAR/EUR/SEM.1/WP.I/3.)
      4. United Nations educational, scientific and cultural organisation. The sources of
          international documentation. (UNITAR/EUR/SEM.1/WP.I/4.)
      5. Cormier, R. The non-confidential documentation produced by the Organisation
          for economic co-operation and development. (UNITAR/EUR/SEM.1/WP.I/5.)
      6. Dimitrov, T. D. International documentation as a source of information.
          (UNITAR/EUR/SEM.1/WP.I/6.)

Panel I: Sources of international documentation.

7.   Loftus, M.   Survey of the documentation and publication programme, including
     available catalogues and lists, of the International monetary fund. (UNITAR/EUR/
     SEM.1/WP.II/7.)
8.   - - Survey of the documentation and publication programme, including available
     catalogues and lists, of the International bank for reconstruction and development.
     (UNITAR/EUR/SEM.1/WP.I/8.)
9.   World health organization.   Office of publications and translation.   Production and
     distribution of WHO documents.   (UNITAR/EUR/SEM.1/WP.I/9.)
10. Auburn, F. M.   United Nations documentation and international law.
     (UNITAR/EUR/SEM.1/WP.I/10.)
11. Mandefield, H. W.   Control, production and distribution of publications in FAO.
     (UNITAR/EUR/SEM.1/WP.I/11.)
12. United Nations. Office, Geneva. Documents division.   Sources of international
     documentation: United Nations. (UNITAR/EUR/SEM.1/WP.I/12.)
13. Rubiato, J. M.   Production of World meteorological organization documentation.
     (UNITAR/EUR/SEM.1/WP.I/13.)

Panel II: Acquisition and organization of international documentation.

1.   Simari, A.   Organization of technical services in a documentation centre or
     specialized library.   (UNITAR/EUR/SEM.1/WP.II/1.)
2.   Kaufmann, H. S.   Publications of the Organization of American States. (UNITAR/EUR/
     SEM.1/WP.II/2.)
3.   Delgado, R. R.   Organization of international documents, principles and conditions
     of implementation of information systems: the problem of regional working
     standards. (UNITAR/EUR/SEM.1/WP.II/3.)
4.   Seymour, H.   The United Nations and modern documentation retrieval. (UNITAR/EUR/
     SEM.1/WP.II/4.)
5.   Zlatich, M.   Acquisition and organization of international documentation within the
     World bank group. (UNITAR/EUR/SEM.1/WP.II/5.)
6.   World health organization.   Library and documentation services.   The World health
     organization Library and documentation services.   (UNITAR/EUR/SEM.1/WP.II/6.)
7.   Martini, G. S.   The Computer assisted indexing programme of the United Nations:
     a brief description.   (UNITAR/EUR/SEM.1/WP.II/7.)
8.   Levy, E.   A computer-produced finding tool for international organization documents:
     the ILO's "Supplementary list".   (UNITAR/EUR/SEM.1/WP.II/8.)
9.   Haden, J. W.   Some previous attempts at organizing international documentation.
     (UNITAR/EUR/SEM.1/WP.II/9.)
10. Clark, D.   Indexing and citation of United Nations material: a critical view.
     (UNITAR/EUR/SEM.1/WP.II/10.)
11. Dimitrov, T. D. Centralized cataloguing of major United Nations and specialized
     agencies documents.   (UNITAR/EUR/SEM.1/WP.II/11.)
12. Faridi, G.   Some problems in the maintenance of United Nations depository
     collections and possible solutions. (UNITAR/EUR/SEM.1/WP.II/12.)
13. Nebehay, E.   United Nations documents and publications not available from usual
     sources: their bibliographical control and source acquisition.   (UNITAR/EUR/
     SEM.1/WP.II/13.)
14. Thompson, G. K.   Approaching a common inter-agency information system
     for library management and document retrieval.   (UNITAR/EUR/SEM.1/WP.II/14.)
15. Woolston, G. E.   Acquisition and organization: two proposals to ameliorate
     the present situation.   (UNITAR/EUR/SEM.1/WP.II/15.)
16. Simari, A.   International trade documentation and the Documentation service
     of the International trade centre UNCTAD/GATT.   (UNITAR/EUR/SEM.1/
     WP.II/16.)
17. Koch, N.   A set of simplified cataloguing rules prepared by the Royal
     library in Copenhagen.   (UNITAR/EUR/SEM.1/WP.II/17.)
18. United Nations educational, scientific and cultural organisation.   The
     computerized documentation service of UNESCO.   (UNITAR/EUR/SEM.1/
     WP.II/18.)
19. Schaaf, R.   International documents at the Library of Congress: an overview
     stressing areas of concern and ideas for improving their availability and
     control.   (UNITAR/EUR/SEM.1/WP.II/19.)
20. Korevaar, J.   Transition to automatic indexing of documents.   (UNITAR/EUR/
     SEM.1/WP.II/20.)
21. Food and agriculture organization.   International information systems in the field
     of agriculture: AGRIS and CARIS. (UNITAR/EUR/SEM.1/WP.II/21.)
22. Bernstein, H.H.   Considérations sur la description "bibliographique" des documents
     des organisations internationales.   (UNITAR/EUR/SEM.1/WP.II/21.)

Panel II: Acquisition and organization of international documentation.(cont'd)

23. Dulong, A. L'index ONU - Maroc du Centre national de documentation de Rabat. (UNITAR/EUR/SEM.1/WP.II/23.)
24. Pease, M. J-01000 through J-09999 - The Plain J - International organization. (UNITAR/EUR/SEM.1/WP.II/24.)
25. Tocatlian, J. UNISIST: implementation, plans and current developments. (UNITAR/EUR/SEM.1/WP.II/25.)
26. Beyerly, H. United Nations documentation in the UNIDO Industrial documentation unit. (UNITAR/EUR/SEM.1/WP.II/26.)

Panel III: Utilization of international documentation.

1.   Mellbye, E. National case study: Norway. (UNITAR/EUR/SEM.1/WP.III/1.)
2.   Delgado, R. R. Facilities at ECLA/CLADES. (UNITAR/EUR/SEM.1/WP.III/2.)
3.   Aladejana, A.   United Nations documents in Nigerian libraries. (UNITAR/EUR/SEM.1/WP.III/3.)
4.   Partan, D. G. International organizations sourcebook. (UNITAR/EUR/SEM.1/WP.III/4.)
5.   Dos Santos, A. Utilisation des documents des Nations Unies dans le cadre du Service question-réponse-développement du Centre de développement de l'OCDE. (UNITAR/EUR/SEM.1/WP.III/5.)
6.   De Schütter, B. Etude de cas nationale: la Belgique. (UNITAR/EUR/SEM.1/WP.III/6.)
7.   Rizzo, G. National case study: the situation of the UN Information centre in Argentina. (UNITAR/EUR/SEM.1/WP.III/7.)
8.   Court, J. La formation des documentalistes. (UNITAR/EUR/SEM.1/WP.III/8.)
9.   Sandeau, M. G. Comment un institut d'enseignement de la gestion utilise la documentation venant des organismes intergouvernementaux. (UNITAR/EUR/SEM.1/WP.III/9.)
10. El-Ayouty, Y. United Nations documentation: guidelines to a study on usage. (UNITAR/EUR/SEM.1/WP.III/10.)
11. Welander, S. Modalités de recherche dans les archives de la Société des nations. (UNITAR/EUR/SEM.1/WP.III/11.)
12. Sprudzs, A. International co-operation and status of information on multilateral treaties in force.   (UNITAR/EUR/SEM.1/WP.III/12.)
13. United Nations educational, scientific and cultural organisation. Working paper for Panel III prepared by the Secretariat. (UNITAR/EUR/SEM.1/WP.III/13.)
14. Bonny, H. The use and treatment of documents produced by international organizations, with the special references to the joint library service conducted for ECE and UNCTAD. (UNITAR/EUR/SEM.1/WP.14.)
15. Dimitrov, T. D. The documentation of the United Nations and other intergovernmental organizations: information and functional purposes, processing and utilization - a bibliography. (UNITAR/EUR/SEM.1/WP.15.)
16. Arshinkova, S. Documentation of the material of international organizations in the National library "Cyril and Methodius". (UNITAR/EUR/SEM.1/WP.III/16.)
17. Erlandsson, A. The United Nations archives and its availability to scholars. (UNITAR/EUR/SEM.1/WP.III/17.)
18. Schaaf, R. Access to the archives of international organizations. (UNITAR/EUR/SEM.1/WP.III/18.)
19. Johnson, E. International documents: use by universities. (UNITAR/EUR/SEM.1/WP.III/19
20. Manning, R. M. Access to the archives of the International labour office. (UNITAR/EUR/SEM.1/WP.III/20.)
21. Cerny, O. Some data and remarks on the use of documentation of the UN and other intergovernmental organizations in small international libraries located in Geneva. (UNITAR/EUR/SEM.1/WP.III/21.)

38.   Die **Internationalen** Wirtschaftsorganisationen im Schrifttum. - T.1-   . - Kiel, 1969-   . -   v. - (Kieler Schrifttumskunden zu Wirtschaft und Gesellschaft. Nr. 5.)

39.   **Judge, A. J. N.** Mapping world problems: a technique illustrated by relations between IGOs and INGOs, particularly for the case of the United Nations system. - International associations=Associations internationales. nos. 8-9, p. 414-417, 1972.

40.   - - - - -   The next step in inter-organizational relationships: for use of information, rather than organization, as the foundation for the inter-organizational activity of the future. - Brussels, Union of international associations, 1971. - 1 v.
At head of title: UAI Study papers ORG/1, February 1971.

41. **Kasme, B.** Les bibliothèques et les publications des Nations Unies.
- Bulletin de l'Unesco à l'intention des bibliothèques=Unesco
bulletin for libraries 8:F31-F36, février-mars 1954.

42. **Lamb, B. P.** Documents of the United Nations. - American journal
of international law 41: 140-145, no. 1, January 1947.

43. **Langrod, G.** La fonction publique internationale: sa genèse, son
essence, son évolution. - Leyde, A.W. Sythoff, 1963. - 387 p.
Bibliography: p. 349-361.
Notes, partly bibliographical, at the end of each chapter.

44. **Libraries** and United Nations publications. - Bulletin de l'Unesco à
l'intention des bibliothèques=Unesco bulletin for libraries: 8:
E32-E36, 1954.

45. **Liebaers, H.** The international librarian. - AIL Newsletter 4:
3-9, 1966.

46. **Meeting on modern documentation techniques, Santiago, Chile, 1971.**
Report on the proceedings, conclusions and recommendations of
the Meeting. - Santiago, Chile, 1971. - iii, 44 p. - (United Nations.
Documents. CLADES/WG.1/L.24.)
At head of title: United Nations. Economic and social council. Economic commission
for Latin America.

47. **Mellbye, E.** Internasjonale organisasjoner og deres publikasjoner.
- Oslo, Norske Nobelinstitutt, 1951. - 28 p.
Bibliography: p. 27 -28.

48. **Meyer, J.** Publications of the United Nations. - College and research
libraries 7:311-318, 1946.

49. **Mikhailov, A. I.** An introductory course on informatics/documentation
/by A. I. Mikhailov and R. S. Giljarevskij. - Paris, 1970. - 208 p.
- (United Nations educational, scientific and cultural organisation.
Documents. COM/WS/147.)
Bibliography at the end of each chapter.

50. **Mikhailov, O. A.** Documentation and international co-operation.
- Libri 18: 161-172, no. 3-4, 1968.

51. **Murra, K. O.** International scientific organizations: a guide to their
library, documentation, and information services. - Washington,
Library of Congress, 1962. - 794 p.

52. **Myrdal, G.** Realities & illusions in regard to inter-governmental
organizations. - London, G. Cumberlege, Oxford university press,
1955. - 28 p. - (L.T. Hobhouse memorial trust lectures. no. 24.)
"Delivered on 25 February, 1954 at Bedford college, London."

53. **New York university. Conference on United Nations documents,
New York, 1952.** Papers. - New York, 1952. - 1 v.

54.   **Organisation for economic co-operation and development.** Information for a changing society: some policy considerations.
- Paris, 1971. - 48 p.
Chapter II concerns current information policies and practices in international
organizations.

55.   - -   **Directorate for scientific affairs.** Activités des principales
organisations internationales dans le domaine de la documentation.
- Paris, Direction des affaires scientifiques, Organisation de
coopération et de développement économiques, 1971. - 185 p.

56.   - -   **Scientific and technical information policy group.** Information
activities of some major international organizations. - Paris, 1969.
- 175 p.

57.   **Organization of American States. Publications and documents office.**
Report on publications and documents. - 1972-   . - Washington,
D.C., 1972-   . -   v. - (Its: Documents. OEA/Ser.D/X, etc.)
Pub. quarterly.

58.   **Padelford, N. J.** The United Nations in the balance: accomplishments
and prospects, edited by Norman J. Padelford and Leland M.
Goodrich. - New York, F.A. Praeger, 1965. - xii, 482 p.
"The essays in this volume originally appeared in a special issue of 'International
organization' entitled 'The United Nations: accomplishments and prospects', vol. XIX,
no. 3 (Summer, 1965)."
Foot-notes, partly bibliographical.

59.   **Palthey, G.** Genève et les organisations internationales. - Genève,
1962. - 21 p. - (United Nations. Office, Geneva. Documents.
MUN/457/62.)

60.   **Peaslee, A. J.** International governmental organizations: constitutional
documents. - v.1-2. - Rev. 2nd ed. - The Hague, M. Nijhoff, 1961. -
2 v.
Contains:
Names of constitutional documents; Age, membership, financial support and headquarters;
Functions; Organs; Membership in specialized agencies of the United Nations; Details of
the International governmental organizations.
Includes bibliographies on some of the organizations listed.

61.   **Poindron, P.** Le contenu, le rôle, l'accessibilité, et la valeur des
communications et comptes rendus de congrès scientifiques.
- Bulletin de l'Unesco à l'intention des bibliothèques. 16: 121-134,
177-189, nos. 3 et 4, 1962.
Rapport d'une enquête effectuée sous les auspices de l'Unesco, par la FID, le CIUS
et l'UAI.

62.   **Roberts, A. D.** The documents and publications of international
organizations. - Revue de la documentation 17: 3-17, fasc.1, 1950.

63.   **Sauget, M. H.** Les principales organisations européennes et leurs
publications. - Bulletin des bibliothèques de France 3: 499-517,
juillet/août 1958.

64. **Saunders, J. F.**   Libraries and the publications of the UN special-
     ized agencies. - Bulletin de l'Unesco à l'intention des biblio-
     thèques=Unesco bulletin for libraries 8: E 102-E 108, août-
     september 1954.

65. **Séminaire sur la documentation des organismes des Nations Unies,
     Geneva, 1971.**   Documents de travail. - no. 1-18. - Genève 1971.
     - 1 v. - (United Nations. Documents. UNITAR/EUR/3/1-18.)
     "Organisé par l'Institut des Nations Unies pour la formation et la recherche (UNITAR)
     en collaboration avec la Bibliothèque et d'autres services de l'Office des Nations
     Unies à Genève, la CEE, la CNUCED, le Centre CNUCED/GATT du commerce
     international et l'Organisation internationale du travail."
     "G. Gribaudo: secrétaire du Séminaire."

     Contents:
     1. El-Ayouty, Y.   United Nations documentation as a research undertaking.
     2. Rózsa, G. Information et culture par rapport aux bibliothèques internationales.
     3. Dimitrov, T. D. La documentation internationale en tant que source d'informa-
        tion.
     4. Casadio, F. A. Quelques considérations préliminaires sur les techniques de l'in-
        formation dans le développement d'une société moderne.
     5. Thompson, G. K. Activités interorganisations dans le domaine de la documenta-
        tion.
     6. Mackay, W. Le centre internationale de calcul électronique.
     7. Seymour, Helen. L'expérience de l'ONU en matière d'informatique dans le
        domaine de la documentation.
     8. Traitler, R. Notes sur les problèmes particuliers que posent aux centres de
        documentation des ONG les systèmes de documentation des Nations Unies.
     9. Not published.
     10. Pernoud, Ch. Le système de la documentation des Nations Unies.
     11. Leckie, H. Suggestions pour une collection de base de publications officielles
        et d'autres ouvrages de référence sur les Nations Unies.
     12. Bonny, H. V. Services fournis par le Service commun des références CEE/
        UNCTAD.
     13. Hennis, C. E. Principes régissant la distribution des documents du BIT aux ONG.
     14. Levy, E. Bref aperçu des documents du BIT.
     15. Thompson, G. K. L'expérience du BIT en matière d'automatisation des services
        de documentation.
     16. Simari, A. La documentation du commerce internationale et le Service de
        documentation du Centre CNUCED/GATT du commerce international.
     17. Questionnaire sur l'évaluation.
     18. Exercices pratiques.

66. **Shatrov, V. P.**   Vsemirnaia organizatsiia intelektual'noi sobstvennosti. -
     Moskva, TSNIIPI, 1969. - 89 p.
     At head of title: Komitet po delam izobretenii i otkrytii pri Sovete ministrov SSSR.
     Information functions of the World intellectual property organization.

67. **Signor, N.**   United Nations versus League of Nations documentation
     - Special libraries 43: 62-64, 70, February 1952.

68. **Speeckaert, G. P.**   Bibliographie sélective sur l'organisation inter-
     nationale, 1885-1964=Select bibliography on international
     organization. - Bruxelles, 1965. - x, 150 p. - (Fédération:
     internationale de documentation. Publications. no. 361.)
     Union des associations internationales, Brussels. Publications. no. 191.
     Title, introduction, headings and index in French and English.

69. -- --- La documentation relative aux organisations, réunions, et
     publications internationales. - Bulletin de l'Unesco à l'intention
     des bibliothèques 15: 155-158, no.3, 1961.

70. -- --- Les travaux de l'Union des associations internationales
     dans le domaine de la documentation internationale. - Revue
     internationale de la documentation 32: 56-58, no. 2, 1965.

71. **Société des nations.** Annuaire. - v.1-8; 1920/27-1938. - Genève, 1927-2938. - 8 v.
Contents:
1. L'organisation constitutionnelle de la Société des nations. 2. Délégués, représentants, juges et fonctionnaires. 3. Historique des événements principaux. 4. Les États.

72. **South Pacific conference.** Report by the Secretary general, South Pacific commission. - 1st-   ; 1950-   . - Noumea, New Caledonia, 1950-   . - v.
Some issues have individual title: Pacific forum.
Contains information on research and publications programms.

73. **Sovet ėkonomicheskoĭ vzaimopomoshchi. Postoiânnaiâ komissiiâ po koordinaŧsii nauchnykh i tekhnicheskikh issledovaniĭ.** Teoriiâ i praktika prognozirovaniiâ razvitiiâ nauki i tekhniki v stranakh-chlenakh SĖV. - Moskva, Izd-vo "Ėkonomika", 1971. -
Materialy Mezhdunarodnogo simpoziuma stran-chlenov SĖV i SFRIŬ po metodologicheskim voprosam prognozirovaniiâ razvitiiâ nauki i tekhniki, sostoiâvshegosiâ v Moskve v marte 1970 g.
Symposium on technological forecasting in CMEA countries.

74. -- --- Upravlenie, planirovanie i organizaŧsiiâ nauchnykh i tekhniche-skikh issledovaniĭ. - t.1-5. - Moskva, Izdanie Vsesoiŭznogo instituta nauchnoĭ i tekhnicheskoĭ informaŧsii, 1970. - 5 v.
Trudy Mezhdunarodnogo simpoziuma stran-chlenov SĖV i SFRIŬ, Moskva, maĭ 1968 g.
International symposium of CMEA countries and Yugoslavia on organization and planning in scientific research and technology.
Includes bibliographies.

75. **Stummvoll, J.** Das Schrifttum der Vereinten Nationen: Gedächtnis und Zeugnis des Weltgewissens. - Biblos 21: 237-250, Hft. 4, 1972.
Les documents des Nations Unies et la conscience mondiale.

76. **Union of international associations.** Centre international, conception et programme de l'internationalisme. Organismes internationaux et Union des Associations internationales, établissements scientifiques installés au Palais Mondial. - Bruxelles, 1921. - 130 p. - (Publication no. 98.)

77. -- --- Documents. - no.1-   . - Bruxelles, 1956-   . - v.

78. -- --- Guide pratique pour la préparation des documents des réunions internationales. - Bruxelles, Union des associations internationales, Fédération internationale de documentation, 1972. - 25 p. F E

79. -- --- Les organisations internationales face à l'aspect budgétaire et économique de leurs congrès. - Bruxelles, 1970. - 160 p. - (Its: Publication. no. 219.)
Compte rendu du 5e Congrès international sur l'organisation des congrès, Barcelone, 6-10 mai 1970.
Analyse de la production de documents par les congrès internationaux.

80. -- --- Study papers. - INF/1-   . - Brussels, Union of international associations, 1969-   . - v.
International agencies. United Nations.

81. **Union of international associations.** Study papers. - PROB/ - . -
Brussels, Union of international associations, 1970- . - v.

82. -- --- L'Union des associations internationales. - Bruxelles, 1912. -
162 p. - (Publications no. 25.)

83. -- --- Union of international associations, 1910-1970: past, present,
future. - Brussels, 1970. - 118 p. - (Union des associations internatio-
nales, Brussels. Publications. no. 214.) ç
"Union des associations internationales, Brussels. Documents. no.17."
On cover: Sixtieth anniversary.
Foot-notes, partly bibliographical.

84. **United Nations.** Organization of the Secretariat. - New York, 1966. -
65 p. - (Its: Documents. ST/SGB/131.) E F S
Contents:
pt. 1. General structure. pt. 2. Offices of the Secretary-general. pt. 3. Other departments
and offices.
Amendments. no.1-31.

85. -- --- Regulations for the control and limitation of documentation. -
New York, 1969-1972. - 1 v. - (Its: Documents. ST/AI/189.)

Add.1. Initiation, approval and execution of the annual programme of United Nations
publications.
Add.2. Covers and title-pages of publications.
Add.3. Distribution from Headquarters of documents, meeting records, official
records and publications.
Add.4. Principles governing the exchange of United Nations documents and
publications.
Add.5. Stock review and disposal: official records and publications.
Add.6. Désignation des auteurs des textes.
Add.7. Documentation workload estimates.
Add.8. Requests for document services.
Add.9. Copyright in United Nations publications: general principles, practice
and procedure.

86. -- --- Structure and organization of the United Nations. - New York,
1959. - 59 p. - (Its: ST/CS/SER.F/160.)
At head of title: Office of conference services. Terminology unit. Terminology bulletin.
no. 160.
1. Committees and commissions. 2. Secretariat. 3. Functional titles of officials.

87. -- **Administrative committee on coordination.** Développement et
coordination des activités des organismes des Nations Unies:
rapport spécial du Comité administratif de coordination. - Genève,
1970. - 7 p. - (United Nations. Documents. E/4893.)
At head of title: Nations Unies. Conseil économique et social. Quarante-neuvième
session. Point 26 b) de l'ordre du jour.

88. -- **Department of conference and general services. Communications and records division.** The archives of the League of Nations
and the United Nations/ prepared by Robert Claus and Irving
P. Schiller. - New York, 1953. - 24 l. - (Its: United Nations
archives special guides. no.1.)

United Nations (Cont'd)

89.   - -   **Economic and social council. Enlarged committee for programme and co-ordination. 2nd session.** Documents. E/AC.51/GR/L.9, etc. General review of the programmes and activities of the United Nations family in the economic, social, technical co-operation and related fields, development of modern management techniques and use of computers.

90.   - -   **European office.** Report on the survey of League of Nations archives and United Nations records and archives held in the Palais des Nations, and proposals for dealing with them. - Geneva, 1957. - 15, 3 p.
Prepared by Henrietta L. Hartmann.

91.   - -   **General assembly.** Documents concerning the publications and documentation of the United Nations. - no. 1-6. - New York, 1966-1971. - 1 v. - (United Nations. Documents. A/6343, etc.)
Symbols: A/6343   A/7359   A/7380   A/8403   A/8501   A/8608
           A/6675   A/7576   A/8319   A/8426   A/8540   A/8624
           A/6872   A/7579   A/8401   A/8429   A/8606   A/8626

92.   - - - - -   Resolutions adopted by the General assembly concerning the publications and documentation of the United Nations. - A/RES/   . - New York, 1951-1971. - 1 v. - (United Nations. General assembly. 6 th session, 1951/52. Official records. Supplements. no. 20, etc.)
United Nations. Documents. A/2119, etc.
Symbols: A/RES/593(VI)   A/RES/2538(XXIV)
              A/RES/1272(XIII)   A/RES/2836(XXVI)
              A/RES/2247(XXI)   A/RES/2839(XXVI)
              A/RES/2292(XXII)

93.   - -   **General assembly. Committee on control and limitation of documentation.** Report. - New York, 1958. - 15 p. - (Its: Documents. A/3888.)
At head of title: Thirteenth session.
Rapporteur: Derek Arnould.

94.   - -   **Library co-ordinating committee of the United Nations organizations. European members working group, Geneva, 1948-1949.** Documents. CO-ORD/LIBRARY/1-9. - Geneva, 1948-1949. - 1 v.

Contents:
1. Summary record of the 1st and 2nd meetings, 10 August 1948.
   Annex I: Rules of procedure of the Library co-ordination committee of the United Nations organizations.
   Annex II: Background information on libraries of the specialized agencies.
2. Indexes and checklists of United Nations and specialized agency documents and publications.
3. Technical assistance to underdeveloped countries.
4. European sub-committee.
5. Co-operative cataloguing.
6. Subject indexes.
7. Trainees.
8. Co-ordination of translations of legal texts and publication of monthly catalogue of newly translated texts.
9. Summary of meeting.

95. **United Nations. Publications board.** Papers. 19 -
- New York, 19 - . - v.

Selected numbers in the series appearing every year:

Programme of United Nations publications.
Publications programme: Department of economic and social affairs.
Publications programme: Economic commission for Africa.
Publications programme: Economic commission for Asia and the Far East.
Publications programme: Economic commission for Europe.
Publications programme: Economic commission for Latin America.
Publications programme: Library internal reproduction programme.

96. -- - - -   Sale of United Nations publications. - 1970-1971.
- (ST/PB/34, etc.)
"Report to the Secretary-General."

97. -- - - -   Work of the Publications board. - 1970-1971.
- (ST/PB/33, etc.)
"Report to the Secretary-General."

98. - -   **Secretary-general.** Annual report of the Secretary-general
on the work of the organization: Meetings and documents
services. - 1965/66-1970/71. - New York, 1966-1971. - 6 v.
- (United Nations. General assembly. 21st session,
1965/66. Official records. Supplements. no. 1, etc.)
Years and symbols:
1965/66. p. 174-175. (A/6301.)   1968/69. p. 214-216. (A/7601.)
1966/67. p. 200-201. (A/6701.)   1969/70. p. 250-252. (A/8001.)
1967/68. p. 226-227. (A/7201.)   1970/71. p. 264-266. (A/8401.)

99. -- - - -   Common services and co-ordination of services at
various centres: draft report. - New York, 1952. - 30 p.
- (United Nations. Documents. COORDINATION/R.137.)
At head of title: Administrative committee on co-ordination, fifteenth session,
New York.

100. **United Nations educational, scientific and cultural organisation.**
Guide des centres nationaux d'information bibliographique.
- 2e éd. - Paris, 1962. - 72 p.

101. -- - - -   Liste des associations de bibliothécaires et documentalistes
=List of library and documentation associations. - Paris, 1972.
- 28 p.

102. **United States. Committee on publications of the Department of
State and the United Nations.** Report. - Lancaster, Pa., 1972.
- p. 393 -409.
"From the Proceedings (April, 1971) of the American society of international law."

103. **World bank group.** Research program. - Washington, D.C., 1972. -
80 p.
Contents:
Development policy and planning. Trade and international finance. Agriculture and
rural development. Industry and mining. Transportation. Public utilities. Urbanization
and regional development. Population and human resources. Other research.
Appendix: Estimated costs of World bank group research program.

104.   **Yearbook** of international organizations. - 1948-1972/73; 1st-14th ed. -
Brussels, Union of international associations, 1948-1972. - 14 v.
Pub. annually, 1948-1950; biannually, 1951/52-1970/71.
Bi-lingual, English/French, 1948-50; monolingual, English, French in alternate eds. 1951/52-
1960/61; English only, 1962/63-1970/71.

Contents:
1. Guide for user. 2. Organization entries. - Indexes: English organization names (Index 1);
Organizations classified by category (Index 2); Geographical location of organization (Index 3);
Initials and acronyms (Index 4); Subjects and keywords (Index 5); Français (Index 6), noms d
organisations suivi de l'Index analytique français.
Supplementary sections: United Nations yearbook and Yearbook of international organizations
membership of the United Nations and the associated agencies and institutes; consultative
relations and the United Nations; international nongovernmental organizations most frequently
recognized by intergovernmental organizations; international NGO groupings; statistics on
international organizations; internationally oriented foundations; international relations: list
of institutes, centres and schools of international affairs; international organization researchers;
bibliography of documents on transnational association networks; international nongovernmental
organization as a field of study.

105.   **Yearbook** of the United Nations. - v.1-24. - 1946/47-1970. - New
York, United Nations, Office of public information, 1957-1972. -
24 v. - (United Nations. Publications. Sales numbers. 1947.I.18, etc.)
Contents of v.24, 1970:
List of abbreviations. Explanatory notes on documents.
Pt. 1.   Political and security questions: Disarmament and related matters: The peaceful
uses of outer space; Questions concerning the uses of atomic energy; Promoting the peaceful
uses of the sea-bed; Review of the question of peace-keeping operations; The strengthening
of international security; 25th anniversary of the United Nations; Questions relating to
Africa; Questions relating to Asia and the Far East; Questions concerning Latin America;
The situation in the Middle East; Assistance to refugees in the Middle East; Other questions
relating to the Middle East; The situation in Cyprus; Other political and security questions;
Questions relating to the United Nations Charter and membership in the United Nations.
Pt. 2.   The second United Nations development decade; The world economic situation;
United Nations operational activities for development; Trade and development; The International
trade centre; The financing of economic development; The economic and social consequences
of disarmament; Industrial development; Regional economic activities; Statistical developments;
The application of science and technology to development; Problems of the environment; The
use and development of natural (non-agricultural) resources; Population questions; Matters
pertaining to food problems; The United Nations children's fund; Assistance to refugees;
Narcotic drugs; Human rights questions; Questions relating to youth; Social questions; Co-
ordination and organizational questions; Consultative arrangements with non-governmental
organizations; Other economic and social questions.
Pt. 3.   Questions relating to trust and non-self-governing territories and the Declaration
on granting independence; The international trusteeship system; The situation with regard
to the implementation of the Declaration on the granting of independence to colonial
countries and peoples; The question of Namibia; The situation in Southern Rhodesia;
Territories under Portuguese administration; Other questions relating to non-self-governing
territories.
Pt. 4.   Legal questions; The International court of justice; Principles of international law
concerning friendly relations and co-operation among States; The question of defining
aggression; Questions concerning the International law commission; Aerial hijacking;
International trade law; United Nations programme of assistance to promote teaching and
knowledge of international law; Treaties and multilateral conventions; Other legal questions.
Pt. 5.   Administrative and budgetary questions.
Pt. 6.   The inter-governmental organizations related to the United Nations:
    I.   The International atomic energy agency;
    II.   The International labour organisation;
    III.   The Food and agriculture organization;
    IV.   The United Nations educational, scientific and cultural organisation;
    V.   The World health organization;
    VI.   The International bank for reconstruction and development;
    VII.   The International finance corporation;
    VIII.   The International development association;
    IX.   The International monetary fund;
    X.   The International civil aviation organization;
    XI.   The Universal postal union;
    XII.   The International telecommunication union;
    XIII.   The World meteorological organization;
    XIV.   The Inter-governmental maritime consultative organization;
    XV.   The Interim commission for the International trade organization (ICITO) and the
        General agreement on tariffs and trade.
Appendices: Roster of the United Nations; The Charter of the United Nations and the
Statute of the International court of justice; The structure of the United Nations; Matters
considered by the principal organs of the United Nations; Delegations to the General
assembly and the Councils; United Nations information centres and offices. - Indices:
Abbreviations used in index. Subject index. Index of names.

II. PROCESSING ASPECTS: ACQUISITIONS, CATALOGUING, INDEXING

106. **Aitchison, J**. Thesaurus construction: a practical manual/ by
Jean Aitchison and Alan Gilchrist. - London, Aslib, 1972. - 95 p.
Bibliography: p. 88-90.
Subject headings. Indexes. Association of special libraries and information bureaux.

107. **Akademiia nauk SSSR. Fundamental'naia biblioteka obshchestvennykh
nauk**. Instructions on the handling of United Nations mimeographed documents in the V. P. Volgin Basic library of social
science of the USSR Academy of sciences. - Approved by
V. I. Shunkov. - Moscow, 1965. - 12, 17 p.
Title and text in English and Russian.

108. - - **Institut filosofii**. Metodika i tekhnika statisticheskoĭ obrabotki
pervichnoĭ sotsiologicheskoĭ informatsii. - Moskva, Izd-vo "Nauka",
1968. - 326 p.
Information in social sciences.

109. **ALA** rules for filing catalog cards. - 2nd ed. - Chicago, American
library association, 1968. - xii, 260 p.
Prepared by the ALA editorial committee's sub-committee on the ALA rules for filing
catalog cards, Pauline A. Seely, chairman and editor.
Pt. 1. Alphabetical arrangement: basic rules; abbreviated forms; variant forms; names -
alphabetization.
Pt. 2. Order of entries: personal name entry arrangement; author entry arrangement;
anonymous classic entry arrangement.
Appendix: initial articles to be disregarded in filing. Glossary. Bibliography. Index.

110. **American library association**. Anglo-American cataloguing rules. - North
American text. - Chicago, 1967. - xxi, 400 p.
Prepared by the American library association, the Library of Congress, the Library
association and the Canadian library association.
Pt. 1. Entry and heading: general rules; works with authorship of mixed character;
related works; certain legal publications; certain religious publications; headings for persons;
choice and form of name; entry of name; general additions to names; special rules for
names in certain languages; headings for corporate bodies; choice and form of name;
subordinate and related bodies; geographical names; governments; government bodies and
officials; conferences, congresses, meetings, etc; religious bodies and officials; uniform titles;
choice and form of title: special rules for bible, other sacred scriptures, liturgical works.
Pt. 2. Description: Principles of descriptive cataloguing; separately published monographs;
serials; incunabula; photographic and other reproductions.
Pt. 3. Non-book materials: manuscripts; single manuscripts, entry description; collections
of manuscripts; maps, atlases, etc.; motion pictures and filmstrips; music; phonorecords;
pictures, designs, and other two dimensional representations.
Appendexes I-VI: Glossary; Capitalization; Abbreviations; Numerals; Punctuation and
diacritics; Rules for entry and heading that differ in the British text. Index.

111. **Aubry, J**. A timing study of the manual searching of catalogs. - The
Library quarterly 42: 399-415, no.4, 1972.
An attempt to identify some parameters relating to ease of manual searching in library
catalogs.

112. **Auerbach** guide to EDP. - Philadelphia, Ps., 1970. - 12 p.
References to Auerbach data handling reports (2 v.); Auerbach data communications
reports (2 v.); Auerbach standard EDP reports (10 v.); Auerbach scientific and control
computer reports (3 v.); Auerbach computer notebook international; Auerbach software
notebook; Auerbach graphic processing reports.

113. **Bakewell, K. G. B**. A manual of cataloguing practice. - Oxford
Pergamon press, 1972. - xiii, 298 p. - (International series of
monographs in library and information science. v. 14.)
Includes 403 bibliographical references.

114.   **Balnaves, J.**   Shared cataloguing. - The Australian library journal: 196-199, October, 1966.

115.   **Bliss, H. E.**   The organization of knowledge in libraries. - 2nd ed. - New York, HW. Wilson, 1939.

116.   **Bracke, J.**   Introduction à l'automation des bibliothèques. - Liège, 1971. - 69 p. - (Liège. Université. Centre d'études, de recherches et d'essais scientifiques du génie civil. Mémoires CERES. no. 31.)

117.   **Breycha-Vauthier, A. C.**   La classification décimale et son application à la Bibliothèque du Palais des Nations. - Journal de Genève, Numéro spécial: 8, 23 mai 1958.

118.   **Burgess, T. K.**   LOLA library on-line acquisitions sub-system, Washington State university/ by T. Burgess and L. Ames. - Washington, D.C., U.S. Dept. of commerce, National bureau of standards, 1968. - 19 l.
Photocopy. Springfield, Va. Clearing house for federal scientific and technical information, n.d., 74 p. (PB 179 892)
Each page represents two pages of the original.
Information storage and retrieval systems - Acquisitions (Libraries). Electronic data processing - Library science. Libraries - Automation.

119.   **Caballero-Marsal, F. A.**   United Nations documents in the United Nations Library: organization and servicing/ by Fernando A. Caballero-Marsal, Jorgen K. Nielsen and Harry N. M. Winton. - Journal of cataloguing and classification 7: 65-72, no. 3, Summer 1951.

120.   **Campbell, B. W.**   A successful microfiche program. - Special libraries 62: 136-142, March 1971.

121.   **Campey, L. H.**   Generating and printing indexes by computer. - London, Aslib, 1972. - 101 p. - (Aslib occasional publications. no.11.)
Bibliography: p. 38-44.

122.   **Canada. National library.**   Canadian MARC: a report of the activities of the MARC task group resulting in a recommended Canadian MARC format for monographs and a Canadian MARC format for serials. - Ottawa, 1972. - x, 242 p.

123.   **Coden** for periodical titles (including non-periodical titles and deleted Coden). - 3rd ed. - Philadelphia, Pa., 1970. - 2045 p.
v.1. Periodical titles arranged by Coden. - v.2. Periodical titles arranged alphabetically by title.
Codes for 102.000 periodical titles and 7.000 other series titles. Codes consist of five letters each.

124.   **Communautés européennes. Bibliothèque scientifique et technique.** Catalogage des périodiques. - Bruxelles, 1969. - 3 1.

125.   -- - - --   Règles de catalogage pour les publications périodiques. - Bruxelles, 1969. - 28 1.

26. **Cutter, C. A.**   Rules for a dictionary catalog. - Washington, D.C., 1904.

27. **Cutter**-Sanborn three-figure author tables. - Swanson-Swift revision, 1969. - Chicopee, Mass., H.R. Hunting company, 1969. - 34 p.
With it: Instruction book on how to use the Cutter-Sanborn table.

28. **Développement** économique et social: liste commune de descripteurs=Economic and social development: aligned list of descriptors=Wirtschaftliche und soziale Entwicklung: Gemeinsames Schlagwortverzeichnis. - v. 1-5. - Paris, Organisation de co-opération et de développement économiques, 1969. - 5 v.
Produced jointly by the ILO, ICSSD, DSE, FAO and OECD.

29. **De Walt, D. D.**   Distribution of documents. - Annual review of the United Nations affairs: 111-119, 1953.

30. **Dimitrov, T. D.**   Some aspects of cataloguing and indexing of United Nations and specialized agencies publications and documents/ by Theodore Dimitrov. - Geneva, 1970. - 24 1.
Lecture given at the Conference on UN publications, organized by the Association of Nordic research librarians at the Norwegian Nobel institute in Oslo, 8th-10th October, 1970.

31. **Divekari, V. D.**   United Nations documents: problems in their arrangement. - Library herald 2: 98-103, 1959.

32. **European atomic energy community.**   EURATOM thesaurus. - 2nd ed. - Brussels, 1966-67. - 1 v.

33. **European communities. Bibliothèque centrale.**   Classification décimale de la Bibliothèque centrale, classe 4:   Organisations internationales= Dezimalklassifikation der Zentralbibliothek, Abt. 4:   internationale Organisationen. - 3e éd.=3. Aufl. - Bruxelles, 1970. - 180 p.   F G
Contents:
1. Généralités. 2. Organisations mondiales. 3. Organisations européennes. 4. Communautés européennes. 5. Autres organisations européennes. 6. Organisations d'autres continents. 7. Tables de concordance. 8. Index alphabetique.

34. **Faure, J. C.**   Emploi des ordinateurs: introduction au software. - Paris, Dunod, 1971. - 122 p. - (Collection du Centre d'études pratiques d'informatique et d'automatique.)

35. **Fédération des associations internationales établies en Belgique.** Un projet de code de signalisation des langues par les couleurs. - Associations internationales=International associations 14: 142-143, no. 2, 1961.

36. **Food and agriculture organization. Terminology and reference section.**   Selected terms in data processing=Choix de termes utilisés dans le traitement de l'information. - Rome, 1970. - ii, 37 p. - (Its: Terminology note. no.3.)

c

137.   **Foskett, D. J.** Classification and indexing in the social sciences. -
       London, Butterworths, 1963.

138.   **Frauendorfer, S. von.** Survey of abstracting services in FAO's
       field of activities. - Rome, 1963. - 37, 2 1.

139.   **Freeman, R. R.** Computers and classification systems. - Journal of
       documentation 20:   137-145, no.3, 1964.

140.   -- --- The management of a classification scheme: modern approache
       exemplified by the UDC project of the American institute of physics.
       Journal of documentation 23: 304-320, no.4, 1967.

141.   **Giliarevskiĭ, R. S.**   La diffusion internationale des fiches de
       catalogue: situation actuelle et perspectives d'avenir/ by
       R. S. Giljarevskij. - Paris, Unesco, 1968. - 94 p. - (United
       Nations educational, scientific and cultural organisation.
       Manuels de l'UNESCO à l'usage des bibliothèques publiques.
       no. 15.)
       Bibliography: p. 50-52.

142.   -- --- Razvitie sovremennykh prinT͡sipov knigoopisaniĭa: kratkiĭ ocherk
       Moskva, Izd-vo Vsesoi͡uznoĭ knizhnoĭ palaty, 1961. - 182 p.
       Added title-page in English: The development of modern cataloguing principles.
       P.t 1. Basic stages in the development of cataloguing theory. Pt. 2. Principles of
       cataloguing in contemporary instructions.

143.   **Groesbeck, J.** Introducing UNDEX (United Nations documents
       index). - Special libraries 61: 165-170, July-August 1970.

144.   **Günther, A.**   A specialized subject index for a mechanized
       library catalogue/ by A. Günther, A. G. Hester and F. Wittmann.
       - Geneva, 1970. - 16 p.
       Report on CERN Library.

145.   **Halm, J. van.** Use of the UDC in a mechanized system: its
       application in a KWIC program. - Special libraries, v. 63, no.10,
       p. 482-486, 1972.
       A special feature of the system is that the KWIC serial number=the program sorting
       number=the encoded UDC form=the storage or shelving number.

146.   **Harris, A. G.** Organizing the United Nations documents collection.
       - College and research libraries 11: no.3, 142-149 August 1951.

147.   **Heaps, W. A.**   A collection on the United Nations. - Library
       journal 80: 1753-1758, September 1955.

148.   **Honoré-Duvergé, S.** Liste internationale de formes approuvées pour le
       catalogage des noms d'Etats=International list of approved forms for
       catalogue entries for the names of States. - Paris, 1964. - v, 53 p.
       At head of title: Fédération internationale des associations de bibliothécaires (F.I.A.B.).
       Conférénce internationale sur les principes de catalogage...
       "Publié avec le concours de l'UNESCO."
       Title and text in French and English. List of forms in English, French, German, Russian,
       and Spanish.

9. **Inter-agency working party on indexing of documents, Geneva, 1966.** Report and Background papers. - no.1-11. - v.p. 1965-1966. - 1 v.
Prepared by the Administrative committee on co-ordination.
Includes bibliographies.

Contents:
A. Report.
B. Background papers.
1. Indexing of agency documents.
2. A survey of indexing, indexes and catalogues of documents and publications of the U.N. and its specialized agencies.
3. Outline of the activities of the U.N. headquarters library...
4. FAO documentation center.
5. International labour office. Central library and documentation branch. ISIS integrated scientific information service progress report June 1965.
6. -- --- Information needs of the users of the Library.
7. -- --- International labour documentation. Index. v.4.
8. Note on the proposed establishment of a department of documentation and libraries (Unesco).
9. Codification and classification of documents and publications.
10. Publications of the United Nations family.
11. List of libraries and information centres receiving U.N. material.

0. **Inter-agency working party on indexing of documents. 2nd, Rome, 1967.** Papers. - v.p. 1967. - 1 v.
At head of title: Administrative committee on co-ordination.

Contents:
A. Meeting papers.
1. Provisional agenda.
2. List of participants.
3. not issued.
4. Extension and coordination of indexing activities.
5. Report of the 2nd meeting.
6. Extension and coordination of indexing activities.

B. Working papers.
1. Control, use and dissemination of United Nations documentation.
2. Co-ordination of indexing approaches and development of a common indexing vocabulary.
3. Implications of wider use of working languages.
4. United Nations. Dag Hammarskjold library. Feasibility of using computer equipment for the preparation of indexes.
5. United Nations public information activities in the economic, social human rights and related fields.
6. International labour office. Central library and documentation branch. Computerised IR and catalogue production within the ISIS system.
7. Proposed inter-agency sub-committee on indexing, documentation and library services.
8. Indexing of publications issued at the International atomic energy agency.
9. Relevant developments at UNESCO.
10. Progress report on FAO's indexing activities.
11. Note by the ITU...
12. Note by GATT on the recommendations in the report of the Inter-agency working party on indexing of documents.
13. Indexing of WHO documentation.

C. Report.

51. **Inter-agency working party on indexing and documentation. 3rd, Paris, 1968.** Working documents - v.p. 1968. - 1 v.
At head of title: Administrative committee on co-ordination.

Contents:

1. Report.
2. List of working documents.
3. Provisional agenda.
4. Provisional list of participants.

Inter-agency working party on indexing and documentation (cont'd).
5. Central index of major documents.
6. An information storage and retrieval system.
7. Central index of major documents on the United Nations system.
8. Outline of proposed U.N. microfiche standards.
9. Unesco's plans for development of the Department of documentation, libraries and archives.
10. Co-ordination of the activities of the U.N. family in the field of documentation, 1968-1969.
11. Report of the Panel of specialists.
12 The FAO documentation centre.
13. General review of the programmes and activities of the U.N. family in the economic, social, technical co-operation.
14. Computer-assisted indexing project: procedural charts.
15. U.N. Dag Hammarskjold library.   Two library projects.
16. Computer-assisted indexing project: samples.
17. -- : input samples.
18. Indexing of U.N. documentation.
19. Draft final report.

152.   **Inter-agency working party on storage and retrieval of documentation to the IOB, Geneva, 1971.**   Report. - Geneva, 1971. - 4, 2 p.
At head of title: Inter-organization board for information systems and related activities.

153.   **International atomic energy agency.**   INIS reference series. - no. 1-13. - Vienna, 1969-1971. - 13 v.
At head of title: IAEA-INIS.

Contents:

IAEA-INIS-1(Rev.I)	INIS: Descriptive cataloguing rules
IAEA-INIS-2(Rev.I)	INIS: Descriptive cataloguing samples
IAEA-INIS-3(Rev.I)	INIS: Subject categories and scope descriptions
IAEA-INIS-4(Rev.0)	INIS: Instructions for submitting abstracts
IAEA-INIS-5(Rev.I)	INIS: Terminology and codes for countries and international organizations
IAEA-INIS-6(Rev.I)	INIS: Authority list for corporate entries
IAEA-INIS-7(Rev.0)	INIS: Magnetic and punched paper tape codes and character sets
IAEA-INIS-8(Rev.0)	INIS: Paper tape specifications and record format
IAEA-INIS-9(Rev.0)	INIS: Magnetic tape specifications and record format
IAEA-INIS-10(Rev.0)	INIS: Transliteration rules for selected non-roman characters
IAEA-INIS-11(Rev.0)	INIS: Authority list for journal titles
IAEA-INIS-12(Rev.0)	INIS: Manual for indexing
IAEA-INIS-13(Rev.0)	INIS: Thesaurus
IAEA-INIS-13A(Rev.0)	INIS: Terminology charts

154.   **International business machines corporation. Advanced systems development division.**   An overview of the experimental library management system (ELMS)/ by R.W. Alexander and R.W. Harvey. - Los Gatos, Calif., 1970. - 19 p. - (Its: Laboratory report. 16.197/1970.)

155.   -- **Data processing division.**   Introduction to IBM data processing systems: student text. - 3rd ed. - White Plains, N.Y., 1969. - 106 p.
Data representation. Storage devices. Central processing unit. Input/output devices. Stored program concepts. Programming languages. Operating systems. Compatibility and emulation. Procedure control. Index.

156.   **International** cataloguing. - v.1-   ; 1972-   . - London, 1972-   . - v.
Quarterly bulletin of the IFLA Committee on cataloguing: A.H. Chaplin (Chairman), Dorothy Anderson (Executive secretary).
Functions: to publish a regular information about cataloguing activities in all parts of the world and draw attention to conferences and meetings and to particular projects under way.

157. **International conference on cataloguing principles, Paris, 1961.** Report. -
London, 1963. - viii, 293 p.
At head of title: International federation of library associations.
Draft statement of principles: functions of the catalogue; structure of the catalogue;
kinds of entry; use of multiple entries; function of different kinds of entry; choice of
standard heading; single personal author; corporate authors; form of heading for corporate
authors; subordinate bodies; multiple authorship; works entered under title; form-headings
and form-subheadings; entry word for personal names.
Resolutions of the conference.
Sectional group meetings reports: Arabic, Indonesian and Malayan names; bilingualism;
Hebrew names; Indic names-of-person (non—Muslim); Iranian names; liturgies and other
religious texts; Muslim names in India and Pakistan; transliteration; terminology; basic
vocabulary of cataloguing terms.
Appendix: working papers:
1. Osborn, A.D. Relation between cataloguing principles and principles applicable to
other forms of bibliographical work.
2. Lubetzky, S. The function of the main entry in the alphabetical catalogue. - one
approach.
3. Verona, E. The function of the main entry in the alphabetical catalogue - a
second approach.
4. Jolley, L.J. A study of the views put forward by Lubetzky and Verona.
5. Vasilevskaia, V.A. Limits to the use of entries under corporate authors; the
cataloguing of laws and treaties.
6. Honoré, S. Corporate authorship: form of heading for corporate authors, treatment
of subordinate bodies.
7. Pierrot, R. Entry of anonymous works under standard or form titles.
8. Dunkin, P.S. Problems in the cataloguing of serial publications.
9. Eisenhart, C. Cataloguing of liturgies and religious texts in the alphabetical catalogue.
10. Braun, H. Multiple authorship.
11. Kalan, P. Choice of entry for authors whose names vary.
12. Ascarelli, F. Compound surnames and surnames with prefixes.
13. Monteiro da Cunha, M.L. Treatment of Brazilian and Portuguese names: problems
and solution.
14. Sengupta, B. Rendering of Indic names -of-person in catalogue entries.
15. Sheniti, M. Treatment of Arabic names.
16. Edelman, R. The treatment of names in Hebrew characters and title entry for
Hebrew books.
17. Gull, C.D. The impact of electronics upon cataloguing rules.

158. **International conference on information processing, Paris, 1959.**
Information processing; proceedings. - Paris, UNESCO, 1960.
- 520 p.
Text partly English, partly French. Abstracts in English, French, German,
Russian and Spanish.
Includes bibliographies.

159. **International congress of libraries and documentation centres, Brussels,
1955.** Rapports=Reports. - v.1-   . - La Haye, M.Nijhoff, 1955-   -
v.
At head of title: International federation of library associations. International federation
for documentation. International association of music libraries.

160. **International federation for documentation.** Classification décimale
universelle. - Éd. moyenne internationale. - t.1-   . - Bruxelles,
Mundaneum, 1967-   . -   v. - (Its: Publications. FID. no.413.)
Ouvrage publié avec l'appui de l'UNESCO.
t.1. Tables systématiques.

161. -- --- FID publications: catalogue 1971. - The Hague, 7 Hofweg,
1971. - 52 p.
General publications. Conferences. Meetings on special topics. Information science.
Documentation literature. Documentation practice. Reproduction. Mechanization.
Linguistics. Training. Information sources. Abstracting and indexing services. Special
bibliographies. Classification. Universal decimal classification. Index to FID publications
numbers.

162.   **International federation of library associations.** Catalogage des publications en série: les éléments en série. - The Hague, 1971. - 11 p.

163.   -- - - - Description bibliographique internationale normalisée des publications en série=International standard bibliographic description for serials. - The Hague, 1972. - 23 p.

164.   -- - - - IFLA communications.
Reprints from Libri, International library review, Copenhagen.

165.   -- **Committee on uniform cataloguing rules.** Newsletter. no.4, October 1969.
Report on the International meeting of cataloguing experts.

166.   **International labour office.** L'introduction des ordinateurs dans les organismes de sécurité sociale: généralités et études préliminaires. - Genève, 1972. - 76 p.

167.   -- **Central library and documentation branch.** CLD internal handbook instructions. - Geneva, 1966-1972. - 1 v.

168.   -- - - - ILO signs agreement with Sweden on computer use. - ILO Press, 28 January 1972.

169.   -- - - - Information retrieval in the computer age: the Constitution of the International labour organisation states that the ILO should be an international clearing house of information on labour questions.

170.   -- - - - ISIS (Integrated Scientific Information System): progress report. - 1965-1967. - Geneva, 1965-1967. - 3 v. - (Its: DOC/NOTES/7, etc.)

171.   -- - - - LD/Notes/1-59. - Geneva, 1966-1972. - 1 v.

Contents of selected numbers:
24.   Processing system for ILO and other intergovernmental organisation documents.
37.   Review of activities in 1968 and guidelines for future development.
39.   Some cost estimates for bibliographical searching in a large-scale social sciences information system/ by G. K. Thompson.
41.   Rules for filling in worksheets and keypunching cards in the ISIS format.
44.   Draft revision of guidelines for writing document analyses (first section).
45.   Etude sur l'utilisation effective de la documentation sur la formation professionnelle enregistrée dans le système ISIS, au Bureau international du travail/ par Catherine Berenstein.
46.   Notes on bibliographical services available from the Central library and and documentation branch of the International labour office.
47.   Proposal for an on-line processing system/ by William D. Schieber.
49.   Guidelines for the formulation of annotations for "International labour documentation".
50.   ISIS - a short guide for librarians and documentalists/ by G. K. Thompson... and others.
52.   Demographic projections to the 1980's (demonstration question - free text search facility).
56.   Instrumentos de trabajo necesarios para permitir el establecimiento de una red latinoamericana de documentación económica y social/ por G. K. Thompson.
59.   Instructions pour la rédaction des notices analytiques de l'"International labour documentation".

72. **International labour office. Central library and documentation branch.**
List of descriptors. - 2nd ed. - Geneva, 1966- . - v. - (Its: LD/NOTES/17.)
Loose-leaf.

73. -- --- Register of research projects.
Pub. bi-annually.

74. -- --- Le traitement de l'information à l'heure de l'électronique. FE

75. - - **Centre international d'informations de sécurité et d'hygiène du travail.** Introduction au service des fiches et schéma de classification - Genève, 1960. - 49 p.

76. - - **Library.** List of subject headings=Répertoire des matières. - Geneva, 1929. - 105 l.
Introduction by André de Maday.

77. **International meeting of cataloguing experts, Copenhagen, 1969.**
Newsletter. no.1-4. London, 1969. - 1 v.

78. -- --- Report and documents. - London, IFLA, 1969. - 1 v.
" Chairman: A. H. Chaplin."

79. **International organization for standardization.** ISO/TC 46:
Normalisation in documentation: recommendations.
- Genève, 1969-1972. - 1 v.

Contents of recommendations:

International code for the abbreviation of titles of periodicals.	R 4-1953
Layout of periodicals.	R 8-1954
International system for the transliteration of slavic cyrillic characters. 2nd edition.	R 9-1968
Short contents list of periodicals or other documents.	R 18-1955
Bibliographical strip.	R 30-1956
Bibliographical references: essential elements.	R 77-1958
Abstracts and synopses.	R 214-1961
Presentation of contributions to periodicals.	R 215-1961
International system for the transliteration of Arabic characters.	R 233-1961
Transliteration of Hebrew.	R 259-1962
Bibliographical references: essential and supplementary elements.	R 690-1968
Abbreviations of typical words in bibliographical references.	R 832-1968
Abbreviations of generic names in titles of periodicals.	R 833-1968
International system for the transliteration of Greek characters into Latin characters.	R 843-1968
Index of a publication.	R 999-1969
Title-leaves of a book.	R1086-1969
Numbering of divisions and sub-divisions in written documents.	ISO2145-1972
Directories of libraries, information and documentation centres.	ISO2146-1971

Documentary reproduction:

Sizes of photocopies (on paper) readable without optical devices.	R 169-1960
Microcopies on transparent bases: sizes of recommended bases.	R 193-1961

International organization for standardization. ISO/TC 46: (cont'd)

Microcopies: scale of 35 mm microfilms for international exchange.	R 218-1961
Terms relating to microcopies and their bases.	R 260-1962
Terms relating to microcopy apparatus.	R 371-1964
ISO conventional typographical character for legibility tests (ISO character).	R 435-1965
Microcopies: legibility tests; description of the ISO mire (ISO test object) and its use in photographic document reproduction.	R 446-1965
Essential characteristics of 35 mm microfilm reading apparatus.	R 452-1965
Microcopies: legibility tests; description and use of the ISO micromire (micro test object) for checking a reading apparatus.	R 689-1968
Microcopy: measurement of the screen luminance of microfilm readers.	R 782-1968
35 mm and 16 mm microfilms, spools and reels.	R1116-1969

180.   **International** standard book numbering: Group 92. - Paris, UNESCO, Distribution division, 1973. - (Pub/105/120173.)

List of Members, January 1973.

Designation	Location	Publisher prefix
European Conference of Ministers of Transport	Paris	821
Field Science Office for South Asia (Unesco)	New Delhi	9001
Food and Agriculture Organization	Rome	5
Inter Governmental Maritime Consultative organization	London	801
International Association of Universities	Paris	9002
International Atomic Energy Agency	Vienna	0
International Institute for Educational Planning	Paris	803
International Labour Office	Geneva	2
International Monetary Fund	Washington	800
International Telecommunications Union	Geneva	61
Organization for Economic co-operation and		64
Development	Paris	6565
Unesco	Paris	3
Unesco Institute for Education	Hamburg	820
United Nations	New York	1
United Nations Institute for Training and Research	New York	802
Universal Postal Union	Geneva	62
World Health Organization	Geneva	4
World Meteorological Organization	Geneva	63

Pending:

ECAFE/Unesco Science and Technology Unit	Bangkok
Economic Commission for Latin America (U.N.)	Santiago de Chile
Regional Educational Building Institute for Africa (Unesco)	Khartoum
Regional Office for Education in Asia (Unesco)	Bangkok
International Civil Aviation Organization	Montreal
Oficina de Ciencias para America Latina (Unesco)	Montevideo
United Nations	Geneva
UNRWA	Beirut
World Intellectual Property Organization	Geneva

181.   **International** standardization is chaotic. - Information retrieval & library automation letter. v.8, no.6, p.1-4.
Analysis of a source document prepared by the Hungarian national committee for IFLA under a contract with UNESCO. The subject is divided into four major areas: layout of documents; library work and equipment; documentation work and services; mechanization of library and documentation processes.

82.   **Inter-organization board for information systems and related
      activities. 4th session, Geneva, 1972.** Report on the library
      management and documentation retrieval system(LIBRIS) to be
      available at ICC. - Geneva, 1972. - 21 p. - (Its: Documents.
      IOB/IV/W.P.3.)
      Working paper for Agenda item no.6.
      Annex: Terms of reference of ILO-SAFAD task force, supplementary agreement
      concerning further development of ISIS. - 8 p.

      Contents:
      1. Background and justification.   2. List of potential applications.   3. Description of
      information retrieval funcations.   4. Description of library management functions.
      5. Implementation of LIBRIS.

83.   **Inter-organization** systems and programme library. - Geneva, 1972. -
      1 v.
      Loose-leaf.
      The present catalogue has been compiled from the answers to the 1969 composite
      questionnaire prepared by the Computer users' committee.
      It is divided into three parts: I. Index by agency.   II. Index by category.   III. Cata-
      logue by agency.
      Worthless to appear in special lists intended to be of value for development of UN
      related information systems.

84.   **Isotta, N. E. C.** International information networks: the
      ESRO (European space research organization) system. - ASLIB
      proceedings 24: 31-37, January 1972.

85.   **Keep** up to date with your UDC. - FID News bulletin 17: 137-138,
      1967.
      Indication of the wide range of editions available and the various associated publications.

86.   **Kyle, B.** The Universal decimal classification: a study of the present
      position and future developments with particular reference to those
      schedules which deal with the humanities, arts and social sciences. -
      Unesco bulletin for libraries 15:   53-69, no.2, 1961.

87.   **Lancaster, F. W.** Vocabulary control for information retrieval. -
      Washington, D.C., Information resources press, 1972. - xiii, 233 p.
      Contents:
      Why vocabulary control?   Vocabulary types: pre-coordination and post-coordination,
      enumeration and synthesis. The classification scheme in vocabulary control. Vocabulary
      control by subject heading. Vocabulary control in post-coordination systems: the
      thesaurus. Generating the controlled vocabulary. Organizing and displaying the vocabulary.
      The thesaurofacet.   Some thesaurus rules and conventions. The reference structure of the
      thesaurus. Computer manipulation of thesaurus data. Vocabulary growth and up-dating.
      The influence of system vocabulary on the performance of a retrieval system. Characteristics
      and components of an index language. Searching natural-language data bases. Creating index
      languages automatically. Compatibility and convertibility of vocabularies. Some further
      controlled vocabularies. The role of the controlled vocabulary in indexing and searching
      operations. Vocabulary use and dynamics in a very large information system. Vocabulary
      in on-line retrieval situation. Some cost-effectiveness aspects of vocabulary control.
      Appendix: Some controlled vocabularies for study or examination.   Index.

88.   **Laver, F. J. M.** Introducing computers. - London, H.M. Stationery
      office, 1965. - 68 p.
      Appendix: reading list. p.63.

89.   **Liebaers, H.** Le catalogage en coopération. - Bulletin de
      l'Unesco à l'intention des bibliothèques 24: 66-78, 139-150;
      mars-avril, mai-juin 1970.
      Bibliography: p. 150-152.

190.   **Magyar tudományos akadémia. Könyvtár.** Vocabularium abbrevia-
        turarum bibliotecarii. - v.1-   . - Budapest, 1961-   . -   v.

191.   **Margot, C.** Notices catalographiques des publications en série:
        analyse de diverses structures de notices catalographiques préconisées
        pour l'éntrée en ordinateur des publications en série. - Lausanne,
        1972. - 60 l.
        Contents:
        1. Glossaire. 2. Problématique des publications en série. 3. Conditions préalables à
        l'établissement d'une structure de notice pour les périodiques à la BCU. 4. Tableaux
        des éléments et exemples. Bibliography
        Bibliography: l. 54-57.

192.   **Melcher, D.** Standard book numbering. - Publishers'
        weekly, April 15, 1968: 39-40.

193.   **Nasatir, D.** Data archives for the social sciences: purposes, operations
        and problems. - Paris, Unesco, 1973. - 126 p. - (United Nations
        educational, scientific and cultural organisation. Reports and papers
        in the social sciences. SS/CH 26.)
        An overview of the archive movement. Operational considerations of archives. Problems
        remaining in the creation of data library infra-structure.

194.   **National microfilm association.** Guide to microreproduction equipment. -
        5th ed. - Silver Spring, Md., 1971. - 793 p.
        Edited by Hubbard W. Ballou.

195.   **Needham, C. D.** Organizing knowledge in libraries: an introduction
        to information retrieval. - 2nd rev. ed. - London, Andre Deutsch,
        1971. - 448 p.
        pt. 1. The author title approach. pt. 2. The subject approach. pt. 3. Description.
        pt. 4. Policy and organization. pt. 5. Examples of practical cataloguing.

196.   **Neville, H. H.** Feasibility study of a scheme for reconciling
        thesauri covering a common subject. - Journal of
        documentation 26: 313-336, December 1970.

197.   La **numérotation** normalisée internationale du livre. - Bulletin de
        l'Unesco à l'intention des bibliothèques 23: 241, no.4, 1969.

198.   **Organization for economic cooperation and development. Library.**
        Plan de classification. - 3e éd. révisée. - Index géographique. -
        Paris, 1972. - 53 p.

199.   **Organization of American States.** Report on publications
        and documents office, Secretariat for management,
        Organization of American States, 1971-1972. - 2 v.
        - (Its: Documents. OEA/Ser.D/X).

200.   **Panel on science and technology. 12th, Washington, D.C. 1971.**
        International science policy: proceedings before the Committee
        on science and astronautics, U.S. House of representatives,
        92nd Congress, 1st sess. - Washington, D.C., 1971. - viii, 373 p.

201.   **Patentnaiā** dokumentaĩsiiā i patentnaiā informaĩsiiā. - vyp. 1-   . -
Moskva, TŜNIIPI, 1969-   . -   v.
At head of title: Komitet po delam izobreteniĩ i otkrytiĩ pri Sovete ministrov SSSR.
R.P. Vcherashniĩ, L.G. Kraveĩs... and others.
International survey of existing processing methods in patents documentation and
patents information.

202.   **Pease, M.**   The plain "J":   a documents classification system. -
Library resources and technical services, v.16, no.3, p. 315-325.
A design of classification scheme for documents as a modification of the Library of
Congress "J" class.

203.   **Penna, C. V.**   The planning of library and documentation
services. - 2nd ed. rev. and enl./ by P. H. Sewell and
Herman Liebaers. - Paris, Unesco, 1970. - 158 p.
- (United Nations educational, scientific and cultural
organisation. Unesco manuals for libraries. no.17.)

204.   **Pierrot, R.**   État présent de la normalisation du catalogage dans la
perspective de l'automatisation. - Bulletin des bibliothèques de
France 15: 127-129, no.3, 1970.

205.   **Pieterse, J.**   The registry in international organizations.
- Revue de la documentation 17: 43-50, February 1950.

206.   **Propositions** du service MARC=MARC record service proposals: détals
de propositions pour la fourniture sur bandes magnétiques de
données catalographiques des publications anglaises. - Grenoble, 1969. -
129 p.
Présenté par R.E. Coward. Trad. par Marc Chauveinc.

207.   **Ranganathan, S.R.**   Classified catalogue code. - 2nd ed. - New York,
H.W. Wilson, 1945. - 328 p. - (Madras library association. Publications series. no.14.)

208.   -- - --   The Colon classification. -   - Rutgers, 1965. -
298 p. - (Rutgers series on systems for the intellectual organization
of information. v.4.)

209.   -- - --   Dictionary catalogue code. - Madras, Thompson & co. ltd.,
1945. - 320 p. - (Madras library association. Publications series.
no.14.)

210.   **Rigby, M.**   Experiments in mechanised control of meteorlogical and
geoastrophysical literature and the UDC schedules in those fields. -
Revue internationale de la documentation 31: 103-106, no.3, 1964.

211.   **Ronquillo, E. M.**   Acquiring publications of the United
Nations and its agencies. - Library herald 8: 64-81, 1965.

212.   **Saint-Paul, M.** Comprendre l'ordinateur. - Paris, Les éditions d'organisation, 1972. - 167 p.
At head of title: Michel Saint-Paul. Albert Perriol.

213.   **Sebestyén, G.** International catalog cards? - Könyvtáros 16: 629-633, November 1966.

214.   **Silva Pôrto, V. da.** Tratamento das publicações das Nações Unidas nas bibliotecas. - Rio de Janeiro, 1957. - p. 231-264.
"Separata da 'Revista do livro' no. 8, dezembro de 1957."

215.   **Sovet ékonomicheskoĭ vzaimopomoslıchi. Postoĭannaĭa komissiĭa po koordinaĭsii nauchnykh i tekhnicheskikh issledovanii.** Primenenie universal'nykh vychislitel'nykh mashin v rabote organov informaĭsii; (trudy simpoziuma). - Moskva, 1970. - 239 p.
"Nastoĭashchiĭ sbornik soderzhit doklady i soobshcheniĭa, sdelannye na Mezhdunarodnom simpoziume stran-chlenov SEV, sostoĭavsheesĭa 19-22 iĭunĭa 1967 goda v g. Moskve."
Bibliographies at the end of some articles.

216.   **Standard book numbering agency.** Standard book numbering: incorporating the recommendations of the Publishers association for implementing the standard book numbering scheme. - 2nd (revised) ed. - London, Standard book numbering agency, 1968. - 10 p. tables.
"Prepared for the Distribution and methods committee of the Publishers association."

217.   **Standardization** for documentation. - Edited by Bernard Houghton. - London, C. Bingley, 1969. - 93 p.

218.   **Standards** - key to progress in developing countries. - ISO bulletin, October 1970, p.6.
Working group of the ISO Development committee (DEVCO) was established at the 1970 Ankara meeting of the International organization for standardization to consider the special needs of developing countries for standards information and the creation of an effective technical information center to meet these needs.

219.   **Strauss, L. J.** Scientific and technical libraries: their organization and administration. - 2nd ed. - New York, Becker and Hayes, 1972. - 450 p.
Includes bibliographies.

220.   **Study session on current developments in cataloguing among the international libraries, Geneva, 1968.** Documents. - Luxembourg, 1967. - (Association of international libraries. Newsletter. no.14.)
Contents:
1. Opening address/ by J. W. Haden.
2. The role of cataloguing in an age of automation/ by Hope Reeder.
3. Philosophy of cataloguing/ by G. K. Thompson.
4. Shared cataloguing/ by E. Johnson.
5. Discussions and conclusions.

221.   **Surin, N. M.** Programmirovanie dlĭa schetno-perforaĭsionnykh mashin. - Moskva, "Statistika", 1968. - 139 p.
Programming for punched cards machines.

22. **Symposium on new techniques in library and documentation work, Geneva, 1963**. Lectures on new techniques in documentation delivered to the Symposium. - Geneva, 1963. - 72 p. - (International institute for labour studies. Lecture series. Série de conférences. ILO/INST/LS.8.)
Text partly English, partly French.

23. **Symposium on the handling of nuclear information, Vienna, 1970**. Handling of nuclear information; proceedings of the Symposium. - Vienna, 1970. - 674 p. - (International atomic energy agency. Proceedings series.)
Texts partly English, partly French, partly Russian. Abstracts of the reports in English at the beginning of each chapter.

24. -- --- Miscellaneous papers. - Vienna, International atomic energy agency, 1969? -1970. - 1 v.
Texts partly English, partly French, partly Russian.

25. **Système** international de données sur les publications en série=International serials data systems, ISDS. - Paris, 1972. - 11 p. - (UNISIST.)
Première réunion du Group d'experts. Point 5 de l'ordre du jour: Organisation de l'ISDS.

26. **Tate, F. A.** Libraries and abstracting and indexing services: - a study in interdependency. - Library trends 16: 353-373, January 1968.

27. **Technical** dictionary of data processing, computers, office machines. - Oxford, Pergamon press, 1970. - 1463 p.
13,000 terms in English, French, German, and Russian.

28. **Tewari, B. C.** Organization and handling of UN publications. - (In Library seminar on research in the social sciences, New Delhi, 1959. Social science research and libraries. London, Asia pub. house, 1960. p. 73-90.).

29. **Thompson, A.** Rules for subject headings, periodicals subject index. - Journal of documentation 9: 169-174, no.3, 1953.

30. **Thompson, G. K.** Abstracting services in education and the social sciences: a study of document analysis techniques useful for the development of a computer-based decentralized labour formation network. - Geneva, International labour office, 1971. - iii, 63 1.
Bibliography: leaves 62-63.

31. **Toerien, B. J.** The treatment of United Nations publications in libraries. - (In Annual conference, South African library association. 19: 1964; Cape town; Reports and proceedings. Potchefstroom, 1964. p. 113-133.)

232. **Union of international associations.** International standard book numbering and its effects on the publications of international organizations. - Brussels, 1969. - 2 p.

233. -- --- Functions of the **Union** of international associations as a standard book **numbering** agency for international organizations (based on the definition of the ISO meeting, Berlin, 17-18 April, 1969.)

234. **United Nations.** Computer-assisted indexing project: input samples. - New York, 1968. - 5 p.

235. -- --- Computer-assisted indexing project: samples. - New York, 1968. - i, 52 p.

236. -- --- Establishment and organization of United Nations archives. - New York, 1961. - 1 v.
"Prepared as working paper for the 4th Round table conference on archives, Warsaw, May 1961."

237. -- --- Filing, discarding and binding of United Nations material. - New York, 1958. - 8 l. - (Its: Documents. ST/LIB/6.)

238. -- --- Forms catalogue. - New York, 1972. -   v, 40 p. - (Its: Documents. ST/ADM/L.1/Rev.4.)

239. -- --- Instructions à l'intention des bibliothèques dépositaires des documents et publications de l'Organisation des Nations Unies. - New York, 1968. - 15 p.   E F
I. Classement et conservation de la documentation déposée. II. Importance du dépôt.
III. Correspondance. IV. Règles à observer pour les demandes de documents.
Annexe A: Modèle de demande de documents.
Annexe B: Principes applicables aux bibliothèques dépositaires des documents et publications de l'Organisation des Nations Unies (ST/PB/4/Rev.2.).

240. -- --- Names of countries and adjectives of nationality. - New York, 1972. - 37 p. - (Its: Documents. ST/CS/SER.F./285.)
At head of title: Office of conference services. Terminology section. Terminology bulletin. no.285.
The bulletin gives a trilingual list, in English alphabetical order, of the names of members of the United Nations, members of specialized agencies and parties to the Statute of the International court of justice.

241. -- --- Supply to the United Nations Library of official material not available through the regular distribution channels. - New York, 1965. - 3 p. - (Its: Documents. ST/AI/165, 27 September 1965.)

242. -- --- United Nations microfiche standard. - Rev. ed. - New York, 1970. - 19 p. - (Its: ST/PB/30.)

243. --   **Dag Hammarskjold library, New York.** Abstracting and indexing services in scientific and technical subjects: a select list. - New York, 1951. - 35 p. - (Its: Miscellaneous bibliographies. no. 12.)
"Prepared for the Technical assistance administration by the United Nations headquarters Library."

244.   **United Nations. Dag Hammarskjold library, New York.** Biblio-
        graphical style manual. - 3rd rev. draft. - New York, 1961. - 70 l.

245.   -- --- Computer-assisted indexing project: instructions for
        the use of the 'indexing data sheet' (form L.30 (1-69)
        - A/B/C/D/E). - New York, 1969. - 66 l. - (Its:
        Instruction/Comp/1.)

246.   -- --- List of United Nations document series symbols.
        - New York, 1970. - iv, 171 p. - (Its: Bibliographical
        series. no.5/Rev.2.)
        United Nations. Publications. Sales numbers. 1970.I.21.
        United Nations. Documents. ST/LIB/SER.B/5/Rev.2.
        The publication contains a list of series symbols in symbol order and
        an alphabetical index consisting of series titles and broad subject categories.
        Additions are included annually in UNDI: Cumulative index, part 2.

247.   -- --- **Index section.** Instructions for the preparation of
        documents for microfiching. - New York, 1967. - 2 p.

248.   -- --- Modifications of COSATI standards part II. E and F
        (utilization of grid areas) to be applied during the pilot
        project of microfiching of United Nations documents.
        - New York, 1967. - 5 p.

249.   -- --- Instructions for analysis of documents.

250.   -- --- Indexing data sheet.

251.   -- **Economic commission for Latin America. Latin American
        centre for economic and social documentation.** La
        computadora y sus sistemas y prógramas aplicados a la
        documentación. (CLADES/WG.1/L.6.). - 1971.

252.   -- --- Economic and social terms in the OECD aligned list
        of descriptors and their translation into Spanish. (CLADES/
        WG.1/L.6.) - 1971.

253.   -- --- Manual para usuarios del KWIC/360. Sistema de
        recuperación e indización bibliográfica. (CLADES/INS/2.)
        - 1972.

254.   -- --- A note on training in documentation and library
        science. (CLADES/WG.1/L.19.) - 1971.

255.   -- --- Report on the proceedings, conclusions and recommendations
        of the Meeting. (CLADES/WG.1/L.24.) - 1971.

256.   -- **Office, Geneva. Division linguistique. Section de terminologie et
        de documentation technique.** Listes terminologiques publiées au
        1er novembre 1972. - Genève, 1972. - 2 p. - (Its: TERM/INF/7/Rev.1.)

257.   **United Nations. Service des conférences et services généraux. Division des documents.** La section de la distribution et des ventes. - Genève, 1968. - 24 p. E F

I.   La Section de la distribution et des ventes dans le Secrétariat de l'Office des Nations Unies à Genève.

II.   Le groupe de la distribution: attributions; organisation; fonctions; modes de distribution; systèmes de distribution et leur application pratique; termes et expressions utilisés dans la Section; mouvement des documents distribués par la section.

III.   Le groupe des ventes: attributions; organisation; fonctions.

IV.   Le groupe de coordinattion et de contrôle des stocks: attributions; organisation; fonctions.

Annexe 1: Organigramme de la Section de la distribution et des ventes.
Annexe 2: Cotes des documents.

258.   -- **Statistical office.** Handbook on data processing methods. - pt.1-2. - Rome, 1959-1960. - 2 v. E F S

Prepared jointly by Statistical office of the United Nations and Statistical division, Food and agriculture organization.
Principal methods of data processing, planning, organizing and administering data processing services, the elements of planning and operating a punch-card installation, manual methods and tools for data processing, punch-card sorting.

259.   -- --- United Nations standard country code. - New York, 1970. - 46 p. - (Its: Statistical papers. series M. no.49.)

United Nations. Publications. Sales number. 1970.XVII.13.
Description and application of country classification.
Annexes: UN numerical country code: three digit code; country classification for international trade statistics; country classification for induatrial and national accounts statistics; standardized abbreviated English country names; standardized abbreviated French country names.

260.   **United Nations educational, scientific and cultural organisation.** Description of the cataloguing and indexing practices of the Unesco library and documentation services. - Paris, 1970. - 4 p.

261.   -- --- Guide to authors on the preparation of scientific and technical reports. (SC/WS/468)

262.   -- --- Guide for the preparation of scientific papers for publication. (SC/MD/

263.   -- --- Guidelines for the establishment and development of monolingual thesauri for information retrieval. - Paris, 1971. - 30 p.

264.   -- --- International standardization of library statistics: proposal for international regulations. - Paris, 1968. - 10 p. - (Its: Documents. 78 EX/8.)

At head of title: Seventy-eighth session. Item 4.5.2. of the provisional agenda.

265.   -- --- Principes directeurs pour l'établissement et le développement de thesaurus scientifiques et techniques multilingues destinés à la recherche documentaire. - Paris, 1971. - 13 p.

266.   -- --- **UNISIST.** International serials data system (ISDS): provisional guidelines for ISDS. - Paris, 1972. - 24 p. - (ISDS/IC/I.6.)

67.   **United Nations industrial development organization.** Thesaurus
      of industrial development terms. - New York, 1971.
      - x, 227 p. - (Its: UNIDO/LIB/SER.C/l.)

68.   **United States. Atomic energy commission. Division of technical
      information extension.** Corporate author headings used by the U.S.
      Atomic energy commission in cataloguing reports. - Oak Ridge,
      Tenn., 1969. - 172 p.
      It conforms to the cataloguing rules adopted by the Committee in scientific and technical
      information (COSATI) of the Federal council for science and technology.

69.   - - **Department of State. Bureau of intelligence and research.** Status
      of the world's nations. - Washington, D.C., 1969. - 20 p. - (Its:
      Publication. no. 7862.)
      Independent States. Quasi-independent States. Irregular categories of political areas and
      régimes. Populations, areas, capitals, and U.N. membership for all independent States.
      Check list of the 66 newly independent States since 1943.

70.   - - **Educational resources information center.** Rules for thesaurus
      preparation. - Washington, D.C., U.S. Department of health,
      education, and welfare, 1971. - 20 p.

71.   - - - - - Thesaurus of ERIC descriptors. - New York, CCM Information
      corporation, 1970. - 546 p.

72.   - - **Library of Congress.** The MARC II format: a communications
      format for bibliographic data. - Prepared by Henriette D. Avram,
      John F. Knapp, and Lucia J. Rather. - Washington, D.C., 1968. -
      167 p.
      Contents:
      1. The communications format.   2. Data organization of monographs in the communications
      format.   Appendixes.

73.   - - - - - Subject headings: used in the dictionary catalogs of the
      Library of Congress. - 7th ed. - Edited by Marguerite V. Quattlebaum. -
      Washington, D.C., Subject cataloguing division, Processing department,
      Library of Congress, 1966. - viii, 1432 p.
      Updated by monthly and cumulative supplements.   January 1966-

74.   - - - - - **MARC development office.** Information on the MARC system. -
      Washington, D.C., 1971. - 1 v.
      Includes Selected bibliography: 56 items.

75.   - - - - - **Processing department. Cataloguing service.** Library of
      Congress policy on shared cataloguing. - Its: Bulletin. no. 75,
      May 1966.

76.   **University microfilms, Ann Arbor, Mich.** Pre-investment reports
      from the United Nations development program=Rapports sur
      les projets de préinvestissement exécutés dans le cadre du
      Programme des Nations Unies pour le développement=Informes
      sobre preinversión del Programa de las Naciones Unidas para
      el desarrollo. - Ann Arbor, Mich., 1970. - 12 p.

D

277.   **Vallee, J.**   Research report no.2. - Stanford, University computation
        center, information systems, 1970. - 46 p.
        Langage de dialogue DIRAC pour banques de données interrogées à distance.

278.   **Vichery, B. C.**   The UDC and technical information indexing. -
        Unesco bulletin for libraries 15:   126-138, 147, no.3, 1961.

279.   **Viet, J.**   Documentation et développement: une expérience
        originale de collaboration internationale dans le domaine
        documentaire. - Social science information=Information sur
        les sciences sociales 8: 183-189, August 1969.
        Etablissement d'une "Liste commune de descripteurs" par différentes
        organisations internationales dont le B.I.T. et la F.A.O.

280.   -- --- Problèmes d'élaboration du thesaurus EUDISED multilingue. -
        Strasbourg, Conseil de l'Europe, 1972.

281.   **Withers, F. N.**   Standards for library service. - Paris, 1970.
        - 228 p. - (United Nations educational, scientific and cultural
        organisation. Documents. COM/WS/151.)

III. HOW TO USE THE INTERNATIONAL DOCUMENTATION

82. **Abdul Rahman, J.** Les organisations économiques internationales,
     1955. - Le Caire, 1956. - 204 p.
     At head of title: Ligue des états arabes. Institut des hatues études arabes.
     Title and text in Arabic.

83. **Akademiiā nauk SSSR.** Trudy i materialy nauchnykh kongressov i
     soveshchaniĭ, opublikovannye za rubezhon. - 1960-   ; vyp. 1-   -
     Leningrad, 1961-   . - v.
     Index of proceedings and materials of science congresses and conferences in the world.

84. -- **Institut Latinskoĭ Ameriki.** Zarubezhnye t͡sentry po izucheniiŭ
     Latinskoĭ Ameriki. - Moskva, 1970. - 4 v.
     Contents:
     vyp. 1. T͡sentry po izucheniiŭ Latinskoĭ Ameriki v SSHA, Kanade.
     vyp. 2. T͡sentry po izucheniiŭ Latinskoĭ Ameriki v stranakh Zapadnoĭ Evropy.
     vyp. 3. Strany Latinskoĭ Ameriki.
     vyp. 4. Strany Latinskoĭ Ameriki.
     Directory of research centers on Latin America.

85. -- **Institut mirovoĭ ėkonomiki i mezhdunarodnykh otnosheniĭ.**
     Kratkiĭ ukazatel' sovetskoĭ literatury po problemam Organizat͡sii
     Ob"edinennykh Nat͡siĭ. - In Its: OON: itogi, tendent͡sii, perspektivy;
     (k 25-letiiŭ OON). - Moskva, 1970. - p. 537-540.

86. -- --- Mezhdunarodnye ėkonomicheskie organizat͡sii: spravochnik. -
     Moskva, Izd-vo Akademii nauk SSSR, 1960. - 980 p.

87. -- **Nauchnyĭ sovet po kibernetike.** Prikladnaiā dokumentalistika. -
     Moskva, Izd-vo "Nauka", 1968. - 197 p. - (Its: Seriiā "Organiza-
     t͡siiā i upravlenie".)
     Documentation in science and technology.

88. **Akademiiā nauk Ukrainskoĭ SSR.** Metody otbora i peredachi
     informat͡sii. - Kiev, 1965. - 183 p.
     Information retrieval.

89. **Alexandrowicz, C. H.** International economic organisations. - London,
     Stevens & sons, 1952. - xii, 263 p. - (Library of world affairs.
     no.19.)
     "Published under the auspices of the London institute of world affairs."

90. The **annual** register: world events in 1971-   - London, Longman,
     1972-   . - v.
     Chapter concerning international organization:
     1. East-West negotiations. 2. The United Nations and specialized agencies. 3. The
     Commonwealth. 4. International defence organizations. 5. Regional economic and
     political organizations. 6. An enlarged European community: the beginning of a new
     stage.

91. **Arntz. H.** Le rôle de la documentation dans les pays en
     voie de développement. - Bulletin de l'Unesco à l'intention
     des bibliothèques 25: 13-19, janvier-février 1971.

92. **Asian** and Pacific council: an introduction. - Wellington, Ministry of
     foreign affairs, 1970. - 17 p. - (New Zealand. Ministry of foreign
     affairs. Foreign affairs publication. no. 375.)

293.   **ASLIB** proceedings. v.23- ; 1971-   . - London, 1971-   . v.
Pub. monthly.
"Incorporating ASLIB information."
Includes bibliographies.
Libraries. Information service. Information storage and retrieval systems. Library
cooperation. Association of special libraries and information bureaux.

294.   **Association of international libraries. Symposium. 5th, Vienna,
1970.** Report on bibliographic systems used in international
libraries from the viewpoint of mutual assistance and
cooperation among libraries and documentation centres of
international organizations. - Luxembourg, 1970? - 1 v.
- (Association of international libraries. Newsletter. no.29.)

295.   **Aufricht, H.** Guide to League of Nations publications: a
bibliographical survey of the work of the League,
1920-1947. - New York, Columbia University Press, 1951.
- 682 p.

296.   **Avicenne, P.** Bibliographical services throughout the world: 1965-69. -
Paris, Unesco, 1972. - 303 p. - (United Nations educational,
scientific and cultural organisation. Documentation, libraries and
archives: bibliographies and reference works. no.1.) E F
Contents:
pt. 1. Development of bibliographical services during the period 1965-69: national
commissions for bibliography, library co-operation, national bibliographies, types of
material, current bibliographies of special subjects, periodicals indexes, training in
bibliography, legal deposit, archives.
pt. 2. Bibliographical activities in the various member States.
Previous surveys:
1951-52   (Unesco bibliographical manuals. no.4.)   EF
1950-59   (Unesco bibliographical manuals. no.9.)   EF
1960-64   (Unesco bibliographical manuals. no.11.)   EF

297:    **Barraine, R.** Institutions internationsles. - Paris, Libr. générale
de droit et de jurisprudence, 1964. - 185 p. - (L'aide-mémoire de
l'étudiant en droit. 1ère année. 2e éd.)

298.   **Basic** documents of African regional organizations. - Edited by
Louis B. Sohn. - v.1-4. - Dobbs Ferry, N.Y., Oceana publications,
1972. - 4 v.
Contents:
v.1. Documents relating to the Organization of African unity, the African development
bank and some of the organizations of French-speaking Africa.
v.2. Documents relating to French-speaking Africa.
v.3. Documents of regional organizations in West, North and East Africa.
v.4. Documents relating to the association of various groups of African States with the
European economic community.

299.   **Bastid, S. (Basdevant).** Institutions internationales. - Paris, Cours
de droit, 1956. - 476.
On cover: Cours d'institutions internationales, rédigé d'après la sténotypie du cours
et avec l'authorisation de Madame Paul Bastid... Licence 1ère année, 1955-1956.

300.   **Begegnung** mit dem Buch: vierundfünfzig Anmerkungen und acht
Zeichnungen=Rencontre avec le livre: cinquante-quatre essais et
huit dessins. - Bern, 1972. - 120 p. - (Nouvelles de l'Association
des bibliothécaires suisses et de l'Association suisse de documentation. Numéro spécial.)
Publié pour l'Année internationale du livre.

01. **Besterman, T.** A world bibliography of bibliographies and of
     bibliographical catalogues, calendars, abstracts, digests, indexes, and
     the like. - 4th ed., rev. and greatly enl. - Lausanne, Societas
     bibliographica, 1965-1966. - 5 v.
     117,000 separately published works, alphabetically arranged under about 16,000 subject
     headings and subheadings, with adequate cross-references, with index to authors, titles
     of serial and anonymous works, libraries and archives, and subjects covered by abstracts
     to British patent specifications.
     Monumental one-man effort.

02. **Bibliographic** index: a cumulative bibliography of bibliographies. -
     1937-   . - New York, Wilson, 1938-   . - v.
     Semi-annual, with cumulations at intervals.
     This subject index gives complete citation for articles devoted wholly or in part to
     bibliography from about 1,500 periodicals, including a number in foreign languages;
     to books and parts of books and pamphlets, indicating whether titles are annotated
     or not. The first cumulation 1937-42 contains about 50,000 bibliographies listed
     under nearly 10,000 subjects.

03. **Bibliothèques** dépositaires des documents de l'Unesco et des
     Nations Unies. - Unesco bulletin for libraries 4: 565-577,
     March 1950.

04. **British standards institution.** Recommendations for the preparation
     of indexes for books, periodicals and other publications. - London,
     1964. - (BS 3700.)

05. **Bureau international pour la publication des tarifs douaniers.** Rapport
     sur le 81ème exercice: 1er avril 1971. - 31 mars 1972. - Bruxelles,
     1972. - 18 p.
     Text in French and English.
     Contains information concerning tariffs published, tariffs in the process of printing,
     tariffs in the process of preparation, tariffs scheduled.

06. **Cadoux, L.** Une expérience de coopérative documentaire de la
     Commission des Communautés européennes et des organismes
     français, le réseau d'information sur l'économie de l'énergie.
     - Bulletin des bibliothèques de France 16: 609-626,
     décembre 1971.

07. **Cain, J.** Le développement des services bibliographiques et de
     la documentation depuis dix ans. - Bulletin de l'Unesco à
     l'intention des bibliothèques 10: 271-277, novembre-décembre
     1956.
     Avec bibliographie p. 277-279.

08. **Carbone, S.** Draft model law on archives: description and text/ by
     Salvatore Carbone and Raoul Guêze. - Paris, 1972. - 225 p. -
     (United Nations educational, scientific and cultural organisation.
     Documentation, libraries and archives: studies and research. no.1.)
     E F

09. **Casadio, F. A.** La politica dell'informazione degli organismi
     internazionali. - In: Il problema dell'informazione nella
     società moderna, Firenze, 1968. - p. 103-109.

10. **Cassidy, T. R.** United Nations documents in the medium-
     sized university: nuisance or necessity? - College and
     research libraries 13: 107-110, April 1952.

311.   **Chamberlin, W.** Material for the undergraduate study of the
        United Nations. - American political science review 48:
        204-211, March 1954.

312.   -- --- The public relations of the United Nations. - Annual review.
        of United Nations: 209-243, 1954.

313.   -- --- The United Nations documents collection at New York
        university. - College and research libraries 12: 52-61, January 1951.

314.   **Cheney, F. N.** Fundamental reference sources. - Chicago, American
        library association, 1971. - vii, 318 p.
        Contents:
        The nature of reference/Information service; Sources of bibliographic information;
        Sources of biographical information; Sources on words; Encyclopedias; Sources of
        statistics; Sources of geographical information; Appendix: additional guidelines for
        reviewing reference books; Readings; Index.

315.   **Cheyney, A. S.** The character and accessibility of office research
        materials. - In: Annals of the American academy of political
        and social science. - v.166, p. 114-118, March 1933.

316.   **Childs, J. B.** Current bibliographical control of international
        intergovernmental documents. - Washington, D. C., Library of
        Congress, Serials division, 1966. - p. 319-330.
        "Reprinted from 'Library resources & technical services, vol. 10, no.3, Summer 1966'."
        Notes, partly bibliographical: p. 330.

317.   **A chronology** and fact book of the United Nations, 1941-1969
        / by Waldo Chamberlin, Thomas Hovet and Erica Hovet.
        - Dobbs Ferry, N.Y., Oceana publications, 1970. - 234 p.

318.   **Coblans, H.** International bibliographical work; some thoughts on
        two Unesco reports. - Journal of documentation 15:
        141-145, Semptember 1959.

319.   **Collection** historique de la Société des nations: guide annoté du
        visiteur. - Préface par Carl J. Hambro. - Genève, 1947. - 38 p.

320.   **Columbia university. School of international affairs.** Special program
        for the study of international organizations in Europe, June 12-
        July 31, 1967. - New York, 1967. - 29 p.
        At head of title: Alice Stetten Fellows.
        International agencies - Study and teaching.

321.   **Conférence des hautes études internationales.** Travaux en cours
        dans le domaine des relations internationales. - Paris, Carnegie
        endowment for international peace, Centre européen, 1952.
        - 59 p.
        "La Conférence des hautes études internationales a préparé la présente
        bibliographie. " - p. 3.

322.   **Conference on the improvement of bibliographical services, Paris,
        1950.** Bibliographical services, their present state and possibilities
        of improvement. - v.1-2. - Paris, 1950. - 2 v.
        Prepared by Unesco/Library of Congress as a working paper for an international
        conference on bibliography.

323.   -- --- General report. - Paris, Unesco, 1950. - 16 p. - (UNESCO/
        CUA/5.) E F S

324.   Conference organized by the Nordic council for international
        organizations in Europe. 2nd, Imatra, 1967. Nordic economic
        and social cooperation. - Stockholm, 1968. - 94 p.

325.   Conférence sur les échanges internationaux de publications en
        Europe, Budapest, 1960. Documents et rapports. Budapest,
        Centre bibliothéconomique et méthodique, 1962. - 240 p.

326.   Council of Europe. Exchange of information on research in European
        law=Échange d'informations sur les recherches en droit européen. -
        Strasbourg, 1972. - vii, 188 p.
        Title and text in English and French.
        This document is issued by the Directorate of legal affairs, Council of Europe, Strasbourg
        France.
        Contents:
        1. Current research projects and studies.   2. Classification system.   3. Classification of
        research projects and studies.

327.   - - European committee on crime problems. International exchange
        of information on current criminological research projects in
        member States=Échange international d'information sur les projets
        de recherches criminologiques dans les États membres. - no.1- . -
        Strasbourg, 1966-   . - v.
        This document is issued by the Directorate of legal affairs, Division of crime problems,
        Council of Europe.
        pt. 1. Current research projects; further information on present position of certain
        projects reported.
        pt. 2. Classification system; index of projects following the classification system;
        index of projects by country.

328.   The delegates world bulletin. - v.2-   ; 1972-   . - New York,
        1972-   . - v.
        Pub. semi-monthly.
        "Dedicated to serving the United Nations and the international community."
        United Nations - Officials and employees. International agencies. International cooperation.

329.   Depository libraries for United Nations documents. - Documents
        of international organizations 3: 1-5, December 1949.

330.   Diallo-Tayiré, A. A. La crise de l'information et la crise de
        confiance des Nations Unies; responsabilités des états membres
        et responsabilités des Nations Unies. - Fribourg, Éd.
        universitaires Fribourg, Suisse, 1971. - 145 p.
        Bibliography: p. 133-138.

331.   Drucker, G. A nemzetközi szervezetek: a nemzetközi organizáciá
        kialakulása: tanulmóny a nemzetközi jog és nemzetközi vonatkozások
        köréböl. - Budapest, Magyar Külügyi társaság, 1933. - 215 p. -
        (Idöszerü kérdések; aktuális problémák. 5. Füzet.)
        Summary in French at end of volume.
        List of international organisations: p. 167-186.
        International agencies.

332.   Encyclopedia of information systems and services. - Edited by
        Anthony T. Kruzas, Anna Ercoli Schnitzer, associate editor,
        Linda E. Varekamp, assistant editor. - Orange, N.J., Academic
        media, 1971. - xii, 1109 p.
        Information services. Directories. Information storage and retrieval systems - Directories.
        Data libraries. - Directories.

333.   **Farmer, G. A. J.** The reprint industry. - The Australian library
        journal 21: 277-283, no.7, 1972.

334.   **Fédération internationale de documentation.** A guide to the
        world's training facilities in documentation and information
        work. - Prepared by Krystana Ostrowska and Anna Lech.
        - The Hague, International federation for documentation,
        1965. - xii, 218 p. - (Its: Publications. 373.)
        At head of title: Central institute for scientific, technical and economic
        information (Warsaw, Poland).

335.   **Filippovskiĭ, E. E.** Patentnaiâ sistema i nauchno-tekhnicheskiĭ
        progress v kapitalisticheskikh stranakh. - Moskva, Izd-vo "Nauka",
        1972. - 124 p.
        Patents and technology development.

336.   **Food and agriculture organization.** FAO fellowships, scholarships,
        study and travel grants 1967-1968: catalogue. - Rome, 1970. -
        342 p.

337.   - - **Terminology and reference section.** List of organizations, meetings,
        programmes, etc. related to fisheries=Lista de organismos, reuniones,
        programas, etc. relacionados cona la pesca. - Rome, 1971. - iii, 35 p. -
        (Its: Terminology note. no.1, Rev.1.)
        At head of title: Publications division. Translation service. Terminology and reference section.

338.   **Garcia del Solar, L.** Rapport sur une rationalisation des
        débats et de la documentation de l'Assemblée mondiale de
        la santé/ par Lucio Garcia del Solar et Joseph Sawe.
        - Genève, 1970. - ii, 68 p. - (World health organization.
        Documents.   JIU/REP/70/8.)

339.   **Gelfand, M. A.** Les bibliothèques universitaires des pays en voie
        de développement. - Paris, 1968. - 178 p. - (United Nations
        educational, scientific and cultural organisation. Manuels de
        l'Unesco à l'usage des bibliothèques. no.14.)   E F

340.   **Glossary** of international conference terminology=Guoji huiyi shuyu
        huibian. - Jean Herbert. - Peking, 1972. - 284 p.
        Title in Chinese only. Texts in Chinese, Russian, German, English, French and
        Spanish in parallel columns.
        Congresses and conventions - Dictionaries.

341.   **Gombocz, I.** Les aspects économiques des échanges inter-
        nationaux de publications. - Bulletin de l'Unesco à l'intention
        des bibliothèques 25:   284-299, septembre-octobre 1971.

342.   - - - - - Evropeĭskaiâ konferentsiiâ po voprosam mezhdunarodnogo
        obmena izdaniiâmi, Vena, aprel' 1972 g. - IFLA General council
        meeting, Budapest, 1972. Documents. IFLA–C/
        European conference on exchange of publications, Vienna, 1972.

343.   **Gray, R. A.**   Serial bibliographies in the humanities and social
        sciences. - Ann Arbor, Mich., Pierian Pr., 1969. - 345 p.
        Ten descriptive codes are used to indicate characteristics of individual titles
        such as language, selectivity, nationality of authors, frequency, publication form,
        and arrangement.   Title: author, publisher, sponsor; subject, keyword-in-context,
        and selected characteristics indexes are appended.

344.   **Great Britain. Central office of information. Reference division.**
        Guide to international organizations. - London, 1949. - 2 v.
        Loose-leaf.

345.   -- **Ministry of information.**   Short guide to some agencies of
        international co-operation. - London, 1945. - 47, 1 p.

346.   **Greene, K. R. C.**   Institutions and individuals: an annotated list
        of directories useful in international administration. - Comp. by
        Katrine R.C. Greene. - Chicago, Public administration clearing
        house, 1953. - 1 v.

347.   **Groesbeck, J.**   United Nations documents and their
        accessibility. - Library resources and technical services 10:
        313-318, 1966.

348.   **Grosse, W.**   Das ABC der Welt-Organisationen: ein aktueller Führer
        durch die internationale Zusammenarbeit. - Ausg. 1954. - Wiesbaden,
        Brandstetter-Verlag, 1954. - 79 p.
        "Anschriften, Abkürzungen, Kommentare."
        International agencies.

349.   Die **grossen** zwischenstaatlichen Wirtschaftsorganisationen: Vorträge
        von Roger Auboin... u.a. gehalten an der Handels-Hochschule,
        St. Gallen. - Zurich, Polygraphischer Verlag, 1955. - x, 176 p. -
        (St. Gallen. Handels-Hochschule. Schweizerisches Institut für
        Aussenwirtschafts- und Marktforschung. Veröffentlichungen. 17.)

350.   **Guide** des institutions européennes. - Paris, Centre européen de
        productions documentaires, 1960. - 116 p. - (Politique et
        économie. no. hors-sér.)

351.   **Guide** to European sources of technical information. - Comp.
        by Colin H. Williams. - 3rd ed. - Guernsey, Channel
        Islands, F. Hodgson, 1970. - 309 p.
        "The earlier ed. of this guide were published by OECD."

352.   A **guide** to the use of United Nations documents; (including
        reference to the specialized agencies and special U.N.
        bodies)/ by Brenda Brimmer... and others. - New York,
        Oceana publications, 1962. - xv, 272 p.
        Bibliography: p. 268-269.

353.   **Haden, J. W.**   Inventaire des listes, index et catalogues de
        publications des organisations intergouvernementales autres
        que l'Organisation des Nations Unies. - Bulletin de l'Unesco
        à l'intention des bibliothèques 21: 289-296, no.5, 1967.

354.   **Hanson, C. W.**   Introduction to science-information work. - London,
        Aslib, 1971. - 199 p.
        Contents:
        The science-information scene; Sources of information; Interlude; Functions of
        information services; Methods of science-information; Appendix; Index.

355.   **Heuline, S.**   Legal collections of the United Nations Library.
        - Law library journal 49: 244-249, 1956.

356.   **Il'in, M. S.**   Informatsionnye poiski v massivakh ekonomicheskikh
        dannykh. - Moskva, "Statistika", 1968. - 95 p.
        Information retrieval in economics.

357.   **Index** translationum: répertoire international des traductions=inter-
        national bibliography of trnaslations. - v.1-   ;   . - Paris,
        Unesco, 19   . -   v.
        Contents:
        1. Classification.   2. System of arrangement of entries.   3. Key to abbreviations
        (languages).   4. Bibliographies arranged by countries.   5. Author index.   6. Statistical
        table of translations.
        The bibliographies arranged by countries are presented under the ten major headings
        of the Universal decimal classification.

358.   **Instituto argentino de derecho internacional.**   Acuerdos internationales. -
        Buenos Aires, Impr. de la universidad, 1945. - 283 p.
        Contents:
        Conferencia monetaria internacional de Bretton Woods.   Conferencia internacional de
        aviación civil.   Conferencia interamericana sobre problemas de la guerra y de la paz.
        Carta de las Naciones Unidas.

359.   **Institute of development studies, Brighton. Library.**   A guide to
        information on developing countries in U.S. government publications,
        1962-1971. - Brighton, 1972. - 81 p. - (Its: Occasional guides. no.2.)

360.   **Institutions** effectuant des travaux dans le domaine de la planification
        économique et sociale en Afrique=Institutions engaged in economic
        and social planning Africa. - Paris, 1965. - 155 p.
        Prepared for Unesco by the International social science council and the Centre d'analyse
        et de recherches documentaires pour l'Afrique noire (Maison des sciences de l'homme),
        under the responsibility of Michèle Cser.

361.   **Intergovernmental conference on cultural policies in Europe, Helsinki,
        1972.**   Final report. - Paris, Unesco, 1972. - 91 p.   E F R S
        Index to the recommendations: p. 89-91.

362.   **International** agreements and conventions. - Tokyo, 1961. - 1059, 23 p.
        Title and text in Japanese, with part translated into English, part into French.

363.   The **International** committee for social sciences: ten years of
        activity. - International social science journal 14: 177-191,
        no.1, 1962.

364.   **International conference on training for information work, Rome, 1971.**
        The proceedings. - Rome, 1972. - 510 p. - (FID. Publications. no.486.
        Joint publications of the Italian national information institute, Rome and the International
        federation for documentation, the Hague.
        Session I: Training of information specialists.
        Session II: Training of information users.
        Includes bibliographies.

365. **International council of scientific unions.** Survey of the
     activities of I.C.S.U. , scientific unions, special and
     scientific committees and commissions of I.C.S.U. in the
     field of scientific information during the year 1969.
     - Paris, I.C.S.U., 1970. - 1 v.
     "Published with the financial assistance of U.N.E.S.C.O."

366. **International federation for documentation.** Directories of science
     information sources: international bibliography=Répertoires de sources
     d'information scientifique et technique: bibliographie internationale=
     Repertorios de fuentes de información cientifica y técnica: biblio-
     grafía internacional. - The Hague, 1967. - 163 p. - (Its: Publication.
     no. 421.)

367. -- --- Guide to world's training facilities in documentation and
     information work. - The Hague, 1965. - (Its: Publications. FID/373.)
     Updated regularly in FID News bulletin.

368. -- --- Statement on a new FID programme: to meet changing
     information patterns. - The Hague, 1966. - 7 p.

369. -- **Secretary-general.** Reports. - 19 -   . - The Hague, 19 -   . -
     v.

370. **International federation of library associations.** Répertoire des
     associations de bibliothécaires membres de la Fédération inter-
     nationale=Repertoire of the associations of librarians members of
     the International federation. - 4th ed. - La Haye, M. Nijhoff,
     1948. - 102 p.
     1st ed. 1931. 2nd ed. 1935. 3rd ed. 1938.

371. **International institute for educational planning.** Educational
     planning: a directory of training and research institutions. -
     Paris, 1968. -

372. **International institute of administrative sciences.** National adminis-
     tration and international organization, a comparative survey of
     fourteen countries: report of an inquiry conducted jointly by the
     International institute of administrative sciences and the United
     Nations educational, scientific and cultural organization. - Brussels,
     1951. - 78 p.   E F

373. **International labour office.** A general description of an
     approach to computerised bibliographical control. - Geneva,
     1971. - ii, 115 p.

374. -- **Centre international d'information de sécurité et d'hygiène du
     travail.** Répertoire-clé alphabétique. - Genève, 1961. - 44 p.
     Contains: Centres nationaux du CIS.

375. **International** organisations. - Amsterdam, J.H. de Bussy, 1960. -
     99 p.

376. The **international** who's who: 1971-1972. - 35th ed. - London,
     Europa publications Ltd., 1972. - 1823 p.
     Biographies of prominent persons in international affairs.

377.   The **internationalist**. - November 1971-   . - Includes bibliographies. -
Wallingford, Berkshire, 1971-   . -   v.
Three issues per year, 1971-72; monthly, 1973-   .
"Sponsored by Christian aid, Oxfam, Third world first, and educational foundations."
Economics. Developing countries. Economic development - Developing countries.
Economic assistance in Developinc countries. Economic policy. Social change -
Developing countries. Third world first, Oxford.

378.   **Jaeger, H. K.**   Science information sources: an international bibliography. - Gent, Association scientifique et technique pour la
recherche en informatique, 1972. - 31 p. - (ASTRID. Series on
information science. no.2.)
Includes guides to sources of information with international coverage.

379.   **Jalava, A.**   YK: ja eräiden sen erityisjärjestöjen
kirjallısuusluettelot, indeksi ja referaattijulkaisut sekä
automaattiset tiedonhakujärjestelmät. - Helsinki, Eduskunnan
kirjasto. - Riksdagsbiblioteket, 1970. - 40 p.
How to use existing catalogues and indexes of international documentation
for computerised systems.

380.   **Johnston, G. A.**   The archives of international organisations, with
special reference to the ILO. - Society of archivists. Journal,
v.4, p. 506-520, October 1972.

381.   **Judge, A. J. N.**   Proceedings of international meetings:
analysis of a bibliography of proceedings of international
meetings. - International associations 16: 462-474, no.8, 1964.

382.   **Kaltwasser, F. G.**   Le contrôle bibliographique universel.
Bulletin de l'Unesco à l'intention des bibliothèques 25: 268-276, no. 5.
septembre-octobre 1971.

383.   **Kanevskiĭ, B. P.**   Bibliografiiâ literatury po mezhdunarodnomu
knigoobmenu. - IFLA General council meeting, Budapest, 1972.
Documents. IFLA-C/EP.
Bibliography on international exchange of publications project.

384.   **Karunatilleke, K.**   Essai d'une classification des accords conclus
par les organisations internationales, entre elles ou avec des
états. - Paris, A. Pedone, 1971. - 80 p.

385.   **Katz, W. A.**   Introduction to reference work. - New York,
McGraw-Hill, 1969. - 1 v. - (McGraw-Hill series in library
education.)
Contents: -v.1.   Basic information sources.

386.   **Koch, T. W.**   The bibliographical tour of 1928. - In: Library
journal. v.54, p. 101-104, February 1929.

387.   **Larsen, K.**   National bibliographical services: their creation and
operation. - Paris, UNESCO, 1953. - 142 p. - (Unesco bibliographical handbooks.)
Prepared in accordance with the recommendation of the International advisory
committee on bibliography.
Contents:
1. The national bibliographical centre: outline of its functions. 2. The current
national bibliography. 3. The retrospective national bibliography. 4. The union
catalogue. 5. Directories. 6. Information service. 7. Administration of the
national bibliographical centre. Appendices.
Bibliography: p. 124-136.

388.   **League of nations.** Handbook of international organisations (associations, bureaux, committees, etc.). - Geneva, 1938. - 491 p. - (Its: Publications. 1937.XII.B.4.)   E F
Contents:
1. Politics and international relations: pacifism. 2. Religion: humanitarianism and morals.
3. Arts and sciences. 4. Education. 5. Studens' and university organisations.
6. Medicine and hygiene. 7. Law and administration. 8. Press. 9. Feminism.
10. Labour and professions. 1. Agriculture. 12. Economics and finance. 13. Trade
and industry. 14. Communications and transit. 15. Sport and tourism. 16. Miscellaneous.
Subject index. Alphabetical index. Geographic index.

389.   - - **International bureau section.** Quarterly bulletin of information on the work of international organisations, comp. by the Section of international bureaux. - no. 1-   ; Oct. 1922-   . - Geneva, 1922. E F
Title varies: v.4- , Bulletin of information on the work of international organisations.

390.   - - **Library.** Guide sommaire des publications de la Société des nations=Brief guide to League of nations publications. - Genève, 1929. - 32 p. E F
The purpose of this guide is to give a brief outline of a system of arrangement which should facilitate the use of the documents.

391.   **Lloyd, G.** Are you stymied by the United Nations documents? - Library journal 72:   1337, 1453, 1529, 1585; 1947.

392.   **Loveday, A.** Reflections on international administration. - Oxford, Clarendon press, 1956. - xxi, 334 p.

393.   **Maass, E.** Interlibrary loan work at the United Nations. - Special libraries 54: 517-521, 1963.

394.   **MacBride, J. H.** A subject approach to United Nations documents. - College and research libraries 15: 42-46, January 1954.

395.   **McConaughy, J. B.** Student's guide to United Nations documents and their use. - Columbia, University of South Carolina, Department of Political Science, 1967. - 15 p.

396.   **Malclès, L. N.** Les sources du travail bibliographique. - v.1: Bibliographies générales. - Genève, E. Droz, 1950. - 370 p.

397.   **Mason, J. B.** Research resources: annotated guide to the social sciences. - Santa Barbara, American bibliographical center, 1968. - 2 v.
Contents: - v.1.   International relations and recent history: indexes, abstracts, and periodicals. -v.2. Official publications: US government, United Nations, international organizations and statistical sources.

398.   **Meeting of the correspondents of the development enquiry service, Geneva, 1970.** Documents. no.1-11. - Paris, Organisation for economic co-operation and development, Development centre, 1970. - 1 v.
Text partly English, partly French.

Contents:
1. Agenda.
2. Liste des participants.

Meeting of the correspondents of the development enquiry service, Geneva, 1970. (Cont'd)

3. Questions transmises aux correspondants pendant la période mars 1969-octobre 1970=Questions sent to correspondents during the period March 1969-October 1970.
4. Tableau recapitulatif des instruments de référence transmis par les correspondants=Recapitulation of reference material transmitted by the correspondents.
5. Les "sommaires".
6. Liste commune des descripteurs: principales conclusions.
7. Summary record.
8. The "Development enquiry service".
9. "DES" Newsletter of the correspondents.
10. The associate expert programme.
11. Conseil de l'Europe. Assemblée consultative. Séminaire de Strasbourg: mobilisation des ressources humaines.

399. **Meyriat, J.** Rapport sur les techniques modernes de documentation dans les sciences sociales et leur application aux pays en voie de développement. - Paris, CIDSS, 1962. - (CIDSS Secr. 62/4.)

400. **Mezhdunarodnye** obshchestvennye organizatsii - profsoiuznye, zhenskie, molodezhnye, studencheskie i dr.; spravochnik. - Moskva, Sotsékgiz, 1962. - 451 p.
"Sostaviteli: Ivanova Z.P., Kriuchkova V.S."
International agencies.

401. **Milam, C. H.** Depository library system. - United Nations bulletin 6: 273-275, 1949.

402. **Monaco, R.** Lezioni di organizzazione internazionale. - 1-   . - Torino, G. Giappichelli, 1957-   . - v.
At head of title: Corsi universitari.

403. **Moor, C. C.** How to use United Nations documents/ by Carol Carter Moor and Waldo Chamberlin. - New York, New York university press, 1952. - iii, 26 p. - (New York university libraries occasional paper. no.1.).

404. **Moore, B.** A B C of the United Nations and international organisations. - London, United Nations association of Great Britain and Northern Ireland, 1949. - 96 p.

405. **Morozov, G. I.** L'O.N.U. a 25 ans/ par G. Morozov et V. Chkounaiev. - Moscou, Ed. de l'Agence de presse Novosti, 1970. - 95 p.
Original ed. pub. under title: K 25-letiiu OON.
"Publié par l'Association soviétique pour les Nations Unies."
Bibliographical foot-notes.
25 years of United Nations.

406. **Munn, R. F.** The use of modern technology in the improvement of information resources and services in developing countries. - International library review 3: 9-13, January 1971.

407. Les **Nations Unies:** chantier de l'avenir. - t. 1-2. - Paris, Presses universitaires de France, 1961-1962. - 2 v. - (Collection "Tiers monde". no. 4-5.)
Contents:
1. Les Nations Unies et les pays sous-développés. 2. Les Nations Unies au service de la paix.

08.   **New Zealand. Ministry of foreign affairs.** The United Nations and
        related agencies handbook: - 1973. - Wellington, 1973. - 186 p. -
        (Its: Publication. no. 435.)
        Contents:
        General assembly, Security council, Economic and social council, International trusteeship
        system and Trusteeship council, International court of justice, Secretariat, Special bodies
        of the United Nations, Inter-governmental agencies, Budget and scale of assessments,
        membership of the United Nations, the specialized agencies, IAEA, and GATT, membership
        of the governing bodies of the specialized agencies and IAEA, summary of current New
        Zealand participation, index.

09.   **Organisation for economic co-operation and development.** International
        scientific organisations; catalogue, preceded by an introduction:
        Some aspects of international scientific co-operation. - Paris, 1965. -
        281 p. E F
        Foot-notes, partly bibliographical.
        Supplement. 1966. 84 p.

10.   -- --- Liste des associations internationales intéressant les industries
        mécaniques et électriques, 1961=List of international associations
        connected with the engineering industries. - 2nd ed. - Paris, Organisa-
        tion de coopération et de développement économiques, 1962. -
        113 p.
        Title and text in French and English.

11.   **Organization of American States.** Conferencias y reuniones: informe
        trimestral=Conference and meetings: quarterly report. - 1972-   . -
        Washington, D.C. 1972-   . - v.
        List of conferences and meetings: General assembly; Meeting of consultation; Permanent
        council; Inter-American commission on human rights; Inter-American economic and
        social council (CIES); Meetings per day and per month; Inter-American council for
        education, science, and culture (CIECC); Specialized conferences; Specialized organizations;
        Other entities; Projections of conferences and meetings.

12.   -- **Council.** Disposiciones que rigen el establecimiento de relaciones
        entre el Consejo de la OEA o sus organos y organismos no
        gubernamentales (al 31 de diciembre de 1955). - Wáshington,
        División de conferencias y organismos, Departamento juridico,
        Unión panamericana, 1955. - iv, 38 p. - (Pan American union.
        Division of conferences and organizations. Serie "Conferencias y
        organismos". no. 49.)

13.   -- --- **Committee on inter-American organizations.** Standards for the
        study of inter-American organizations. - Rev. ed. - Washington, 1949. -
        6 p. - (Pan American union. Division of conferences and organizations.
        Conferences and organizations series. no.1.)

14.   **Overbergh, C. van.** Enquêtes sur les structures sociales; l'association
        internationale. - Bruxelles, A. de Wit, 1907. - 329 p. - (Le Mouve-
        ment sociologique international; Enquête no. 3.)

15.   **Pan American union.** Organizations with which the Organization of
        American states has established cooperative relations as of June 1959. -
        Washington, 1959. - 11 l.

16.   -- **Governing board.** Report on specialized inter-American organizations,
        submitted to the ninth International conference of American states. -
        Washington, 1947. 0 35 l.

417.   **Pan American union. Office of public relations.** Pan American
        societies in the United States: 1 list with supplementary lists of
        other associations, inter-American and general. - 1st-   ed. -
        Washington, D.C., 1957-   . -   v.

418.   **Paris. Université. Faculté de droit et des sciences
        économiques. Bibliothèque.** Service des publications
        internationales. - Paris, 1969. - 6 p.

419.   **Patch, W. H.** The use of United Nations documents.
        - Urbana, Ill., 1962. - 29 p. - (Illinois. University.
        Library school. Occasional papers. no.64.)
        Bibliography: p.26-27.

420.   **Pérotin, Y.** Facilitating access to the League of nations
        archives. - The American archivist: 23-34. no.1. January 1972.

421.   **Potter, P. B.** The League of nations and other international organiza-
        tions: an analysis of the evolution and position of the League in
        cooperation among States. - Geneva, Research center, 1934. -
        22 p. - (League of nations association of the United States. Geneva
        research committee. Geneva special studies. v.5 no.6. 1934.)

422.   **Premier** colloque de l'Association des bibliothèques internationales. -
        Bulletin de l'Unesco à l'intention des bibliothèques 20: 349-350,
        no.6, 1966.
        Le projet d'index général des publications et documents des organisations intergouverne-
        mentales autres que l'Organisation des Nations Unies.

423.   **Raeymaeker, O. de.** Nouveaux aspects de l'organisation internationale. -
        München, Isar, 1955. - 33 p.
        Detached from: Internationales Jahrbuch der Politik, 1955. 1. Lieferung: April 1955.
        Text in French and German on opposite pages.

424.   **Rao, Y. V. L.** La pratique de la grande information. - Paris, Unesco,
        1972. - 56 p. - (United Nations educational, scientific and cultural
        organisation. Etudes et documents d'information. no.65.) E F
        Bibliography: p. 55-56.

425.   **Reinsch, P. S.** International unions and their administration. - (In:
        American journal of international law. New York, 1907. v.1,
        p. 579-623.)

426.   **Roussier, M.** Où trouver le texte des traités européens:
        bibliographie établie par Michel Roussier. - New York,
        Carnegie endowment for international peace, 1958. - 53 p.
        Edited by M. A. C. Breycha-Vauthier.

427.   **Rózsa, G.** L'échange international de publications avec les
        pays afro-asiatiques. - Bulletin de. l'Unesco à l'intention des
        bibliothèques 16: 150-154, no.3, mai-juin 1962.

428.   **Sabor, J. E.** Méthodes d'enseignement de la bibliothéconomie. -
        Paris, Unesco, 1969. - 154 p. - (Manuels de l'Unesco à l'usage des
        bibliothèques. no. 16.) E F S
        Avec une étude préliminaire de Ricardo Nassif.
        Includes bibliographies.

429.   **Scientific** thought: some underlying concepts methods and procedures. -
        Paris, Unesco, 1972. - xii, 252 p.
        Includes bibliographies.

430.   **Servan-Schreiber, J. L.** Le pouvoir d'informer. - Paris, R. Laffont,
        1972. - 510 p. - (Le monde qui se fait.)
        Press. Television. Information. Communication.

431.   **Shaw, R.** Outline of governments: history, civics, economics, men. -
        New York, Review of reviews corporation, 1934. - 212 p.

432.   **Simsova, S.** A handbook of comparative librarianship/ by S. Simsova
        & M. Mackee. - London, Clive Bingley, 1970. - 413 p.
        Pt. 1. Comparative librarianship and comparative method.
        Pt. 2. Guide to sources.

433.   **Speeckaert, G. P.** Méthodes de diffusion des résultats obtenus
        par les organisations internationales dans leurs activités.
        - Associations internationales=International associations 16:
        205-214, no.4, 1964.
        Rapport établi pour la 10e Conférence des organisations internationales
        pour l'étude en commun des plans d'activités dans le domaine de l'agriculture
        en Europe, Paris, 1964.
        English text: Associations internationales=International associations 16:
        398-406, no.7, 1964.

434.   **Sprudzs, A.** Treaty sources in legal and political research:
        tools, techniques, and problems; the conventional and the
        new. - Tucson, Ariz., University of Arizona press, 1971.
        - 63 p. - (Arizona, University. Institute of government
        research. International studies. 3.)
        Bibliographical foot-notes.

435.   **Stern, H. A.** Handbook to the use of United Nations documents.
        - New York, 1952. - 63, 29 p.
        Thesis - New York University.

436.   **Systematic** bibliography: a practical guide to the work of compilation. -
        3rd ed. rev. by A.M. Lewin Robinson. - London, Clive Bingley,
        1971. - 123 p.
        The meaning of bibliography and its varied forms, the collection of material and the
        mechanics of compilation, arrangement, layout, the use of computers in bibliographical
        compilation, recommended books, list of plates, index.

437.   **Szapiro, J.** The newspaperman's United Nations: a guide for
        journalists about the United Nations and specialized agencies. -
        Bibliographies at the end of some chapters. - Paris, UNESCO,
        1961. - 229 p.   E F S

438.   **Thompson, G. K.** From boiler room to data bank: some problems
        facing documentalists in sociology. - Geneva, 1966. - 11 1. - (LD/NOTES/18.)
        "Paper prepared for the Roundtable on documentation in sociology, 6th World
        congress, International sociological association, Evian, 4-11 September 1966."

439.   -- - -- -   ISIS for ILO information. - Management and productivity 34:
        40-44, no.3, 1970.

440.   -- - ---   United Nations documents: a manual for their use in the
        library. - Cleveland, Ohio, University libraries, Western reserve
        university, 1951. - 192 1.
        Bibliography: leaves 190-192.

E

441.   The **Unesco** clearing house for publications. - Unesco
bulletin for libraries 4:   481-487, January 1950.

442.   **Union of international associations.** Annual international congress,
calendar. - 13th ed.: 1973-1985. - Brussels, 1973. - 336 p.
This calendar gives: A chronological listing; A geographical listing; An international
organization index; An analytical index; A listing of international associations.

443.   -- --- Tableau de l'Organisation internationale: organismes internationaux
et activités internationales. - n.p., 1924. - 34 p. - (Publication no. 114.)
Pref. signed: Paul Otlet.

444.   -- --- Yearbook of international congress proceedings. - 1st-2nd ed. -
1960-1969. - Brussels, 1968-1970. - 2 v.
1st ed. :   1960-1967.
2nd ed.:   1962-1969.
French ed. has title: Bibliographie des comptes rendus des réunions internationales:
1957-1959. 3 v.

445.   **United Nations.** Access to League of nations archives. - New York,
1969. - 2 p. - (Its: Secretary-General's bulletin. ST/SGB/1/ .
26 December 1969

446.   -- --- Guide de la collection historique de la Société des nations,
1919-1948. - Genève, 1946. - 8 p.
Guide du premier musée international d'histoire diplomatique établi à la Bibliothèque
des Nations Unies à Genève.

447.   -- --- Guide to official recipients of United Nations documents;
methods of obtaining and making the best use of those documents. -
New York, 1957, - 16 p.

448.   -- --- Instructions for depository libraries receiving UN material. -
New York, 1968. - 15 p. - (Its: Documents. ST/LIB/13.Rev.1.)

449.   -- --- List of depository libraries receiving United Nations material=
Liste des bibliothèques dépositaires recevant les documents et
publications de l'Organisation des Nations Unies=Lista de bibliotecas
depositarias que reciben documentos y publicaciones de las Naciones
Unidas. - New York, 1971. - 27 p. - (Its: Documents. ST/LIB/12/Rev.5.)
Each entry contains the name and the address of the depository and parliamentary
library or informtion centre, the extent and language of the material deposited, the
depository or parliamentary library code number; the beginning date of deposit.

450.   -- **Administrative committee on co-ordination.** Compendium of
decisions and actions related to co-ordination within the United
Nations system. - New York, 1970. - 11 p. - (Its: Documents.
Co-ORDINATION/R.813.)
Designed primarily for the use of delegations and secretariats, but should be of value
also to students and research workers. It should be a self-contained document,
summarizing or quoting from the basic texts on co-ordination so as to make each
subject understandbale, and should give references, including dates, to the main
sources. An anlytical index should give cross-references to the other UN indexes;
it should also give full references to the documents analysed so as to serve for the
retrieval of information.

United Nations (Cont'd)

51.   -- **Economic commission for Europe.** L'échange de résumés
       analytiques de documents scientifiques dans le domaine de
       l'économie appliquée; rapport établi par le Secrétaire
       exécutif en exécution de la résolution 3(XVII). - Genève,
       1963. - 7 p. - (E/ECE/474.)
       Annexe 1: Exposé succint des conclusions des consultations conjointes
       CEE/UNESCO sur les résumés analytiques dans le domaine de l'économie
       appliquée.
       Annexe 2: Renseignements bibliographiques concernant quelques uns des
       services de documentation existant dans le domaine de l'économie appliquée.

52.   -- **Information office, New York.** Guide to United Nations and
       allied agencies, April 1945. - New York, 1945. 0 1 v.
       "Revised edition of a survey of ...agencies originally issued in April 1945... It is
       limited to agencies set up as a direct outcome of the war..."
       Bibliography at end of each article.

53.   -- **Library co-ordinating committee of the United Nations
       organizations, Geneva, 1951.** A reference guide to the
       documents and publications of the United Nations and the
       specialized agencies. - Geneva, 1951. - 2 p. - (Its: Documents.
       CO-ORD/Library/L.15.)

54.   -- **Library, Geneva. Historical collections' section.** Guide
       to the archives of the League of Nations, 1919-1946. - Geneva,
       1969. - 78 p.

55.   -- --- **League of nations archives project.** Rapport sur
       l'ouverture des archives et projet de réglementation. - Genève,
       1967. - 75 p. - (Groupe de consultants des archives de la
       Société des nations. Comptes rendus. 1967 (mai) sess.
       no. 12.)
       Editor: Yves Pérotin.
       Bibliographical notes: p. 68-75.

56.   -- **Library, New York.** A select bibliography of
       directories and lists of international organizations and
       conferences. - Issued 1945 to date. - Lake Success, N.Y.,
       1950. - 7 1. - (Its: Miscellaneous bibliographies. no.11.)

57.   -- --- Supplement 1st-   ; 1951-   . v.

58.   -- **Office, Geneva. Division des documents. Section de la distribution
       et des ventes.** Liste des adresses officielles=List official addresses. -
       Geneva, 1970. - 65 1. - (Its: ST/Geneva/SER.H/L.1/Rev.1.)
       Communications addressed to members of the United Nations. Communications addressed
       to non-member states. Addresses of the UN commissions and missions, information centres,
       offices, specialized agencies and others.

59.   -- **Publications board.** Principles governing United Nations depository
       libraries. - New York, 1967. - 3 p. - (Its: Documents. ST/PB/4,Rev.2.)

460.   **United Nations educational, scientific and cultural organisation.**
Directory of international scientific organizations. - Paris, 1950. -
xiii, 224 p. - (Its: Publications. 619.)
Prepared by the Department of natural sciences and the Department of exchange
of information.

461.   -- --- Guide for the establishment of national social sciences
documentation centres in developing countries. - Paris, 1969. -
72 p. - (Its: Reports and papers in the social sciences. no. 24.)
E F
Contents:
1. Preliminary definitions and considerations. 2. Collection of documents. 3. Identification and handling of documents. 4. Analysis of documents. 5. Use and distribution.
6. Recapitulation.
Annex I: Some works of reference. Annex II: Instructions for making a card index.
Annex III: Modern techniques for archives in tropical countries.

462.   -- --- International repertory of institutions specializing in research
on peace and disarmament. - Paris, 1966. 0 77 p. - (Its: Reports
and papers in the social sciences. no. 23.)
A definition of peace research and criteria for selection of institutions. Present trends
in peace research. The United Nations and the specialized agencies - activities relating
to peace research. International peace research organizations. National peace research
institutions. Institutions promoting or supporting peace research.
Appendix 1: Attitudes to research projects. Appendix 2: List of research fields. Index.

463.   -- --- Politiques scientifiques nationales en Europe=National science
policies in Europe. - Paris, 1970. - 489 p. - (Its: Études et
documents de politique scientifique=Science policy studies and
documents. no.17.)

464.   -- --- La promotion du livre en Afrique: problèmes et perspectives. -
Paris, 1969. 0 41 p. - (Its: Études et documents d'information.
no. 56.)

465.   -- --- Science policy research and teaching units=Unités de recherche
et d'enseignement en politique scientifique: Europe et Amérique du
Nord: 1967-1970. - Paris, 1971. - 378 p. - (Its: Science policy
studies and documents=Etudes et documents de politique scientifique.
no. 28.)
Contains the findings of a survey of science policy research and teaching units in
European and North American member States of the organisation.

466.   -- --- World guide to technical information and documentation
services=Guide mondial des centres de documentation et d'information techniques. - Paris, 1969. - 287 p. - (Its: Documentation and
terminology of science=Documentation et terminologie scientifique.)
1. International technical documentation centres. 2. Nations institutions providing
technical information and documentation services. 3. List of international regional and
national directories to technical information and documentation services. 4. Alphabetical
list of institituons. 5. Subject index.

467.   **United Nations industrial development organization.** Guide to industrial
directories=Guide des répértoires de materiel industriel=Guîa de anuarios
industriales. - New York, 1970. - xvi, 137 p. - (United Nations.
Publications. Sales numbers. 1970.II.B.20.)
UNIDO. Documents. ID/53.

468.   **United Nations industrial development organization.** Industrial
        information. - New York, 1969. - ix, 56 p. - (Its: UNIDO mono-
        graphs on industrial development; industrialization of developing
        countries: problems and prospects. no.13.)   E F R S
        United Nations. Publications. Sales numbers. 1969.II.B.39, vol. 13.
        United Nations. Documents. ID/40/13.
        "Based on the Proceedings of the International symposium on industrial development
        (Athens, November-December 1967.)"
        Bibliography: p. 53-56.

469.   **United States. Board on science and technology for international
        development.** Scientific and technical information for developing
        countries: a report of an ad hoc advisory panel. - Washington,
        D.C., National academy of sciences, 1972. - xiii, 80 p.
        Contents:
        1. Scientific and technical information: rationale for assistance.   2. Information transfer
        and information infrastructure.   3. Information needs in priority fields.   4. Recommendations.
        Appendices: A. Diagram: Situational definition of decision maker's need for information.
        B. Annotated bibliography, ch.III. International organizations (intergovernmental, non-
        governmental).

470.   - - **Bureau of international commerce.** Agribusiness organization
        directory; a selected list of government and private organizations
        engaged in or concerned with international agribusiness. - Washington,
        D.C., U.S., Department of commerce, 1968. - 50 p.

471.   - - **Bureau of United Nations affairs. Office of United Nations
        economic and social affairs.** Patterns of cooperation: achievements
        of international organizations in the economic and social field. -
        Washington, 1950. - v, 130 p. - (United States, Department of
        state. Publication 3735. International organization and conference
        series I, 9.)
        "Prepared in the Office of United Nations economic and social affairs... edited by
        Anne Winslow." - p. iii.

472.   - - **Congress. House. Committee on foreign affairs.** International
        organizations and movements. - Hearings before the Subcommittee
        on international organizations and movements of the Committee
        on foreign affairs... 83rd Congress, 1st sess... - Washington, 1953. -
        vi, 299 p.
        Hearings: March 27-July 29, 1953.

473.   - - - - - Special study mission on international organizations and
        movements: report/ by Chester E. Merrow... and others. -
        Washington, 1945. - xiv, 240 p.
        At head of title: 83rd Congress, 2nd session. Committee print.
        "Printed for the use of the Committee on foreign affairs."

474.   - - - - - **Special study mission on international organizations and
        movements.** Report/ by Chester E. Merrow... and others. -
        Washington, 1954. - xiv, 240 p.
        At head of title: 83rd Congress, 2nd session. Committee print.

475.   - - - - - **Department of labor.** Occupations in electronic computing
        systems. - Washington, D.C., 1972. - x, 130 p.

476.   - - **National bureau of standards.** A computer terminal network
        for transparent stimulation of the user of an on-line retrieval
        system/ by Siegfried Treu. - Washington, D.C., 1972. - 33 p.

477. **University microfilms ltd.** Publications in the field of library science= Publicazioni nel campo della biblioteconomia=Publications dans la sphère de la bibliothéconomie. - Buckinghamshire, 1972. - 18 p.

478. **Use** of computers, documentation and the social sciences. - International social science journal. - v.22, no.2, 1971.

479. **Viet, J.** Documentation and development. - Industrial research and development news 4: 32-35, no.2, 1969.
Transfer of experience and documentation, automatic data processing, establishment of specialized information centres. Aligned list of descriptors, use of descriptors in UNIDO, use of the Aligned list.

480. -- - -- An international documentation network. - Industrial research and development news 6: 6-10, 25-29, no.2, 1972.
Establishment of an international documentation network as a result of the Development inquiry service being set up at the Development centre of OECD. Composition of the network: international organizations, operating on a regional basis, intergovernmental, non-governmental, national institutions. The mechanism of information exchange, questions and answers, information tools, computerized documentation and the "Aligned list of descriptors", example of inquiry and reply, future developments.

481. **Villacrés Moscoso, J. W.** Organismos internacionales especializados (material didáctico). - Guayaquil, Escuela de diplomacia, Secretaría, 1965. - 94 l.
At head of title: Universidad de Guayaquil. Escuela de diplomacia, servicio consular y funcionarios internacionales. Dr. Jorge W. Villacrés M.

482. **Vorob'ev, G. G.** Informatsionnaia kul'tura upravlencheskogo truda. - Moskva, Izd-vo "Ėkonomika", 1971. - 106 p.
Nature of information and retrieval systems in scientific management.

483. **Walford, A.** Guide to reference material. - 2nd ed. - v.1-3. - London, 1966-1970. - 3 v.

484. **Weitz, H.** An approach to the analysis of resolutions of the Economic and social council/ by Harold Weitz, Marchall Childs, Jose Glasserman. - New York, 1972. - 113 p. - (UNITAR. Research reports. no.16.)

485. **Wieder, J.** Select bibliography on union catalogues and international loans. - Unesco bulletin for libraries 22: 33-35, no.1, 1968.

486. **Williams, E. E.** Exchanges, national and international. - Library trends 2: 562-572, April 1954.

487. **Winchell, C.** Guide to reference books. - 8th ed. - Chicago, American library association, 1967. - 741 p.
7,5000 entries.

488. **Winton, H. N. M.** Documentation of the United Nations. - 1949-1952. - Annual review of United Nations affairs: 1950-1953.
Guide to UN documentation.

489. -- - -- Documents and publications of the United Nations. - College and research libraries 9: 6-14, 1948.

490. -- - -- Publications of the United Nations system: a reference guide. - New York, R. R. Bowker, 1972. - 202 p.

491. -- - -- United Nations documents. - Drexel library quarterly 1: 32-41, October 1965.

2.   **World** guide to library schools and training courses in documentation=
       Guide mondial des écoles de bibliothécaires et documentalistes. -
       Paris, London, Unesco, Clive Bingley, 1972. - 245 p.
       The present guide contains information on 306 schools and other institutions in 60
       countries offering higher education in documentation and librarianship.
       Prepared by Unesco from the responses to questionnaires.

3.   **World health organization.** World directory of schools of public
       health. - 1971-   . - Geneva, 1972-   . -   v.

4.   - - **Working group on the review of the organizational study of
       medical literature services to members, Geneva, 1971.** Review
       of the organizational study on medical literature services to
       members: report. - Geneva, 1971. - 20 p.

5.   The **world** of learning: 1970-71. - 21st ed. - London, Europa.
       publications ltd., 1971. - 1,868 p.
       Part one covers international organizations.

6.   The **world** this year, 1972: governments and intergovernmental
       agencies as of January 1, 1972. - Edited by Richard P. Stebbins
       and Alba Amoia. - New York, Published for the Council on
       foreign relations by Simon and Schuster, 1972. - 181 p.
       Supplement to the Political handbook and atlas of the world.

7.   **Yearbook** of international congress proceedings. - 1st - 2nd ed.
       1960/67-1962/69. - Brussels, Union of international
       associations, 1969-1970. - 2v.
       Title on spine: 1960/67-   , Yearbook; international meeting reports.

8.   The **year** book of world affairs. - 1947-   . - London, Stevens,
       1947-   . -   v.
       Published under the auspices of the London Institute of world affairs.
       Contents of 1972 issue:
       Research programs; Trends and events; The British confront their European test;
       U Thant and his critics; President Nixon's arms supply policies; The continuity of
       French policy; Sino-Soviet relations; Alliance, deterrence and defence: the changing
       context of security; The limitation of strategic armaments; External involvement
       in civil strife: the case of Chad; the Pearson and Jackson reports in the context of
       development ideologies; the Washington monetary agreement; the World council of
       churches; the International hydrological decade; international law and the environment;
       equality and discrimination in international economic law: the UNCTAD scheme for
       generalised preferences; immunities of officials associated with permanent United Nations
       establishments; Eastern European approaches to public international law; equity in
       international law.

99.   **Zagari, M.** Informazione assistenza tecnica ai paesi in via di
       sviluppo. - Rivista dell'informazione=Information review 2:
       no.1. February 1971.

00.   **Zagayko, F. F.** International documentation and treaty
       problems. - Law library journal 43: no. 3, August 1950.

IV. BIBLIOGRAPHIC CONTROL

Note: In the first part of the following chapter are presented complete or partial recurrent catalogues and indexes covering international documentation. They are arranged alphabetically according to the issuing intergovernmental organization. The second and third parts contain specialized bibliographies and indexes covering particular areas which contribute to general bibliographic control. The fourth part consists of the accessions lists, lists of periodicals and selected articles published by international libraries. Part five deals with national surveys of international documentation. Journals reviewing international documentation and library journals theoretically concerned with it, in part six, are presented on a very selective basis.

A. CURRENT CATALOGUES AND INDEXES OF INTERNATIONAL DOCUMENTAT

COUNCIL OF EUROPE

501. **Council of Europe**. Catalogue of the publications.
- 1964-   . -   v.
A. European Treaty Series. B. Consultative assembly: I. Records of proceedings; II. Other publications. C. Records of proceedings of the European conference of local authorities. D. Political and economic surveys by the Secretariat. E. Human rights. F. Legal problems and criminology. G. Population and refugees. H. Public health. I. Partial agreement in the social field. J. Publications of the Directorate of education and scientific and cultural affairs on education youth and cultural problems. E F

502. -- ---   List of information material and facilities free and immediately available on written request to the Information directorate. - 1965. v. E F

503. -- ---   List of the Council of Europe fellowship holders. - 1953-1964.

504. -- ---   Liste des documents parus (section de la reproduction et de la distribution des documents). Internal circulation; daily (number dated 8 mars 1966-   .)

505. --   **Committee of ministers**. Documents of the Committee of ministers=Documents du Comité des ministres. - 1963-   .
English and French texts separately, alphabetical index.

506. --   **Consultative assembly**. Index of the official records.
- 1st session-18th session; 1949-1966/67.
1. A general index of the Official records of proceedings. 2. An index of speakers. 3. A list of documents indexed according to category. 4. A list of texts adopted by the Assembly. E F

507. --   **Council for cultural co-operation**. Education in Europe; publications. - 1965.

508. -- ---   Record of European art exhibitions held under the auspices of the Council of Europe. - 1965. E/F

509. --   **Documentation section and Library**. Selected list of reports and proceedings of meetings and conferences held by the Council of Europe 1960-1968 for the inclusion in the Yearbook of international congress proceedings. - Strasbourg, 1968. - 11 p. - (ET/DOC/1968/16.)
Contents:
1. Records of proceedings of the Consultative assembly. 2. European conference.
3. Seminars, symposia, etc.

10. **European court of human rights.** Publications de la Cour européenne des droits de l'homme=Publications of the European court of human rights=Veröffentlichungen des Europäischen Gerichtshofes für Menschenrechte. - Strasbourg, Registry of the Court, Council of Europe, Greffe de la Cour, Conseil de l'Europe, Kanzlei des Gerichtshofes, Europarat, 1972. - 4 p.

Contents:
1. Series A: Judgments and decisions.
2. Series B: Pleadings, oral arguments and documents.

DANUBE COMMISSION

11. **Danube commission.** List of publications available in United Nations Library, Geneva. - Geneva, 1968. - 3 l.
At head of title: United Nations Library, Geneva.

EUROPEAN ATOMIC ENERGY COMMUNITY

12. **European atomic energy community. Information and documentation centre.** Euratom information. - Düsseldorf, Verlag Handelsblatt, 1963-   . G/F/I/D/E
Pub. monthly.
Contents:
I. Scientific and technical publications; II. Patents; III. Research contracts; IV. The Euratom/United States Joint research and development program ('Quarterly digest'); Abbreviations. Abstracts in original language and English.

EUROPEAN COMMUNITIES

13. **Communautés européennes.** Catalogue des publications, 1952-1971. - Bruxelles, 1972. - 306 p. - (Its: Bulletin. Supplément hors série.)

Contents: v.1.ç
A. Publications des Communautés: traités, Journal officiel des Communautés européennes, Recueil d'actes;
B. Publications des institutions et organes communautaires: Parlement européen, Conseil des Communautés européennes - Comité consultatif CECA, Cour de justice des Communautés européennes, Comité économique et social, Banque européenne d'investissement.

14. -- --- Index 1971: Bulletin des Communautés européennes. - Bruxelles, 1972. - 138 p.

Contents:
1. Problèmes généraux. 2. Fonctionnement du marché commun. 3. Progrès de l'Union économique et monétarie. 4. Elargissement et relations extérieures de la Communauté. 5. Vie des institutions et organes communautaires. 6. Discours et exposés des membres de la commission. 7. Interventions devant le Parlement européen. This index is a documentary guide to the contents of the Bulletin of the European communities in 1971. The index covers two of the three parts of the Bulletin, pt.1. Features and documents and pt. 2. the classified survey of Community activities during the month under report. E F

Communautés européennes. (Cont'd)

515.   -- ---   List of the publications of the European communities in English: supplement to the French edition of the "Catalogue of publications of the European communities, 1952-1971". - Brussels, 1972. - 135 p.

Contents:
Publications of the Communities. Publications of the institutions and organs. Annexes.

516.   -- ---   Publications des Communautés européennes. - 1962-1971. - Luxemburg, 1962-1972.   E F

Contents:
1. Journal officiel des Communautés européennes; 2. Parlement européen; 3. Cour de justice des Communautés européennes; 4. Communauté économique européenne; 5. Communauté européenne de l'énergie atomique; 6. Communauté européenne du charbon et de l'acier; 7. Office statistique des Communautés européennes; 8. Service de presse et d'information des Communautés européennes. Liste des publications mises en vente; titres classés par institutions et, à l'intérieur du chapitre concernant une institution donnée, par catégories de documents ou par grands sujets, suivant le cas.

517.   -- ---   Relevé bibliographique mensuel=Monatliches Veröffentlichungsverzeichnis. - 1962-   .

518.   --   **Statistical office.**   Agrarstatisches Jahrbuch=Annuaire de statistique agricole=Annuario di statistica agricola=Landbouwstatistisch jaarboek= Yearbook of agricultural statistics. - List of publications: p. 209-226. - Luxembourg, 1972. - 226 p.

519.   -- ---   Veröffentlichungen=Publications=Pubblicazioni=Uitgaven=Publications. - In its: Aussenhandel=Commerce exterieur=Buitenhandse handel= Commercio estero=Foreign trade.

520.   -- ---   Veröffentlichungen=Publications=Pubblicazioni=Uitgaven=Publications. - In its: Sozialstatistik=Statistiques sociales.

EUROPEAN FREE TRADE ASSOCIATION

521.   **European free trade association.**   EFTA publications. - In: EFTA Information. - 1960-1972.

EUROPEAN ORGANIZATION FOR NUCLEAR RESEARCH

522.   **European organization for nuclear research.**   List of CERN publications. - 1955-1972. - Geneva, 1955-1972.
Pub. monthly.

523.   -- ---   List of forthcoming conferences=Liste des conférences prévues. - April 1972-April 1973.

524.   -- ---   List of reprints=Liste de tirés à part. - 1955-1971.

525.   -- ---   List of scientific publications=Liste des publications scientifiques. - 1955-1970.
Pub. annually.

FOOD AND AGRICULTURE ORGANIZATION

26.   **Food and agriculture organization.** Abstracts of Special fund
      and EPTA reports=Résumés analytiques des rapports
      d'assistance technique et du Fonds spécial des Nations Unies.
      - Oct. 1965. - xiv, 91, 129 p. - (MI/PU:QL 65/4).

27.   -- --- Catalogue of FAO publications, 1945/1964.
      Classified by large subjects with author and subject-title indices. E F S
      Quarterly supplement.

28.   -- --- Quarterly list, publications and main documents=Liste
      trimestrielle, publications et documents principaux. - 19 -   .
      Publications: monographs, annuals, periodicals. Main documents listed by
      departments and divisions responsible for their issue. EPTA final reports,
      listed in chronological order by countries.
      Publications: monographies, publications annuelles, périodiques. Documents
      principaux, énumérés par départements et divisions responsables de la
      publication. Rapports finaux du PEAT, énumérés dans l'ordre chronologique,
      par pays.

29.   -- --- Weekly documents list. - no. 1-9. - Rome, 1962-   .
      Restricted to Secretariat (and specialized agencies since 26 Feb. 1966). Main
      documents. Working documents and internal Secretariat papers.

30.   -- **Agrarian research and intelligence service.** FAO
      publications and documents on agrarian structure. - Rome, 1963.
      - 61 p.
      Systematic arrangement with subject index.

31.   -- **Documentation centre.** Current index=Index courant=Indice
      corriente. - Rome, 1967-1972.
      Contents:
      DC/67/6   Cumulative (Jan-June 67)=Cumulatif (jan-juin 67)=Acumulativo
                   (Enero-Junio 67). - 277 p. - 650 doc. - 12500 index ref.
      67/12   Cumulative (July-Dec. 67)=Cumulatif (juil-déc. 67)=Acumulativo
                   (Jul-Dic. 67). - 425 p. - 1240 doc. - 18000 index ref.
      68/6   Cumulative (Jan-June 68)=Cumulatif (jan-juin 68)=Acumulativo
                   (Enero-Junio 68). - 451 p. 1550 doc. - 17000 index ref.
      68/12   Cumulative (July-Dec. 68)=Cumulatif (juil-déc. 68)=Acumulativo
                   (Jul-Dic. 68). - 450 p. - 1485 doc. - 16800 index ref.
      69/12   Cumulative (Jan-Dec.' 69)=Cumulatif (jan-déc. 69)=Acumulativo
                   (Enero-Dic. 69). - 1048 p. - 3505 doc. - 40000 index ref.
      70/12   Cumulative (Jan-Dec. 70)=Cumulatif (jan-déc. 70)=Acumulativo
                   (Enero-Dic. 70). - 1090 p. - 3846 doc. - 40100 index ref.
      71/12   Cumulative (Jan-Dec. 71)=Cumulatif (jan-déc. 71)=Acumulativo
                   (Enero-Dic. 71). - 1200 p. - 4445 doc. - 41500 index ref.

32.   -- --- Special indexes=Index speciaux=Indices especiales.
      Contents:
      DC/SP 1   FAO technical assistance reports=Rapports   1951-1965
                   d'assistance technique de la FAO=Informes de asistencia
                   tecnica de la FAO. - 244 p. - 2120 doc. - 1100 index ref.
      SP 2   Fisheries=Peches=Pesca. - 432 p. - 2551 doc. - 13800 index   1945-1966
                   ref.
      SP 3   FAO/UNDP (SF) project reports=Rapports de projets
                   FAO/PNUD(FS)=Informes de proyectos FAO/PNUD (FE)   1963-1966
                   - 82 p. - 139 doc. - 4200 index ref.
      SP 4   Forestry=Fôrets=Montes. - 656 p. - 2325 doc. - 26000
                   index ref.   1945-1966
      SP 5   Plants=Plantes=Plantas. - 606 p. - 2423 doc. - 23500
                   index ref.   1945-1966
      SP 6   Animals=Animaux=Animales. - 408 p. 1617 doc. -
                   - 15000 index ref.   1945-1966
      SP 7   Nutrition=Nutrición. - 372 p. - 1354 doc. - 14000 index
                   ref.   1945-1966
      SP 8   Land and water=Terres et eaux=Tierras y aguas. -
                   424 p. - 1308 doc. - 17600 index ref.   1945-1966

Food and agriculture organization. Documentation centre.
Special indexes. (Cont'd)

SP 9	Rural institutions=Institutions rurales=Instituciones rurales. - 320 p. - 1185 doc. - 11500 index ref	1945-1966
SP 10	Statistics=Statistiques=Estadisticas. - 371 p. - 1320 doc. - 12700 index ref.	1945-1966
SP 11	Commodities=Produits=Productos básicos. - 297 p. - 945 doc. - 10000 index ref.	1945-1966
SP 12	Economic analysis=Analyse economique=Análisis económicos. - 260 p. - 873 doc. - 9200 index ref.	1945-1966
SP 13	FAO/UNDP(SF) project reports and documents - 1 (Guyana, Kenya, Korea, Sudan, Syria, Tunisia, Zambia, Interregional Desert Locust project)=Rapports et documents de projets FAO/PNUD(FS) - 1=Informes y documentos de proyectos FAO/PNUD(FE) - 1. - 189 p. - 517 doc. - 6500 index ref	
SP 14	Fisheries=Pêches=Pesca. - 2 vol. - 1114 p. - 4504 doc. - 40900 index ref.	1945-1969
SP 15	FAO/UNDP (SF) project reports and documents - 2 (Afghanistan, Brazil, British Guiana, Chile, China (Taiwan). Colombia, Cyprus, Ecuador, Honduras, Peru, Philippines, Saudi Arabia, Turkey, United Arab Republic)=Rapports et documents de projets FAO/PNUD (FS) - 2=Informes y documentos de proyectos FAO/PNUD (FE) - 2. - 172 p. - 284 doc. - 6000 index ref.	
SP 16	FAO/UNDP (SF) project reports and documents - 3 (Chile, Costa Rica, Ethiopia, Greece, Iran, Lebanon, Mexico, Nicaragua, Somalia, Sudan, Togo, Turkey)=Rapports et documents de projets FAO/PNUD (FE) - 3=Informes y documentos de proyectos FAO/PNUD (FE) - 3. - 184 p. - 359 doc. - 6300 index ref.	
SP 17	Food and agricultural industries (1945-1970)=Industries alimentaires et agricoles (1945-1970)=Industrias de la agricultura y la alimentación (1945-1970). - 504 p. - 1512 doc. - 20800 index ref.	
SP 18	FAO/UNDP (SF) Project reports and documents - 4 (Bolivia, Ecuador, El Salvador, Ghana, Greece, Haiti, Israel, Peru, Syria, Thailand, Tunisia, U.A.R., Regional Africa, Regional Latin America)=Rapports et documents de projets FAO/PNUD (FS) - 4=Informes y documentos de proyectos FAO/PNUD (FE) - 4. - 209 p. - 544 doc. - 8700 index ref.	
SP 19	FAO/UNDP (SF) Project reports and documents - 5 (Sebou River Basin)=Rapports et documents de projets FAO/PNUD (FS) - 5=Informes y documentos de proyectos FAO/PNUD (FE) - 5. - 350 p. - 789 doc. 12725 index ref.	
SP 20	Land reform (1945-1970)=Reforme agraire(1945-1970)=Reforma agraria(1945-1970). - 257 p. - 909 doc. - 7750 index ref.	
SP 21	Environment (1967-1970)=Environnement(1967-1970)=Medio ambiente(1967-1970). - 728 p. - 1982 doc. - 28750 index ref.	
SP 22	Agricultural engineering (1967-1971)=Machinisme agricole (1967-1971)=Maquinaria agrícola(1967-1971). - 195 p. - 489 doc. - 7500 index ref.	
SP 23	Micro-economics of agriculture (1967-1971)=Micro-economie de l'agriculture(1967-1971)=Micro-economía de la agricultura (1967-1971). - 303 p. - 792 doc. - 12250 index ref.	
SP 24	Agricultural cooperation (1945-1971)=Cooperation agricole (1945-1971)=Cooperación agrícola(1945-1971). - 306 p. - 814 doc. - 12250 index ref.	
SP 25	Education and training: annotated bibliography=Education et formation: bibliographie annotée=Educación y capacitación: bibliografía anotada. - 388 p. - 1,272 doc. - 13,100 index ref.	

533.   -- **Fisheries division.** FAO catalogue of fisheries publications and documents=Catalogue FAO des publications et documents sur les pêches=Catálogo FAO de publicaciones y documentos de pesca. - 1948-May 1962. - (FID/C).
Supplement. 1-2, May 1962/Feb. 1963-Feb. 1963/Nov. 1963. 1963. 8,6 p. (FID/C, Supp.).
Arranged by categories, series, etc.; no alphabetical index.

534. **Food and agriculture organization. Forestry and forest products division.** List of technical assistance reports. - 1964. - (PCS/3/Rev.9.)
Supplement: 1965. Arranged by continents and countries.

535. -- **Plant production and protection division.** Publications and documents. - 1947/63- .

GENERAL AGREEMENT ON TARIFFS AND TRADE

536. **General agreement on tariffs and trade.** Documents index. - (INF/-). - Geneva, 1963- . E F
Annual.
Alphabetical subject-author index with short title of document given under each heading.

537. -- --- List of documents issued. - 1963- . - (INF/105, etc.). E F
Annual.
Arranged by document number.

538. -- --- List of official material published by the Secretariat of the General agreement on tariffs and trade (GATT). - 1965. E F
Text of the General agreement on tariffs and trade. Basic instruments and selected documents series. Reports on international trade. GATT programme for expansion of international trade. Publications concerning quantitative restrictions, customs tariffs. GATT tariff schedules and protocols. GATT International trade centre. Miscellaneous publications. Information papers and brochures.

539. -- --- Publications: GATT et Centre du commerce international CNUCED/GATT. - 1969-1970. - Geneva, 1970-1971. E F
Contents:
1. Instruments juridiques. 2. Rapports sur le commerce international et sur l'application de l'Accord général. 3. Programme pour l'expansion du commerce international. 4. Textiles et coton. 5. Protocoles et listes tarifaires annexeées à l'Accord général. 6. Publications diverses. 7. Documents d'information gratuits. 8. Centre du commerce international CNUCED/GATT.

INTER-GOVERNMENTAL MARITIME CONSULTATIVE ORGANIZATION

540. **Inter-governmental maritime consultative organization.** Conferences, documents and publications. - p. 22-23. - Its: Annual report. 1971/1972. - London, 1972. - 36 p.

541. -- --- IMCO publications=Publications de l'OMCI. - In: IMCO/OMCI. - Bulletin, no.1, Sept. 1962- .

542. -- --- List of documents issued during the session of the Assembly. - London, 1962- . -(A.I- /INF-). - 1962-
Appears as a document in the Conference series.

543. -- --- List of sales publications. - 1962-1972.

INTERNATIONAL ATOMIC ENERGY AGENCY

544.   **International atomic energy agency.**   Publications: catalogue,
        1972. - Vienna, 1972. - 165 p.
        "This catalogue lists all publications of the International atomic energy agency
        issued since 1958 till the end of December 1971."
        Contents: pt.1. Publications, by subject:
                        I. Life sciences.
                       II. Health, safety and waste management.
                      III. Physics.
                       IV. Chemistry, geology and raw materials.
                        V. Reactors and nuclear power.
                       VI. Industrial applications.
                      VII. Miscellaneous.
                  pt.2. Periodicals of the IAEA.
                  pt.3. Publications en français.
                  pt.4. Publikatsii na russkom íazyke.
                  pt.5. Publicaciones en español.
                  pt.6. Series index (lists the titles of publications in each series, with
                         the publication number).
                  pt.7. Alphabetical index (four sections: English, French, Russian and
                         Spanish.
        Supplement. - 1972-   .

545.   -- --- INIS atomindex=INIS atomindeks. - v.1-   . - Vienna,
        International atomic energy agency, 1970-   .

INTERNATIONAL BANK FOR RECONSTRUCTION AND DEVELOPMENT

546.   **International bank for reconstruction and development.**
        Free publications of the World bank group. - 1971.
        - Washington, D.C., 1971.
        Contents:
        1. International bank for reconstruction and development (World bank or
        IBRD). 2. International finance corporation (IFC). 3. International
        development association (IDA). 4. International centre for settlement of
        investment disputes (ICSID).

547.   -- --- List of recent additions. - no.1-   ; March 1947-
        Contains Bank, Fund, IDA and IFC publications.
        Arrangement: general, alphabetical part, followed by a geographical,
        alphabetical part.

548.   -- --- Sale publications. - 1966-1971. - leaflets.

INTERNATIONAL BUREAU OF EDUCATION

549.   **International bureau of education.**   List of publications.
        - Geneva, 1965-1971. E F
        Sales catalogue.

INTERNATIONAL CIVIL AVIATION ORGANIZATION

550.   **International civil aviation organization.** Catalogue of
        salable publications. - 1946-1963. - Montreal, 1963. E F
        1. Aeronautical agreements and arrangements. 2. Annexes to the Convention
        on international civil aviation. 3. Procedures for air navigation services.
        4. Communication codes and abbreviations. 5. Manuals. 6. Facility and
        service documents. 7. Air navigation plans. 8. Implementation panel.
        9. Assembly Official records. 10. Council Official records. 11. Reports of
        air navigation meetings. 12. Reports of air transport meetings. 13. Legal
        meetings Official records. 14. Statistical publications. 15. ICAO circulars.
        16. Public information. 17. Indexes of ICAO publications. 18. Miscellaneous.

551.   -- ---   Index of ICAO publications: cumulated edition.
        - 1947/1951; 1952/1966; 1967/1969 (planned).
        Supplemented by annual cumulations.

552.   -- ---   Index of ICAO publications. - Fascicle no.1, Jan./Apr.
        1965-   .
        I. Analytical index of ICAO publications. II. Working papers of council.
        III. ICAO basic documents.
        Includes list of documents and working papers by number.

553.   -- ---   New ICAO publications. E F S

554.   -- ---   Weekly list of publications. - no. 1/2-   .
        - 1963-   .

555.   -- **Council.** Indexes to action of the Council. - 1971-

INTERNATIONAL COURT OF JUSTICE

556.   **International court of justice.** Annuaire. - 19 -   . - La Haye,
        19 . -   v.
        Contains a chapter: Publications de la Cour. Séries publiées par la Cour internationale
        de justice: Recueil des arrêts, avis consultatifs et ordonnances; Mémoires, plaidoiries
        et documents; actes et documents relatifs à l'organisation de la Cour; Annuaire;
        Bibliographie de la Cour internationale de justice.

557.   -- ---   Publications of the International court of justice: catalogue. -
        The Hague, 1963-   . E F
        Includes list by sales numbers.

INTERNATIONAL LABOUR ORGANISATION

558.   **International labour office.** ILO new publications. - Geneva,
        1972. E F R S

559.   -- ---   Legislative series: chronological index of laws,
        1919-1962. - 1964. - 218 p.

560.   -- ---   Legislative series; general subject index, 1919-1959.
        - 1961. - 128. E F

International labour office. (Cont'd)

561.   -- --- Publications of the International labour office.
        - 1944-1972. E F S
        Sales catalogue.

562.   -- **Central library and documentation branch.** Subject guide
        to publications of the International labour office, 1919-1964.
        - (Its: Bibliographical contributions. no.25.)

INTERNATIONAL MONETARY FUND

563.   **International monetary fund.** Catalogue of publications: 1946-71. ·
        Washington, D.C., 1972. - vii, 104 p.
        Contents:
        1. General publications. 2. Periodicals. 3. Pamphlet series. 4. Books. 5. Primarily
        for use within the Fund. 6. Information for the press.
        Translations: Français - p. 35, Español - p.45, Deutsch - p.54, Português - p.56.
        Appendices: I. Staff papers: contents by subject, v.I-XVIII (1950-71). II. The
        International monetary fund, 1945-1965: twenty years of international monetary
        cooperation. III. Finance and development: selected contents by subject, v.1-8
        (1964-71). IV. How to order Fund publications.

INTERNATIONAL ORGANIZATION FOR STANDARDIZATION

564.   **International organization for standardization.** Catalogue:
        1972. - Geneva, 1972. - 162 p.

INTERNATIONAL TELECOMMUNICATIONS UNION

565.   **International telecommunications union.** Catalogue of films on
        telecommunication. - 2nd ed. - Geneva, 1973. - 37 p. E F S
        Contents:
        1. Conditions for loan of films. 2. Films arranged by number. 3. Subject index.
        4. Alphabetical title index. 5. Country index. 6. Language index.

566.   -- --- List of recent and forthcoming publications of the ITU. -
        In: Telecommunication journal, Geneva, 1965-   .

567.   -- --- Publications of the General secretariat of ITU. - 1965-   .
        E F S

568.   -- --- Rapport sur les activités de l'Union internationale des
        télécommunications. - 1948-1972. - Genève, 1948-1972. -   v.
        E F
        Contains: Liste des publications éditées par l'Union. 1948-1972.

INTERNATIONAL TRADE CENTRE

69. **International trade centre.** Publications for developing countries
     on export promotion techniques, export marketing and export
     markets. - Geneva, 1972. - 8 p.

70. -- --- Publications: GATT et Centre du commerce international
     CNUCED/GATT. - 1970.

NORDISK RÅD

71. **Nordisk råd.** Bibliography. - Comp. by Magnus Sørensen. - Kobenhavn,
     1966. - 10 p.
     Indices to publications of the Northern council are found in Danmarks Institut for
     international usveksling, published annually.

72. -- --- Nordiska rådets publikationer. - Stockholm, 1972. - 5 l.
     Contents:
     1. Periodiskt utkommande publikationer. 2. Informationsmaterial. 3. Nordiska statuter.

73. -- --- Publications of the Nordic council. - Copenhagen, 1971.
     - leaflet.

NORTH ATLANTIC TREATY ORGANIZATION

574. **North Atlantic treaty organization.** NATO publications.
      - In: NATO letter, Brussels, 1954-   .

575. -- --- Official publications of the North Atlantic treaty
      organization. - In: NATO bibliography, Brussels, 1963,
      p. 65-68.

ORGANISATION FOR ECONOMIC CO-OPERATION AND DEVELOPMENT

576. **Organisation for economic co-operation and development.**
      Catalogue of publications. - 1964-1972. - Paris, 1964-1972.
      The Catalogue contains an alphabetical index of titles, authors and series
      indicating the page on which full details are given.
      Contents:
      1. Economic and financial affairs. 2. Statistics. 3. Development. 4. Agriculture -
      food - fisheries. 5. Energy - industry - transport - tourism. 6. Environment - land-
      use planning. 7. Manpower and social affairs. 8. Science and technology.
      9. Education. 10. Information. 11. Index of titles, authors and series.

577. -- --- Supplements. - 1972-   .

578. -- --- Just out: OECD publications. - 1968-   . - Paris, 1968-   . -
      v.
      The folder contains detailed information on new publications of the OECD.

579. -- --- OECD at work. - Paris, 1968. - 149 p.   E F
      Chapter: OECD publications, p.145-149.

F

ORGANISATION OF AFRICAN UNITY

580.   **Organisation of African unity. Scientific, technical and research
        commission.** Liste des publications en vente=Price list of
        publications. - Niamey, Publications bureau, Maison de l'Afrique,
        1972. - 6 p.
        At head of title: Organisation de l'unité africaine.
        Publications obtainable from the Publications bureau, OAU/STRC, PMB 2359, Lagos,
        Nigeria.

ORGANIZATION OF AMERICAN STATES

581.   **Organization of American States.** Catalog of publications about
        the American Republics and reports on the strengthening of
        our Inter-American community=Catálogo de publicaciones sobre
        las Repúblicas Americanas e informes acerca del fortalecimiento
        de nuestra comunidad interamericana, 1965-1966. - Washington,
        1965. - 27,5 p.
        Contents:
        I. Technical and informational publications (by subjects). II. Official records,
        OAS. Title and country index.
        Publications out of print are not listed.

582.   -- --- Catalog of publications=Catálogo de publicaciones. - 1971/72.
        - Washington, D.C., 1972.   E /S

583.   -- --- Documentos oficiales.   S
        ser.Z/I:
            1. Its: Documentos oficiales. Lista.
                1959.   Lista general. enero-dic.   1959.
                v.1.   Indice y lista general. enero-dic.   1960.
                v.2.   see Z/II.1, v.2, 1961.
                v.3.   see Z/II.1, v.3, 1962.
                v.4.   no.1-2.   Lista general. enero-dic. 1963.
                v.5.   no.1-2.   ”   ”   ”   1964.
                v.6.   no.1-2.   ”   ”   ”   1965.
                v.7.   no.1-2.   ”   ”   ”   1966.
                v.8.   no.1-2.   ”   ”””   ”   1967.
                v.9.   no.1-2.   ”   ”   ”   1968.
                v.10.   no.1-2.   ”   ”   ”   1969.
                v.11.   no.1-3.   ”   ”   ”   1970.

        ser.Z/II:
            1. Its: Documentos oficiales. Indice.
                v.1. Indice y lista general. enero-dic. 1960.
                v.2. Indice y lista general. enero-dic. 1961.
                v.3. Indice y lista general. enero-dic. 1962.
                v.4. no.3. Indice analitico. Enero-Dic. 1963.
                v.5. no.3.   ”   ”   ”   1964.
                v.6. no.3.   ”   ”   ”   1965.
                v.7. no.3.   ”   ”   ”   1966.
                v.8. no.3.   ”   ”   ”   1967.
                v.9. no.3.   ”   ”   ”   1968.
                v.10.no.3.   ”   ”   ”   1969.

584.   -- --- Informe anual del Secretario general. - 19 . - Washington,
        D.C., 19 . - v.
        Contains list of publications issued during the year.

UNITED NATIONS

85. **United Nations.** Daily list of documents distributed at Headquarters=Liste quotidienne des documents distribués au Siège.- 1948- . - New York, 1948- . - v. - (Its: Documents. ST/CS/SER.D/1- .)

86. -- --- Publications des Nations Unies: Administration internationale, stupéfiants, démographie, droits de l'homme. - 1971-

87. -- --- Publications des Nations Unies: Droit, tutelle, administration publique, transports, énergie atomique. - 1971-

88. -- --- Publications des Nations Unies: Economie mondiale. - 1971-

89. -- --- Publications des Nations Unies: Economies régionales. - 1971-

90. -- --- Publications des Nations Unies: Finances et fiscalités, statistiques, périodiques, documents miméographiés. - 1971-

91. -- --- Publications des Nations Unies: Questions générales. - 1971-

92. -- --- Publications des Nations Unies: Questions sociales. - 1971-

93. -- --- Publications périodiques.
English title: United Nations periodicals and recurrent publications. - 1971.

94. -- --- United Nations official records. 1948/1962- . - New York, 1963- . - v. F E
A listing by organ.

95. -- --- United Nations publications; catalogue of Sales numbers and of publications of the International court of justice. 1945/66- . - New York, 1967- . - v. F E

96. -- --- United Nations publications, 1945-1963; a reference catalogue. - 1964. - 71 p. - (ST/CS/SER.J/3)
A listing by sales number categories.

97. -- --- United Nations publications, 1964: a reference catalogue. - 1965. - 14 p. - (ST/CS/SER.J/3/Add.1.)
Supplemented by Monthly sales bulletin.
Title and text in English, French and Spanish.

98. -- **Advisory committee on the application of science and technology to development.** List of documents. - In Its: Annual reports to ECOSOC.

99. -- **Archives section.** Index to microfilm of United Nations documents in English, 1946-1961. - New York, 1963. - 279 p. - (Archives special guide, no.14.)

600.   **United Nations. Children's fund.** Index to UNICEF documents. -
        v.1-2; 1949/63-1963/70. - New York, 1963-1970. - 2 v. - (United
        Nations. Documents. E/ICEF/INDEX/1 and Add.1.)

        Documents issued subsequent to August 1970 are indexed periodically in
        loose-leaf form at the close of each Board session. At some future time they
        will be replaced by another consolidated Index (which will be issued as
        E/ICEF/INDEX/1/Add.2.)

601.   - - **Commission for social development.** List of documents.
        - In Its: Annual reports to ECOSOC.

602.   - - **Commission on human rights.** List of documents. - In
        Its: Annual reports to ECOSOC.

603.   - - **Commission on international trade law (UNCITRAL).** Checklist of
        documents. - In Its: Yearbooks, v.1.

604.   - - - - - List of documents. - In Its: Annual reports to the General
        Assembly.

605.   - - **Commission on narcotic drugs.** List of documents. - In
        Its: Annual reports to ECOSOC.

606.   - - **Commission on the status of women.** List of documents. - In
        Its: Annual reports to ECOSOC.

607.   - - **Committee for development planning.** List of documents. - In
        Its: Annual reports to ECOSOC.

608.   - - **Committee on housing, building and planning.** List of documents.
        - In Its: Annual reports to ECOSOC.

609.   - - **Committee on natural resources.** List of documents. - In
        Its: Annual reports to ECOSOC.

610.   - - **Dag Hammarskjold library, New York.** Check list of United
        Nations documents. - Pt. 1-9. - (ST/LIB/SER.F/1-   )

        The Check list is intended to fill the gap between 1946 and 1950 when UNDI began.

611.   - - - - - Index to proceedings of the Economic and social council.
        - 14th session-   ; 1952-   . 1953-   .
        - (ST/LIB/SER.B/E.5-   ). Sessional.

612.   - - - - - Index to proceedings of the General assembly.
        - 5th session-   ; 1950/51-   . 1953-   .
        - (ST/LIB/SER.B/A.1-   ). Sessional.

613.   - - - - - Index to proceedings of the Security council. - 19th year
        -        ; 1964-   . 1965-   . - (ST/LIB/SER.B/S.1-   ).
        Annual.

United Nations. Dag Hammarskjold library, New York, (Cont'd)

615. -- --- Index to proceedings of the Trusteeship council.
- 11th session-   ; 1952-   . 1953-   .
- (ST/LIB/SER.B/T.6-   ). Sessional.
The indexes to proceedings offer a bibliographical guide to the proceedings and
documentation of the General Assembly and the three councils.
Each index consists of the following parts:
- Introduction , including list of officers and check lists of meetings;
- Agenda, with reference to the relevant subject headings used in the Subject index;
- Subject index, with reference to the documentation, discussion and disposition
  of each agenda item;
- Index to speeches;
- Numerical list of documents, arranged by documents symbols.
The draft pages of the indexes to proceedings are circulated internally (daily), and
to fourteen United Nations Information centres (weekly).

616. -- --- Index to resolutions of the General assembly, 1946-1970.
- New York, 1972. - iii, 146 p. - (Its: Indexes to resolutions.
no.1.)
United Nations. Publications. Sales numbers. 1972.I.3.
United Nations. Documents. ST/LIB/SER.H/1, part 1.

617. -- --- UNDEX. - New York, 1970-   . -   v. - (ST/LIB/SER.I/A-
etc.)
Contents:

SERIES	TITLE	CONTENTS	FREQUENCY	LANGUAGE VERSIONS
A -	Subject index	Subjects - Type of document - Symbol of document	20 issues a year with quarterly and annual cumulations	E F S R
B -	Country index	Country - Type of action - Subject - Symbol of document	20 issues a year with quarterly and annual cumulations	E F S R
C -	List of documents	Symbol of document - Title - Author - Date - Number of pages	10 issues a year	E (F S R)
D -	List of issuances	Symbol of document - Language versions - Republication - Microfiche No. - Category of distribution	4 issues a year with annual cumulations	E only
E -	Index to reports	Subjects - Author - Symbol of document	One issue a year with 3-year cumulations	E F S R
F -	Index to resolutions and decisions	Subjects - Symbol of document	One issue a year with 3-year cumulations	E F S R
G -	Compendium of resolutions	Subjects - Symbol of document - Full text of operative paragraphs	One issue a year	E only
H -	Index to speeches	Country - Name of representative - Subjects - Symbol of document	Two issues a year	E F S R

United Nations.   Dag Hammarskjold library, New York. (cont'd)

618.   -- --- United Nations documents index. - v. 1, no. 1- ;
            January 1950-   . - (ST/LIB/SER.E/1-   ).
            Monthly with annual cumulations.
            The index lists and indexes all documents and publications of the United Nations,
            except restricted material and internal papers, and all printed publications of the
            ICJ.
            Up and till v. 13, 1962 it also included documents and publications of the
            specialized agencies.
            Prior to v. 14, 1963, only the subject index was issued in an annual cumulative
            edition.   From v. 14, 1963, an annual cumulative edition supersedes the monthly
            issues.   It consists of the Cumulative checklist and the Cumulative index.   The
            latter is issued in two parts (part one: Subject index; part two: Lists of
            documents issued in all languages, republication in Official Records, sales
            publications, list of new document series symbols, list of libraries and information
            centres receiving UN material).

619.   -- **Department of public information.**   Ten years of United
            Nations publications, 1945-1955; a complete catalogue. - New
            York, 1955. - viii, 271 p. - (United Nations. Publications.
            Sales numbers. 1955.I.8).   E F
            Supplement: Publications. 1955-   .

620.   -- --- **Library services.**   Check list of United Nations documents.
            - pt. 1-   . - Lake Success, N.Y., 1947-   . -   v.
            - (United Nations. Publications. Sales numbers. I. 1949, etc.)

621.   -- **Economic and social council.**   Checklist of documents.
            - In Its: Official records, main volume.

622.   -- **Economic commission for Africa.**   List of documents by subjects.
            - 1965. -   v. - (E/CN.14/DOC/9, etc.)

623.   -- --- List of documents. - In Its: Annual reports to ECOSOC.

624.   -- --- List of ECA documents distributed up to   1964. - General
            series 1964. -   . - (E/CN.14/DOC/1, etc.)

625.   -- --- List of ECA documents issued. - 1962-   .
            - (E/CN.14/DOC/35, etc.)

626.   -- **Economic commission for Asia and the Far East.**   Checklist of
            ECAFE documents. - 1947/1953-   .
            Includes documents not listed in UNDI.

627.   -- --- List of documents. - In Its: Annual reports to ECOSOC.

628.   -- --- List of ECAFE printed publications. - 1966-   .

629.   -- **Economic commission for Europe.**   Compendium of resolutions
            and decisions of the ECE, 1947-1964. - Geneva, 1965. - 179 p.
            - E/ECE/574).   E F
            Includes alphabetical subject index.

630.   -- --- List of documents. - In Its: Annual reports to ECOSOC.

631.   -- --- List of ECE documents distributed. - (E/ECE/DOCS/120,
            etc.)

32. **United Nations. Economic commission for Europe.** Studies and
     other publications issued under the auspices of the Economic
     commission for Europe, 1947-1966. - New York, 1967. - viii,
     81 p. - (United Nations. Publications. Sales numbers. 1967.II.E.4.)
     United Nations. Documents. E/ECE/642.

33. - - **Economic commission for Latin America.** List of documents. In Its:
     Annual reports to ECOSOC.

34. - - **Library.** Indice de trabajos preparados por la Comisión
     económica para América Latina. - (E/CN.12/LIB/1/add.4, etc.)

35. - - - - - List of ECLA documents distributed. (E/CN.12/DOC/3,
     etc.)

36. - - **General assembly.** Checklist of documents. - In Its:
     Official records, Annexes, Plenary meetings.

37. - - **International law commission.** List of documents. - In
     Its: Yearbook.

38. - - **Office, Geneva. Distribution and sales section.** List of
     new publications available=Liste des nouvelles publications
     disponibles=Lista de nuevas publicaciones disponibles. 1968-1972.
     - Geneva, 1968-1972. -   v.

39. - - - - - List of mimeographed documents of the Economic
     commission for Europe put on sale.- 1968-1972. - Geneva,
     1968-1972.   -   v. E F

40. - - **Population commission.** List of documents. - In Its:
     Annual reports to ECOSOC.

41. - - **Security council.** Checklist of documents. - In Its:
     Official records, supplements.

42. - - **Trusteeship council.** Checklist of documents. - In Its:
     Official records.

43. **United Nations administrative tribunal.** Indexes of judgements.
     1-70:   AT/DEC/1-70 (Sales no. 1958.X.1.)
     71-86: AT/DEC/71-86 (Sales no. 1963.X.1.)

44. **United Nations conference on consular relations, Vienna,
     1963.** Index to the documents of the Conference. - In
     Its: Official records. v.2.

     A/CONF.25/16/Add.1.   (Sales no. 1964.X.1.)

45. **United Nations conference on diplomatic intercourse and
     immunities, Vienna, 1961.** Index to the documents of the
     Conference. - In: Its: Official records. v.2.

     A/CONF.20/14/Add.1   (Sales no. 1962.X.1.)

646.   **United Nations conference on the application of science and
        technology for the benefit of the less developed areas.** Science
        and technology for development: report. - v.8: Plenary
        proceedings, list of papers and index. - New York, 1963.
        - viii, 295 p. - (United Nations. Publications. Sales numbers.
        1963.I.28.)
        Contents:
        pt.1.   Plenary proceedings.
        pt.2.   Reports and papers considered by the Conference.
                  List of reports of the Secretary-general of the Conference and of the
                  rapporteurs. List of papers considered by the Conference.
        pt.3.   Subject-index to the series of eight volumes.

647.   **United Nations conference on the human environment,
        Stockholm, 1972.** Conference bibliography. - Geneva, 1972.
        - 60 p. - (A/CONF.48/13/Rev.1.)
        Contents: A. Basic documents contributed to the conference secretariat from
        States invited to the Conference in accordance with General assembly
        resolution 2850(XXVI): national reports on environmental problems, case studies,
        other basic documents; B. Basic documents prepared within the United Nations
        system; C. Basic documents received from other sources; D. Draft position papers;
        E. Other papers.

648.   **United Nations conference on the law of the sea. 1st-2nd,
        1958-1960.** Index to documents of the Conference. - In:
        Summary records of plenary meetings and the meetings of the
        Committee of the whole.

        1st.   A/CONF.13/ 37   (Sales no. 1958.V.4, v.1.)
                       "   38   ("   "   "   "   v.2.)
                       "   39   ("   "   "   "   v.3.)
                       "   40   ("   """   "   "   v.4.)
                       "   41   ("   "   "   "   v.5.)
                       "   42   ("   "   "   "   v.6.)
                       "   43   ("   "   "   "   v.7.)
        2nd: A/CONF.19/8   (Sales no. 1960.V.6.)

649.   **United Nations conference on the law of treaties, Vienna,
        1968-1969.** Index to the documents of the Conference.
        - In Its: Official records.

        A/CONF.39/11/Add.2.   (Sales no. 1970.V.5.)

650.   **United Nations congress on the prevention of crime and the
        treatment of offenders. 1st-4th, 1955-1970.** List of
        documents. - In: Reports prepared by the Secretariat.
        - (United Nations. Publications. Sales numbers. 1971.IV.8, etc.)

        A/CONF.43/5, etc.
        A/CONF.6/1, 1956.IV.4.

651.   **United Nations institute for training and research.** Publications. -
        New York, 1972. - 14 p.
        Contents:
        1. Maintenance of peace and security. Peaceful settlement of disputes. International
        law.   2. Promotion of economic and social development. Environment. Economic
        development. Transfer of technology. Technical assistance. Brain drain. Racial
        discrimination. Communications.   3. The United Nations.
        Lists of publications in English, French and Spanish. Author index.

52. **United Nations regional cartographic conference for Asia and the Far East, Mussoorie, India, 1955.** List of documents issued for the Conference.

E/CONF.18/6.   (Sales no.1955.I.29.)

53. -- **2nd, Tokyo, 1958.** List of documents issued for the Conference.

E/CONF.25/3.   (Sales no. 1959.I.9.)

54. -- **3rd, Bangkok, 1961.** List of documents issued for the Conference.

E/CONF.36/2.   (Sales no.1962.I.14.)

55. **United Nations technical conference on the international map of the world on the millionth scale. Bonn, 1962.** List of documents issued for the Conference.

E/CONF.40/8.   (Sales no. 1964.I.4.)

UNITED NATIONS CONFERENCE ON TRADE AND DEVELOPMENT

556. **United Nations conference on trade and development.** Checklist of the documents of the United Nations conference on trade and development, including documents of the Preparatory committee of the Conference, and other documents referred to in the proceedings. - In: Proceedings of the United Nations conference on trade and development, Geneva, 1964, v. 1, Final act and report, p. 331-362.
All mimeographed documents.
Contents:
A. Conference documents. B. Documents of the General committee and of the Drafting committee for the Final act. C. Main committee documents. D. Preparatory committee documents. E. Documents of the General assembly and the Economic and social council referred to in the Proceedings of the Conference.

557. -- --- Checklist of documents. - In: Proceedings of the United Nations conference on trade and development, second session, New Delhi, 1968, v.1, Report and annexes, p. 462-482.

558. -- --- Cumulative list of documents. - Geneva, 1971-   .
Contents:
1. Trade and development board. TD/B/DOCS/1-2.
2. Ad hoc bodies of the Trade and development board. UNCTAD inter-governmental group on the second UN development decade. Group of experts on multilateral payments arrangements. Intergovernmental group on trade expansion. TD/B/AC/DOCS/1-   .
3. Commodities. Committee on commodities. Advisory committee to the Trade and development board and to the Committee on commodities. Permanent sub-committee on commodities. Permanent group on synthetics and substitutes. Ad hoc meeting on iron ore. Exploratory meeting on rubber. Committee on tungsten. Ad hoc working party on international organization of commodity trade. TD/B/C.1/DOCS/1-   .

United Nations conference on trade and development. (cont'd)

- - - - - Cumulative list of documents. - Geneva, 1971- .
Contents:
4. Manufactures. Committee on manufactures. Joint UNCTAD/FAO working party on forest and timber products. Intergovernmental group of experts on tariff reclassification. TD/B/C.2/DOCS/1- .
5. Invisibles and financing related to trade. Committee on invisibles and financing related to trade. Expert group on reinsurance. Intergovernmental group on supplementary financing. TD/B/C.3/DOCS/1- .
6. Shipping. Committee on shipping. Working group on international shipping legislation. TD/B/C.4/DOCS/1- .
7. Generalized system of preferences. Special committee on preferences. Group on preferences. Special committee on preferences. Working group on rules of origin. TD/GSP/DOCS/1- .
8. United Nations conference on trade and development, 2nd session, 1968. TD/DOCS/2- .

659.   - - - - - Guide to documentation: UNCTAD II, New Delhi, 1968. - New York, 1968. - 2 v. - (TD/INF.3 and Add.1.)
Contents:
- pt.1. Classification by provisional agenda items of the documents before the second session of the Conference and summary list of their contents. - pt. 2. Subject index of the documents before the second session of the Conference.

660.   Guide to UNCTAD publications; 1964-1969.
Supplement. - 1970- .

661.   - - - - - Pre-session documents prepared for UNCTAD III. - Geneva, 1971.

UNITED NATIONS EDUCATIONAL, SCIENTIFIC AND CULTURAL ORGANISATIC

662.   **United Nations educational, scientific and cultural organisation.**
Catalogue général des publications de l'Unesco et des publications parues sous les auspices de l'Unesco=General catalogue of Unesco publications and Unesco sponsored publications: 1946-1959. - Paris, 1962.
Supplement. - 1960/1963- .
Title, preliminary matter, classification headings and indexes in English and French. Listing by UDC classification with alphabetical index (author, subject, title).

663.   - - - - - Catalogue of Unesco publications. - no.1-15; December 1949-1962. E/F

664.   - - - - - Index. - In: UNESCO. Records of the General conference. 1st- session; 1946- .
Alphabetical name-subject index.

665.   - - - - - List of UNESCO documents and publications. - (UNESCO/ARC/List/1-). E F
Quarterly.
Contents:
pt.1 lists:
(a) Documents of the General Conference; documents of the Executive Board; documents of the Secretariat.
(b) UNESCO periodicals; UNESCO non-periodical publications;
(c) Publications issued by other publishers:
(i)   Translations of UNESCO publications;
(ii) Works published for UNESCO;
(iii) Works published with the assistance of UNESCO;
pt.2. is a combined alphabetical subject-author index to the documents and publications listed in pt.1.
A cumulative index is contained in the list for the last quarter.

United Nations educational, scientific and cultural organisation. (Cont'd)

666.   -- --- Resolutions index. - In: UN ESCO. Records of the
General conference. 4th-   session; 1949-   .
Alphabetical author-subject index.

667.   -- --- Selected list of Unesco statistical publications=Liste sélective
d'ouvrages de statistiques publiés par l'Unesco. - Unesco statistical
yearbook=Unesco annuaire statistique 1971:   889-890.

668.   -- --- Subject list of UNESCO documents. - 1949-1962.
E F

669.   -- --- Unesco publications catalogue. - 1968-1972.
Contents:
1. Alphabetical list of all Unesco publications available. 2. Subject lists.
3. List of national distributors.

670.   -- --- UNESCO publications checklist. - no.1-   ;
Alphabetical listing by title and series.

671.   -- **Executive board.** Cumulative subject index of resolutions
and decisions. - (Ex/Index/3, etc.).

672.   **International institute for educational planning.** IIEP book list. -
In its: Financing educational systems: specific case studies. no.1,
etc. - Paris, 1972-   . - v.

UNITED NATIONS INDUSTRIAL DEVELOPMENT ORGANIZATION

673.   **United Nations industrial development organization.** Checklist
of UNIDO documents distributed. - (ID/SER.G/32,etc.)

674.   -- --- Documents list: cumulative list for the period 1 January 1967
to 31 December 1971. - New York, 1972. - 110 p. - (Its: ID/SER.G/30.)

"This list incorporates and supersedes lists previously issued in documents
ID/SER.G/2 to ID/SER.G/29."
Contents:
I.   Major printed publications.
II.   Industrial development board. Working group on programme and
co-ordination.
III.   Meetings
A. Conferences.
B. Expert working groups, workshops and seminars.
IV.   Information series.
V.   Major studies and reports.
VI.   Recurrent publications and series.

675.   -- --- Index to UNIDO documents and publications.
- ID/SER.G/1-30.

UNIVERSAL POSTAL UNION

676.   **Universal postal union.** Catalogue de l'UPU. - 1954-   .
        Loose-leaf.
        B. Bibliothèque. C. Cinémathèque. E. Etudes en cours, etc. G. Rapports
        de gestion. I. Iconothèque. J. Journal L'Union postale.

677.   -- ---- Catalogue de l'UPU; cinémathèque, films postaux
        destinés à l'orientation du personnel, à l'enseignement, à
        la propagande, etc. - Berne, 1971. - 54 p.

678.   -- ---- Indexes.
        The following official documents of the UPU have alphabetical indexes:
        (a) Documents of the Postal congresses;
        (b) Documents of the Executive councils;
        (c) Documents of the Consultative committee for postal studies;
        (d) The Union postale;
        (e) Circulars of the International Bureau.

679.   -- ---- Liste des documents et publications parus en 1970. -
        Berne, 1971. - 1 v.

680.   -- ---- Liste des publications du Bureau international. - Berne, 1966. -
        44 p.
        Contents: 1. Histoire de l'Union postale universelle. 2. Renseignement
        d'ordre général. 3. Actes de l'Union. 4. Recueils se rapportant à l'exécution
        des Actes de l'Union et documents assimilés. 5. Taxes. 6. Communications
        de surface. 7. Communications aériennes. 8. Statistiques. 9. Revue.
        10. Collection d'études postales. 11. Divers.

WORLD HEALTH ORGANIZATION

681.   **World health organization.** World health organization
        publications: catalogue, 1947-1971. - Geneva, 1971.
        - 171 p. EF
        Contents: 1. Publications grouped by subject. 2. Periodicals and series.
        3. Official publications. 4. Publications of the International agency for
        research on cancer. 5. Indexes: Author index; Subject index.
        Supplement. - 1972-   .

682.   -- ---- Index. - In: Official records of the WHO: World
        health assembly. pt.1: Resolutions and decisions, annexes.
        - 1st-   ; 1948-   . E F

683.   -- ---- Index. - In: Official records of the WHO: World health
        assembly. pt.2: Plenary meetings; verbatim records. Committees;
        minutes and reports. - 1st-   ; 1948-   . E F

684.   -- ---- Index. - In: Official records of the WHO: Executive
        board. Resolutions, annexes. - 1st-   ; 1948-   . E F
        The above three publications have alphabetical subject-name indexes.

685. **World health organization.** Publications of the World health organization. - v.1: 1947-1957; v.2: 1958-1962; v.3. 1963-1967.

Contents:
1. Technical articles and publications. 2. Administrative and general articles and publications. 3. Author index. 4. Country index. 5. List of WHO publications by series.

686. -- --- Subject index and numerical index to resolutions. - In: Handbook of resolutions and decisions of the World health assembly and the Executive board. - 7. ed. - 1948-1963. - p. 419-444.

WORLD INTELLECTUAL PROPERTY ORGANIZATION

687. **World intellectual property organization.** Publications de l'Organisation mondiale de la propriété intellectuelle=Publications of the World intellectual property organization=Publicaciones de la Organización mundial de la propriedad intelectual. - 1972- .
- Genève, 1972- . - v. E/F/S
Contents:
1. Periodicals. 2. Manuals of conventions and agreements. 3. Booklets of conventions and agreements. 4. Instruments adopted by the Stockholm conference, 1967. 5. Documents of diplomatic conferences. 6. International classification of goods and services for the purposes of the registration of marks. 7. Collections of laws. 8. Model laws. 9. Miscellaneous.
10. Information papers.

688. -- **Library.** Catalogue des publications et documents d'archives des BIRPI. - Genève, 1966. - 1 v. - (Its: Etudes bibliographies. no.4.)
Liste complète avec cotes bibliographiques de tous les documents de conférences ou de comités d'experts, de toures les publications ronéographiées ou imprinées émanant des BIRPI et conservés à la Bibliothèque.
Contient dix chaptires:
1. Historique des BIRPI. 2. Administration des BIRPI. 3. Propriété industrielles.
4. Marques. 5. Dessins et modèles. 6. Droit d'auteur. 7. Nouveautés végétales.
8. Caractères typographiques. 9. Brochures et publications diverses. 10. Périodiques.

WORLD METEOROLOGICAL ORGANIZATION

689. **World meteorological organization.** Publications of the WMO.
- 1965- . - Geneva, 1965- .

690. -- --- Recent WMO publications. - In: WMO Bulletin. v.1- , no.1- : 1952- . E F

B. STRUCTURE AND ACTIVITIES OF INTERNATIONAL ORGANISATIONS

691. **Abboushi, W. F.** The Secretary-general of the United Nations: constitutional powers and developments. - Bibliography: p. 187-196. - Cincinnati, Ohio, 1959.
Microfilm copy of typewritten manuscript. Postive.
Collation of the original: 196 p. diagrs.
Diss. - Univ. of Cincinnati.

692. **Abdorrahman-Boroumand,** La licéité constitutionnelle de la conclusion des traités instituant une communauté supranationale. - Bibliography: p. 206-217. - Téhéran, Impr. Cherkat Sahami Tchapp, 1956. - 221 p.
Thèse - Univ. de Genève.

693. **Adam, H. T.** Les établissements publics internationaux. - Notes, partly bibliographical. - Paris, Libr. générale de droit et de jurisprudence, 1957. - ix, 323 p. - (Bibliothèque de droit international. t.3.)
"Ouvrage publié avec le concours du Centre national de la recherche scientifique."

694. -- --- Les organismes internationaux spécialisés: contribution à la théorie générale des établissements publics internationaux. - Notes, partly bibliographical. - 1-3. - Paris, Libr. générale de droit et de jurisprudence, 1965-1967. - 3 v. - (Bibliothèque de droit international. t. 29, etc.).
"Ouvrage publié avec le concours du Centre national de la recherche scientifique."

695. **Adiseshiah, M. S.** Let my country awake; the human role in development thoughts on the next ten years. - Bibliography: p. 345-362. - Paris, Unesco, 1970. - 375 p.

696. **Agoston, I.** Le Conseil d'assistance économique mutuelle (C.A.E.M.); analyse de l'expérience régionale de la coopération économique internationale en Europe de l'Est. - Bibliography: p. 335-347. - Genève, E. Droz, 1964. - xii, 353 p.
Thèse - Univ. de Genève.

697. **Ahluwalia, K.** The legal status, privileges and immunities of the specialized agencies of the United Nations and certain other international organizations. - Bibliography: p. 209-220. - The Hague, M. Nijhoff, 1964. - xiii, 230 p.
First pub. 1960 as dissertation of Columbia university.

698. **Ahmed, L. N.** Administrative committee on coordination (ACC): an inter-secretariat coordinating machinery of the United Nations family of agencies. - Bibliography: v.2, p. 467-470. - Lawrence, Kan., 1955.
Microfilm copy of typewritten manuscript. Negative.
Collation of the original: 2v. on 1 reel. (484 p.)
Diss. - Univ. of Kansas.
Notes, partly bibliographical, at the end of each chapter.

699. **Akademiía nauk SSSR. Institut mezhdunarodnogo rabochego dvizheniía.** Sotsial'naía deíatel'nost' OON: Organizatsiía Ob''edinennykh Natsii i sotsial'nye problemy trudíashchikhsía. - Moskva, Izd-vo "Mezhdunarodnye otnosheniíâ" 1970. - 232 p.

700. **Akademiîã nauk SSSR. Institut mirovoĭ ėkonomiki i mezhdunarodnykh otnosheniĭ.** OON; itogi, tendenfsii, perspektivy; (k 25-letiĭû OON). - Bibliographical notes: p. 496-540. - Moskva, Izd-vo "Mezhdunarodnye otnosheniîã", 1970. - 543 p.
25 years UN.

701. **Alcock, A. E.** History of the International labour organisation. - Bibliography: p. 365-372. - London, Macmillan, 1971. - x, 384 p.

702. **Alekseev, D. M.** Evropeĭskoe ob"edinenie uglîã i stali. - Bibliography: p. 251-261. - Moskva, Izd-vo Instituta mezhdunarodnykh otnosheniĭ, 1960. - 282 p.
At head of title: D. M. Alekseev. A. P. Mikhaĭlov.

703. **Alexander, Y.** International technical assistance experts: a case study of the U.N. experience. - Bibliography: p. 207-221. - New York, F.A. Praeger, 1966. - xx, 223 p. - (Praeger special studies in international economics and development.)
Notes, partly bibliographical, at the end of each chapter.

704. **Alterman, R.** Le Marché commun: histoire et grands problèmes. - Bibliography: p. 207. - Paris, Éd. Universitaires, 1971. - 207 p. - (Encyclopédie universitaire.)

705. **Amaducci, S.** La nature juridique des traités constitutifs des organisations internationales. - Bibliography: l. 152-156. - Bruxelles, 1971. - 156 l.
Diplôme - Institut universitaire de hautes études internationales de Genève.

706. **Ameli, M.** La procédure d'enquête aux Nations Unies. - Bibliography: p. 196-198. - Paris, 1954.
Microfilm copy of typewritten manuscript. Negative.
Collation of the original: 201 p.
Thèse - Univ. de Paris.

707. **America Latina:** el pensamiento de la CEPAL. - Bibliography: p. 297-299. - Santiago de Chile, Ed. universitaria, 1969. - 298 p. - (Colección tiempo latinoamericano.)

708. **American association for the United Nations.** "We the peoples..." A brief history of the United Nations, 1948 - 3rd rev. ed. - Bibliography: p. 71-75. - New York, 1948. - 80 p. - (Commission to study the organization of peace, New York. Publications. no. 18.)

709. **Amundsen, G. L.** Le Conseil d'entraide économique: structure, réalisations, perspectives. - Bibliographie sommaire: p. 760-808. - Strasbourg, 1971. - 835 p.

710. **Ananiadès, L. C.** L'association aux Communautés européennes. - Bibliography: p. 337-342. - Paris, Libr. générale de droit et de jurisprudence, 1967. - iii, 352 p. - (Bibliothèque de droit international. t. 38.)
"Ouvrage publié avec le concours du Centre national de la recherche scientifique."

711. The **anatomy** of influence: decision making in international organization/ by Robert W. Cox and Harold K. Jacobson and Gerard and Victoria Curzon... and others. - Includes bibliographies. - New Haven, Yale university press, 1973. - xiii, 497 p.

712.   **Aquino, C.**   Migration: bibliography. - Rome, 1971. - 43 1.
        - (United Nations social defence research institute.   Documents.
        Doc/UNSDRI/1971/13.)

713.   **Arsenov, S. I.**   Izdaniiâ organov nauchno-tekhnicheskoĭ informa͡tsii
        stran-chlenov SĖV na 1971 g. - Katalog. - Moskva, 1971.
        Catalogue of scientific publications of the Council for mutual economic assistance.

714.   **Ascher, C. S.**   Program-making in Unesco, 1946-1951; a study in the
        processes of international administration. - Notes, partly bibliographica〔
        Chicago, 1951. - ix, 84 p. - (Public administration service, Chicago.
        Special publication no. 59.)
        "Published under the auspices of Public administration clearing house."

715.   **Associazione bancaria italiana.**   Organizzazioni internazionali economiche
        e sociali; compendio segnaletico a cura di Leo Trovini. - Roma, 1949〔
        42 p.

716.   **Aufricht, H.**   The International monetary fund: legal bases, structure,
        functions. - Notes, partly bibliographical. - London, Stevens, 1964. -
        126, viii p. - (Library of world affairs.   no. 63.)
        "Published under the auspices of the London institute of world affairs."

717.   **Ausch, S.**   Theory and practice of CMEA co-operation. - Notes, partly
        bibligoraphical. - Budapest, Akadémiai Kiadó, 1972. - 279 p.
        Original ed. pub. under title A KGST-együttmuködés helyzete, mechanizmusa, távlatai
        (nemzetközi munkamegosztás és gazdasági mechanizmus.)
        "Translated by J. Rácz."
        Economic cooperation - Europe, Eastern.   Economic integration - Europe, Eastern.
        East-West trade (1945-   ).

718.   **Bailey, S. D.**   The Secretariat of the United Nations. - Notes, partly
        bibliographical. - New York, 1962. - 113 p. - (Carnegie endowment f〔
        international peace. United Nations studies. no. 11.)

719.   -- --- The United Nations; a short political guide. - Bibliography:
        p. 135-136. - London, Pall Mall press, 1963. - 141 p.

720.   -- --- Voting in the Security countil. - Bibliography: p. 237-239. -
        Bloomington, Indiana university press, 1969. - vii, 275 p. - (Indiana
        university.   International studies.)

721.   **Baker, J. C.**   The international finance corporation; origin, operations a〔
        evaluation. - Bibliography: p. 251-262. - New York, F. A. Praeger, 1〔
        xxi, 271 p.

722.   **Barros, J.**   The United Nations: past, present and future. - Notes, par〔
        bibliographical at the end of each chapter. - New York, Free press,
        1972. - 279 p.

723.   **Bartlett, T. A.**   The United Nations Secretariat at work. - Bibliography:
        p. 396-423. - Stanford, Calif., 1958.
        Microfilm copy of typewritten manuscript.   Positive.
        Collation of the original: viii, 423 p.
        Diss. - Stanford university.

24. **Bauer, G.** Towards a theology of development; an annotated
     bibliography/ compiled by Fr. Gerhard Bauer for Sodepax.
     - Lausanne, Impr. La Concorde, 1970. - viii, 201 p.
     "Sponsored by the Committee on society, development and peace of the World
     council of churches and the Pontificial commission justice and peace (Sodepax)."

25. **Becker, B. M.** Is the United Nations dead? - Bibliography: p. 161-163. -
     Philadelphia, Pa., Whitmore, 1969. - xvii, 163 p.

26. **Beeler, A (Boise).** The ILO, 1935-1955: changes in its structure, function
     and policy. - Bibliography: p. 197-218. - Ithaca, N.Y., 1956.
     Microfilm copy of typewritten manuscript. Made in 1956 by University microfilms
     (Publication no. 16,994). Positive.
     Collation of the original: iv, 218 p. tables
     Thesis - Cornell university.

27. **Benar, G.** Le Conseil de l'Europe. - Bibliography: v. 1, p. 1. - 5 v in 1. -
     (Juris-classeur de droit international. l'organisation politique et administrative
     internationale.   fasc. 155A-155E.)

28. **Bender, F.** Unesco na zes jaren. - Bibliography: 1 p. following p. 47. -
     Amsterdam, Contact, 1952. - 37 p.

29. **Benhamouda, B.** L'Association internationale de développement. -
     Bibliography: l. 251-254. - Alger, 1971. - vi, 26o l.
     Thèse - Univ. d'Alger.

30. **Berberian, N. G.** Le Conseil de sécurité: ses différences fondamentales
     avec le Conseil de la S.D.N. - Bibliography: p. 327-329. - Paris, n.d.
     Microfilm copy of typewritten manuscript. Positive.
     Collation of the original: 333 p.
     Thèse - Paris.

31. **Berkov, R.** The World health organization; a study in decentralized
     international administration. - Bibliography: p. 163-173. - Genève,
     E. Droz, 1957. 0 x, 173 p.
     Thèse - Genève.

32. **Bernadet, P.** L'O.A.C.I.: service public international. - Bibliography:
     p. 110-113. - Paris, 1953.
     Microfilm copy of typewritten manuscript. Negative.
     Collation of the original: 116 p.
     Thèse - Univ. de Paris.

33. **Bernhard, J. T.** United Nations reform: an analysis. - Bibliography:
     p. 230-251. - Los Angeles, 1950.
     Microfilm copy of typewritten manuscript. Negative.
     Collation of the original: 251 p.
     Diss. - Univ. of California (Los Angeles).

34. **Berthoud, J. L.** Plans et accords monétaires des Nations Unies. Des
     plans Keynes et White au projet d'accord monétarie de Bretton Woods. -
     Bibliography: p. 9-11. - Neuchâtel, Impr. Richème, 1946. - 132 p.
     United Nations monetary and financial conference, Bretton Woods, 1944.

35. **Besterman, T.** UNESCO, peace in the minds of men. - Bibliographies
     at the end of some chapters. - London, Methuen, 1951. - xi, 132 p.

G

736.   **Bibié, M.** La communauté internationale et ses institutions: les juridic
        internationales, l'Organisation internationale du travail, l'organisation de
        Nations Unies, les ententes régionales (avec les textes essentiels). - Par
        Recueil Sirey, 1949. - 248 p.

737.   **Bibliografía** de Centroamérica y del Caribe. 1956-   . - Habana,
        1958-   . - v.
        "Compilada bajo los auspicios de la Unesco por la Agrupación bibliográfica cubana
        José Toribio Medina, y realizada por la Dirección general de archivos y bibliotecas
        de España."

738.   **Bibliographie** géographique internationale. - 1893-   . - Paris,
        Centre national de la recherche scientifique, 1893-   . v.
        1897-1914, pub. as September issue of Annales de géographie.
        At head of title: 1915-   , Association de géographes français.
        Pub. under auspices of Union géographique internationale, with assistance from
        UNESCO, 1947-   .
        Title varies: 1893-98, Bibliographie; 1899-1930, Bibliographie géographique annuelle
        (varies); 1931-   , Bibliographie géographique internationale.

739.   **Bibliographie** linguistique des années 1939-1947. - Pub.   par le
        Comité international permanent de linguistes avec une
        subvention de l'Organisation des Nations Unies pour l'éducation
        la science et la culture. - v. 1-   . - Cambridge, W. Heffer, 1949-
             . - v.

740.   **Bindschedler, R. L.** La délimitation des compétences des Nations Unies.
        - Bibliography: p. 419-421. - (In Academy of international law, The
        Hague. Recueil des cours, 1963, I. Leyde (Pays-Bas), A.W. Sijthoff,
        1964. v. 108, p. 307-423.)

741.   **Blagojević, B. T.** Bibliographie du droit yougoslave, 1945-1967.
        - 2e ed. - Paris, Mouton, 1970. - 155 p. - (Maison des
        sciences de l'homme, Paris.   Service d'échange d'informations
        scientifiques.   Publications.   sér. A: Bibliographies. 2.)
        "Établie pour le Comité international pour la documentation des sciences sociales
        sous le patronage de l'Association internationale des sciences juridiques."
        "Publié avec le concours financier de l'Unesco."

742.   **Blaisdell, D. C.** International organization. - Bibliography: p. 405-418. -
        New York, Ronald press, 1966. - vi, 531 p.

743.   **Bloch, R.** La fonction publique internationale et européenne. - Biblio-
        graphy: p. 213-214. - Paris, Libr. générale de droit et de jurisprudence
        1963. - 219 p. - (Economie et législation européennes. 1.)

744.   **Blümel, W. L.** Deutsches und ausländisches Schriftum über die
        Organisation der Vereinten Nationen unter besonderer Berücksichti-
        gung des Schrifttums zur Revision der UN-Charta. - Zusammen-
        gestellt und bearb. von Willi L. Blümel. - Frankfurt am Main,
        Institut für europäische Politik und Wirtschaft, 1955. - iii, 63 l. -
        (Europa-Archiv. Aktuelle Bibliographien. Hft. 9.)

745.   **Boen, S. E.** The leadership role of the Secretary-general in times of
        international crisis. - Bibliography: p. 407-418. - Charlottesville, Va.,
        1965.
        Microfilm copy of typewritten manuscript. Positive.
        Collation of the original: iii, 418 p.
        Diss. - Univ. of Virginia.

746. **Böhme, K. H.** Die internationale Organisation der zivilen Luftfahrt in ihrem geschichtlichen Werdegang. - Bibliography: p. viii-xviii. - Göttingen, 1956. - xxi, 256 l.
Diss. - Georg August Universität, Göttingen.

747. **Börner, B.** Die Entscheidungen der Hohen Behörde; eine Studie zum supranationalen Verwaltungsprozess. - Bibliography: p. 201-214. - Tübingen, J.C.B. Mohr (Paul Siebeck), 1965. - xv, 225 p.
"Die Schrift hat im Dezember 1960 der Rechts- und staatswissenschaftlichen Fakultät der Wilhems-Universität in Münster zur Habilitation vorgelegen." - Vorwort.
European coal community.

748. **Boisson, H.** La Société des nations et les bureaux internationaux des Unions universelles postale et télégraphique. - Bibliography: p. 131-134. - Paris, A. Pedone, 1932. - xiii, 134 p.
Thèse - Faculté de droit de Paris.

749. **Borisov, K. G.** Mezhdunarodnye organizat͡sii. - vyp. 1- . - Bibliographical notes. - Moskva, 1967- . - v.
At head of title: Universitet druzhby narodov imeni Patrisa Lumumby. Kafedra mezhdunarodnogo prava.
International organisations.

750. **Bottenberg, P.** Die politischen Leitungsfunktionen der Generalsekretäre internationaler Organisationen. - Bibliography: l. viii-xvii. - Göttingen, 1959. - xvii, 169 l.
Diss. - Georg-August-Universität in Göttingen.

751. **Boutros-Ghali, B. Y.** L'Organisation de l'unité africaine. - Bibliography: p. 185-189. - Paris, A. Colin, 1969. - 196 p. - (Collection U. sér.: "Institutions internationales".)

752. **Boyd, W. S.** The veto in the Security council. - Bibliography: l. 130-136. - Washington, 1951.
Microfilm copy of typewritten manuscript. Negative.
Collation of the original: ii, 136 l.
Thesis. - Georgetown university (Washington, D.C.).

753. **Božić, N.** Ekonomske sankcije u kolektivnoj bezbednosti Drustva naroda i Ujedinjenih nacija. - Bibliography: p. 209. - Beograd, Izdanje Instituta za medunarodnu politiku i privredu, 1971. - 254 p.
Summaries in English and Russian: p. 213-229.
Economic sanctions.

754. **Breycha-Vauthier, A. C.** Internationales Sekretariat. - Bibliography: p. 136. - Berlin, W. de Gruyter, 1961. - p. 134-136.
"Sonderdruck aus: Strupp-Schlochauer 'Wörterbuch des Völkerrechts', 2. Auflage, Band II."

755. **Briggs, H. W.** The International law commission. - Notes, partly bibliographical. - Ithaca, N.Y., Cornell university press, 1965. - xv, 380 p.

756. **Brogan, P.** The Common market. - Bibliography: 1 p. following p. 20. - London, Times' education services, 1970. - 20 p. - (Issues of today. no.3.)

757. **Buerstedde, S.** Der Ministerrat im konstitutionellen System der Europäischen Gemeinschaften. - Bibliography: p. 15-28. - Bruges, De Tempel, 1964. - 251 p. - (Cahiers de Bruges. N.S.9.)
On cover: College of Europe.

758.   **Bureau international d'éducation.**   Annual educational bibliography.
        - 1955-   . - Geneva, International bureau of education,
        1956-   . -   v. - (Its: Publications. no.178, etc.)

759.   **Burnett, H. J.**   The United Nations and commodities: a study of U.N.
        promoting of economic cooperation in fulfilling its basic purposes. -
        Bibliography: p. 271-282. - New York, 1965.
        Microfilm copy of typewritten manuscript.   Positive.
        Collation of the original: vii, 283 p. tables, diagrs.
        Diss. - New York university.

760.   **Burnhauser, P.**   Die Entwicklung der Rechtsstellung internationaler
        Beamten. - Bibliography: p. i-vii. - Erlangen, 1953.
        Microfilm copy of typewritten manuscript.   Negative.
        Collation of the original: xii, 127 p.
        Inaug. Diss. - Friedrich-Alexander-Universität zu Erlangen.

761.   **Caillot, J.**   Le C.A.E.M.:   aspects juridiques et formes de coopération
        entre les pays socialistes. - Bibliography: p. 381-404. - Paris, Libr.
        générale de droit et de jurisprudence, 1971. - 413 p. - (Bibliothèque
        de droit international.   t. 62.)
        "Ouvrage honoré d'une subvention du Ministère de l'éducation nationale."

762.   **Cale, E. G.**   Latin American free trade association: progress, problems,
        prospects. - Bibliography: p. 56-58. - Washington, D.C., 1969. - v,
        61 p. - (United States. Department of state. Inter-American series. no.9
        "A report prepared under contract for the Office of external research."

763.   **Calmann, J.**   The common market; the Treaty of Rome explained, edited
        by John Calmann. - Bibliography: p. 75. - London, A. Blond, 1967. -
        80 p. - (The great society. 5.)

764.   **Calzada Flores, M.**   La organización interamericana dentro de la organizac
        mundial. - Bibliography: p. 101-104. - Mexico, 1949. - 104 p.
        Thesis - Mexico.

765.   **Campolongo, A.**   Organizzazioni economiche internazionali. - Includes
        bibliographies. - Padova, CEDAM, 1969. - x, 455 p.
        At head of title: Centro studi sulle Comunità europee delle Facoltà di giurisprudenza,
        scienze politiche, economia e commercio dell'Università di Pavia.

766.   **Carmoy, G. de.**   Les organisations économiques internationales. -
        Bibliography: p. 334-335. - Paris, Cours de droit, 1950. - 2 v. in 1.
        At head of title: Université de Paris.   Institut d'études politiques, 1949-1950.

767.   **Carnegie endowment for international peace.**   Coordination of economic
        and social activities of the United Nations. - Bibliography: p. 105-109. -
        New York, 1948. - 109 p. - (Its: United Nations studies. 2.)
        "Walter R. Sharp... did the basic research and prepared the initial draft of the study."

768.   **Carreau, D.**   Le Fonds monétaire international. - Bibliography: p. 257-260
        Paris, A. Colin, 1970. - 270 p. - (Collection U. sér.: "Droit internationa
        économique".)

769.   **Carroll, M. J.**   Key to League of nations documents placed on
        public sale 1920-1929. - Boston, World peace foundation, 1930. -
        340 p.
        -- -- --   1st suppl. 1930. Boston, World peace foundation, 1930, xi, 107 p.
        -- - ---   2nd suppl. 1931 and check list of catalog cards issued by the Library
        of Congress for League publications 1920-1931. Boston, World peace
        foundation, 1933. xii, 127 p.
        -- -- --   3rd suppl. 1932/33. 1934
        -- -- --   4th suppl..., 1934/36. New York, Columbia univ. press, 1938. xxi, 188 p.

70. **Carroz, J.** La personnalité juridique internationale de l'Organisation des Nations Unies. - Bibliography: l. 168-175. - Paris, 1952. - 177 l.
At head of title: Université de Paris. Faculté de droit.
Thèse - Univ. de Paris.

71. **Casco Nuñez, A.** El principio de unanimidad de los miembros permanentes del Consejo de sguridad. - Bibliography: p. 85. - México, D.F., "Impr. económica", 1950.
Microfilm copy. Negative.
At head of title: Universidad nacional autonoma de México. Facultad de derecho y ciencias sociales.
Collation of the original: 85 p.
Tesis - Mexico.

72. **Catalogue** des sources de documentation juridique dans le monde=A register of legal documentation in the world.
1953-   . - Paris, UNESCO, 1953-   . -   v.
At head of cover-title: Documentation dans les sciences sociales. Documentation in the social sciences.
Issued by: International committee for social sciences documentation.
Joint issueing body varies: 1953, International committee of comparative law; 1957-   , International association of legal science.

73. **Chase, E. P.** The United Nations in action. - Bibliography: o. 395-400. - New York, McGraw-Hill, 1950. - xii, 464 p. - (McGraw-Hill series in political science.)
"Charter of the United Nations": p. 403-434.
"Statute of the International court of justice": p. 435-451.

74. **Chaumont, C. M.** L'Organisation des Nations Unies. - Bibliography: p. 126. - Paris, Presses universitaires de France, 1957. - 128 p. - ("Que sais-je?" Le point des connaissances actuelles. no. 748.)

75. **Cheever, D. S.** The Security council: its interpretations of the United Nations charter. - Bibliography: p. 348-361. - Cambridge, Mass., 1948.
Microfilm copy of typewritten manuscript. Negative.
Collation of the original: 361, 7 p.
Thesis - Harvard university.

76. **Chen, Wen-chao.** The personnel system of the United Nations; a study of international civil service. - Bibliography: l. 399-427. - St. Louis, 1951.
Microfilm copy of typewritten manuscript. Negative.
Collation of the original: ii, iv, 434 l.
Diss. - St. Louis university.

77. **Chumakova, M. L.** Organizatsiiā tsentral'noamerikanskikh gosudarstv. - Bibliographical notes. - Moskva, Izd-vo "Mezhdunarodnye otnosheniiā", 1970. - 126 p.
Organization of Central American States. Charter.

78. **Claude, I. L.** The changing United Nations. - Bibliography: p. 131-136. - New York, Random house, 1967. - xix, 140 p. - (Studies in political science, PS 58.)

79. **Codding, G. A.** The International telecommunication union; an experiment in international cooperation. - Bibliography: p. 479-496. - Leiden, E.J. Brill, 1952. - xiv, 496 p.
Thèse - Genève.

780.   **Codding, G. A.** The Universal postal union: coordinator of the international mails. - Bibliography: p. 267-285. - New York, New York, university press, 1964. - ix, 296 p.
"Publication of this work was aided by a partial subvention from the Ford foundation."

781.   **Cohen, B. V.** The United Nations: constitutional developments, growth and possibilities. - Notes, partly bibliographical. - Cambridge, Mass., Harvard university press, 1961. - 106 p. - (Oliver Wendell Holmes lectures. 1961.))

782.   **Cohen Orantes, I.** Central American integration, 1950-1968. - Bibliography: p. 107-122. - Lexington, Mass., D.C. Heath, 1972. - xiii, 126 p. - (Lexington books.)
Thèse - Univ. de Genève, Institut universitaire de hatues études internationales.

783.   **Colliard, C. A.** Institutions internationales. - Includes bibliographies. - Paris, Dalloz, 1956-   . - (Petits précis Dalloz.)   v.

784.   -- - --- Mezhdunarodnye organizaťsii i uchrezhdeniiâ. - Includes bibliographies. - Moskva, Izd-vo, "Progress", 1972. - 631 p.
At head of title: K. Kol'iar.
"Perevod s franťsuzskogo Z.I. Lukovnikovoĭ i A.S. Malikova."
Added title-page with title: Institutions internationales.
International agencies. League of nations. United Nations - Specialized agencies.

785.   **Commission to study the organization of peace, New York.** Strengthenin the United Nations. - Notes, partly bibliographical. - New York, Harpe 1957. - xii, 276 p.
"Arthur N. Holcombe, chairman."

786.   **Communauté européenne du charbon et de l'acier. Haute autorité. Biblioghèque.** Études régionales=Regionalbegrenzte Studien; Bibliographien. - 1950/55-   . - Luxembourg, 1955-   . - v. - (Communauté européenne du charbon et de l'acier. Haute autorité. Bibliographies de la Haute autorité. nos.3, etc.)

787.   **Communautés européennes.** Bibliographie sur le marché commun et la Turquie=Ortak pazar ve Türkiye bibliografyasi. - Bruxelles, Service de presse et d'information des Communautés européennes, 1967. - 38 p. - (Its: Dossiers bibliographiques.)

788.   -- - --- Bibliographie sur les transports dans l'intégration européenne=Bibliographie über den Verkehr im europäischen Integrationsprozess=Bibliografia sui trasporti nell'integrazione europea=Bibliografie over het vervoer in de Europese integratie. - 1967. - iii, 119 p.

789.   -- - --- Droit d'établissement et libre prestation des services: bibliographie. - Bruxelles, 1968. - 30 1. - (Its: Cahier bibliographique. no.1)

790.   -- - --- L'enseignement dans les pays de la Communauté européenne. - Bruxelles, Communautés européennes, Direction générale presse et information, 1970. - ix, 223 p. - (Its: Références bibliographiques.)

791.   **Communautés européennes.**   Literaturhinweise zur Koordinierung des
        Währungspolitik im gemeinsamen Mark=Bibliographie concernant la
        coordination des politiques monétaires dans le marché commun. -
        1968. - 44 p.

792.   - - - - -   Le marché commun et les consommateurs: références
        bibliographiques=Der gemeinsame Markt und die Verbraucher=
        Il mercato comune e i consumatori=De gemeenschappelijke
        markt en de verbruikers. - 1968-   . -

793.   - - - - -   La politique économique à moyen terme de la CEE.
        - Bruxelles, Communautés européennes, Service de presse et
        d'information, Division des publications, 1966. - 22 p. - (Its:
        Dossiers bibliographiques.)

794.   - - - - -   La politique régionale des Communautés européennes.
        - Bruxelles, Communautés européennes, Service de presse et
        d'information, Division des publications, 1966. - 35 p. - (Its:
        Dossiers bibliographiques.)

795.   - - - - -   La politique scientifique en Europe. - Bruxelles,
        Communautés européennes, Service de presse et d'information,
        Division des publications, 1967. - 54 p. - (Its: Dossiers
        bibliographiques.)

796.   - - - - -   Rapports entre le droit communautaire et le droit
        national. - Bruxelles, Service de presse et d'information des
        Communautés européennes, Division des publications, 1966. - 32 p.
        - (Its: Dossiers bibliographiques.)

797.   - - - - -   Le travail féminin en Europe: références bibliographiques=
        Die Frauenarbeit in Europa=Il lavoro femminile in Europa=De
        vrouwenarbeid in Europa. - 1968-   . - 1968-   . -   v.

798.   **Conferéncia especializada sobre a aplicaçao da ciéncia e da tecnologia
        para o desenvolimento da América Latina, Brazilia, 1972.** Relatório
        final. - Washington, D.C., 1972. - iii, 180 p. - (Organization of American
        States. Documents. OEA/Ser.C/VI.22.1.)
        Lista de documentos: 1. Documentos nacionais, outros documentos de paises, autores
        individuais, publicaçoes de instituçoes. -. 139-180.

799.   **Connell-Smith, G.**   The inter-American system. - Bibliography: p. 346-360. -
        London, Oxford university press, 1966. - xix, 376 p.
        "Issued under the auspices of the Royal institute of international affairs."

800.   **Cordovez, D.**   UNCTAD and development diplomacy; from confrontation
        to strategy. - Bibliographical notes. - London, 1971. - 167 p.
        "Published by The Journal of world trade law."
        "This work covers developments in the legislative history and institutional framework of the
        UNCTAD during the last five years."
        United Nations conference on trade and development - History. United Nations conference on
        trade and development. 2nd session, New Delhi, 1968. Contracting parties to the General
        agreement on tariffs and trade. Economic development. Commerce.

801.   **Cormier, R.** Les sources des statistiques actuelles: guide de documenta
         Paris, Gauthier-Villars, 1969. - 283 p. - (Institut national des techniqu
         de la documentation. Documentation et information.)
         Organismes centraux d'études et de recherches statistiques. Enseignement de la statistique.
         Bibliographies générales. Sources des statistiques générales. Sources des statistiques démo-
         graphiques et sanitaires. Sources des statistiques économiques. Sources des statistiques
         culturelles. Sources des statistiques politiques et juridiques.
         Annexe A: Sources bibliographiques des statistiques nationales de divers pays. Liste indicati
         Annexe B: Les classifications documentaires dans le domaine des statistiques.
         Index alphabétique des matières. Index des sigles d'organismes.

802.   **Cosgrove, C. A.** The new international actors: the United Nations and
         the European economic community, edited by Carol Ann Cosgrove an
         Kenneth J. Twitchett. - Bibliography: p. 257-266. - London, Macmilla
         1970. - 272 p. - (Readings in international politics.)

803.   **Council of Europe.** Bibliographie des traductions des codes
         de droit privé des états membres du Conseil de l'Europe
         et de la Conférence de la Haye de droit international
         privé=Bibliography of translations of codes of private law.
         - Strasbourg, 1967. - 355 p.
         "The necessary research was carried out and the references collected were
         checked, edited and arranged by Mrs. G. Van der Espt."

804.   - - - - - Documentation sur le Conseil de l'Europe=Documentation
         on the Council of Europe. - Strasbourg. Centre de
         documentation, 1952. - 40 p.
         At head of title: Conseil de l'Europe. Direction des études. Council of
         Europe. Research directorate.

805.   - - **Conseil de la coopération culturelle.** Bibliographie d'ouvrages
         sur l'Europe à l'intention des enseignants. - Strasbourg, 1965-   .
         -   v.
         "Cette bibliographie sera mise à jour et la suite paraîtra sous forme de bulletin
         trimestriel du Service d'information de la Campagne d'éducation civique européenne."
         - Préf. 1965.

806.   - - **Documentation section.** Documentation sur l'enfance;
         quelques aspects sociaux=Documentation on childhood; a few
         social aspects. - Strasbourg, 1959. - 22 p.

807.   - - **Section documentation et bibliothèque.** Bulletin d'information
         sur la politique sociale. - no.1-11. - Strasbourg, 1967-1972. -   v.
         Ce bulletin est publié une ou deux fois par an, sur la base de contributions
         fournies par les gouvernements membres.

808.   - - - - - Bulletin de bibliographie. - v.1-10.

809.   **Crabol, J.** L'Organisation mondiale de la santé. - Bibliography: p.xxvii-
         xxxi. - Grenoble, 1951.
         Microfilm copy of typewritten manuscript. Negative.
         Collation of the original: 106, xxxi, p.
         Thèse - Univ. de Grenoble.

810.   **Cremer, G.** Die Verfassung der Internationalen Arbeitsorganisation. -
         Bibliography: p. iii-iv. - Berlin, Hiehold & Co., 1929. - iv, 50 p.
         Inaug. -Diss. - Kiel.

311. **Curzon, G.** Hidden barriers to international trade/ by Gerard Curzon and Victoria Curzon. - Bibliographical notes. - London, Trade policy research centre. Thames essays. no.1.)

312. -- --- Multilateral commercial diplomacy; an examination of the impact of the General agreement on tariffs and trade on national commercial policies and techniques. - Bibliography: p. 337-355. - London, En vente chez: M. Joseph, 1965. - xii, 367 p.
Thèse - Univ. de Genève.

313. **Cutajar, M. Z.** The less developed countries in world trade; a reference handbook of world trade, and the work of two international organizations concerned with trade policies: The General agreement on tariffs and trade (GATT), and the UN Conference on trade and development (UNCTAD) / by Michael Zammit Cutajar and Alison Franks. - Notes, partly bibliographical. - London, Overseas development institute, 1967. - 209 p.
On cover: ODI.

314. **Dag Hammarskjöld seminar on the structure, role and functions of the UN system, Uppsala, 1968.** Essays presented by the seminar participants. - Includes bibliographies. - pt. 1-2. - Uppsala, Dag Hammarskjöld foundation, 1969. - 2 v.

315. -- --- Lectures/ by Georges Abi-Saab... and others. - Notes, partly bibliographical, at the end of some papers. - pt. 1-2. - Uppsala, Dag Hammarskjöld foundation, 1969. - 2 v.

316. **Daillier, P.** Les institutions du développement. - Bibliography: p. 94-95. - Paris, Presses universitaires de France, 1972. - 95 p. - (Dossiers Thémis. sér. "Institutions et droit internationa.".)
Economic assistance in Developing countries. Technical assistance in Developing countries. Development programme. Regional co-operation.

317. **Dajany, O.** The world bank and the International finance corporation; the last look in international organizations. - Bibliography: p. 161-169. - Washington, 1956.
Microfilm copy of typewritten manuscript. Negative.
Collation of the original: xv, 268 p.
Thesis - American university.

318. **Dam, K. W.** The GATT: law and international economic organization. - Notes, partly bibliographical. - Chicago, Univ. of Chicago press, 1970. - xvii, 480 p.

319. **Davis, E. E.** Attitude change: a review and bibliography of selected research. - Paris, Unesco, 1965. - 63 p. - (United Nations educational, scientific and cultural organisation. Reports and papers in the social sciences. no. 19.)
Pt.1. Experimental research on attitude change. Personality-oriented research. Group-oriented research. Persuasive communications research. Theoretical problems of attitude change research.
Pt.2. Action research on intergroup attitudes. Educational programmes in intergroup relations. Intergroup contact and community studies. Cultural influences and the role of society.
Index of authors.

820. **Day, G.** Le droit de veto dans l'Organisation des Nations Unies. - Bibliography: p. 239-241. - Paris, A. Pedone, 1952. - iv, 244 p.
"Ouvrage couronné par la Faculté de droit de l'Université de Paris."

821. **Delvaux, L.** La Cour de justice de la Communauté européenne du charbon et de l'acier; exposé sommaire des principes: organisation, compétence, procédure, le droit en vigueur dans la Communauté. - Bibliography: p. 321-325. - Gembloux, J. Duculot, 1956. - 334 p.

822. **Dembiński, L.** Samostanowienie w prawie i praktyce ONZ. - Bibliograpł p. 253-267. - Warszawa, Państwowe wydawnictwo naukowe, 1969. - 274. p.
A summary in English entitled: "Self-determination in the law and practice of the United Nations": p. 268-272.

823. **Dendias, M.** Les principaux services internationaux administratifs. - Bibliography: p. 359-363. - (In Hague, Academy of international law. Recueil des cours, 1938. v. 63, p. 243-366.)

824. **Detter, I.** Law making by international organizations. - Bibliography: p. 330-345. - Stockholm, P. A. Norstedt, 1965. - 353 p.
Added title-page inserted has thesis note: Akademisk avhandling - Stockholm univ.

825. **Deutsche Liga für die Vereinten Nationen.** Die Organisation der Vereinten Nationen; Dokuments. T.1- . - Notes, partly bibliographical. - Berlin, Deutscher Zentralverlag, 1961- . - v.

826. **Dharma, P.** The advisory jurisdiction of the International court. - Bibliography: p. 274-283. - Oxford, Clarendon press, 1972. - xvi, 292 p.

827. **Digest** of legal activities of international organizations and other institutions=Répertoire des activités juridiques des organisations internationales et autres institutions. - Dobbs Ferry, N.Y., Oceana publications, 1968- . - v.
At head of title: Unidroit. International institute for the unification of private law. Institut international pour l'unification du droit privé.
Loose-leaf.

828. **Dimitrijevic, P.** L'Organisation internationale du travail: histoire de la représentation patronale. - Bibliography: p. 459-491. - Genève, 1972. - x, 512 p.

829. **Dollfus, D. F.** A propos de: Euratom. - Bibliography: p. 209. - Paris, Productions de Paris, 1959. - xix, 221 p.
At head of title: Daniel F. Dollfus. Jean Rivoire.

830. **Dossier** de l'Europe des six du plan Schuman à la commission Rey: où en est la Communauté? où va-t-elle? - Bibliography: p. 320-326. - Verviers (Belgique), Gérard, 1969. - 336 p. - (Marabout université. v. 176.)
"Dossier établi par Maryse Charpentier, avec la collaboration de H. Brugmans... et d'autres."

831. **Dougall, R.** The archives and documents of the Preparatory Commission of the United Nations. - American archivist 10: 25-34, no.1, January 1947.

2. **Dreier, J. C.** The Organization of American states and the hemisphere crisis. - Notes, partly bibliographica. - Harper & Row, 1962. - xii, 147 p.
"Published for the Council on foreign relations."

3. **Duckworth-Barker, V.** Breakthrough to tomorrow: the story of international co-operation for development through the United Nations. - Bibliography: p. 69-70. - New York, 1970. - iii, 70 p. - (United Nations. Publications. Sales numbers. 1971.I.5.) E F S
At head of title: United Nations centre for economic and social information.

4. **Duclos, P.** La réforme du Conseil de l'Europe. - Bibliography: p. 503-505. - Paris, Libr. générale de droit et de jurisprudence, 1958. - 525 p. - (Union européenne des fédéralistes. Bibliothèque de textes et études fédéralistes. t.2.)

5. **Dufau, J.** La F.A.O. et l'action internationale en matière d'alimentation et d'agriculture. - Bibliography: 6th p. before the end. - Paris, 1952.
Microfilm copy of typewritten manuscript. Negative.
Collation of the original: 1 v.
Thèse - Univ. de Paris.

36. **Dupuy, R. J.** Le Pacte de Varsovie/ par René Jean Dupuy et Mario Bettati. - Bibliography: p. 95-96. - Paris, A. Colin, 1969. - 96 p.

37. **Durante, F.** L'ordinamento interno delle Nazioni Unite. - Bibliography: p. xxi-xxxviii. - Milano, A. Giuffrè, 1964. - xli, 448 p. - (Catania. Università. Facoltà di giurisprudenza. Pubblicazioni. 44.)

38. **Durdenevskiĭ, V. N.** Organizat͡sii͡a Ob"edinennykh Nat͡siĭ; sbornik dokumentov, otnosi͡ashchikhsi͡a k sozdanii͡u i dei͡atel'nosti. - Moskva, Gos. izd-vo iurid. lit-ry, 1956. - 374 p.
At head of title: V.N. Durdenevskiĭ. S.B. Krylov.
Documents on UN activities.

39. **Economic development institute, Washington, D.C.** Selected readings and source materials on economic development; a list of books, articles and reports included in a small library/ assembled by the Economic development institute. Washington, D.C., International bank for reconstruction and development, 1962. - vi, 66 p.

40. **Einzig, P.** A textbook on monetary policy. - Bibliography: p. 447-461. - London, Macmillan, 1972. - xi, 461 p.

41. **Elbialy, F.** La Société financière internationale. - Bibliography: p. 307-318. - Genève, E. Droz, 1963. - 323 p.
Thèse - Univ. de Genève.

42. **Elian, G.** The International court of justice. - Bibliographical notes. - Leiden, A.W. Sijthoff, 1971. - 150 p.

43. **Engle, H. E.** A critical study of the functionalist approach to international organization. - Bibliography: p. 542-565. - New York, 1957.
Collation of the original: 3, vi, 565 p.
Thesis - Columbia university.

844.   **Ennals, D.** United Nations on trial. - Notes, partly bibliographical. -
        London, 1962. - 33 p. - (Fabian society, London. Research series.
        no. 227.)
        At head of title: Fabian International bureau.

845.   **Az ENSZ-** rol. - Bibliography: p. 163-175. - Budapest, Országgyülési
        könyvtár és az MTI kiadása, 1961. - 194 p.
        "Szerkesztette Vértes György... Lektorálta...Sebestyén Pál."
        Tables of contents in English, French, Russian and Hungarian. Text only in Hungarian.
        United Nations.

846.   **Entezami, F.** L'organisation de l'U.N.E.S.C.O. et ses rapports avec
        l'O.N.U. - Bibliography: p. 201-202. - Paris, 1952.
        Microfilm copy of typewritten manuscript. Negative.
        Collation of the original: 202, 3p.
        Thèse - Univ. de Paris.

847.   **Enukidze, D.** The United Nations. - Bibliography: 3rd p. following
        p. 49. - Tbilisi, 1959.
        Microfilm copy. Negative.
        Title and text in Georgian. Translation of title-page supplied.
        Collation of the original: 49 p.

848.   **Erichsen, H. U.** Das Verhältnis von Hoher Behörde und Besonderem
        Ministerrat nach dem Vertrage über die Gründung der Europäischen
        Gemeinschaft für Kohle und Stahl. - Bibliography: p. 291-297. -
        Hamburg, Hansischer Gildenverlag, 1966. - x, 297 p. - (Kieler
        rechtswissenschaftliche Abhandlungen. Nr. 6.)
        Foot-notes, partly bibliographical.
        European coal community.

849.   Die **Europäische** Wirtschaftsgemeinschaft im Ausbau: Bilanz und
        Perspektiven. - Bibliography: p. 257-261. - Baden-Baden, Nomos
        Verlagsgesellschaft, 1972. - 261 p. - (Schriftenreihe europäische
        Wirtschaft. Bd. 60.)
        At head of title: Pierre Maillet. Gerhard Hipp. Hugo Krijnse Locker. Robert Sunnen.
        Communauté économique européenne.

850.   **Evans, C.** Interpretations of part IV to include preferences: a
        possible solution to the conflict between the General agreement
        and preferential arrangements in favor of developing countries. -
        Bibliography: l. 80-87. - Geneva, 1970. - ii, 87 l.
        Mémoire - Institut universitaire de hautes études internationales.
        Contracting parties to the General agreement on tariffs and trade. Favoured nation clause.
        Developing countries - Commerce and economic development.

851.   **Evans, G.** UN's mutual aid: an introduction to the United Nations
        programme of technical and economic assistance. - Bibliography:
        p. 55. - Rochester, Kent, Staples printers, 1951. - 55 p. - (United
        Nations association of Great Britain and Northern Ireland. Peace-
        finder series. no. 11.)

852.   **Evans, J. W.** The Kennedy round in American trade policy; the
        twilight of the GATT? - Bibliography: p. 329-366. - Cambridge,
        Mass., Harvard university press, 1971. - xiii, 383 p.
        "Written under the auspices of the Center for international affairs, Harvard university."

853.   **Faddeev, N. V.** Sovet ėkonomicheskoĭ vzaimopomoshchi. - Biblio-
        graphical notes. - Moskva, Izd-vo "Ėkonomika", 1964. - 166 p.
        Council for mutual economic assistance.

4. **Fakher, H.** The relationships among the principal organs of the United
    Nations. - Bibliography: p. 195-200. - Genève, Impr. centrale, 1950. -
    200 p.
    Thèse - Genève.

5. **Falk, R. A.** The United Nations. - Notes, partly bibliographical. -
    Edited by Richard A. Falk and Saul H. Mendlovitz. - New York,
    World law fund, 1966. - xv, 848 p. - (Strategy of world order. v. 3.)

56. **Fanshawe, M.** Reconstruction; five years of work by the League of
    nations. - Bibliography: p. 321-326. - London, G. Allan & Unwin
    ltd., 1925. - 326 p.

57. **Faroughy, A.** L'Acte constitutif de l'Unesco (ses origines). - Bibliography:
    p. 185-186. - Paris, 1953.
    Microfilm copy of typewritten manuscript. Negative.
    Collation of the original: 193 p.
    Thèse - Univ. de Paris.

58. **Fasihpour, H.** L'Organisation mondiale de la santé. - Bibliography:
    p. 4-8. - Paris, 1951.
    Microfilm copy of typewritten manuscript. Negative.
    Collation of the original: 193 p.
    Thèse - Univ. de Paris.

59. **Feld, W.** The Court of the European communities: new dimension in
    international adjudication. - Bibliography: p. 123-125. - The Hague,
    M. Nijhoff, 1964. - viii, 127 p.

60. The **first** U.N. development decade and its lessons for the 1970's. -
    Edited by Colin Legum. - Includes bibliographies. - New York,
    Praeger, 1970. - xxviii, 312 p. - (Praeger special studies in inter-
    national economics and development.)
    "Published in cooperation with the Vienna institute for development".
    "Consists of selected contributions from a conference sponsored by the Vienna institute
    for development and held June, 1968".

61. **Fischer, F.** Die institutionalisierte Vertretung der Verbände in der
    Europäischen Wirtschaftsgemeinschaft. - Bibliography: p. 203-207. -
    Hamburg, Hansischer Gildenverlag, 1965. - 207 p. - (Kiel. Universität.
    Institut für internationales Recht. Veröffentlichungen. 54.)

62. **Fischer, G.** Les rapports entre l'Organisation international du travail et
    la Cour permanente de justice internationale. Contribution à l'étude
    du problème de la séparation des pouvoirs dans le domaine inter-
    national. - Bibliography: p. 367-380. - Berne, Impr. des hoirs
    C.-J. Wyss, 1946. - 388 p.
    Thèse - Genève.

63. **Flory, T.** Le G.A.T.T., droit international et commerce mondial. -
    Bibliography: p. 291-296. - Paris, Libr. g-enéral de droit et de
    jurisprudence, 1968. - iv, 306 p. - (Bibliothèque de droit inter-
    national. t. 46.)
    Serie Organisations internationales. no.2.

864.   **Food and agriculture organization.** Aquatic sciences & fisheries
        abstracts. - v.1-   ; 1971-   . - London, 1971-   . -   v.
        Pub. monthly.
        "Compiled by the Food and agriculture organization of the United Nations with the
        collaboration of Institut für Dokumentationswesen, Frankfurt, Bundesforschungsantalt
        für Fischerei, Hamburg, INRA, Département d'hydrobiologie, Biarritz, Information
        retrieval limited, London."
        Superseded in part: July 1971, Its: Current bibliography for aquatic sciences and
        fisheries. (1958-1971.)

865.   -- --- Bibliography on demand analysis and projections=Biblio-
        graphie de l'analyse et des projections de la demande=Bibliografía
        sobre el análisis y las proyecciones de la demanda. - Rome, 1959.
        - xv, 167 p.

866.   -- --- Bibliography on land and water utilization and conservation
        in Europe/ by C. H. Edelman and B. E. P. Eeuwens. - Rome,
        1955. - 347 p.

867.   -- --- Bibliography on land tenure=Bibliographie des régimes
        fonciers=Bibliografía sobre tenencia de la tierra. - Rome, 1955.
        - 386 p.
        "This bibliography has been compiled by the Food and agriculture organization...
        in collaboration with the University of Wisconsin and with the support of the
        United Nations, the International labour office and the United Nations educational,
        scientific and cultural organization."

868.   -- --- Bibliography on the analysis and projection of demand and
        production. - Rome, 1963. - xii, 279 p. - (Its: Commodity
        reference series.2.)

869.   -- --- Food aid: a selective annotated bibliography on food
        utilization for economic development. - Rome, United Nations,
        Food and agriculture organization of the United Nations, 1964.
        - vii, 203 p. E F
        "Prepared for the World food program by Elizabeth Henderson."

870.   -- --- World fisheries abstracts; a quarterly review of technical
        literature on fisheries and related industries. - v.1-   ; 1950-   .
        - Rome, 1950-   . -   v. E F S
        Pub. bi-monthly, 1950-61; quarterly, 1962-   .

871.   -- **Fisheries resources and exploitation division. Biological data
        section.** North Atlantic bibliography and citation index. - Rome,
        1968. - 1 v. - (Food and agriculture organization. Fisheries
        resources and exploitation division. FAO fisheries technical paper.
        no. 54.)

872.   -- **Fishery resources division.** Current bibliography for aquatic
        sciences and fisheries. Taxonomic classification; alphabetic key
        to 8 digit code=Classification taxonomique...=Clasificacion
        taxonomica... - Rome, 1970. - v, 175, 122 p. - (Its: FAO
        fisheries technical reports. no.12, rev.1.)

873.   -- **General commemorative conference, Rome, 1970.** Report. -
        Includes bibliographies. - Rome, 1970. - 1 v.
        At head of title: Twenty-fifth anniversary of the Food and agriculture organization
        of the United Nations.

74.   **Fosdick, R. B.**   The League and the United Nations after fifty years: the six secretary-generals. - Bibliography: p. 195-196. - Newtown, Conn, 1972. - xv, 203 p.

75.   **Friedeberg, A. S.**   The United Nations Conference on trade and development of 1964; the theory of the peripheral economy at the centre of international political discussions. - Bibliography: p. 227-232. - Rotterdam, Universitaire pers, 1968. - xv, 240 p.
Praefschrift - Nederlandse economische hogeschool.
Summary in Dutch: p. 237-240.
Bibliographical notes at the end of each chapter.

76.   **Friedmann, W. G.**   De l'efficacité des institutions internationales. - Texte inédit tr. de l'anglais et adapté par Simone Dreyfus. - Bibliography: p. 184-185. - Paris, A. Colin, 1970. - 199 p. - (Collection U. sér.: "Relations et institutions internationales".)

77.   **Friis, F. T. B.**   FN: status efter 25 ar. - Bibliography: p. 178. - Odense, 1970. - 182 p. - (Fremads fokusbøger.)
"Udgivet med støtte af Udenrigsministeriet."

78.   **Furey, J. B.**   Voting alignment in the General assembly. - Bibliography: p. 232-235. - New York, 1953.
Microfilm copy of typewritten manuscript.   Made in 1954 by University microfilms
(Publication no. 6620).   Positive.
Collation of the original: 235 p. tables.
Diss. - Columbia university, New York.

79.   **Gandolfi, A.**   Institutions internationales: première année. - Bibliography at the end of each chapter. - Paris, Masson, 1971. - 204 p. - (Premier cycle. sér.:   Droit et sciences économiques.)
International law.   International relations.   International agencies.   United Nations.   Economic assistance in Developing countries.

80.   **Ganiûshkin, B. V.**   Vsemirnaîa organizt͡siîa zdravookhraneniîa. - Bibliographical notes. - Moskva, 1959. - 77 p. - (Institut mezhdunarodnykh otnosheniĭ, Moscow.   Mexhdunarodnye organizat͡sii.)
Study on WHO.

81.   **Garchon, C.**   Le droit de veto: étude positive du mode de vote dans les organismes internationaux. - Bibliography: p. 181-184. - Alger, Imp. Charras, 1949.
Microfilm copy.   Negative.
At head of title: Université d'Alger. Faculté de droit. Année 1949 - no. 3.
Collation of the original: 184 p.
Thèse - Alger.

82.   **Gardner, R. N.**   The global partnership: international agencies and economic development. - Edited by Richard N. Gardner and Max F. Millikan. - Bibliography: p. 459-474. - New York, F.A. Praeger, 1968. - vii, 498 p.
"The essays in this volume originally appeared in a special issue of 'International organization' entitled 'The global partnership: international agencies and economic development', vol. XXII, no. 1 (Winter, 1968)."

83.   **Gegenwarstprobleme** der Vereinten Nationen. - Notes, partly bibliographical. - Göttingen, Musterschmidt, 1955. - 196 p. - (Göttinger Beiträge für Gegenwartsfragen. Bd. 10.)
"Vorträge gehalten im Rahmen der vom Institut für Völkerrecht der Universität Göttingen gemeinsam mit der Deutschen Gesellschaft für die Vereinten Nationen, Landesverband Niedersachsen, vom 25. bis 29. Oktober 1954 in Göttingen veranstalteten Seminarwoche über die Vereinten Nationen."

884.   **Geisendorf, A. L.**   Vade-mecum des principales organisations internationale
       tenant compte spécialement de leurs rapports avec l'agriculture, et des
       organisations agricoles internationales et institutions internationales
       apparentées à l'agriculture; aide-mémoire. - Bibliography: p. 121. -
       Brugg, 1951. - 125 p. - (Confédération européenne de l'agriculture.
       Publications. fasc. 5.)

885.   **General agreement on tariffs and trade.**   Checklist of books on
       international trade, economic development and related matters.
       - 4th-   ed. - Geneva, 1968-   . -   v.

886.   -- **Information and library service.**   GATT bibliography: 1st-
       supplement; 1954-   . - Geneva, 1954-   . -   v.

       It lists books, pamphlets, articles in periodicals, newspaper reports and editorials (including
       texts of lectures which refer to the General agreement on tariffs and trade), as well as the
       titles of press releases issued by the GATT secretariat. The purpose of the list is to provide
       sources of reference for historians, researchers and students on the operations of the GATT.
       The publications prepared by the GATT secretariat are not included. These are contained in
       the Publications list issued every year.

887.   **Geneva research centre.**   The United States, League of nations and
       Internationa labour organisation during 1937. - Bibliographical notes. -
       Geneva, 1938. - 72 p. - (Its Geneva studies, v. 9, no. 1, Jan. 1938.)

888.   **Gerbet, P.**   Les organisations internationales. - Bibliography: p. 126. -
       Paris, Presses universitaries de France, 1958. - 128 p. ("Que sais-je? "
       no. 792.)

889.   **Giannini, A.**   La convensione di Chicago 1944 sull'aviazione civile
       internazionale. - Bibliography: p. 95. - Roma, Associazione culturale
       aeronautica, 1953. - 130 p.

890.   **Gillespie, J. S.**   The role of the director in the development of the
       International labour organisation. - Bibliography: p. 480-498. -
       New York, 1956.
       Microfilm copy of typewritten manuscript. Positive.
       Collation of the original: iv, 498 p.
       Thesis - Columbia university.

891.   **Giraud, E.**   La révision de la Charte des Nations Unies. - Notes, partly
       bibliographical. - (In Academy of international law, The Hague.
       Recueil des cours, 1956. II. Leyde (Pays-Bas), A.W. Sijthoff, 1957.
       v. 90, p. 307-467.)

892.   -- --- Le secrétariat des institutions internationales. - Bibliography:
       p. 503-506. - (In Academy of international law, The Hague. Recueil
       des cours, 1951, II. Paris, 1952. v. 79, p. 369-509.)

893.   **Göttelmann, W.**   Die Delegation hoheitlicher Befugnisse internationaler
       Organisationen und ihrer Organe; ein Vergleich mit dem deutschen
       Recht. - Bibliography: p. ix-xxxvi. - München, Dissertationsdruck
       "Schön", 1968. - xl, 95 p.
       Inaug. - Diss. - Universität des Saarlandes.

894.   **Gold, J.**   The stand-by arrangements of the International monetary fund: a commentary on their formal legal, and financial aspects. - Bibliography: p. 213. - Washington, D.C., International monetary fund, 1970. - xii, 295 p.

895.   **Goodrich, L. M.**   The United Nations. - Bibliography at the end of each chapter. - New York, T.Y. Crowell, 1959. - x, 419 p.

896.   **Goodspeed, S. S.**   The nature and function of international organization. - Bibliography: p. 625-640. - New York, Oxford university press, 1959. - xi, 676 p.
        Diagr. on front lining-paper.

897.   **Gordenker, L.**   The UN secretary-general and the maintenance of peace. - Notes, partly bibliographical: p. 345-369. - New York, Columbia university press, 1967. - xx, 380 p. - (Columbia university studies in international organization. no. 4.)

898.   **Gori, U.**   L'organizzazione internazionale dalla S.d.N. all N.U. - Bibliography: p. 190-196. - Padova, CEDAM, 1969. - 200 p. - (Società italiana per l'organizzazione internazionale. Pubblicazioni.)

899.   **Gosovic, B.**   UNCTAD: conflict and compromise: the third world's quest for an equitable world economic order through the United Nations. - Bibliography: p. 335-339. - Leiden, A.W. Sijthoff, 1972. - xiv, 349 p.
        "This study represents the abridged and updated version of a doctoral thesis in political science, submitted at the University of California in Berkeley."

900.   **Goudarznia, S.**   La Commission de droit international des Nations Unies. - Bibliograpjy: p. 144-146. - Paris, 1952.
        Microfilm copy of typewritten manuscript.   Negative.
        Title-page missing.
        Collation of the original: iii, 147 p.
        Thèse - Univ. de Paris.

901.   **Graiver, B. Z.**   Mezhdunarodnyĭ bank i razvivaiũshehiesĩa strany. - Bibliographical notes. - Moskva, Izd-vo, "Nauka" 1972. - 198 p.
        Half-title: Akademiĩa nauk SSSR.   Institut mirovoĭ ėkonomiki i mezhdunarodnykh otnosheniĭ. Banks and banking in Developing countries.   International bank for reconstruction and development in Developing countries.   International finance corporation in Developing countries. International development association in Developing countries.

902.   **Grassi, C.**   Le unioni internazionali amministrative e la Società delle nazioni. - Bibliography: p. 425-433. - Catania, V. Giannotta, 1919. - 433 p. - (Biblioteca della Società internazionale degl'intellettuali. N. 9.)

903.   **Gray, C. H.**   A bibliography of peace research, indexed by key words/ comp. by Charles H. Gray, Leslie B. Gray and Glenn W. Gregory. - Eugene, Or., General research analysis methods, 1968. - x 164 p.

904.   **Green, A. W.**   Political integration by jurisprudence; the work of the Court of justice of the European communities in European political integration. - Bibliography: p. 545-559. - Leyden, A.W. Sijthoff, 1969. - xxvii, 847 p.

H

905.   **Greene, M. A.** The transfer of a functioning international agency from
        one physical location to another (with special reference to FAO). -
        Bibliography: p. 281-301. - Washington, D.C., 1960.
        Microfilm copy of typewritten manuscript. Positive.
        Collation of the original: x, 321 p.
        Thesis - American university.

906.   **Gregg, R. W.** The United Nations and the limitation of opium productio
        Bibliography: p. 368-380. - Ithaca, N.Y., 1956.
        Microfilm copy of typewritten manuscript. Positive.
        Collation of the original: viii, 380 p.
        Thesis - Cornell university.

907.   -- --- The United Nations system and its functions: selected readings
        edited by Robert W. Gregg and Michael Barkun. - Notes, partly
        bibliographical. - Princeton, N.J., D. Van Nostrand, 1968. - iv, 460 p. -
        (Van Nostrand political science series.)

908.   **Gross, E. A.** The new United Nations. - Bibliography: 58-62. - New
        York, N.Y., 1957. - 62 p. - (Foreign policy association. Department of
        popular education. Headline series. no. 125.)

909.   **Gross, L.** The International court of justice and the United Nations. -
        Bibliography: p. 436-438. - (In Academy of international law, The
        Hague. Recueil des cours, 1967, I.   Leyde (Pays-Bas), A.W. Sijthoff,
        1968. v. 120, p. 313-440.)

910.   **Grüber, H. R.** Die Beziehungen zwischen den Vereinten Nationen und
        den Sonderorganisationen. - Bibliography: p. i-vii. - Berlin, 1953.
        Microfilm copy of typewritten manuscript. Negative.
        Collation of the original: ix, 172 p.
        Diss. - Freie Universität, Berlin.

911.   **Gunzenhäuser, M.** Der Genfer Völkerbund 1920-1946. - Frankfurt/Main,
        Bernard & Graefe Verlag für Wehrwesen, 1969. - p. 425-536.
        Sonderdruck aus Jahresbibliographie Bibliothek für Zeitgeschichte, Stuttgart, Jahrgang 41, 1969.
        Contents: 1. Bibliographien und Kataloge. 2. Jahrbücher, Zeotschriften, Handbcher.
        3. Allgemeine Werke über den Völkerbund. 4. Geschichte des Völkerbundes. 5. Satzung des
        Völkerbundes. 6. Organisation des Völkerbund. 7. Völkerbundsversammlung. 8. Völkerbunds
        rat.   9. Generalsekretariat.   10. Komittes und Kommissionen.   11. Finanzverwaltung.
        12. Spezielle Tätigkeit (All.).   13. Völkerbundsmandate.   14. Minderheitenschutz.   15. Wirt-
        schaftliche Tätigkeit. 16. Soziale Tätigkeit. 17. Geistige Zusammenarbeit. 18. Politische
        Fragen.   Sicherheit u. Abrüstung.   19. Beziehungen einzelner Staaten zum Völkerbund.

912.   **Gvozdarev, B. I.** Organizatsiiã amerikanskikh gosudarstv. - Bibliography:
        p. 309-321. - Moskva, Izd-vo Instituta mezhdunarodnykh otnosheniĭ,
        1960. - 322 p.
        Organization of American states.

913.   **Haas, E. B.** Beyond the nation-state; functionalism and international
        organization: the International labor organization. - Notes, partly
        bibliographical: p. 517-586. - Stanford, Calif., Stanford university
        press, 1964. - x, 595 p.

914.   **Hagras, K. M.** United Nations conference on trade and development;
        a case study in U.N. diplomacy. - Bibliography: p. 158-167. - New
        York, F.A. Praeger, 1965. - xiii, 171 p. - (Praeger special studies in
        international economics and development.)
        Notes, partly bibliographical: p. 139-157.

5. **Hahn, H. J.** Constitutional limitations in the law of the European organisations. - Bibliography: p. 299-304. - (In Academy of international law, The Hague. Recueil des cours, 1963, I. Leyde (Pays-Bas), A.W. Sijthoff, 1964. v. 108, p. 189-306.)

6. **Halpérin, J.** L'organisation internationale agit-elle sur la pensée et les politiques économiques contemporaines? - Bibliography: p. 431-432. - Bruxelles, Univ. libre de Bruxelles, Ed. de l'Institut de sociologie, 1968. - p. 421-432.
Extrait des "Mélanges offerts à G. Jacquemyns".

7. **Hambridge, G.** The story of FAO. - Bibliography: p. 264-277. - New York, D. Van Nostrand, 1955. - xii, 303 p.

8. **Han, H. H.** International legislation by the United Nations: legal provisions, practice and prospects. - Bibliography: p. 172-185. - New York, Exposition press, 1971. - 221 p.
"An exposition-university book."

9. **Harley, J. E.** Documentary textbook on the United Nations; humanity's march towards peace: a volume emphasizing official co-operation for world peace, especially the United Nations and related specialized agencies. - Bibliography: p. 853-912. - Los Angeles, Calif., Center for international understanding, 1947. - xx, 952 p.

0. **Heilperin, M. A.** International monetary reconstruction. The Bretton Woods agreements. - Bibliography: p. 103-109. - New York, American enterprise association, 1945. - 112 p. - (American enterprise association. National economic problems. no. 407.)
United Nations monetary and economic conference, Bretton Woods, 1944.

1. **Henderson, W. O.** The genesis of the common market. - Bibliography: p. 179-192. - London, F. Cass, 1962. - xv, 201 p.

2. **Henriquez, H.** Las Naciones Unidas. - Bibliography: p. 307-308. - Ciudad Trujillo, Ed. "Arte y cine", 1952. - 321 p.

3. **Hexner, E. P.** Das Verfassungs- und Rechtssystem des Internationalen Währungsfonds. - Bibliography: p. 112-115. - Frankfurt am Main, V. Klostermann, 1960. - 115 p. - (Institut für ausländisches und internationales Wirtschaftsrecht, Frankfurt am Main. Schriften. Bd. 14.)

4. **Heyman, J. F.** Les juridictions administratives internationales. - pt. 1-2. - Bibliography: pt. 2, p. 429-437. - Dijon, 1958. - 2 v.
Thèse - Univ. de Dijon.

5. **Higgins, R.** The development of international law through the political organs of the United Nations. - Bibliography: p. 384-395. - London, Oxford university press, 1963. - xxi, 402 p.
"Issued under the auspices of the Royal institute of international affairs."

6. **Higham, J.** The United Nations International law commission: a guide to the documents, 1949-59. - Oxford, University press, 1961. - p. 384-397.
"Reprinted from the British year book of international law, 1960."

927.   **Hiitonen, E.**   La compétence de l'Organisation internationale du travail.
        Bibliography: v. 1, p. ix-xlvii. - Paris, Rousseau & cie., 1929-   .

928.   **Hill, N. L.**   International organization. - Bibliography: p. 609-617. -
        New York, Harper, 1952. - xii, 627 p.

929.   **Hoffmann, E.**   COMECON: der gemeinsame Markt in Osteuropa. -
        Bibliography: p. 173-174. - Opladen, C.W. Leske, 1961. - 174 p. -
        (Die grossen Märkte der Welt. Bd. 3.)

930.   **Holt, S.**   The common market; the conflict of theory and practice. -
        Bibliography: p. 199-200. - London, H. Hamilton, 1967. - xiii,
        207 p. - (Hamilton management studies.)

931.   **Hoog, G.**   Die Genfer Seerechtskonferenzen von 1958 und 1960:
        Vorgeschichte, Verhandlungen, Dokumente. - Bibliography: p. 128-
        138; - Frankfurt am Main, A. Metzner, 1961. - 138 p. - (Hamburg.
        Universität.   Forschungsstelle für Völkerrecht und ausländisches
        öffentliches Recht.   Dokumente.   Bd. 36.)
        "Dokumente" in English and German.   Rest of text German only.

932.   **Horie, S.**   The International monetary fund; retrospect and prospect. -
        Notes, partly bibliographical. - London, Macmillan, 1964. - xii, 208 |

933.   **Horsefield, J. K.**   The International monetary fund, 1945-1965; twenty
        years of international monetary cooperation. - v.1-3. - Includes
        bibliographies. - Washington, D.C., International monetary fund, 1969
        3 v.
        v.1. Chronicle.   v.2. Analysis.   3. Documents.

934.   **Houben, P. H. J. M.**   Les Conseils de ministres des Communautés
        européennes. - Bibliography: p. 247-254. - Leyde, A.W. Sythoff,
        1964. - 259 p. - (Aspects européens. sér. C: Politique. no. 17.)
        "Cette étude a été réalisée avec l'aide d'une bourse accordée par le Conseil de l'Europe."

935.   **Imbach, J.**   Contribution de l'Organisation des Nations Unies au
        relèvement économique de l'Europe. - Bibliography: 402-403. -
        Strasbourg, 1950.
        Microfilm copy of typewritten manuscript.   Negative.
        At head of title? Université de Strasbourg.   Faculté de droit et des sciences politiques.
        Collation of the original: 405 p. tables, diagr.
        Thèse - Strasbourg.

936.   **Institut de la Communauté européenne pour les études universitaires.**
        Etudes universitaires sur l'integration européenne=University studies on
        European integration. - no. 1-7. - Bruxelles, 19   . -   v.
        European integration.   The European communities: the institutions.   European communities
        general studies.   European communities: sector studies.   The European communities and th
        world.

937.   **Inter-American council for education, science and culture.   2nd special
        meeting, Washington, D.C., 1972.**   Final report. - Lista de document
        p. 37-42. - Washington, D.C., Organization of American States, 1972.
        42 p. - (OAS. Official records. OEA/Ser.C/V.13.)

938.   **Inter-American institute of international legal studies.**   The inter-Americ
        system: its development and strengthening. - Bibliography: p. 523-
        527. - Dobbs Ferry, N.Y., Oceana publications, 1966. - xxxvi, 530 p

9. **Inter-American institute of international legal studies.** Instruments relating to the economic integration of Latin America. - Bibliography: p. 419-450. - Dobbs Ferry, N.Y., Oceana publications, 1968. - ix, 452 p.
Original ed. pub. under title: Instrumentos relativos a la integración económica de América Latina.

0. **Intergovernmental committee for European migration.** Migrants and refugees: a bibliography on legal matters (articles not included). - Geneva, 1961. 22 p.

1. **Inter-governmental maritime consultative organization.** L'OMCI et ses activités; informations sommaires. - Bibliography: p. 61-65. - Londres, Organisation intergouvernemental consultative de la navigation maritime, 1971. - 65 p.

2. **International African institute. Research information liaison unit.** International register of organisations undertaking Africanist research in the social sciences and humanities=Répértoire international des organisations poursuivant des recherches africanistes en sciences humaines. - 1970. - London, 1971. - 65 l.
African countries. Other countries. International organisations.

3. **International atomic energy agency.** Bibliographical series. - no.1-   . - Vienna, 1960-   . - v.
Contents:
1.   Application of high energy radiations in therapy. 1960.
2.   Nuclear reactors. 1960.
3.   Nuclear propulsion. 1961.
4.   Geology of uranium and thorium. 1962.
5.   Disposal of radioactive wastes into marine and fresh waters, 1962.
6.   Effects of neutron irradiation in non-fissionable metals and alloys. 1962.
7.   Research on controlled thermonuclear fusion. 1962.
8.   Semiconductor nuclear particle detectors. 1962.
9.   Radioisotopes and ionizing radiation in entomology. 1963.
10. Photonuclear reactions. 1964.
11. Chromatographic separation of the lanthanide and actinide elements. 1964.
12. Capture relations. 1964.
13. Nuclear power economics. 1964.
14. Uranium carbides, nitrides and silicides. 1965.
15. Radioisotopes and ionizing radiations in entomology (1961-1963).
16. The Mössbauer effect. 1965.
17. Organic coolants and moderators. 1965.
18. Neutron detectors. 1966.
19. Chemistry of transplutonium elements. 1966.
20. Radioisotope instruments in industry and geophysics. 1966.
21. Uranium carbides, nitrides and silicides (1963-1965).
22. Fast reactors. 1966.
23. Solid-state dosimetry. 1967.
24. Radioisotopes and ionizing radiations in entomology, vol. 3. (1964-1965).
25. Recovery of fission products. 1967.
26. Nonaqueous reprocessing of irradiated fuel. 1967.
27. Photonuclear reactions. v. 2 (1963-1966).
28. Thermal diffusion. 1967.
29. Radiation stability of nuclear fuels. (1962-1966).
30. Nuclear power economics. v.2 (1964-1967).
31. Geology of uranium and thorium. v.2 (1961-1966).
32. Isotopes techniques in hydrology. v.1 (1957-1965).
33. Uranium carbides, nitrides and silicides. v.3 (1966-1967).
34. Recurring inspection of nuclear reactor steel pressure vessels (1960-1966).
35. Laser applications in plasma physics (1962-1968).
36. Radioisotopes and ionizing radiations in entomology. v.4 (1966-1967).
37. Heavy-water reactors. 1970.
38. Peaceful uses of nuclear explosions. 1970.
39. Thorium fuel cycle. 1970.
40. Neutrons in radiation biology and therapy. 1971.

944.   **International atomic energy agency.** Bibliography on research on
        controlled thermonuclear fusion. - Vienna, 1961. - 260 p.

945.   -- --- Publications in the nuclear sciences, 1964-   . - Vienna,
        1964-   . - v.

946.   -- --- Radioisotope applications in industry; a survey of
        radioisotope applications, classified by industry or economic
        activity, with selected references to the international literature.
        - Vienna, 1963. - 129 p.

947.   -- **General conference.** Cumulative index to resolutions and
        decisions. - 1957/1965-   . - (GC/RES/INDEX/3, etc.)

948.   **International bank for reconstruction and development.** List of
        national development plans. - 2nd ed. n.p. Development services
        department, 1968. - p.587-685.
        "Reprinted from: Albert Waterston 'Development planning: lessons of experience'."

949.   -- --- Selected readings and source materials on economic
        development. - Washington, D. C., 1965. - 2,v,54 p.

950.   -- --- Suggested bibliography on economic development. - n.p.,
        1960. - 78 1.

951.   **International** bibliography of economics=Bibliographie internationale
        de science économique... works published. - 1952-   ;
        v. 1   . - Paris, UNESCO, 1955-   .   v.
        v.9 (1960) ceased to be pub. by UNESCO.
        At head of cover-title: Documentation in the social sciences. Documentation dans
        les sciences sociales.
        "Prepared by the Fondation nationale des sciences politiques... with the assistance
        of the International economic association and the International committee for
        social documentation."
        Series note varies as follows:
        v.1-8,   Documentation in the social sciences.
        v.4,   International bibliographies of the social sciences.
        v.5-8,   International social science bibliographies.
        v.9.   International bibliography of the social sciences.

952.   **International** bibliography of political science=Bibliographie
        internationale de science politique... (works published. - 1952-
        .) - v.1-   . - Paris, UNESCO. 1954-   . - v.
        v.9 (1960)-   , ceased to be pub. by UNESCO.
        Pub. annually.
        At head of cover-title: Documentation in the social sciences. Documentation
        dans les sciences sociales.
        "Prepared by the International political science association in co-operation
        with the International committee for social sciences documentation, and with the
        support of the International studies conference."

953.   **International** bibliography of social and cultural anthropology=
        Bibliographie internationale d'antropologie sociale et culturelle.
        - v.1-   ; 1955-   . - Paris, UNESCO, 1958-   . - v.
        - (International social science bibliographies.)
        v. 6. (1960) ceased to be pub. by UNESCO.
        Pub. annually.
        At head of cover-title: Documentation in the social sciences.
        "Prepared by the International committee for social sciences documentation in
        co-operation with the international congress of anthropological and ethnological
        sciences."

54.   **International** bibliography of sociology=Bibliographie internationale
de sociologie. - v.5-   ; 1965-   . - Paris, UNESCO, 1957-   .
-   v.
v.10 (1960) ceased to be pub. by UNESCO.
Vols. 1-4 (1951-1954), pub. in: Current sociology.
At head of cover-title: v.5-   , Documentation in the social sciences.
Documentation dans les sciences sociales.
Prepared by the International committee for social sciences documentation in
co-operation with the International sociological association.

55.   **International chamber of commerce.** Quelques publications de la CCI. -
In: Guide pour les investissements internationaux. - Paris, 1972. -
16 p. - (Its: Publications. no. 272.)

56.   **International civil aviation organization. Assembly.** Resolutions
adopted by the Assembly and Index to documentation. - 1st
session-
Doc. 8528 A15-5/6, etc.

57.   **International committee for social science documentation.** Retrospective
bibliography of social science works published in the Middle East
(U.A.R., Iraq, Jordan, Lebanon), 1945-1955=Bibliographie retrospective
des travaux de sciences sociales publiés au Moyen-Orient. - Cairo,
Unesco Middle East science cooperation office, 1959. - vi, 299 p.
Cover-title: Social science bibliography: Egypt, Iraq, Jordan, Lebanon, Syria.

58.   **International conference on human rights, Teheran, 1968.**
List of documents before the Conference. - In Its:
Final act. - A/CONF.32/41. (Sales no. 1968.XIV.2.)

59.   **International council of voluntary agencies.** Profiles of some
selected clearing houses dealing with development aid.
- Geneva, 1969. - 69 p.
Includes cross-reference tables by country, organization and type of aid,
850 national agencies, 150 international agencies.

60.   **International court of justice. Library.** Bibliography. - no.1-25.
- The Hague, 1947-1972.
Contents:
A.   Official and private draft plans (Dumbarton Oaks, 1944. Committee of
      jurists, 1945.)
B.   Conference of San Francisco.
C.   Ratification of Charter and Statute, legislative instruments of various countries,
      new members of the U.N.
D.   Accession to the Statute of the Court of States not members of the United
      Nations.
E.   Conditions under which the Court shall be open to States not parties to
      the Statute.
F.   Organs of the United Nations other than the Court. Publications.
      Commentaries. Reports of delegations.
G.   The International court of justice.
H.   Cases brought before the Court.
I.   Proposed references to the Court.
J.   Works and review articles on the Court in general.
K.   Pacific settlement of international disputes. Arbitration and judicial
      decision.
L.   Miscellaneous works and documents containing references to the Court.
      Alphabetical index of authors' names.
      Alphabetical index of subjects.

961.   **International institute for education planning.** Educational planning: a
        bibliography. - Paris, 1964. -

962.   **International institute for labour studies. Library.** Bibliografía sobre
        los problemas del trabajo en América Latina: 1960-1970.
        - Ginebra, 1971. - xii, 132 p.

963.   -- - -- Bibliographie sur la participation populaire au développement
        dans les pays africains francophones situés au sud du Sahara.
        - 1971. - 34 p.

964.   -- - -- Bibliographie sur le travail et les problèmes annexes,
        spécialement en Algérie, Haute-Volta, Mauritanie, Tunisie, au
        Mali, Maroc, Niger, Tchad et dans les pays du Maghreb. - 24 p.

965.   -- - -- Bibliography on labour problems and related fields. - no.1-   .
        - Geneva, 1968-   .

966.   -- - -- Bibliography on peasant movements, 1950-1967. - pt.1-2.
        - 70 p.

967.   -- - -- International educational materials exchange. - no.1- .
        - Geneva, 1968-   . -   v.   .

968.   -- - -- Library catalogue: 1962. - Geneva, 1962. - 1v.

969.   -- - -- List of readings on labour problems and related fields
        (with special emphasis on Ceylon, India, Malaysia, Pakistan
        and Singapore).

970.   -- - -- Selected bibliography on the Gambia, Ghana, Liberia, Nigeria and
        Sierra Leone: economic and social aspects with special reference to
        labour problems. - Geneva, 1972. - 69 p. - (Its: International education
        materials exchange. IEME. 7008.)

971.   -- - -- Workers' participation in management: selected bibliography,
        1950-1970. - vii, 108 p.

972.   **International labour office.** The ILO and the United Nations: twenty-
        five years of a partnership of service. - Notes, partly bibliographical. -
        Geneva, International labour office, 1970. - 54 p.
        "Supplement to the Report of the Director-general to the International labour conference,
        fifty-fourth session, 1970."

973.   -- - -- Labour faces the new age: purposes, structure and work of the
        I.L.O.; a workers' education manual. - Bibliography: p. 225-227. -
        Geneva, International labour office, 1965. - v, 227 p.
        Later ed. issued with title: The ILO in the service of social progress.

974.   -- - -- L'O.I.T. au service du progrès social. - Notes, partly bibliographic
        Genève, Bureau international du travail, 1969. - iv, 230 p.
        "Le présent ourvrage, publié à l'occasion du cinquantenaire de l'OIT, est une version révisée
        du volume publié en 1965 sous le titre: Le monde du travail face à l'âge nouveau.

75.   **International labour office. Central library and documentation branch.** Bibliographical contributions. - no.1-28. - Geneva, 1949-1968. -   v.
Contents:
1.   Catalogue-dictionnaire des publications en langue française, 1919-1948, and supplement.   1949.
2.   Catalogue of Russian periodicals in the International labour office, Library. 1951.
3.   List of periodicals indexed in the International labour office, Library during 1950.
4.   International management institute. Library. Catalogue. 1953.
5.   Muller, M. Catalagoue of publications in English of the International labour office, 1919-1950.
6.   Muller, M. Catalogue des publications en langue française du Bureau international du travail, 1919-1950.
7.   Bibliography on the International labour organisation. 1954.
8.   Bibliography on labour law. 1953. and supplements. 1-   .
9.   Falcy, M. Bibliographie de périodiques internationaux.   1952.
10. Bibliography of industrial relations. 1955.
11. Bibliography on workers' education.   1950.
12. Bibliography on vocational training.
13. Bibliography on labour law. (rev.)   1958.
14. Bibliography on cooperation. 1958.
15. Index de la Revue internationale du travail. v.31 à 73. (1935 à 1956).
16. Africa. 1958.
17. International labour review index. vols. 31 to 75 (1935 to 1957). 1959.
18. Bibliography on non-manual workers. 1959.
19. Bibliography on the International labour organisation. 1959.
20. Bibliography on social security. 1963.
21. Bibliography on vocational guidance . 1961.
22. Catalogue of publications of the International association for labour legislation. International association on unemployment. 1962.
23. Cooperation. Rev. ed. 1964.
24. Bibliographie des sources de documentation sur le travail. 1965.
25. Subject guide to publications of the International labour office, 1919-1964.
26. -- --- Suppl. Geographical index. 14 p. 1968.
27. Nicolas, S. Bibliography on women workers = Bibliographie sur le travail des femmes. 200 p. 1969.
28. Bibliography on the ILO, 1919-1968 = Bibliographie sur l'OIT, 1919-1968. 170 p. 1968.

76.   -- --- Cumulative list of microfilms available for consultation. - Geneva, 1964.

77.   -- --- National plans for economic and social development. - Geneva, 1969. - (Its: LD/NOTES/34.)

78.   -- --- Reference lists prepared from machine-readable records. - no.1-5300.
Sample titles of computerised information retrieval:

Search no.	Number of references	Title
666	143	Economic policy in respect of various aspects of development in Africa as a region, with particular reference to rural development.
669	94	Technological change and automation in the USA, the UK, France and Japan.
693	28	Comparative studies of labour management relations and labour legislation.
728	288	Income distribution, poverty and unemployment in the USA, with some reference to minority groups.
736	114	Natural resources, human resources and manpower in African countries.
772	54	Brain drain, with particular reference to brain drain migration from developing countries into the USA.

979.   **International labour office. Library.** Bibliographical reference list-
        Liste de références bibliographiques. - Genève, 1936-1958. - 86 fascs.
        Pre-war and postwar bibliographic activities of ILO Library.

980.   **-- Public information branch.** Bibliography of the ILO fiftieth
        anniversary=Bibliographie du cinquantenaire de l'OIT=Bibliografía
        del cincuentenario de la OIT. - Geneva, 1970. - 67 p.
        "Prepared by Joseph Wilson Haden."

981.   **International labour organisation. Conference.** Alphabetical
        author-subject index. - In Its: Record of proceedings. 1st-57th
        session; 1919-1972.

982.   **-- Governing body.** Alphabetical author-subject index. - In
        Its: Minutes. 1st-187th session; 1919-1972.

983.   **International monetary fund.** Central banking legislation;
        a collection of central bank monetary and banking laws.
        - Washington, D.C., 1962-   . -   v. - (Its: Monograph
        series. no.1, v.1-   .)

984.   The **international** register of current team research in the social
        sciences... a tentative survey=Répertoire international des
        recherches collectives en cours dans le domaine des sciences
        sociales... essai de classification (1950-1952). - Paris, UNESCO,
        1955. - 312 p.
        At head of cover-title: Documentation in the social sciences. Documentation dans
        les sciences sociales.
        "Compiled with the assistance of: Organization of American states, Washington, D.C.,
        National institute of economic and social research, London, Comité international
        pour la documentation des sciences sociales, Paris."

985.   **International trade centre, Geneva.** Analytical bibliography: market
        surveys by products and countries. - Geneva, 1969. - ix, 203 p.
        At head of title: International trade centre. UNCTAD, GATT.
        "This bibliography has been financed by a grant from the Swedish international
        development authority (SIDA)."

986.   -- - --- Annotated directory of product and industry journals.
        - Geneva, 1970. - xi, 359 p.

987.   -- - --- Annotated directory of regional and national trade and
        economic journals. - Geneva, 1971. - vii, 153 p.

988.   -- - --- A bibliography of market surveys by products and
        countries=Bibliographie études de marché par produits et par
        pays=Bibliografía estudios sobre los mercados por productos
        y paises. - Geneva, 1967. - xix, 187 p.

989.   -- - --- L'exportation vers les pays socialistes de l'Europe de l'Est:
        manuel des techniques de commercialisation. - Bibliography: p.437-500.
        Genève, 1971. - x, 504 p. - E F S
        "La préparation du présent manuel a été financé par un don accordé par l'Office central
        suédois pour l'aide au développement (SIDA)."

International trade centre, Geneva (Cont'd)

990.
-- --- A select bibliography for export promotion services in developing countries=Sélection bibliographique destinée aux services de promotion des exportations des pays peu développés= Selección bibliográfica para los servicios de fomento de la exportación de los países en vías de desarrollo. - Geneva, 1966. - v, 37 p.

991.
International union of official travel organisations. Tourist documentation centre. Tourist bibliography: publications. - CDT/1- . - Geneva, 1959- . - v.
Contains publications on the scientific, technical, organizational, economic and managerial aspects of tourism, published throughout the world.

992.
Islam, R. International economic cooperation and the United Nations. - Bibliography: p. 122-129. - Groningen, J.B. Wolters, 1956. - 129 p.
Proefschrift - Nederlandsche economische hoogeschool, Rotterdam.

993.
Jaehne, G. Landwirtschaft und landwirtschaftliche Zusammenarbeit im Rat für gegenseitige Wirtschaftshilfe (COMECON). - Bibliography: p. 307-327. - Wiesbaden, O. Harrassowitz, 1968. - 327 p. - (Hesse. Hochschule. Osteuropastudien. Reihe 1: Giessener Abhandlungen zur Agrar- und Wirtschaftsforschung des europäischen Ostens. Bd. 41.)
Summary in English: p. 303-306.

994.
James, R. R. Staffing the United Nations secretariat. - Bibliographical notes. - Brighton, 1970. - 30 p. - (University of Sussex. Institute for the study of international organisation. ISIO monographs. 1st ser., no. 2.)

995.
Jenks, C. W. The headquarters of international institutions: a study of their location and status. - Bibliography: p. 91-102. - London, 1945. - 102 p. - (Royal institute of international affairs. Post-war problems. no. 8.)

996.
-- --- International immunities. - Bibliographical notes: p.173-174. - London, Stevens, 1961. - xxxviii, 178 p. - (His: The law of international institutions.)

997.
-- --- The International labour organisation in the U.N. family. - Notes, partly bibliographical. - New York, 1971. - 48 p. - (United Nations institute for training and research. UNITAR lecture series. no. 3.)
"An address given on 23 January, 1969, at U.N. Headquarters, New York for the UNITAR seminars in international organization and multilateral diplomacy."

998.
-- --- A new world of law? a study of the creative imagination in international law. - Bibliography: p. 301-326. - London, Longmans Green, 1969. - x, 341 p.

999.
-- --- The proper law of international organisations. - Notes, partly bibliographical. - London, Stevens, 1962. - xli, 282 p. - (His: The law of international institutions.)

000.
-- --- Social justice in the law of nations: the ILO impact after fifty years. - Bibliography: p. 89-90. - London, Oxford university press, 1970. - ix, 94 p. - (Oxford paperbacks. 225.)
Hersch Lauterpacht lectures, 1969.
"Issued under the auspices of the Royal institute of international affairs."

1001.   **Jensen, F. B.** The common market: economic integration in Europe/ b
        Finn B. Jensen and Ingo Walter. - Bibliography: p. 255-267. - Phila-
        delphia, J. B. Lippincott, 1965. - vii, 278 p. - (Preceptor. P-13.)

1002.   **Jessup, P. C.** Parliamentary diplomacy; an examination of the legal
        quality of the rules of procedure of organs of the United Nations. -
        Bibliography: p. 317-318. - (In Academy of international law, The
        Hague. Recueil des cours, 1956, I. Leyde (Pays-Bas), A.W. Sijthoff,
        1957. v. 89, p. 181-320.)

1003.   **Johnston, G. A.** The international labour organisation; its work for
        social and economic progress. - Bibliography: p. 351-352. - London,
        Europa publications, 1970. - xii, 363 p.

1004.   **Joint FAO/WHO expert committee on food additives.** Reports and other
        documents resulting from previous meetings. - In Its: Evaluation of c
        food additives: 16th report. p. 29-31. - Rome, 1972. - 32 p. - (FAO
        Nutrition meetings report series. no.51.)
        WHO Technical report series. no.505.

1005.   **Joyce, J. A.** World of promise; a guide to the United Nations decade
        of development. - Bibliography: p. 149-152. - Dobbs Ferry, N.Y.,
        Oceana publications, 1965. - xii, 163 p. - (The Oceana library on the
        United Nations. Study guide series. v.6.)

1006.   **Judge, A. J. N.** Bibliography of documents on transnational
        association networks: international nongovernmental organization
        as a field of study. - In: Yearbook of international organizations:
        1972-1973, Brussels, Union of international associations, 1972.
        Ca. 1000 entries.

1007.   **Juillerat, V.** Evaluation de la coopération technique de l'Organisation
        des Nations Unies, et Guide to the United Nations documentation on
        evaluation of technical co-operation. - Genève, 1970. - 21, iv, 102 l.

1008.   **Julien-Laferrière, F.** L'Organisation des états américains. - Bibliography:
        p. 94-95. - Paris, Presses universitaires de France, 1972. - 95 p. -
        (Dossiers Thémis. ser. "Institutions et droit international".)

1009.   **Junckerstorff, H. A. K.** International manual on the European economic
        community, edited by Henry Alfred Kurt Junckerstorff, assisted by
        Clement S. Mihanovich. - Bibliography: p. 494-505. - St. Louis, Mo.,
        Saint Louis university press, 1963. - xvi, 521 p.

1010.   **al-Kadhim, N. M.** Privileges and immunities of international organizations
        and their personnel. - Bibliography: p. 297-315. - Los Angeles, 1957.
        Microfilm copy of typewritten manuscript. Positive.
        Collation of the original: xi, 379 p.
        Diss. - Univ. of Southern California.

1011.   **Kapp, E.** The merger of the executives of the European communities. -
        Bibliography: p. 13-16. - Bruges, De Tempel, 1964. - 113 p. -
        (Cahiers de Bruges. N.S. 10.)
        On cover: College of Europe.

012.   **Karp, B.**   The development of the philosophy of UNESCO. - Bibliography:
        p. 195-206. - Chicago, 1951.
        Microfilm copy of typewritten manuscript.   Positive.
        Collation of the original: vii, 206 p.
        Diss. - Univ. of Chicago (thesis no. 1349.)

013.   **Karunatilleke, K.**   Essai d'une classification des accords conclus par les
        organisations internationales, entre elles ou avec des états. - Bibliography:
        p. 78-80. - Paris, A. Pedone, 1971. - 80 p.
        "Extrait de la 'Revue générale de droit international public', janvier-mars 1971, no.1."

014.   -- - -- Le Fonds des Nations Unies pour l'enfance; étude de droit des
        organisations internationales. - Bibliography: p. xl-lii. - Paris, 1966. -
        315, lx p.
        Thèse - Univ. de Paris.

015.   **Kasme, B.**   La capacité de l'Organisation des Nations Unies de conclure
        des traités. - Bibliography: p. 201-210. - Paris, Libr. générale de droit
        et de jurisprudence, 1960. - 214 p.
        Thèse - Univ. de Genève.

016.   **Kellogg, E. H.**   The 7th General assembly "Nationalization" resolution:
        a case in United Nations economic affairs. - Bibliography: p. 18. -
        New York, 1955. - 20 p. - (Woodrow Wilson foundation.   Miscellaneous
        publications. no. 13.)

1017.   **Kelsen, H.**   The law of the United Nations; a critical analysis of its
        fundamental problems. - Bibliographical notes. - London, Stevens &
        sons, 1950. - xvii, 903 p. - (Library of world affairs. no.11.)
        "Published under the auspices of the London institute of world affairs."
        Supplement: Recent trends in the law of the United Nations. - London, Stevens & sons,
        1951.   909-994 p.

1018.   **Kenworthy, L. S.**   Studying the United Nations and its specialized
        agencies. - Bibliography: p. 18-42. - Brooklyn, N.Y., Author, Brooklyn
        college, 1953. - 44 p.

1019.   **Kern, E.**   The changing role of the Secretary-general of the United Nations. -
        Bibliography: p. 101-102. - Chicago, Ill., 1958.
        Microfilm copy of typewritten manuscript.   Positive.
        Collation of the original: 102 p.

1020.   **Kerno, I. S.**   L'Organisation des Nations Unies et la Cour internationale
        de justice. - Bibliography: p. 571-572. - (In Academy of international
        law, The Hague. Recueil des cours, 1951, I.   Paris, 1952.   v. 78,
        p. 507-574.)

1021.   **Kim, Y. H.**   Technical assistance programs of the United Nations and of
        the United States; a comparative study. - Bibliography: p. 390-420. -
        Los Angeles, Calif., 1960.
        Microfilm copy of typewritten manuscript.   Positive.
        Collation of the original: iii, 445 p. tables.

1022.   **King, J. A.**   Economic development projects and their appraisal;   cases
        and principles from the experience of the world bank. - Notes, partly
        bibliographical. - Baltimore, Md., Johns Hopkins press for the Economic
        development institute, International bank for reconstruction and develop-
        ment, 1967. - xii, 530 p.

1023.   **Kirdar, U.** The structure of United Nations economic-aid to under-
         developed countries. - Bibliography: p. 348-356. - The Hague,
         M. Nijhoff, 1966. - xxiv, 361 p.

1024.   **Kiser, M.** Organization of American states; a handbook for use in schoo
         colleges and adult study groups. - Bibliography: p. 69-74. - 4th ed. -
         Washington, Pan American union, 1955. - iv, 74 p.

1025.   **Kitzinger, U. W.** The European common market and community/ by
         Uwe Kitzinger. - Bibliography: p. 218-219. - London, Routledge &
         K. Paul, 1967. - xiii, 226 p. - (World studies series.)

1026.   **Kock, K.** International trade policy and the Gatt, 1947-1967. - Notes,
         partly bibliographical: p. 305-324. - Stockholm, Alqvist & Wiksell,
         1969. - xv, 334 p. - (Acta Universitatis Stockholmiensis. Stockholm
         economic studies. new series, no.11.)

1027.   **Kohlmeyer, F. W.** The movement toward international cooperation in
         food and agriculture; background of the FAO of the UN. - Biblio-
         graphy: p. 413-430. - Minneapolis, Minn., 1954.
         Microfilm copy of typewritten manuscript. Made in 1954 by University microfilms
         (Publication no. 8461). Positive.
         Collation of the original: iv, 430 p.
         Thesis - Univ. of Minnesota.

1028.   **Kouzbari, W. Y.** Les pouvoirs politiques du Secrétaire général des
         Nations Unies. - Bibliography: p. 291-299. - Paris, 1959. - iii, 305 p.
         At head of title: Université de Paris.   Faculté de droit et des sciences économiques.
         Thèse - Univ. de Paris.

1029.   **Krasnov, G. A.** Torgovliâ uslugami ili ekspluatatsiiâ? - Bibliography:
         p. 171-173. - Moskva, Izd-vo "Mezhdunarodnye otnosheniiâ", 1971. -
         173 p.
         Developing countries - Commerce.   United Nations conference on trade and development.

1030.   **Krezdorn, F. J.** Les Nations Unies et les accords régionaux. - Biblio-
         graphy: p. 167-176. - Speyer am Rhein, Jaegersche Buchdr. 1954. - 176
         Thèse - Genève.

1031.   **Krylov, S. B.** Istoriiâ sozdaniiâ Organizatsii Ob"edinennykh Natsiĭ;
         razrabotka teksta Ustava Organizatsii Ob"edinennykh Natsiĭ (1944-
         1945). - Pod red. G.I. Tunkina. - Bibliography: p. 337-339. -
         Moskva, Izd-vo IMO, 1960. - 342 p.
         At head of title: Institut mezhdunarodnykh otnosheniĭ.
         "Nastoiâshchaiâ kniga iavliâetsiâ vtorym, dopolnennym izdaniem knigi 'Materialy k istorii
         Organizatsii Ob"edinennykh Natsiĭ'. Vyp. 1. ... 1949."
         United Nations - History.

1032.   **Kutzner, G.** Die Organisation der amerikanischen Staaten (OAS). -
         Bibliography: p. 379-392. - Hamburg, Hansischer Gildenverlag, 1970. -
         399 p. - (Kiel. Universität. Institut für Internationales Recht.
         Veröffentlichungen. 62.)

1033.   **Labeyrie-Ménahem, C.** Des institutions spécialisées: problèmes juridiques
         et diplomatiques de l'administration internationale. - Bibliography:
         p. 163-164. - Paris, A. Pedone, 1953. - 168 p.

034.   **Lamoureux, F.** Un exemple de coopération intergouvernementale: le
        Conseil de l'Europe/ par François Lamoureux et Jacques Molinié. -
        Bibliography: p. 94-95. - Paris, Presses universitaires de France, 1972. -
        95 p. - (Dossiers Thémis. sér. "Institutions et droit international". 17.)

035.   **Landy, E. A.** The effectiveness of international supervision; thirty years
        of I.L.O. experience. - Bibliography: p. 257-261. - London, Stevens,
        1966. - x, 268 p.
        Thèse - Univ. de Genève.

036.   **Langrod, G.** La fonction publique internationale: sa genèse, son essence,
        son évolution. - Bibliography: p. 349-361. - Leyde, A.W. Sythoff, 1963. -
        387 p.
        Notes, partly bibliographical, at the end of each chapter.

037.   **Larson, A.** Appointment of the Secretary-general of the United Nations
        without a recommendation of the Security council. - Notes, partly
        bibliographical. - n.p., 1962. - 24 l.

038.   **Lavalle, R.** La Banque mondiale et ses filiales: aspects juridiques et
        fonctionnement. - Bibliography: p. 255-259. - Paris, Libr. générale de
        droit et de jurisprudence, 1972. - 323 p. - (Bibliothèque de droit
        international. t. 65.)
        Bibliothèque de droit international. sér. "Organisations internationales". 4.
        International bank for reconstruction and development. International bank for reconstruction
        and development - Legal aspects.

039.   **Laves, W. H. C.** UNESCO: purpose, progress, prospects/ by Walter H.C.
        Laves and Charles A. Thomson. - Bibliography: p. 451-455. - Blooming-
        ton, Indiana university press, 1957. 0 xxiii, 469 p.
        Bibliographical notes: p. 359-414.

040.   **Lawson, R. C.** International regional organizations; constitutional foun-
        dations. - Bibliography: p. 387. - New York, F.A. Praeger, 1962. -
        xviii, 387 p. - (Books that matter.)
        Notes, partly bibliographical, and bibliography at the end of each chapter.

041.   **League of nations.** Bibliographie sommaire des publications de la
        Société des nations. - Genève, 1930. - 18 p.
        Tirage à part de "Dix ans de coopération internationale".

042.   -- --- Catalogue of publications, 1920-1935. - Geneva, 1935. - 312 p.
        Supplement, 1935/36-1940/46. 5 v. in 1 v.

043.   -- --- Catalogue of selected publications on economic and
        financial subjects: a guide to the documents of value in
        connection with the formulation of postwar economic
        policies. - Princeton, Princeton university press, 1943. - 69 p.

044.   -- --- Guide sommaire des publications de la Société des nations=
        Brief guide to League of nations publications. - Genève, 1949.
        - 32 p.

045.   -- --- Index to Council documents/ prepared by the Library.
        Provisional English ed. - Geneva, 1920. - 81 p.

League of nations (Cont'd)

1046.   -- --- Répertoire analytique des documents distribués au
             Conseil et aux membres de la Société au cours de 1925.
             - Genève, 1926. - 188 p. - (Publications de la Société des
             nations. Questions générales. 1926.10.)
             At head of title: Société des nations.
             Official no.: C.400.M.141.1926.

1047.   -- --- Subject list of documents distributed to the Council and
             members of the League during 1925. - Geneva, 1926. - 183 p.
             - (Publications of the League of nations. General. 1926. 10.)

1048.   -- **Secretariat. Library.** Ouvrages sur la Société des nations
             catalogués à la Bibliothèque du Secrétariat, 1920-1925=Books on the
             League of nations received in the Library of the Secretariat, 1920-
             1925. - Genève, 1926. - 31 p.
             At head of title: Supplément au Résumé mensuel, février 1926. Supplement to the
             Monthly summary, February 1926.
             Supplément. 1927. - 11 p.

1049.   **League of nations union, London.** The International labour organisation
             of the League of nations; being a short account of its organisation
             and activities, together with a summary of the work of the Internatio
             labour conferences at Washington, 1919, Genoa, 1920, and Geneva, 19
             Bibliography: p. 23-24. - London, League of nations union, 1922. -
             23, 1 p.

1050.   **Legal** documents index and bibliography of the United Nations and
             related intergovernmental organizations. - United Nations juridical
             yearbook, 1970. - p. 199-262. E F S R
             Main headings: General assembly and subsidiary organs (Plenary General assembly and
             main committees, Executive committee of the Programme of the UNHCR, Committee
             on the peaceful uses of outer space, Special committee on principles of international
             law concerning friendly relations and co-operation among States, United Nations council
             for Namibia, Special committee on the question of defining agression, Committee on the
             peaceful uses of the sea-bed and the ocean floor beyond the limits of national jurisdiction,
             International law commission, UNCITRAL. - Security council and subsidiary organs. -
             Economic and social council (Sessional committees, Commission on human rights, Commis-
             sion on the status of women, Economic commission for Europe. - UNCTAD. - International
             court of justice. - Specialized agencies.

1051.   **Legault, A.** Peace-keeping operations; bibliography. - Paris,
             International information center on peace-keeping operations,
             1967. - 203 p.

1052.   **Le Guiner, F.** Le Conseil de sécurité de l'O.N.U. son rôle dans les
             conflits internationaux depuis 1946. - Bibliography: p. 390-393. -
             Paris, 1964. - 401 p.
             Thèse - Univ. de Paris.

1053.   **Le Pan de Ligny, G.** Marché commun. - Bibliography; p. 251-260. -
             Paris, Dunod, 1961. - xxii, 266, lxiv p. - (Aide-mémoire Dunod.)

1054.   **Levison, M. E.** The ideas and operations of the cultural activities
             programme of Unesco, 1945-1952, in the context of the Unesco
             programme as a whole. - Bibliography: p. 450-473. - New York, 1958
             Microfilm copy of typewritten manuscript. Positive.
             Collation of the original: 4, ix, 473 p.
             Diss. - Columbia university.

055.   **L'Huillier, J. A.** La coopération économique internationale, 1957-1959. - Notes, partly bibliographical. - Paris, Libr. de Médicis, 1959. - 138 p.
Supplement to the author's "Théorie et pratique de la coopération économique internationale."

056.   -- --- Les organisations internationales de coopération économique et le commerce extérieur des pays en voie de développement. - Notes, partly bibliographical. - Genève, 1969. - 105 p. - (Geneva. Institut universitaire de hautes études internationales. Etudes et travaux.no.9.)

057.   -- --- Théorie et pratique de la coopération économique internationale. - Notes, partly bibliographical. - Paris, Libr. de Médicis, 1957. - 603 p.

058.   **Liebich, F. K.** Das GATT als Zentrum der internationalen Handelspolitik, unter Anschluss insbesondere der Texte des Allgemeinen Zoll- und Handelsabkommens (GATT), des Baumwolltextilabkommens und des Anti-dumping Kodex. - Bibliography: p. 211-224. - Baden-Baden, Nomos Verlagsgesellschaft, 1971. - 224 p. - (Schriftenreihe europäische Wirtschaft. Bd. 46.)

059.   -- --- Grundriss des Allgemeinen Zoll- und Handelsabkommens (GATT), mit Texten des GATT, des Baumwolltextilabkommens und anderer wichtiger Dokumente. - Bibliography: p. 163-171. - 2. neubearb. Aufl. - Baden-Baden, Nomos Verlagsgesselschaft, 1967. - 177 p. - (Handbuch für europäische Wirtschaft. Schriftenreihe. Bd. 19.)
Earlier ed. issued with title: Das GATT; eine Textausgabe des Allgemeinen Zoll- und Handelsabkommens....

060.   **Lima, F. X. de.** Intervention in international law, with a reference to the Organisation of American states. - Bibliography: p. 219-229. - Den Haag, Uitgeverij Pax Nederland, 1971. - ix, 229 p.
Summary in Dutch: 9 p. at end.

061.   **Lindberg, L. N.** The political dynamics of European economic integration. - Bibliography: p. 351-360. - Stanford, Calif., Stanford university press, 1963. - xiv, 367 p.
"Published with the assistance of the Ford foundation."
Notes, partly bibliographical: p. 317-350.

062.   **Loftus, M. L.** The International monetary fund, 1962-1965: a selected bibliography.
Contains a list of IMF publications.
Reprinted from the November 1965 issue of IMF Staff papers.

063.   -- --- The International monetary fund, 1968-1971: a selected bibliography. - Washington, 1972. - p. 174-258.
Reprinted from the March 1972 issue of the International monetary fund Staff papers.
This bibliography covers books, pamphlets, reports, and periodical articles dealing with the functions, organization, and activities of the International monetary fund. It is a continuation of the bibliographies published in Staff papers, v.1, no.3 (April 1951), v.3, no.1 (April 1953), v.4, no.3 (August 1955), v.6, no.3 (November 1958), v.9, no.3 (November 1962, v.12, no.3 (November 1965), and v.15, no.1 (March 1968). Although most of the Fund's official publications are included, this is not intended to be a complete bibliography of such publications.

064.   **Lokanathan, P. S.** ECAFE - the economic parliament of Asia. - Bibliographical notes. - Madras, Diocesan press, 1954. - 24 p.
"Reprinted from the Indian year book of international affairs, 1953."

1

1065.   **Lopez Paez, F. J.**   Del Consejo de la Liga al de la Organización de las
         Naciones Unidas. - Bibliography: p. 68-69. - Mexico, Facultad de
         derecho y ciencias sociales, Univ. autonoma de Mexico, 1949. - 69 p
         Tesis - Mexico.

1066.   **Luard, D. E. T.**   The evolution of international organizations. - Biblio-
         graphy at the end of each chapter. - London, Thames and Hudson,
         1966. - 342 p. - (Studies in international order.)

1067.   **Lusignan, G. de.**   L'Organisation internationale du travail (1919-1959). -
         Bibliography: 1 p. following p. 133. - Paris, Ed. Ouvrières, 1959. -
         133 p. - (Collection "Vous connaîtrez".)

1068.   **Malinowski, W. R.**   Centralization and decentralization in the United N;
         economic and social activities. - Bibliographical notes. - n.p., 1962. -
         p. 521-541.
         "Reprinted from 'International organization', volume XVI, number 3, 1962."

1069.   **Malmgren, H. B.**   International economic peacekeeping in phase II. -
         Notes, partly bibliographical. - New York, Quadrangle books, 1972. -
         xv, 267 p.
         "Published for the Atlantic council of the United States."
         Commercial policy. Economic relations. International agencies. Economics - Societies.
         Contracting parties to the General agreement on tariffs and trade.

1070.   **Manin, A.**   L'Organisation de l'aviation civile internationale; authorité
         mondiale de l'air. - Préface de Suzanne Bastid. - Bibliography: p 329
         332. - Paris, Libr. générale de droit et de jurisprudence, 1970. - iii,
         339 p. - (Bibliothèque de droit international. t.56.)
         Série Organisations internationales. no.3.

1071.   **Manno, C. S.**   Weighted voting in the United Nations General assembly
         a study of feasibility and methods. - Bibliography: p. 300-311. -
         Washington, D.C., 1964.
         Microfilm copy of typewritten manuscript. Positive.
         Collation of the original: x, 319 p.
         Diss. - American university.

1072.   **Marcus, M. M.**   Voting procedures and practices in the Security council
         of the United Nations. - Bibliography: p. 431-477. - Ann Arbor, Mic
         1958.
         Microfilm copy of typewritten manuscript. Positive.
         Collation of the original: vii, 477 p.
         Diss. - Univ. of Michigan.

1073.   **Marseillan, L.**   L'Organisation des Nations Unies pour l'alimentation et
         l'agriculture (O.A.A.). - Bibliography: p. 8-13 at end. - Paris, 1951.
         Microfilm copy of typewritten manuscript. Negative.
         Collation of the original: xii, 268, 13 p.
         Thèse - Univ. de Paris.

1074.   **Mason, H. L.**   The European coal and steel community; experiment in
         supranationalism. - Bibliography: p. 145-147. - The Hague, M. Nijhof
         1955. - xi, 153 p.

1075.   **Matiátegui Arellano, J. C.**   Manual de organismos internacionales/ por
         José Carlos Mariátegui A. - Bibliography: p. 321-329. - Lima, Perú,
         Libr. internacional del Peru, 1967. - 347 p.
         At head of title: Academia diplomática del Perú.

076. **Mayne, R.**   The institutions of the European community. - Bibliography: p. 80-82. - London, Chatham house and PEP, 1968. - 82 p. - (European series. no.8.)

077. **Meerhaeghe, M. A. G. van.**   International economic institutions. - Bibliography at the end of each chapter. - London, Longmans, 1966. - xx, 404 p.
Original ed. pub. under title: Internationale economische betrekkingen en instellingen.

078. **Meeting of experts on the United Nations programme in public administration. 2nd, New York, 1971.**   Public administration in the 2nd United Nations development decade; report. - Bibliography: p. 144-147. - New York, 1971. - v. 163. p. - (United Nations. Publications. Sales numbers. 1971.II.H.3.)
United Nations. Dcouments. ST/TAO/M/57.
At head of title: Department of economic and social affairs. Public administration division.

079. **Meigs, C. L.**   The great design; men and events in the United Nations from 1945 to 1963. - Bibliography: p. 307-311. - Boston, Little, Brown, 1964. - x, 319 p.
Notes, partly bibliographical: p. 297-305.

080. **Mellor, R. E. H.**   COMECON: challenge to the West. - Bibliography: p. 148-150. - New York, Van Nostrand Reinhold, 1971. - vii, 152 p.
"A Searchlight original".

081. **Meyer, J. U.**   Die zweite Entwicklungsdekade der Vereinten Nationen: Konzept und Kritik einer globalen Entwicklungsstrategie. - Bibliography: p. 191-200. - Düsseldorf, Bertelsmann Universitätsverlag, 1971. - 218 p. - (Bochumer Schriften zur Entwicklungsforschung und Entwicklungspolitik. Bd. 10.)
At head of title: Jörg-Udo Meyer. Dieter Seul. Karl Heinz Klingner.
United Nations development decade. 2nd (1971-1981).

082. **Mezerik, A. G.**   Economic development aids for underdeveloped countries: UN sources, national and international agencies, financial and technical assistance, edited by A.G. Mezerik. - Bibliography: p. 47-49. - New York, 1961. - ii, 108 p. - (International review service. v.7, no.63.)

083. **Mezhdunarodnye** politicheskie, èkonomicheskie i obshchestvennye organizafsii: slovar'-spravochnik. - Moskva, Politizdat, 1966. - 270 p.

084. **Mikheev, IÛ. IA.**   Primenenie prinuditel'nykh mer po Ustavu OON. - Bibliographical notes. - Moskva, Izd-vo "Mezhdunarodnye otnosheniiã", 1967. - 205 p.

085. **Mir Eskandari, A. N.**   L'Institution internationale spécialisée des P.T.T. (UPU). - Bibliography: p. 108. - Paris, 1951.
Microfilm copy of typewritten manuscript. Negative.
Collation of the original: 110 p.
Thèse - Univ. de Paris.

1086.   **Molavi, M. A.** La Banque pour la reconstruction et le développement
         (Bretton-Woods) et la politique du développement des pays sous-
         développés. - Bibliography: l. 472-498. - Paris, 1957.
         Microfilm copy of typewritten manuscript. Negative.
         Collation of the original: 505 l.
         Thèse - Univ. de Paris.

1087.   **Monaco, R.** Commento allo statuto delle Nazioni Unite; con i testi
         della carta di S. Francisco e dello statuto della Corte internazionale
         di giustizia. - Bibliography: 2 p. following p. 169. - Torino, A. Viglongo,
         1946. - 169 p. - (Attualita' e proplemi. 3.)

1088.   **Montceau, M.** L'Organisation internationale du travail (1919-1959). -
         Bibliography: 1 p. following p. 125. - Paris, Presses universitaires de
         France, 1959. - 125 p. - ("Que sais-je? " no. 836.)

1089.   **Morard, N.** Fonctionnement et perspectives de la Communauté européenn
         du charbon et de l'acier. - Bibliography: p. 229-233. - Fribourg, Suisse,
         Éd. universitaires, 1962. - x, 233 p. - (Fribourg. Universität. Institut
         des sciences économiques et sociales. Chaiers. 10.)

1090.   **Morozov, G. I.** Organizatsiia Ob"edinennykh Natsii; (osnovnye mezh-
         dunarodno-pravovye aspekty struktury i deiatel'nosti). - Bibliography:
         p. 492-510. - Moskva, Izd-vo IMO, 1963. - 510 p.
         At head of title: Institut mezhdunarodnykh otnoshenii.
         United Nations: legal aspects, structure and activities.

1091.   **Mosin, I. N.** Mezhdunarodnyi valiutnyi fond. - Bibliographical notes. -
         Pod red. G.S. Lopatina. - Moskva, Izd-vo "Mezhdunarodnye otnosheniia"
         1964. - 238 p.
         At head of title: Institut mezhdunarodnykh otnoshenii.
         International monetary fund.

1092.   **Mostafavi, R.** Le fonctionnement technique du Secrétariat des Nations
         Unites. - Bibliogrpahy: p. 188,bis. - Paris, 1952.
         Microfilm copy of typewritten manuscript. Negative.
         Collation of the original: 195 p.
         Thèse - Univ. de Paris.

1093.   **Mourad, M. H.** Le rôle et l'activité du Fonds monétaire international. -
         Bibliography: p. 383-389. - Paris, 1949.
         Microfilm copy of typewritten manuscript. Negative.
         Collation of the original: 395 p.
         Thèse - Univ. de Paris.

1094.   **Murray, J. N.** The formation and functioning of the trusteeship system
         of the United Nations. - Bibliography: p. 306-312. - Urbana, Ill., 1953.
         Microfilm copy of typewritten manuscript. Made in 1953 by University microfilms
         (Publication no. 5992). Positive.
         Collation of the original: 3, iii-iv, 358 p.
         Thesis - Univ. of Illinois.

1095.   **Muyden, M. L. (Holthausen) van.** Documents ronéographiés
         de la Société des nations; liste topographique. - Genève, 1958.
         - 22 l.

1096.   - - - - - Les documents officiels à consultation restreinte de la
         Société des nations (1920-1946). - Genève, 1958. - 18 l.
         Diplôme - École de bibliothécaires (Genève)

097.   **Myrdal, G.**   The research work of the Secretariat of the Economic
        commission for Europe. - Bibliography: p. 24-27. - n.p., 1957. -
        27 p.   E F
        From "25 economic essays in honour of Erik Lindahl".

098.   **el-Naggar, S.**   The United Nations conference on trade and development;
        background, aims and policies. - Bibliography: p. 344-345. - (In Academy
        of international law, The Hague. Recueil des cours, 1969, III.   Leyde,
        (Pays-Bas), A.W. Sijthoff, 1970. - p. 241-345.

099.   **Negin, M.**   Organizatsiia Ob"edinennykh Natsiĭ po voprosam prosve-
        shcheniiã, nauki i kul'tury (IUNESKO). - Bibliographical notes. -
        Moskva, Izd-vo Instituta mezhdunarodnykh otnoshenii, 1959. - 106 p.-
        (Mezhdunarodnye organizatsii.)
        UNESCO activities.

100.   **Nême, J.**   Organisations économiques internationales. - Bibliography at
        the end of each chapter. - Paris, Presses universitaires de France, 1972. -
        482 p. - (Thémis: sciences économiques.)
        At head of title: Jacques Nême. Colette Nême.

101.   **Netherlands. Departement van buitenlandsche zaken.**   Het ontstaan der
        Verenigde Naties, San Francisco, 25 April-25 Juni 1945. - Biblio-
        graphical notes. - 's-Gravenhage, 1950. - 282 p. - (Its: Uitgaven. no.23.)
        United Nations conference on international organization, San Francisco, 1945.

102.   **Nordisk råd.**   Nordiska rådets verksamhet, 1952-1961; översikt över-
        rådets rekommendationer och radspresidiets framstallningar, sammanställd
        inom Nordiska rådets sekretariat under redaktion av Gustaf Petrén. -
        Notes, partly bibliographical. - Stockholm, 1962. - 335 p. - (Nordisk
        utredningsserie. 1962:8.)

103.   **Norske Nobelinstitutt, Oslo. Biblioteket.**   Nordisk litteratur om de
        Forente Nasjoner; et utvalg böker og tidsskriftartikler skrevet i arene
        1959-1964, utarb. ved Nobelinstituttets bibliotek av Agot Brekke. -
        Oslo, Norsk samband for de Forente Nasjoner, 1965. - 43 l.

104.   -- - -- -   Penge- og valutapolitikken i de Europeiske fellesskap: bibliografi. -
        Oslo, Nobelinstituttets bibliotek, 1971. - 6 l.
        Bibliography on monetary policy in Europe.

105.   **Oliver, R. W.**   Early plans for a world bank. - Notes, partly biblio-
        graphical. - Princeton, N.J., International finance section, Department
        of economics, Princeton university, 1971. - 57 p. - (Princeton
        studies in international finance. no.29.)
        Banks and banking. Keynes plan. Keynes, John Maynard, 1883-1946. White, Harry Dexter.
        International bank for reconstruction and development.

106.   -- - -- -   The origins of the International bank for reconstruction and
        development. - Bibliography: p. 762-792. - Princeton, N.J., 1952.
        Microfilm copy of typewritten manuscript. Positive.
        Collation of the original: 4, x, 792 p.
        Diss. - Princeton university.

1107.   **Onno, E.** L'U.N.E.S.C.O.: organisation et œuvre. - Bibliography:
            3 p. at the end. - Montpellier, "Renex", 1954. - 2, 371, 3, 7 p.
            Thèse - Univ. de Toulouse.

1108.   **Organisation européenne pour la recherche nucléaire.** Répertoire
            des communications scientifiques=Index of scientific publications,
            1955-1959. - Genève, 1960. - 77 p. E/F

1109.   **Organisation for economic co-operation and development.** Migrations
            internationales de la main-d'œuvre: bibliographie=International
            migration of manpower: bibliography. - Paris, Organisation de
            coopération et de développement économiques, 1969. - 137 p.

1110.   -- --- OECD at work for environment. - OECD publications on the
            environment: 31-32. - Paris, 1971. - 32 p.

1111.   -- --- OECD at work for science and education. - OECD publications
            on science, technology and education: p. 57-68. - Paris, 1972. - 68 p.

1112.   -- --- Pays en voie de développement=Countries in process of
            development. - 1958/61-   . - Paris, 1962-   . - v.
            - (Its: Bibliographies spéciales. Special bibliographies. no.37,etc.)
            Superseded: Organisation for European economic co-operation. Pays en voie de
            développement. 1954/59-1959/61.

1113.   -- --- Science policy document exchange scheme: bibliography.
            - 4th-   ; 1966-   . - Paris, Directorate for scientific affairs,
            Organisation for economic co-operation and development, 1966.
            - v.

1114.   -- --- Systems analysis for educational planning: selected
            annotated bibliography=Méthodes analytiques appliquées à
            la planification de l'enseignement: bibliographie choisie et
            annotée. - Paris, Organisation de coopération et de développement
            économiques, 1969. - 219 p.

1115.   -- **Development centre.** International comparison of real incomes. -
            Bibliography: p. 59-62. - Paris, 1966. - 62 p.
            At head of title: Wilfred Beckerman.

1116.   -- --- Inventaire de catalogues d'institutions et d'ouvrages de
            référence=List of catalogues of institutions and reference books. -
            Paris, 1968. - 38 l.
            Catalogues. Ouvrages de référence. Bibliographie. Films.

1117.   -- --- Occupational training: annotated bibliography. - Paris,
            O.E.C.D., 1970. - iv, 102 p.

1118.   -- --- Réévaluation des politiques d'aide à l'étranger. - Bibliography:
            p. 127-134. - Paris, 1961. - 134 p. - (Its: Etudes du Centre de
            développement.)
            At head of title: Goran Ohlin.

19.   **Organisation for economic co-operation and development. Library.**
Bibliographies spéciales analytiques=Special annotated bibliographies. -
no.1-   ; 1964-   . - Paris, 1964-   . -   v.
Contents:
1.   Pays en voie de développement. Developing countries. v, 41 p. 1964.
2.   Automation. iv, 38 p. 1964.
3.   Planification économique. Economic planning. v. 57 p. 1964.
4.   Payements internationaux. International Payments. v, 51 p. 1964.
5.   Conférence des Nations Unies sur le commerce et le développement. United
Nations Conference for trade and development. v, 58 p. 1965.
6.   Inflation. v, 84 p. 1965.
7.   Les relations commerciales est-ouest. East-West trade relations. v, 95 p. 1966.
8.   Politique régionale. pt.1. v, 124 p. 1966.
9.   -- --- pt.2. v, 74 p. 1966,
10.   L'éducation dans le développement économique. The educational factor
for development. pt.1. v. 130 p. 1966.
11.   -- --- pt.2. v, 117 p. 1966.
12.   L'alimentation et l'agriculture dans les pays en voie de développement. Food
and agriculture in developing countries. pt.1. v, 124 p. 1967.
13.   -- --- pt.2. iii, 110 p. 1967.
14.   European recovery program (Marshall plan). Programme de relèvement
européen.   v, 99 p. 1967.
15.   Système d'arbitrage des conflits du travail. Labour arbitration systems.
v, 106 p. 1967.
16.   International monetary system. Système monétaire international. vii, 130 p. 1967.
17.   Its: Croissance économique. Economic growth. v.1.   1968.
18.   -- --- v.2. 1968.
19.   Its: Les investissements étrangers et leurs effets dans les pays en voie de
développement. Foreign investment and its impact in developing countries. 1968.
25.   Its: Intégration régionale. Regional integration. t. 1/1969/.
26.   -- --- t.2 /1970/.
27-28. -- La politique agricole. Agricultural policy. v. 1-2. 1970.
29.   Environnement et urbanisation. Environment and urbanisation. t.1. 1970.
31.   Problèmes du commerce extérieur des pays en voie de développement. Trade
problems of developing countries. 1971.
32.   L'inflation. 1972.
33.   -- --- v.2. 1972.

20.   -- --- Catalogue des sources bibliographiques disponibles au
Service de documentation-bibliothèque au 1er janvier 1967. -
Paris, 1967. - 63 p.
Inventaire de 443 documents bibliographiques concernant le développement économique.

21.   **Organization of American States. Comité jurídico interamericano.**
Informes y documentos: serie CIJ - 1-   . - Lista de publicaciones
de la División de codificación e integración jurídica. - In: Its:
Trabajos realizados por el Comité jurídico interamericano durante
su período extraordinario de sesiones. - Washington, D.C., Secretaria
general de la Organización de los estados americanos, 1949-   .

22.   **Organization of the petroleum exporting countries.** Selected
documents on the international petroleum industry. - 19   . -
Vienna, OPEC, 19   . -   v.

23.   **Organski, A.** The veto as viewed by the United States and the Soviet
world. - Bibliography: p. 314-317. - New York, 1951.
Microfilm copy of typewritten manuscript. Copy 1, positive. Copy 2, negative.
Collation of the original: 317 p.
Thesis - New York university.

1124.   **Ornatskiĭ, I. A.** Amerikanskaĩa diplomatiĩa i ėkonomicheskaĩa deĩatel'
         nost' OON. - Bibliography: p. 325-333. - Moskva, Izd-vo "Mezh-
         dunarodnye otnosheniĩa", 1972. - 333 p.
         Bibliography on economic activities of UN.

1125.   **Osterreichische Liga für die Vereinten Nationen.** Universality of the
         United Nations organization and its special organization; report
         drawn up by the Austrian league for the United Nations/ by Lujo
         Tončić Sorinj. - Bibliographical notes. - n.p. 1955. - 20 leaves.

1126.   **Overstreet, A. B.** Sovereignty in the constitutions of some international
         organizations: a comparative study of certain aspects of the League
         of nations, International labor organization, United Nations relief and
         rehabilitation administration, and United Nations. - Bibliography:
         leaves 311-327. - Cambridge, Mass., 1948.
         Microfilm copy of photostat copy of typewritten manuscript. Positive.
         Collation of the original: x, 327 l.
         Diss. - Harvard.

1127.   **Paklous, L. L.** Bibliographie européenne=European bibliography.
         - Bruges, De Tempel, 1964. - 217 p. - (Cahiers de Bruges. N.S.8.)

1128.   **Pan American union.** Catalogue of Pan American union
         publications in English, Spanish, Portuguese and French.
         - 19 -   . - Washington, 19 -   . - v.
         "Contains publications for sale, issued or sponsored by the Pan American union."
         - p.vi.

1129.   -- - -- Catalogue of publications about the American republics and
         reports on the strengthening of our inter-American community=
         Catálogo de publicaciones sobre las républicas americanas, 1965-
         1966. - Washington, D.C., 1966. - 27 p.
         Pt.1: Technical and informational publications.
         Pt.2: Official records, Organization of American States.

1130.   -- - -- Repertorio de publicaciones periódicas actuales
         latinoamericanas=Directory of current Latin American periodicals=
         Répertoire des périodiques en cours publiés en Amérique latine.
         - Paris, UNESCO, 1958. - xxv, 266p; - (United Nations educational,
         scientific and cultural organisation. Bibliographical handbooks.no.8.)
         Title and text in Spanish, English and French. Subject index also in Portuguese.

1131.   -- **Columbus memorial library.** Bibliografía de la literatura sobre
         educación de adultos en la América latina. - Wáshington, Departament(
         de asuntos culturales, Unión panamericana, 1952. - xi, 88 p.
         - (Its: Bibliographic series 37.)

1132.   -- - -- Bibliografía de las conferencias interamericanas. - Washington,
         Departamento de asuntos culturales, Unión panamericana, 1954.
         - x, 277 p. - (Its: Bibliographic series. no.41.)

1133.   -- - -- Bibliographic series. - no.1.-   . - Washington, D.C.,
         1930-   . - v.
         Set partly English, partly Spanish, partly Portuguese.

Pan American union. Columbus memorial library. (Cont'd)

34.   -- --- Bibliography on public administration in Latin America.
- 2nd ed. - Comp. by/ Jorge Grossmann. - Washington, Department
of cultural affairs, Pan American union, 1958. - xii, ¹98 p.
- (Its: Bibliographic series. no. 43, 2nd ed.)

35.   -- --- Indice general de publicaciones periódicas latinoamericanas;
humanidades y ciencias sociales=Index to Latin American
periodicals. - v. 1-6; 1961-1966. - Boston, Mass., G. K. Hall,
1963-66. - 6 v.
Title and text in Spanish and English.

36.   -- --- Selected references on the Inter-American treaty of
reciprocal assistance, signed at Rio de Janeiro, Brazil, on
September 2, 1947. - n.p., 1950. - 11 1.

37.   -- **Division of education.** Bibliography on education and economic
and social development; (American sources). - Washington, D.C.,
Documentation and information service, Division of education,
Department of cultural affairs, Pan American union, 1962.
- 62 p. - (Its: Education in the Americas information series;
bulletins. 1962: no.2.)

38.   **Patch, D. I.** The International bank for reconstruction and development:
its establishment and its use of the developmental loan in Latin
America. - Bibliography: p. 69-71. - Mexico, 1950.
Microfilm copy of typewritten manuscript. Positive.
Collation of the original: 71 p.
"Special topic paper" - Mexico City college.

39.   **Peacock, L. C.** Policies and operations of the International monetary
fund, 1947-1956. - Bibliography: p. 228-242. - Austin, Texas, 1958.
Microfilm copy of typewritten manuscript. Positive.
Collation of the original: iv, 243 p. tables.
Diss. - Univ. of Texas.

40.   **Pellecer Cruz, L. F.** La juridicidad de las Naciones Unidas. - Bibliography:
2nd p. following p. 36. - Guatemala, 1951. - 36 p.
Tesis - Universidad de San Carlos de Guatemala.

41.   **Pickard, B.** The greater United Nations; an essay concerning the place
and significance of international non-governmental organizations. - Notes,
partly bibliographical. - New York, Carnegie endowment for international
peace, 1956. - 86 p.

42.   **Pochkaeva, M. V.** Pravovye voprosy ėkonomicheskogo sotrudnichestva
gosudarstv v sisteme OON: Ekonomicheskaiã komissiiã OON dlíã
Evropy. - Notes, partly bibliographical. - Moskva, Gosiūrizdat, 1962. -
74 p.
United Nations. Economic commission for Europe.

43.   **Polach, J. G.** Euratom: its background, issues and economic implications. -
Bibliography: p. 211-223. - Dobbs Ferry, N.Y., Oceana publications,
1964. - xxiv, 232 p.

1144. **Potter, P. B.**   An introduction to the study of international organization.
       Bibliography: p. 602-636. - New York, Century co., 1922. - xiv,
       647 p. - (Century political science series.)
       "Documents illustrating the development of international organization": p. 511-601.

1145. **Poujade, D.**   La Commission économique pour l'Amérique Latine. -
       Bibliography: 4 p. at the end. - Paris, 1953.
       Microfilm copy of typewritten manuscript.   Negative.
       Collation of the original: 1 v. (various pagings.)
       Thèse - Univ. de Paris.

1146. **Practical** manual of LAFTA. 1969/70. - Bibliography: p. 246. - Monte-
       video, CENCI: Centre of national statistics and international trade
       of Uruguay, 1969. - 246 p.
       At head of title: Latin American free trade association (LAFTA-ALALC).
       "This book is the translation from the Spanish original 'Manual práctico de la ALALC'".
       p. 3.

1147. **Prieur, R.**   La Communauté européenne du charbon et de l'acier:
       activité et évolution. - Bibliography: p. 14-16. - Paris, Ed. Mont-
       chrestien, 1962. - 496 p.
       Reproduced from typewritten copy.

1148. **Public** papers of the secretaries-general of the United Nations. - v.1- -
       Notes, partly bibliographical. - New York, Columbia university press,
       1969-   . -   v.
       Editor: v.1-   , Andrew W. Cordier and Wilder Foote.

1149. **Puryear, E. F.**   Communist negotiating techniques: a case study of
       the United Nations Security council Commission of investigation
       concerning the Greek frontier incidents. - Bibliography: p. 333-357. -
       Princeton, N.J., 1959.
       Microfilm copy of typewritten manuscript.   Positive.
       Collation of the original: 357 p.
       Diss. - Princeton university.

1150. **Račic, O.**   Odnos izmedu Ujedinjenih Nacija i specijalizovanih
       ustanova. - Bibliography: p. 269-273. - Beograd, Izdanje Instituta
       za medunarodnu politiku i privredu, 1966. - 303 p.
       Summaries in English and Russian: p. 275-303.
       UN and specialized agencies.

1151. **Rafajlovic, D.**   Veto, met-il en question l'existence même de l'ONU:
       son reflet historique et son importance politique actuelle. -
       Bibliography: p. 151-157. - Singen, Druckerei und Verlagsanstalt,
       1951. - 157 p.

1152. **Rainaud, J. M.**   L'Agence internationale de l'énergie atomique. -
       Bibliography: p. 187-188. - Paris, A. Colin, 1970. - 237 p. -
       (Collection U. sér.:   "Relations et institutions internationales".)

1153. **Rapisardi-Mirabelli, A.**   Théorie générale des unions internationales. -
       Bibliographie: p. 391. - (In: Hague. Academy of international law.
       Recueil des cours, 1925, II. Paris, 1926. v.7, p. 341-393.)

1154. **Rauzières, E.**   La crise financière de l'O.N.U. - Bibliography: leaves
       248-250. - Lille, Imprimerie-coopérative de l'A.G.E.L., 1966. - 250 l.
       Thèse - Univ. de Montpellier.

55. **Reuter, P.**   La Communauté européenne du charbon et de l'acier. - Bibliography: p. 312-313. - Paris, Libr. générale de droit et de jurisprudence, 1953. - 320 p.

56. -- --- Instituciones internacionales. - Bibliography: p. 5-8, and at the end of each chapter. - Versión española de Cristóbal Massó Escofet. - Barcelona, Bosch, 1959. - 372 p.
"Título del libro en su edición original: 'Institutions internationales', 1956."

57. -- --- Institutions internationales. - Bibliography at the end of each chapter. - Paris, Presses universitaires de France, 1955. - 426 p. - ("Thémis"; manuels juridiques, économiques et politiques.)

58. -- --- International institutions. - Bibliography: p. 305-310. - London, G. Allen & Unwin, 1958. - 316 p. - (Minerva series of students' handbooks. no.1.)
"Translated from the French 'Institutions internationales', published by Presses universitaires de France, 1955."

59. -- --- Les organes subsidiaires des organisations internationales. - Notes, partly bibliographical. - (In Hommage d'une génération de juristes au président Basdevant. Paris, A. Pedone, 1960. p. 415-440.)

60. -- --- Les organisations internationales. - Bibliography: p. 5-7. - Paris, 1955. - 501 p.
On cover: Année 1954-55: Droit international public (doctorat); cours professé par M. Reuter.

61. **Richards, J. H.**   International economic institutions. - Bibliography: p. 310-318. - London, Holt, Rinehart and Winston, 1970. - xv, 334 p.

62. **Robertson, A. H.**   The Council of Europe, its structure, functions and achievements. - Bibliography: p. 239-241. - London, Stevens & sons, 1956. - (Library of world affairs. no.32.)   E F
"Published under the auspices of the London institute of world affairs."

63. **Robins, D. B.**   The UN story; toward a more perfect world/ by Dorothy B. Robins and Frederic A. Weed. - Bibliography: p. 95-99. - New York, Education committee for school and college activities, American association for the United Nations, 1950. - 103 p.

64. **Robinson,, J.**   Metamorphosis of the United Nations. - Bibliography: p. 585-589. - (In Academy of international law, The Hague. Recueil des cours, 1958, II. Leyde (Pays-Bas), A.W. Sijthoff, 1959. v.94, p. 493-592.)

65. **Robinson, J. W.**   The roots of international organization. - Bibliography: p. 42-45. - Washington, D.C., Public affairs press, 1968. - 76 p.

66. **Ros, E. J.**   Organisation et personnalité juridique de l'O.A.C.I. - Bibliography: p. 180-189. - Paris, 1953.
Microfilm copy of typewritten manuscript. Negative.
Collation of the original: 195 p.
Thèse - Univ. de Paris.

1167.   **Rosenne, S.**   United Nations treaty practice. - Bibliography: p. 439-442. - (In Academy of international law, The Hague.   Recueil des cours, 1954, II.   Leyde (Pays-Bas), A.W. Sijthoff, 1955. v.86, p. 275-444.)

1168.   **Rosner, G. E.**   The United Nations emergency force. - Bibliography: p. 271-282. - New York, Columbia university press, 1963. - xiv, 294 p. - (Columbia university studies in international organization. no.2.)
        Notes, partly bibliographical: p. 223-270.

1169.   **Ross, A.**   Constitution of the United Nations: analysis of structure and function. - Bibliographical notes. - Kφbenhavn, E. Munksgaard, 1950. - 236 p.
        "Text of the Charter of the United Nations": p. 200-232.

1170.   -- --- The United Nations: peace and progress. - Bibliography at the end of each chapter. - Totowa, N.J., Bedminster press, 1966. - xi, 443 p.
        Original ed. pub. under title: De Forenede Nationer: fred or fremskridt.

1171.   **Roussier, M.**   Les publications officielles des institutions européennes: bibliographie/ établie par Michel Roussier, avec la collaboration de Maryvonne Stephan. - Paris, Carnegie endowment for international peace, Centre européen, 1954. - 73 p.

1172.   **Rouyer-Hameray, B.**   Les compétences implicites des organisations internationales. - Notes, partly bibliographical. - Paris, Libr. générale de droit et de jurisprudence, 1962. - 110 p. - (Bibliothèque de droit international. t. 25.)
        "Ouvrage publié avec le concours du Centre national de la recherche scientifique."

1173.   **Rovine, A. W.**   The first fifty years: the secretary-general in world politics, 1920-1970. - Bibliography: p. 465-468. - Leyden, A.W. Sijtho 1970. - 498 p.

1174.   **Rozanov, L. L.**   Sotͦsial'no-ėkonomicheskie i politicheskie aspekty deiͦatel'nosti Vsemirnoǐ organizatͦsii zdravookhraneniiͦa. - Moskva, Izd-vo "Nauka", 1972. - 183 p.
        At head of title: Akademiiͦa nauk SSSR.   Institut mirovoǐ ėkonomiki i mezhdunarodnykh otnoshenii.
        Includes important bibliographical foot-notes.

1175.   **Rubanik, K. P.**   Mezhdunarodno-pravovye problemy IͦUNESKO. - Bibliographical notes. - Moskva, Izd-vo "Mezhdunarodnye otnosheniiͦa", 1969. - 164 p.
        Legal aspects of UNESCO.

1176.   **Russell, R. B.**   A history of the United Nations charter; the role of th United States, 1940-1945/ by Ruth B. Russell assisted by Jeannette I Muther. - Notes, partly bibliographical. - Washington, D.C., Brookings institution, 1958. - xviii, 1140 p.

1177.   **Ruzié, D.**   Les fonctionnaires internationaux. - Bibliography: p. 88-95. - Paris, A. Colin, 1970. - 95 p. - (Dossiers U2. t.95.)

1178.   -- --- Organisations internationales et sanctions internationales. - Bibliography: p. 214. - Paris, A. Colin, 1971. - 223 p. - (Collection U. sér.:   "Relations et institutions internationales".)

1179. **Saba, H.** Les accords régionaux dans la Charte de l'O.N.U. -
Bibliography: p. 717-718. - (In Academy of international law,
The Hague. Recueil des cours, 1952, I. Paris, v.80, p. 635-720.)

1180. -- --- L'activité quasi-législative des institutions spécialisées des
Nations Unies. - Bibliography: p. 687-688. - (In Academy of
international law, The Hague. Recueil des cours, 1964, I. Leyde,
(Pays-Bas), A.W. Sijthoff, 1964. v. 111, p. 603-690.)

1181. **Salomon, A.** Le préambule de la Charte, base idéologique de l'O.N.U. -
Bibliography: p. 213-219. - Genève, Ed. des Trois Collines, 1946. -
228 p. - (Etudes juridiques et sociales.)

182. **Sand, H. B.** COMECON: Struktur und Entwicklungen. - Bibliographical
notes. - Köln, Deutsche Industrieverlags-GMBH, 1972. - 91 p. -
(Beiträge des Deutschen Industrieinstituts. 1972.Hft. 10/11.)

183. **Sar, C.** Le financement des activités de l'O.N.U., 1945-1961. - Biblio-
graphy: p. 257-260. - Ankara, Ankara üniversitesi basimevi, 1963. -
xv, 260 p. - (Ankara. Université. Faculté des sciences politiques.
Publications. no. 169-151.)
"Ouvrage couronné par la Faculté de droit et des sciences économiques de Paris:
Prix Georges Scelle."

184. **Sasse, H.** Der Weltpostverein. - Bibliography: p. 37-46. - Frankfurt am
Main, A. Metzner, 1959. - 126 p. - (Hamburg. Universität. Forschungs-
stelle für Völkerrecht und ausländisches öffentliches Recht. Dokumente.
Hft. 31.)
Text partly German, partly French.

185. **Savage, K.** The story of the United Nations. - Bibliography: p. 185-186. -
London, Bodley head, 1964. - 191 p.

186. **Schachter, O.** The relation of law, politics and action in the United
Nations. - Bibliography: p. 251-252. - (In Academy of international
law, The Hague. Recueil des cours, 1963, II. Leyde (Pays-Bas),
A.W. Sijthoff, 1964. v.109, p. 165-256.)

187. -- --- Toward wider acceptance of UN treaties: a UNITAR study/ by
Oscar Schachter, Mahomed Nawaz and John Fried. - Notes, partly
bibliographical. - New York, Arno press, 1971. - 190 p.
At head of title: United Nations institute for training and research.

188. **Schaeffer, U.** Die Vereinigten Staaten und das Veto in den Vereinten
Nationen. - Bibliography: p. 126-139. - Freiburg i. Br., Rota-Druck:
J. Krause, 1961. - iv, 139 p.
Inaugural-Diss. - Albert-Ludwigs-Univ. zu Freiburg im Breisgau.

189. **Schenkman, J.** International civil aviation organization. - Bibliography:
p. 399-410. - Genève, E. Droz, 1955. - viii, 410 p. - (Études
d'histoire économique, politique et sociale, 14.)

90. **Schermers, H. G.** International institutional law. - v.1- . - Leiden,
A.W. Sijthoff, 1972. - v.
"Selected bibliography on individual international organizations." - p. 270-288.

1191.   **Schwebel, S. M.** The secretary-general of the United Nations; his
         political powers and practice. - Bibliography: p. 279-285. -
         Cambridge, Harvard university press, 1952. - xiv, 299 p.

1192.   **Seavey, W. A.** Dumping since the war: the GATT and national laws. -
         Bibliography: p. 183-197. - Oakland, Calif., Office services co., 1970. -
         x, 219 p.
         Thèse - Univ. de Genève.

1193.   **Semenov, E. K.** ĖKADV: voprosy ėkonomicheskogo razvitiiâ i
         sotrudnichestva molodykh gosudarstv Azii. - Bibliography: p. 164-165. -
         Moskva, Izd-vo "Nauka", 1971. - 165 p.
         At head of title: Akademiiâ nauk SSSR. Institut mirovoĭ ėkonomiki i mezhdunarodnykh
         otnosheniĭ.
         United Nations. Economic commission for Asia and the Far East.

1194.   **Sen, S.** United Nations in economic development: need for a new
         strategy. - Bibliography: p. 345-346. - Dobbs Ferry, N.Y., Oceana
         publications, 1969. - xiv, 351 p.

1195.   **Seniwong, P.** The work of the United Nations' International law
         commission in codifying and developing international law. - Biblio-
         graphy: p. 86-90. - Chicago, Ill., 1956.
         Microfilm copy of typewritten manuscript. Made in 1956 by Library Department of
         photographic reproduction, Univ. of Chicago (Thesis no. 3179). Positive.
         Collation of the original: 90 p.
         Diss. - Univ. of Chicago.

1196.   **Sewell, J. P.** Functionalism and world politics: a study based on
         United Nations programs financing economic development. -
         Bibliography: p. 333-338. - Princeton, N.J., Princeton university
         press, 1966. - xii, 359 p.

1197.   **Seyersted, F.** Objective international personality of intergovernmental
         organizations: do their capacities really depend upon the conventions
         establishing them? - Notes, partly bibliographical. - Copenhagen,
         1963. - 112 p.
         Also pub. as fasc. 1-2 of "Nordisk tidsskrift for international ret og jus gentium", v. 34, 1964

1198.   **Sharp, W. R.** Field administration in the United Nations system; the
         conduct of international economic and social programs. - Notes,
         partly bibliiographical. - New York, F.A. Praeger, 1961. - xiv, 570 p. -
         (Carnegie endowment for international peace. United Nations studies.
         no.10.)
         Books that matter.

1199.   -- --- Implications of expanding membership for United Nations
         administration and budget. - Notes, partly bibliographical: p. 32-34. -
         New York, Carnegie endowment for international peace, 1956. - 31 p.

1200.   **Shibaeva, E. A.** Mezhdunarodnye organizat͡sii v oblasti transporta i
         svi͡azi. - Bibliographical notes. - Moskva, Izd-vo, Instituta mezhdunarod-
         nykh otnosheniĭ, 1960. - 105 p.
         IMCO. ITU. ICAO.

201.   **Shingiro, V.** La coopération régionale en matière industrielle: l'exemple de l'UDEAC et ses leçons. - Bibliographie: l. 144-152. - Genève, 1972. - 152 l.
At head of title: Institut universitaire de hautes études internationales. - The Graduate institute of international studies.
Contents: - ch.1. Le contexte historique de la coopération industrielle dans l'UDEAC. - ch.2. Les dispositions du Traité touchant la coopération industrielle. - ch.3. Impace du marché de l'UDEAC sur l'industrialisation de la région. - ch.4. La réaction de l'investisseur à L'UDEAC et le rôle de l'initiative privée. - ch.5. Appréciation des réalisations et projets à finalité régionale : l'action des gouvernements. - ch.6. La position des Etats moins développés dans l'UDEAC. - ch.7. Leçons d'une integration: en termes d'évaluation; les questions qui restent posées.

202.   **Shippen, K. B.** The pool of knowledge: how the United Nations share their skills. - New and rev. ed. - Bibliography: p. 85-91. - New York, Harper & Row, 1965. - xiv, 99 p.

203.   **Shkunaev, V. G.** Mezhdunarodnaia organizatsiia truda vchera i segodnia. - Bibliography: p. 243-245. - Moskva, izd-vo "Mezhdunarodnye otnosheniia", 1968. - 246 p.
At head of title: Akademiia nauk SSSR. Institut mirovoĭ ėkonomiki i mezhdunarodnykh otnosheniĭ.
History of ILO.

204.   **Shuster, G. N.** UNESCO: assessment and promise. - Bibliography: p. 122-123. - New York, Harper & Row, 1963. - xiv, 130 p.
"Published for the Council on foreign relations."

205.   **Sidjanski, D.** Dimensiones institucionales de la integración latinoamericana: instituciones, proceso de decisión, proyecciones. - Bibliography: p.157-159. - Buenos Aires, Instituto para la integración de América Latina (INTAL), B.I.D., 1967. - 164 p.

206.   **Sierra Nava, J. M.** El Consejo de Europa. - Bibliography: p. 303-310. - Madrid, Instituto de estudios politicos, 1957. - xix, 335 p.

207.   **Singer, J. D.** Financing international organization; the United Nations budget process. - Bibliography: p. 180-182. - The Hague, M. Nijhoff, 1961. - xvi, 185 p.

208.   -- --- The United Nations fiscal process; development and practice. - Bibliography: p. 445-457. - New York, 1955.
Microfilm copy of typewritten manuscript.   Negative.
Collation of the original: iv, 457 p.
Thesis - New York university.

209.   **Singh, J. B.** Domestic jurisdiction and the law of the United Nations. - Bibliography: p. 301-326. - Ann Arbor, Mich., 1954.
Microfilm copy of typewritten manuscript.   Positive.
Collation of the original: iv, 326 p.
Diss. - Univ. of Michigan.

210.   **Siotis, J.** La Commission économique pour l'Europe et la reconstruction du système européen. - Notes, partly bibliographical. - New York, Dotation Carnegie pour la paix internationale, 1967. - 91 p.
"Traduit de l'anglais. L'original a paru dans notre revue 'International conciliation', no.561."

1211.   **Skolnikoff, E. B.**   The international imperatives of technology:
        technological development and the international political system. -
        Bibliography: p. 187-194. - Berkeley, 1972. - ix, 194 p. - (Cali-
        fornia. University. Institute of international studies. Research
        series. no.16.)
        Technological innovations. World politics. International cooperation. Developing countries.
        International agencies.

1212.   **Skubiszewski, K.**   Les organisations régionales. - pt. 1-2. - Biblio-
        graphical notes: pt. 2, l. 68-69. - Strasbourg, 1966. - 2 v. in 1. -
        (Strasbourg. Université. Faculté internationale pour l'enseignement
        du droit comparé. Publications. no. 564-565.)

1213.   **Smouts, M. C.**   Le secrétaire général des Nations Unies: son rôle
        dans la solution des conflits internationaux. - Bibliography: p.283-
        298. - Paris, A. Colin, 1971. - 298 p. - (Fondation nationale des
        sciences politiques. Travaux et recherches de science politique. 16.)
        "Ouvrage publié avec le concours du Centre national de la recherche scientifique."

1214.   **Sobakine, V.**   L'Unesco: problèmes et perspectives. - Bibliographical
        notes. - Moscou, Ed. de l'Agence de presse Novosti, 1972. - 133 p.

1215.   **Società italiana per l'organizzazione internazionale.**   Contributi allo
        studio della organissasione internazionale. - Notes, partly bibliogra-
        phical. - Padova, CEDAM, 1957. - 290 p.

1216.   **Sohn, L. B.**   Basic documents of the United Nations. - 2nd ed. -
        Brooklyn, Foundation press, 1968. - xi, 329 p.

1217.   -- --- Cases and other materials on world law: the interpretation
        and application of the Charter of the United Nations and of the
        constitutions of other agencies of the world community. - Biblio-
        graphy: p. 1-14. - Brooklyn, Foundation press, 1950. - xxii, 1363 p.
        (University casebook series.)

1218.   **Sommer, A.**   Les finances de l'organisation des Nations Unies. -
        Bibliography: p. 7-10. - Zürich, Juris-Verlag, 1951. - 128 p.
        Thèse - Zurich.

1219.   **Sonnenfeld, R.**   Art. 2 Ziff. 7 der UN-Satzung in der Praxis der
        politischen Organe der UN. - Notes, partly bibliographical: p. 30-32. -
        n.p., 1967. - p. 19-32.
        At head of title: Wiss. Z. Univ. Halle, XVI'67 G, H. 1, S. 19-32.

1220.   **Sørensen, M.**   Le Conseil de l'Europe. - Bibliography: p. 198. -
        (In Academy of international law, The Hague. Recueil des cours,
        1952, II. Paris, 1953. v. 81, p. 117-200.)

1221.   -- --- Grundtraek af international organisation. - Bibliography:
        p. 179-180. - København, Munksgaard, 1952. - 184 p.

1222.   **Soto, J. de.**   La Communauté européenne du charbon et de l'acier
        (C.E.C.A.). - Bibliography: 1 p. following p. 124. - Paris, Presses
        universitaires de France, 1958. - 124 p. - ("Que sais-je?" no. 773.)

23. **Speeckaert, G. P.**   Connaissance de la coopération internationale: liste de quelques études documentaires et articles publiés dans la revue "Associations internationales" de 1949 à 1965. - Associations internationales 18:   87-92, no.2, 1966.

24. -- --- International institutions and international organization: a select bibliography/ comp. by G. P. Speeckaert. - Brussels, 1956. - 116 p. - (Fédération internationale de documentation. Publications. no.292.)
Union des associations internationales, Brussels. Publications. no. 151.
"Published with assistance from UNESCO."

25. -- --- Les organismes internationaux et l'organisation internationale: bibliographie sélective/ établie par G. P. Speeckaert. - Bruxelles, 1956. - 116 p. - (Fédération internationale de documentation. Publications. no.290.)
Union des associations internationales, Brussels. Publications. no. 150.
"Publiée avec l'aide de l'UNESCO."

26. **Spefsializirovannye** uchrezhdeniiâ OON v sovremennom mire. - Biblio-graphical notes. - Moskva, Izd-vo, "Nauka", 1967. - 401 p.
Half-title: Akademiiâ nauk SSSR.   Institut mirovoĭ ekonomiki i mezhdunarodnykh otnosheniĭ.

27. **Stege, W.**   Die Wirkungsmöglichkeit der Internationalen Organisation der Arbeit (Teildruck). - Bibliographical notes. - Berlin, E. Ebering, 192 . - 42 p.
Inaug.-Diss. - Berlin.

28. **Steinberger, H.**   GATT und regionale Wirtschaftszusammenschlüsse; eine Untersuchung der Rechtsgrundsätze des Allgemeinen Zoll- und Handelsabkommens vom 30. Oktober, 1947 (GATT) über die Bildung regionaler Wirtschaftszusammenschlüsse. - Bibliography: p. 229-248. - Köln, C. Heymann, 1963. - xv, 248 p. - (Max-Planck-Institut für ausländisches öffentliches Recht und Völkerrecht. Beiträge zum ausländischen öffentlichen Recht und Völkerrecht. 41.)

29. **Stelzl, D.**   Entwicklung und Problematik der Verrechnungsbeziehungen zwischen den Mitgliedsländern des COMECON. - Bibliography: 52 p. at end. - München, 1971. - 1 v.
Inaugural-Diss. - Ludwig-Maximilians-Univ. zu München.
Clearing - Europe, Eastern.   Clearing - Communist countries.   Sovet ekonomicheskoi vzaimopomoshchi - Clearing.   Europe, Eastern - Commerce.

30. **Stepanenko, S. I.**   Organizatsiiâ sotrudnichestva stran-chlenov SĖV v oblasti standartizatsii. - Bibliography: p. 96-98. - Moskva, Izd-vo Komiteta standartov, mer i izmeritel'nykh priborov pri Sovete ministrov SSSR, 1968. - 98 p.
CMEA and standardization.

31. **Stoessinger, J. G.**   Financing the United Nations system/ by John G. Stoessinger with the collaboration of Gabriella Rosner Lande... and others. - Bibliography: p. 327-332. - Washington, D.C., Brookings institution, 1964. - 348 p.

K

1232. **Stoetzer, O. C.** The Organization of American states; an introduction. - Bibliography: p. 211-213. - New York, F.A. Praeger, 1965. - viii, 213 p.
"The German-language edition of this work, 'Panamerika: Idee und Wirklichkeit; die Organisation der amerikanischen Staaten' was published in 1964."

1233. **Stošić, B.** Les organisations non gouvernementales et les Nations Unies. Bibliography: p. 319-328. - Genève, E. Droz, 1964. - 367 p.
Thèse - Univ. de Genève.

1234. **Strasbourg. Université. Faculté internationale pour l'enseignement du droit comparé.** Les organisations régionales internationales: recueil de cours. - fasc. 1-2. - Bibliographies at the end of some chapters. - Paris, Éd., Montchrestien, 1971. - 2 v.

1235. **Summer institute on international and comparative law, University of Michigan, 1955.** International law and the United Nations. - Bibliographical notes: p. 403-404, 462-468, 504-511. - Ann Arbor, Mich., Univ. of Michigan, Law school, 1957. - 566 p.
"Published under the auspices of the University of Michigan Law school."

1236. **Symonds, R.** The United Nations and the population question, 1945-1970/ by Richard Symonds and Michael Carder. - Includes bibliographies. - London, Sussex university press, 1973. xviii, 236 p.

1237. **Szalai, A.** The United Nations and the news media: a survey of public information on the United Nations in the world press, radio and television/ by Alexander Szalai with Margaret Croke and associates. - Bibliography: p. 285-309. - New York, UNITAR, 1972. - vi, 323 p.

1238. **Szapiro, J.** Nations Unies et institutions spécialisées; guide à l'intention des journalistes. - Bibliographies at the end of some chapters. - Paris, UNESCO, 1962. - 255 p.

1239. **Szasz, P. C.** The law and practices of the International atomic energy agency. - Bibliography: p. 1141-1146. - Vienna, 1970. - 1176 p. - (International atomic energy agency. Legal series. no.7.)

1240. **Taguaba, L.** L'Association des états de l'Afrique de l'est à la Communauté économique européenne. - Bibliography: l. 294-307. - Paris, 1970. 317 l.
Thèse - Univ. de Paris.

1241. **Tammes, A. J. P.** Hoofdstukken van internationale organisatie. - Bibliographical notes. - s'Gravenhage, M. Nijhoff, 1951- . - v.

1242. **Teich, G.** Der Rat für Gegenseitige Wirtschaftshilfe, 1949-1963; fünfzehn Jahre wirtschaftliche Integration im Ostblock; Bibliographie. - Kiel, 1966. - v, 445 p. - (Kieler Schrifttumskunden zu Wirtschaft und Gesellschaft; Arbeiten der Bibliothek des Instituts für Weltwirtschaft. Bd. 14.)

1243. **Tew, B.** The International monetary fund: its present role and future prospects. - Notes, partly bibliographical. - Princeton, N.J., 1961. - 41 p. - (Princeton university. International finance section. Essays in international finance. no.36.)

44. **Thomas, A. (Van Wynen).** The Organisation of American states/ by Ann Van Wynen Thomas and A. J. Thomas. - Notes, partly bibliographical: p. 435-504. - Dallas, Southern Methodist university press, 1963. - xii, 530 p.
"Law institute of the Americas study."
"Published with the assistance of a grant from the Southwestern legal foundation."

45. **Thomas, J.** U.N.E.S.C.O. - Bibliographical notes. - Paris, Gallimard, 1962. - 266 p. - (Problèmes et documents.)

46. **Tinbergen, J.** Towards a better international economic order. - Bibliography: p. 27-28. - New York, 1971. - 28 p. - (United Nations institute for training and research. UNITAR lecture series. no. 2.)
"A special lecture sponsored by UNITAR and given at U.N. Headquarters, New York, on 27 May, 1970..."

47. **Tobiassen, L. K.** The reluctant door: the right of access to the United Nations. - Bibliographical notes at the end of each chapter. - Washington, D.C., Public affairs press, 1969. - vi, 413 p.

48. **Tomasini, L.** Le rôle du Conseil de sécurité dans le maintien de la paix. - Bibliography: p. i-vii. - Dijon, 1952.
Microfilm copy of typewritten manuscript. Negative.
Collation of the original: 188, ix p.
Thèse - Univ. de Dijon.

49. **Tonts, R. L.** Foreign agricultural trade; selected readings/ Edited by Robert L. Tontz. - Ames, Iowa State university press, 1966. - xx, 500 p.

50. **Toward** a better world for children: the rising generation and its stake in world development. - Suggested reading for teachers. Suggested reading for students: p. 60-61. - Dobbs Ferry, N.Y., Oceana publications, Inc., 1963. - 61 p.
This series is designed for use in libraries and by teachers, group leaders and students.

51. **Toward** mankind's better health: the WHO and the UNICEF. - Bibliography: p. 102-103. - Dobbs Ferry, N.Y., Oceana publications, 1963. - 103 p. - (The Oceana library on the United Nations. Study guide series. v.3.)
"Assembled by the UNESCO Youth institute under the auspices of UNESCO."

52. **Ubertazzi, G. M.** Contributo alla teoria della conciliazione delle controversie internazionali davanti al Consiglio di sicurezza. - Notes, partly bibliographical. - Milano, A. Giuffrè, 1958. - vii, 143 p. - (Studi di diritto internazionale. 23.)

53. **Ul'ianova, N. N.** Mezhdunarodnye demokraticheskie organizaĩsii. - Bibliographical notes. - Kiev, 1956. - 208 p.
At head of title: Akademia nauk Ukrainskoĭ SSR. Sektor gosudarstva i prava.
International agencies.

1254.   **Union des associations internationales, Brussels.** The 1,978 (one thousan
         nine hundred and seventy eight) international organizations founded
         since the Congress of Vienna; chronological list. - Brussels, Union of
         international associations, 1957. - xxviii, 204 p. - (Its: Documents.
         no.7.) E F

1255.   -- - - - Petit répertoire des organisations internationales. - Bruxelles,
         1965. - 160 p. - (Its: Publications. no.194.)

1256.   **Union internationale des télécommunications.** Del semáforo al
         satélite. - Bibliography: p. 343. - Ginebra, Unión internacional de
         telecomunicaciones, 1965. - 343 p.
         "Se publica este libro en ocasión del centenario de la Unión internacional de tele-
         comunicaciones."

1257.   **Union of Soviet Socialist Republics. Komissiiā po delam IUNESKO.**
         IUNESKO i sovremennost': k 20-letiiu IUNESKO. - Pod red. S.K.
         Romanovskogo... i dr. - Bibliographical notes. - Moskva, Izd-vo
         "Mezhdunarodnye otnosheniiā", 1966. - 285 p.
         At head of title: Komissiiā SSSR po delam IUNESKO.

1258.   **Union postale universelle.** Echanges d'information - études
         techniques: catalogue général des informations de toute nature
         concernant le service postal et des documents disponibles pour
         le service de prêt. - Berne, 1949. - 1 v.

1259.   -- - - - Guide to technical cooperation: United Nations technical
         cooperation programmes. - Bibliography: 1 p. following p. 11. -
         Berne, 1949. - 12 p.
         Original ed. pub. under title: Guide concernant la coopération technique.

1260.   **United** Nations. Editor, John D. Balcomb. Contributing editor,
         Anita R. Horwich. - Bibliographies at the end of some chapters. -
         New York, Worldmark press, 1967. - xxvi, 278 p. - (Worldmark
         encyclopedia of the nations. v.1.)

1261.   **United Nations.** Catalogue of economic and social projects;
         annotated list of work planned, in progress or completed by
         United Nations and specialized agencies. - no.1-   . - Lake
         Success, N.Y., 1949-   .   v.
         "Replaces the Directory of economic and statistical projects."

1262.   -- - - - Preparatory study concerning a draft declaration on the rights
         and duties of States: memorandum submitted by the Secretary-gener
         Bibliography: p. 133-138. - Lake Success, United Nations, General a
         sembly, International law commission, 1948.   - vi, 228 p. - (United
         Nations. Documents. A/CN.4/2. 15 Dec. 1948.)
         United Nations. Publications. Sales numbers. 1949.V.4.

1263.   -- - - - A study of the capacity of the United Nations development
         system. - v.1-2. - Bibliography: p. 483-485 (v.2). - Geneva, 1969. -
         2 v. - (Its: Publications. Sales numbers. 1970.I.10.)   E F R S
         United Nations. Documents. DP/5.

United Nations (Cont'd)

54. -- --- Treaty series, treaties and international agreements registered or filed and recorded with the Secretariat of the United Nations: cumulative index. - no.1-8; v.1-600. - New York, 1946/47-1971.

55. -- --- Ways and means of making the evidence of customary international law more readily available: preparatory work within the purview of article 24 of the statute of the International law commission, memorandum submitted by the Secretary-general. - Lake Success, United Nations, General assembly, International law commission, 1949. - v, 114 p. - (United Nations. Documents. A/CN.4/6.)
United Nations. Publications. Sales numbers. 1949.V.6.
"Corrigendum. A/CN.4/6/Corr.1.": leaf inserted.

66. -- **Commission on international trade law. (UNCITRAL).** Bibliography on arbitration law=Bibliographie concernant la legislation relative à l'arbitrage=Bibliografiia po arbitrazhnomu pravu=Bibliografía relative a la legislación sobre arbitraje. - New York, 1969. - (A/CN.9/24/Add.1.)

67. -- --- Bibliography on international trade law: report of the Secretary-general. - Geneva, 1971. - 4 p. - (United Nations. Documents. A/CN.9/L.20.). E F
At head of title: United Nations. General assembly. United Nations Commission on international trade law. 4th session, Geneva, 29 March 1971. Item 9 of the provisional agenda.
Addendum: Survey of bibliographies relating to international trade law. 1. General legal bibliographies. 2. National legal bibliographies. 19 p. (A/CN.9/L.20/Add.1.) E F

68. -- **Commission on narcotic drugs.** The question of cannabis: cannabis bibliography. - New York, 1965. - 250 p. - (Its: Documents. E/CN.7/479.)
At head of title: United Nations. Economic and social council. Commission on narcotic drugs. 20th session. Item 8 of the provisional agenda.
Prepared by Nathan B. Eddy.
An index by subject has been included at the end to facilitate the use of the bibliography.

69. -- **Dag Hammarskjold library, New York.** Apartheid: a selective bibliography on the racial policies of the Government of the Republic of South Africa. - 52 p. - (ST/LIB/22.)

70. -- --- Bibliographical series. - no.1-12. - New York, 1949-1969.
Contents:

1.	Selected bibliography of the specialized agencies related to the United Nations	49.I.16
2.	Latin America, 1939-1949. A selected bibliography.	52.I.12
3.	A bibliography of the Charter of the United Nations.	55.I. 7
4.	Index to microfilm of UN documents in English, 1946-1950.	55.I.24
5/Rev.2	List of United Nations document series symbols	E.70.I.21
6.	Bibliography on industrialization in under-developed countries	56.II.B.2
7.	List of periodicals and newspapers currently received. Mar. 1957	- -
8.	Bibliographical style manual.	63.I.5
9.	Economic and social development plans. Africa, Asia and Latin America. Jun. 1964.	64.I.16
10.	Government Gazettes. An annotated list.	64.I.24
11.	Economic and social development plans. Centrally-planned economies; developed market economies. Mar. 1966.	66.I.10.
12.	Disarmament: a select bibliography, 1962-1967.	E.68.I.10.

United Nations.   Dag Hammarskjold library.   New York.   (Cont'd)

1271.   -- --- Legal bibliography of the United Nations and related
            intergovernmental organizations. - In: United Nations juridical
            yearbook, 1969, p. 283-311. - (ST/LEG/SER.C/7.)
            Sales no. 1971.V.4.

1272.   -- --- Miscellaneous bibliographies.
            Contents:
            1.   Division of social activities. Technical reference and documentation
                 section.   Acquisition list 9.   1949.
            2.   Selected bibliography of the Caribbean commission, June 1950.
            3.   Transjordan: a bibliography from 1922-   .
            4.   Publications of the Headquarters library, 1949.
            5.   Department of public information.   Division of library services.
                 Selected list of periodical articles, June through December 1948.
            6.   Bibliography on social welfare... 1949.
            7.   A selected bibliography on the theory and future of trusteeship and
                 non-self-governing territories.   1949.
            8.   Selected bibliography on the development of education in trust and
                 non-self-governing territories.   Suppl. no.1.   1949.
            9.   Public finance and related matters: selected list of publications to be
                 found in the United Nations central library.   1949.
            10. Selected list of references to the legal relations between the Union of
                 South Africa   and the mandated territory of South West Africa as
                 contained in the records of the Permanent mandates commission, the
                 Council and the Assembly of the League of Nations.   1949.
            11. A selected bibliography of directories and lists of international
                 organizations and conferences, issued 1945 to date.   1950.
            12. Abstracting and indexing services in scientific and technical subjects:
                 a select list.   1951.
            13. Administrative tribunals; a tentative list of references.   1951.
            14. World peace congress and related movements; 1948 to date.   1951.
            15. A select bibliography of directories and lists of international
                 organizations and conferences issued 1945 to date.   1st supplement,
                 July 1951.
            16. Catalogue of the library of the Legal department.   1950.
            17. Catalogue of the library of the Department of social affairs.   1950.
            18. Acquisition unit.   List of periodicals and newspapers currently received,
                 Oct.   1950.
            19. Saudi Arabia; a select bibliography, chiefly concerned with economic
                 and social conditions.   1951.
            20. Servicios de indices y extractos sobre asuntos cientificos y tecnicos; lista
                 seleccionada.   1951.
            21. Selected bibliography on the development of education in trust and
                 non-self-governing territories.   Sept.   1949.
            22. A select bibliography on the admission of members to the United
                 Nations.   Dec.   1951.
            23. A selection of material on the trust territories in the Pacific area.
                 January 30th, 1952.
            24. Multilateral international agreements of 1951; provisional list. March 1952.
            25. Tunisia; a selected bibliography.   3 March 1952.
            26. The League of Arab states; a bibliography.   April 18, 1952.
            27. Professional conduct of civil servants; a selected bibliography.   April 1952.
            28. Selected references on the Schuman plan.   1952.
            29. Selected references on public administration in Latin America.   1952.
            30. Repatriation of prisoners of war on the cessation of hostilities;
                 selected references.   1952.
            31. Full employment; selected references.   1953.
            32. Commercial relations between Canada, the United Kingdom and the
                 United States; selected references.   1953.
            33. Reference books recommended to United Nations information
                 centres.   List no.4.   1953.
            34. Selected list of teaching materials; popular and juvenile books and
                 pamphlets on the United Nations.   1953.
            35. Selected references on the question of defining aggression.   1953.
            36. Reference books recommended to United Nations information centres.
                 (Superseding list no.4. of 1 July 1953)   1954.
            37. Irrigation in the Jordan Valley region, with references to some other areas;
                 a selected bibliography.   1954.

United Nations. Dag Hammarskjold library. New York.
Miscellaneous bibliographies.
(cont'd)

38. Reference books recommended to United Nations information centres.
    1954. (List no.6.)
39. Representation of China in the United Nations; selected references. 1954.
40. Reference books recommended to United Nations information centres.
    1955. (List no.7.)
41. Antarctica; a selected bibliography. 1956.
42. Administrative tribunals; a supplementary list of references. 1956.
43. Jammu and Kashmir; a bibliography. 1957.
44. Annotated list of official gazettes in the U.N. headquarters library. 1959.
45. A bibliography of the law of outer space. 1958.
46. Africa: a list of books suggested for the Congo mission. 1960.
47. Selective bibliography on the law relating to the utilization and use of
    international rivers (excluding navigation). 1963.
48. Apartheid; a selective bibliography on the racial policies of the government
    of South Africa (since June 1962).
49. Angola; a bibliography. 1963.
50. Bibliography on consular relations. 1963.

1273. -- --- Occasional reading list. - New York, 1969-   .
Contents:
2. Regime of the sea and the sea-bed: a bibliography.
3. People's Republic of China and the United Nations membership.

1274. -- --- Reference aid. - New York, 1971-   .   v.
Contents:
1. Environmental law: a partial list of national and international legislation.
2. Organ transplantation; a partial list of national legislation.
3. The diplomatic recognition of China.
4. The diplomatic recognition of the divided countries.

1275. -- --- Selected bibliography. - In: Consideration of principles of
international law concerning friendly relations and cooperation
among States in accordance with the Charter of the United
Nations, New York, 1964, p. 69-84, 157-165, 203-209, 236-240. -
(A/C/L.537/Rev.1.)

1276. -- --- Statutes and subsidiary legislation: a selected source
list of collections, bibliographies and other aids. - New York,
1969. - 76 p. - (United Nations. Documents. ST/LIB/24.)

1277. -- **Department of economic affairs.** Classified list of publications
and documents on the post-war economic situation in European
countries. - New York, 1947. - 1 v.

1278. -- --- Directory of economic and statistical projects: a
classified list of work completed in progress or planned by
United Nations and specialized agencies. - no.1. - Lake Success,
1958. - vi, 130 p.
"United Nations. Publications. Sales no. 1948.II.D.1."
Replaced by Catalogue of economic and social projects, issued by the Department of
economic affairs and the Department of social affairs (later by Economic and social
council.)

1279. -- --- List of multilateral conventions, agreements, etc., relating
to transport and communications questions. - Lake Success,
1948. - 92 p.
"United Nations publications. Sales no.: 1948.VIII.1."

1280.   -- **Department of public information.** Helping economic development
in Asia and the Far East; the work of ECAFE. - Bibliography:
p. 20-22. - New York, 1954. - 22 p.
"United Nations publications. 1953.I.40."

1281.   -- **Department of public information. Library services.** Selected
bibliography of the specialized agencies related to the United
Nations. - Lake Success, Library services, Dept. of public
information, 1949. - 28 p. - (United Nations. Library.
Bibliographical series, no.1.).
"United Nations publications. Sales no.: 1949.I.16."

1282.   -- **Department of social questions.** Liste des publications sur l'éducation
politique des femmes reçues par le Secrétariat des Nations Unies. - In:
Its: Éducation politique des femmes. New York, 1951. p. 21-39.

1283.   -- **Development programme.** An index to information sources at
UNDP Headquarters. - New York, Management information service
((MIS), Bureau for policy planning, 1971. - 17 p. - (Its: Documents.
DP/AI/123)
This document describes some 100 sources of information relating to current operations of
the United Nations Development programme. An A-to-Z index, it is designed to help
Headquarters personnel locate basic source material. - Chapter IV, B.

1284.   -- --- **Fund of the United Nations for the development of West Irian.**
The role of forest-based industries in the economic and social
development of West Irian. - Bibliography: p. 172-173. - New York,
1968. - 173 p. - (Its: Documents. UN/DP/FUNDWI/2.)

1285.   -- **Division for public administration. Information and reference
unit.** Reference list of United Nations documents related to
public administration and public finance administration.
- New York, 1961. - 28 p.   .

1286.   -- **Economic commission for Africa. Library.** Bibliography: economic
and social development plans of African countries=Bibliographies: plans
de développement économique et social des pays africains. - Addis-
Ababa, 1968. - 40 p. - (Its: Publications. E/CN.14/LIB/SER.C/4.)

1287.   -- --- Bibliography of African statistical publications, 1950-1965=
Bibliographie des publications statistiques africaines. - Addis-Ababa,
1966. - 256 p. - (Its: Documents. E/CN.14/LIB/SER.C/2.)

1288.   -- --- Bibliography of African statistical publications=Bibliographie
des publications statistiques africaines. - Addis Ababa, 1971.
- 19 p. - (United Nations. Documents. E/CN.13/LIB/SER.C/
2/Add.1.)

1289.   -- --- Selected bibliography: manpower and training problems
in economic and social development=Choix de bibliographie:
problèmes de main-d'œuvre et de formation dans le
développement économique et social. - New York, 1967.
- (E/CN.14/LIB/SER.C/3.)

1290.   -- --- Selected subject bibliography: model schemes of small scale
industries. - Addis-Ababa, 1969. - 67 p. - (Its: Documents.
E/CN.14/LIB/SER.C/5.)

291.   **United Nations. Economic commission for Africa. Library.**   Africa
       index: selected articles on socio-economic development=Catalogue
       Afrique: articles choisis sur le développement économique et
       social. - no.1-   ; 1971-   . - Addis Ababa, 1971-   . -   v. -
       (Its: Documents. E/CN.14/LIB/SER.E/1, etc.)
       Pub. quarterly.
       Title and text in English and French.

292.   - -   **Economic commission for Asia and the Far East.**   Family
       planning, internal migration and urbanization in ECAFE
       countries: a bibliography of available materials. - New York,
       1968. - (Its: Asian population studies series. no.2.)
       Contents:
       pt.1. Family planning. pt.2. Internal migration and urbanization.

293.   - - - - -   Fertility studies in the ECAFE region: a bibliography of
       books, papers, and reference materials. - New York, 1971.
       - v, 54 p. - (Its: Asian population studies series. no.6.)
       United Nations. Publications. Sales numbers. 1972.II.F.3.
       United Nations. Documents. E/CN.11/992.

294.   - - - - -   A selected bibliography on economic planning in Asia
       and the Far East, 1952-58. - Bangkok, 1959. - 60 p.

295.   - - - - -   **Library.**   Asian bibliography. - v.1-   ;   1952-   .
       - Bangkok, 1952-   . -   v.
       Pub. semi-annually.

296.   - -   **Economic commission for Europe.**   Bibliographical index
       of works published on hydro-electric plant construction=Index
       bibliographique des ouvrages publiés au sujet de la construction
       d'installations hydro-électriques=Bibliograficheskiĭ ukazatel'
       trudov, opublikovannykh v oblasti gidroènergeticheskogo
       stroitel'stva. - Geneva, United Nations, 1957-   . - v.
       - (United Nations. Document. E/ECE/295, E/ECE/EP/188).
       "United Nations publication. Sales number: 1957.II.E/Mim.24."

297.   - - - - -   **Technical assistance office.**   Selected training courses
       specially designed for developing countries=Liste de cours
       sélectionnés conçus spécialement à l'intention des pays en voie
       de développement. - 8th ed. - Geneva, 1972. - xii, 294 p. -
       (Its: Documents. MTAO/1/72.)   E F
       Public administration. Economic development, planning and statistics. Economic development,
       finance, banking, taxation, insurance. Economic development, tourism and hotel management.
       Housing, building, physical planning and environment. Industrial development. Natural resources
       and energy. Social development. Trade and customs. Transport and communications.

298.   - -   **European office. Bureau des affaires sociales.**   Service de prêt de
       films relatifs au service social: catalogue général. - Genève, 1962. -
       210 p. - (Its: Documents. SOA/FILM/62.)
       At head of title: Programme européen de service social.
       Comment utiliser le catalogue. Utilisation des films documentaires traitant de questions
       sociales. Instructions à l'intention des organisations qui désirent emprunter des films. Index
       méthodique. Notices descriptives des films du service de prêt. Index alphabetique des films.

299.   - -   **General assembly. Special committee for the review of the United
       Nations salary system.**   List of documents. - In: Its: Report. v.1,
       p. 230-244. - (United Nations. General assembly. 27th session, New
       York, 1972. Official records. Suppl. no. 28.)
       United Nations. Documents. A/8728.

1300.   **United Nations. Information office, New York.** Guide to United Nations and allied agencies, April 1945. - Bibliography at the end of each article. - New York, 1945. - 1 v.
"Revised edition of a survey of... agencies originally issued in April 1945... It is limited to agencies set up as a direct outcome of the war."

1301.   - - **Latin American centre for economic and social documentation.** Bibliografia analitica de la Comisión especial de coordinación latinoamericana (CECLA); documentos básicos y resoluciones hasta marzo de 1972. - Santiago de Chile, 1972. - ii, 65 p. - (Its: Colección: Bibliografias. v.1, no.1.)
UN Economic and social council. Documents. CLADES/BBG/5.
Elaboración electrónica. - Chapter IV, B.

1302.   - - **Library, Geneva.** Listes de références=Reference lists. - no.1-4. - Geneva, 1970-1972. - 4v.
Contents:
1.   East-West trade: a selective bibliography. 1970.
2.   International law commission; a guide to the documents, 1949-1969.
3.   List of seminars, study groups, expert groups, symposia and workshops held under the UN auspices, 1946-69
4.   Science policy in ECE countries; a selective bibliography. 1971.

1303.   - - **Library, Geneva. Processing section.** Legal aspects of C.M.E.A.: selective bibliography. - Geneva, 1970. - 1 v.
Supplements. no.1-2.

1304.   - - **Library, New York.** A select bibliography of directories and lists of international organizations and conferences. - Issued 1945 to date. Lake Success, N.Y., 1950. - 7 l. - (Its: Miscellaneous bibliographies. no. 11.)
Supplement 1st-   : 1951-   .   v.

1305.   - - **Office of public information.** The work of the International law commission. - Bibliography: p. 240-243. - New York, 1972. - viii, 243 p. - (United Nations. Publications. Sales numbers. 1972.I.17.)

1306.   - - **Secretary-general, 1961-1971 (Thant).** The external financing of economic development: international flow of long-term capital and official donations. - 1964/68-   . - Notes, partly bibliographical. - New York, 1970-   . - v. - (United Nations. Publications. Sales numbers. 1970.II.A.3.)
United Nations. Documents. E/4815, etc.
At head of title: Department of economic and social affairs.

1307.   - - **Secretary-general, 1972-   (Waldheim).** Participation of women in community development: report. - Notes, partly bibliographical. - New York, 1972. - iv, 68 p. - (United Nations. Publications. Sales numbers. 1972.IV.8.)
United Nations. Documents. E/CN.6/514/Rev.1.
At head of title: Commission on the status of women.

1308.   - - **Social reference centre.** Bibliography of publications of the United Nations and specialized agencies in the social welfare field, 1946-1952. - New York, Department of economic and social affairs, 1955. - 270 p. - (ST/SOA/SER.F /10:3)

309. **United Nations. Statistical commission.** Methodological problems of international comparison of levels of labour productivity in industry. - Bibliography: p. 1-2. (at end). - New York, 1971. - iii, 99, 2 p. - (Conference of European statisticians. Statistical standards and studies. no.21.)
United Nations. Publications. Sales numbers. 1971.II.E/Mim.3.
United Nations. Documents. ST/CES/21.
At head of title: United Nations. Statistical commission and Economic commission for Europe.

310. -- **Statistical office.** Bibliography of industrial and distributive trade statistics. - New York, United Nations, 1962. - 58 p. - (Its: Statistical papers. ser.M.no.36.)
United Nations. Documents. ST/STAT/ser.M/36.
"United Nations publication. Sales no.:62.XVII.5."

311. -- --- Bibliography of inquiries and selected statistical series, industrial and distributive units. - New York, 1960. - 64 p. - (Its: Documents. ST/STAT/6.1960.)

312. -- --- Concepts and definitions of capital formation. - Bibliography: p. 20. - New York, 1953. - 20 p. - (Its: Statistical papers. ser.F, no.3.)
United Nations. Documents. ST/STAT/ser.F/3.
United Nations. Publications. Sales numbers. 1953.XVII.6.

313. -- --- Handbook of statistical organization. - Bibliography: p. 125-138. - New York, 1954. - iii, 138 p. - (Its: Studies in methods. ser.F, no.6.)
United Nations. Documents. ST/STAT/ser.F/6.
"United Nations publication. Sales no.: 1954.XVII.7."

314. -- --- Input-output bibliography, 1963-1966. - New York, 1967. - vii, 259 p. - (United Nations. Publications. Sales numbers. 1967.XVII.19.)
Its: Statistical papers. Series M. no.46.

315. -- --- Input-output bibliography, 1966-1970. v.1-3. - New York, 1972. - 3 v. - (Its: Statistical papers. Series M, no.55, v.1-3.)
United Nations. Publications. Sales numbers. 1972.XVII.6, etc.
United Nations. Documents. ST/STAT/SER.M/55, v.1-3.

316. **United Nations association of the United States of America.** Read your way to world understanding: a selected annotated reading guide of books about the United Nations and the world in which it works for peace and human welfare. - New York, Scarecrow press, 1963. - 320 p.

317. **United Nations conference on the law of treaties.** Selected bibliography on the law of treaties=Bibliographie d'ouvrages choisis sur le droit des traités=Bibliografía seleccionada sobre el derecho de los tratados. - New York, 1968. - (A/CONF.39/4.)

318. **United Nations conference on trade and development.** Analysis of resolutions adopted at UNCTAD III. - Geneva, 1972. - 32 p. - (Its: Documents. UNCTAD/CA/229.) E F R S
Information structure: 1. Reference. 2. Title of resolution. 3. Contents. 4. Voting.
5. Action by UNCTAD permanent machinery and/or the secretariat. 6. Action by other UN bodies. 7. Action by governments, GATT, etc.

1319.   **United Nations conference on trade and development. ECE/UNCTAD reference unit.**   Third United Nations conference on trade and development (UNCTAD III):   publications for consultation in the UNCTAD reference room in Santiago. - Geneva, 1972. - (UNCTAD III/REF. no.1 and Add.1.)

1320.   **United** Nations documents concerning development and codification of international law. - Bibliographical notes. - Lancaster, Pa., Lancaster press, 1947. - p. 29-148.
"Supplement to American journal of international law, volume 41, no.4, October, 1947."

1321.   **United Nations educational, scientific and cultural organisation.**   The activities of Unesco in science and technology. - Bibliography: p. 21-22. - Paris, 1964. - 23 p.
"A Unesco information manual."

1322.   -- --- Bibliographies in the social sciences: a selected inventory of periodical publications. - Paris, 1951. - 129 p. - (Its: Publications. no.798.)

1323.   -- --- **Bibliographie hydrologique africaine**=Bibliography of African hydrology. - Paris, 1963. - 166 p. - (Its: Recherches sur les ressources naturelles. no.2.)

1324.   -- --- Bibliography of interlingual scientific and technical dictionaries=Bibliographie de dictionnaires scientifiques et techniques multilingues=Bibliografia de diccionarios cientificos y técnicos plurilingües. - 5th ed. - Paris, Unesco, 1969. - 250 p. - (Its: Documentation and terminology of science. no. 11.)
Title, introductory material and headings in English, French and Spanish.

1325.   -- --- Bibliography of monolingual scientific and technical glossaries=Bibliographie de vocabulaires scientifiques et techniques monolingues.../ by Eugen Wüster. - v.1-2. - Paris, 1955-59. - 1 v. - (Its: Documentation and terminology of science. no.2.).

1326.   -- --- Bibliography of publications designed to raise the standard of scientific literature. - Paris, 1963. - 83 p. - (Its: Documentation and terminology of science. no.7.)

1327.   -- --- Catalogue de films d'intérêt archéologique, ethnographique ou historique. - Paris, Unesco, 1970. - 546 p.

1328.   -- --- Catalogue de reproductions en couleurs de peintures=Catalogue of colour reproductions of paintings=Catálogo de reproducciones en color de pinturas.   1860/1949-   . - Paris, 1949-   . -   v.

1329.   -- --- Catalogue sélectif international de films ethnographiques sur la région du Pacifique. - 1er-   . - Paris, Unesco, 1970-   . -   v.

1330. **United Nations educational, scientific and cultural organisation.**
Current official publications containing statistics relating to
education. - Paris, 1961. - 28 p. - (Its: Publications. UNESCO/ST/
R/21.)

1331. -- --- Current official publications containing statistics
relating to education. - Paris, 1961. - 28 p. - (Its: Publications.
UNESCO/ST/R/21.)

1332. -- --- Index of cultural agreements=Index des accords
culturels=Indice de los acuerdos culturales. - Paris, UNESCO,
1962. - 267 p. E/F/S.

1333. -- --- An international bibliography of technical and vocational
education. - Paris, 1959. - 72 p. - (Its: Educational studies
and documents, no.31.)

1334. -- --- International guide to educational documentation.
- 1955/60- . - Paris, UNESCO, 1963- . - v.

1335. -- --- Liste mondiale des périodiques spécialisés dans les sciences
sociales=World list of social science periodicals. - Paris, 1953.
- 161 p. - (Its: Documentation dans les sciences sociales.)

1336. -- --- Liste mondiale des périodiques spécialisés dans les sciences
sociales=World list of social science periodicals. - 3rd ed., rev. and
enl. - Paris, 1966. - 448 p. - (Documentation dans les sciences
sociales=Documentation in the social sciences.)
"Préparé par le Comité international pour la documentation des sciences sociales."

1337. -- --- Literacy: 1967-1969; progress achieved in literacy throughout
the world. - Laws and decrees concerning literacy which have been
adopted since September 1967: p. 110-112. - International conferences
and meetings on literacy, 1968-1969: p. 112-113. - Paris, 1970. 113 p.

1338. -- --- Monthly bulletin on scientific documentation and
terminology. May 1952-Nov./Dec. 1960. - Paris, 1952-1960.
- 9 v.

1339. -- --- New trends in integrated science teaching=Tendences nouvelles
de l'intégration des enseignements scientifiques. - v.1- ; 1969/70-
. - Includes bibliographies. - Paris, Unesco, 1971- . - v. -
(Its: The teaching of basic. L'enseignement des sciences fondamentales.
no.6.)

1340. -- --- Teaching agriculture: a selected bibliography/ prepared
by the United Nations educational, scientific and cultural
organisation (Unesco) and the Food and agriculture organisation (FAO). - Paris, Education clearing house, United Nations
educational, scientific and cultural organisation, 1952. - 52 p.

1341. -- **Department of mass communication. Clearing house.**
Tentative international bibliography of works dealing with
press problems (1900-1952). - Paris, 1954. - 96 p.
- (Its: Reports and papers on mass communication. no.13.)

1342.   **United Nations educational, scientific and cultural organisation. Director general.** Long-term outline plan for 1971-1976. - Notes, partly bibliographical. - Paris, Unesco, 1970. - 80 p. E F R S
At head of title: General conference. Sixteenth session, Paris, 1970.

1343.   -- **Education clearing house.** Education for community development: a selected bibliography/ prepared by UNESCO and United Nations, Division of social affairs. - Paris, 1954. - 49 p. - (Its: Educational studies and documents, 7.)

1344.   -- --- Literacy education: a selected bibliography. - Paris, 1950. - 43 p. - (Its: Occasional papers in education.5.)

1345.   -- --- Literacy teaching: a selected bibliography. - Paris, UNESCO, 1956. - 48 p. - (Its: Educational studies and documents. no.18.)

1346.   -- **Field science cooperation office, Middle East.** Middle East social science bibliography; books and articles on social sciences published in Arab countries of the Middle East in 1955-1960. - Cairo, Unesco, Middle East science cooperation office, 1961. - iv, 152 p.
Title on cover: Social science bibliography; Arab countries of the Middle East, 1955-1960.

1347.   -- **Research centre on the social implications of industrialization in Southern Asia.** Southern Asia social science bibliography (with annotations and abstracts). no.8-   ; 1959-   .
- Calcutta, 1960-   . - v.
Published annually.
Superseded: 1959, Its: South Asia social science bibliography, and Its: South Asia social science abstracts.
Issued by: no.9-   , UNESCO. Research centre on social and economic development in Southern Asia.

1348.   -- **Social science clearing house.** International organizations in the social sciences; a summary description of the structure and activities of non-governmental organizations in consultative relationship with UNESCO and specialized in the social sciences. - Includes bibliographies. - Paris, UNESCO, 1956. - 100 p. - (Its: Reports and papers in the social sciences. no.5.)

1349.   -- **South East Asia science cooperation office.** Scientific and technical journals of East and South East Asia (Hong Kong, Japan, Indonesia, Macao, Malaya, North Borneo, the Philippines, Sarawak, Thailand, Vietnam). - 2nd ed. - Manila, 1953. - ii, 233 p.

1350.   -- **Statistics division.** Current official publications containing statistics relating to education. - 1961-   . - Paris, UNESCO, 1961-   . - v. - (United Nations educational, scientific and cultural organisation. Documents. UNESCO/ST/R/21, etc).

1. **United Nations industrial development organization.** Chemical
    fertilizer projects: their creation, evaluation and establishment. -
    Bibliography: p. 28-29. - New York, 1968. - 52 p. - (Its:
    Fertilizer industry series; monograph no.1.) E F S
    United Nations. Publications. Sales numbers. 1968.II.B.17.
    United Nations. Documents. ID/SER.F/1.

2. -- --- Coopération régionale dans l'industrie. - Bibliography: p. 52-53. -
    New York, Nations Unies, 1971. - viii, 53 p. - (Its: Monographies
    de l'ONUDI sur le développement industriel: l'industrialisation des
    pays en voie de développement, problèmes et perspectives. no.18.)
    E F S
    United Nations. Publications. Sales numbers. 1969.II.B.39, vol.18.
    United Nations. Documents. ID/40/18.
    "Etude fondée sur les travaux du Colloque international sur le développement industriel,
    (Athènes, novembre-décembre 1967)."

3. -- --- Estimation of managerial and technical personnel requirements
    in selected industries. - Includes bibliographies. - New York, United
    Nations, 1968. - 250 p. - (Its: Training for industry series. no.21.)
    E F S
    United Nations. Publications. Sales numbers. 1968.II.B.16.
    United Nations. Documents. ID/SER.D/2.

4. -- --- Guides to information sources. - Vienna, 1972-   .
    -   v.
    Contents:
    1. Information sources on the meat-processing industry. 1972. (UNIDO/LIB/
    SER.D/1).
    2. Information sources on the cement and concrete industry. 1972.

55. -- --- Industrial development abstracts. - 1971-   .
    - Vienna, 1971-   . -   v. - (Its: Documents. ID/LIB/SER.B/1,
    etc.)

56. -- --- Industrial location and regional development: an
    annotated bibliography. - New York, 1970. - 165 p.
    - (United Nations. Publications. Sales numbers. 1970.II.B.15.)
    United Nations. Documents. ID/43.

57. **United Nations institute for training and research.** UNITAR: what
    it is, what it does, how it works. - New York, 1971. - 29 p.
    Contains information on its research and publications.

58. -- --- Status and problems of very small states and territories. -
    Notes, partly bibliographical. - New York, 1969. - v, 230 p. - (Its:
    UNITAR series. no. 3.)

59. -- --- Wider acceptance of multilateral treaties. - Notes, partly
    bibliographical. - New York, 1969. - xiv, 213 p. - (Its: UNITAR
    series. no. 2.)

60. **United Nations research institute for social development.**
    Research notes: a review of recent and current studies
    conducted at the Institute. - no.1-   . - Geneva, 1968-
            . -   v.

61. -- --- A working bibliography on the child in developing
    communities/ prepared by P. E. Mandl. - n.p., 1968.
    - 114 p. - (Its: Documents. UNRISD/68/C.7.)

1362.   **United Nations research institute for social development.** Distribution
        of income and economic growth: concepts and issues. - Bibliography:
        p. 77-80. - Geneva, 1970. - vii, 80 p. - (United Nations. Publications.
        Sales numbers. 1970.IV.8.)
        "Report on an Institute study by Nancy Baster."

1363.   **United Nations seminar on aerial survey methods and equipment,
        Bangkok, Thailand, 1960.** Proceedings. - Includes bibliographies. -
        Bangkok, 1960. - vii, 167 p. - (United Nations. Economic commission
        for Asia and the Far East. Mineral resources development series.
        no.12.)
        United Nations. Documents. E/CN.11/536.
        "United Nations publications. Sales no.: 60.II.F.5."
        "Convened by the United Nations in co-operation with the Government of Thailand."

1364.   **United Nations seminar on planning techniques, Moscow, 1964.** Report.
        Bibliography: p. 177-179. - New York, 1966. - iv, 190 p. - (United
        Nations. Publications. Sales numbers. 1966.II.B.13.)
        United Nations. Documents. ST/TAO/SER.C/76.
        "Organized by the United Nations in co-operation with the government of the Union of
        Soviet Socialist Republics."

1365.   **United Nations social defence research institute.** Commentary
        and bibliography on capital punishment. - Rome, 1971.
        - 11, 32, 1. - (Its: Documents. Doc/UNSDRI/1971/4.)

1366.   -- --- Manpower and training in the field of social defence: a
        commentary and bibliography. - Prepared by Franco Ferracuti and
        Maria Cristina Giannini. - Rome. UNSDRI, 1970. - 152, iii p. -
        (Its: Publication. no.2.) E F S
        Classification of bibliographical items: I. Manpower. II. Area. III. Training.
        Index by area: O. General. 1. Police. 2. Courts. 3. Prisons. 4. Non-institutional.
        5. Volunteers. 6. Research workers.

1367.   **United Nations war crimes commission.** History of the United Nations
        war crimes commission and the development of the laws of war. -
        Bibliography: p. 557-573. - London, H.M. Stationery off. 1948. -
        xx, 592 p.

1368.   **United States. Congress. Senate. Committee on the judiciary.** United
        Nations headquarters site status of agreement resolutions. Hearings
        before the Sub-committee to investigate the administration of the
        internal security act and other internal security laws... 90th Congress,
        1st sess. - Bibliographical notes. - Washington, D.C., 1967. - 126 p.

1369.   -- **Department of state.** Regional organizations; a description of their
        development and functions: Europe and the North Atlantic area. -
        Bibliography: p. 33-34. - Washington, 1953. - 34 p. - (Its: Publication
        4944. International organization and conference series II. B. European
        and British commonwealth 3.)

1370.   -- **Library of Congress. General reference and bibliography division.**
        United Nations educational, scientific and cultural organization (UNESC
        a selected list of references. - Comp. by Helen Dudenbostel Jones. -
        Washington, 1948. - iv, 56 p.

1371. **United States. Library of Congress. International organization section.**
International scientific organizations: a guide to their library,
documentation, and information services/ prepared under the direction
of Kathrine O. Murra. - Bibliography of general sources of information:
p.731-740. - Washington, D.C., General reference and bibliography
division, Reference department, Library of Congress, 1962. - xi,
794 p.

1372. -- **Office of education.** The United Nations and related organizations:
a bibliography/ prepared in the International educational relations
branch. - Washington, D.C., U.S. Department of health, education, and
welfare, Office of education, 1960. - 17 p.

1373. **Valentine, D. G.** The Court of justice of the European communities. -
Bibliography: v.1, p. 573-580. - v. 1-2. - London, Stevens, 1965. -
2 v.
Jurisdiction and procedure. Judgements and documents, 1954-1960.

1374. **Vas-Zoltán, P.** United Nations technical assistance. - Bibliography:
p. 397-404. - Budapest, Akadémiai kiadó, 1972. - 404 p.
"Translated by Pál Félix."

1375. **Vela M. C.** Estrategia para el desarrollo: las iglesias, las Naciones
Unidas, los expertos. - Bibliographical notes. - Madrid, 1972. -
xxxii, 542 p.

1376. **Vermeylen, M.** Les opérations pour le maintien de la paix dans
le cadre des Nations Unies: travaux du Comité spécial. - Bibliography: l. 256-272. - Louvain, 1967. - vi, 278 l.
Mémoire - Univ. catholique de Louvain.

1377. **Vetere. E.** Cybernetics and law: bibliography. - Rome, 1971.
- ii, 67 l. - (United Nations social defence research
institute. Documents. Doc/UNSDRI/1971/8.)

1378. **Viet, J.** Assistance to under-developed countries: an annotated
bibliography=L'assistance aux pays sous-développés: bibliographie
commentée. - Paris, UNESCO, 1957. - 83 p. (Reports and
papers in the social sciences. Rapports et documents de
sciences sociales, no.8.)
United Nations educational, scientific and cultural organization. Document
SS/CH 8 AF.

1379. -- --- International co-operation and programmes of economic
and social development=Coopération internationale et
programmes de développement économique et social: an
annotated bibliography. - Paris, UNESCO, 1962 i.e. 1961.
- 107 p. - (United Nations educational, scientific and cultural
organisation. Social science clearing house. Reports and
papers in the social sciences. no.15.)

1380. **Vignes, D.** La Communauté européenne du charbon et de l'acier;
un exemple d'administration économique internationale. - Bibliography:
p. 189-191. - Paris, Libr. générale de droit et de jurisprudence,
1956. - 196 p. - (Recherches européennes.)

L

1381.　**Virally, M.**　Les missions permanentes auprès des organisations inter-
nationales/ par M. Virally, P. Gerbet, J. Salmon, avec la collaboration
de V.-Y. Ghébali. - v.1-　　. - Notes, partly bibliographical. - Bruxelles,
E. Bruylant, 1971-　　. -　v.
At head of title: Dotation Carnegie pour la paix internationale.

1382.　-- --- L'organisation mondiale. - Bibliographie générale: p.533-547. -
Paris, Librarie Armand Colin, 1972. - 587 p. - (Collection U:
série droit international public.)
Contents:
Le dispositif institutionnel. (La fondation des Nations Unies. Le système des Nations
Unies. La structure de l'ONU: les organes intergouvernementaux; les organes intégrés.)
Les pouvoirs institutionnels. (Le pouvoir de débattre. Le pouvoir de décider. Le
pouvoir d'agir. Le dynamisme institutionnel.)　Les Nations Unies comme instrument
d'universalisation. (Le décolonisation. La déségrégation. L'unification du système
international. L'unification idéologique. L'unification juridique. L'unification fonction-
nelle. L'action opérationnelle. Les activités normatives. La stratégie international du
développement.)　La planification de la vie internationale. (L'élimination des causes
de conflit. La mise à l'écart des moyens militaires. La répression. L'échec de la
sécurité collective. Les opérations de maintien de la paix. La capacité de l'ONU à
préserver la paix.)

1383.　**Vladigerov, T.**　Evropeĭska ikonomicheska obshtnost: izmeneniĭa v
kapitalizma:　teoriĭa i praktika. - Bibliography: p. 390-397. -
Sofiia, Izd-vo na Bŭlgarskata akademiĭa na naukite, 1967.
At head of title: Bŭlgarska akademiĭa na naukite. Ikonomicheski institut.
Added title-page in French.　Text in Bulgarian only.　Sumary in French.
European economic community.

1384.　**Vogel-Polsky, E.**　Du tripartisme à l'Organisation internationale du
travail. - Bibliography: p. 339-347. - Bruxelles, 1966. - xv, 352 p. -
(Brussels. Université libre. Institut de sociologie. Centre national du
droit social. Etudes.)
"Publié avec l'appui du Ministère de l'éducation nationale et de la culture."

1385.　**Walter, I.**　The Central American common market; a case study on
economic integration in developing regions/ by Ingo Walter and
Hans C. Vitzthum. - Bibliography: p. 71. - New York, 1967. -
72 p. - (New York university.　Graduate school of business
administration.　Institute of finance.　Bulletins. no.44.)
Notes, partly bibliographical.

1386.　**Wang, C. M.**　The development of I.L.O. procedures for making and
implementing international labor conventions between 1945 and
1957. - Bibliography: p. 296-303. - New York, 1959.
Microfilm copy of typewritten manuscript. Positive.
Collation of the original: 3, 303 p.
Thesis - Columbia university.

1387.　**Weaver, J. H.**　The International development association; a new
approach to foreign aid. - Bibliography: p. 258-268. - New York,
F.A. Praeger, 1965. - ix, 268 p. - (Praeger special studies in
international economics and development.)
Bibliographical notes: p. 225-257.

1388.　**Weidenmann, H. U.**　Entstehung und Aufgabe der Ernährungs- und
Landwirtschaftsorganisation der Vereinigten Nationen (FAO). -
Bibliography: p. ix-xii. - Aarau, H. Dengler, 1951. - xx, 159 p.
Diss. - Basel.

89. **Weil, G. L.** A handbook on the European economic community, edited by Gordon L. Weil. - Bibliography: p. 465-479. - New York, F.A. Praeger, 1965. - xiv, 479 p. - (Praeger special studies in international economics.)
"Published in cooperation with the European community information service, Washington, D.C."

90. **Wendelin, E. C.** Subject index to the economic and financial documents of the League of nations, 1927-1930. - Boston, Mass., World peace foundation. - 1932. - ix, 190 p.

91. **Wendt, F. W.** The Nordic council and cooperation in Scandinavia. - Bibliography: p. 237-240. - Copenhagen, E. Munksgaard, 1959. - 247 p.
"Translated from the Danish by Askel A. Anslev."

92. **Werners, S. E.** The presiding officers in the United Nations. - Bibliography: p. 204-207. - Haarlem, Erven F. Bohn, 1966. - viii, 212 p.
Proefschrift - Univ. van Amsterdam.

93. **White, L. C.** International non-governmental organizations: their purposes, methods, and accomplishments/ by Lyman Cromwell White assisted by Marie Ragonetti Zocca. - Bibliography: p. 312-314. - New Brunswick, Rutgers university press, 1951. - xi, 325 p.
Notes, partly bibliographical: p. 279-304.

94. -- --- The structure of private international organizations. - Bibliography: p. 324-326. - Philadelphia, Pa., G.S. Ferguson co., 1933. - ix, 327 p.

95. **Wightman, D.** Economic co-operation in Europe; a study of the United Nations Economic commission for Europe. - Bibliography: p. 269-274. - London, Stevens & sons, 1956. - xi, 288 p. - (Carnegie endowment for international peace. European center. Prizes in international organization.)

96. -- --- Toward economic co-operation in Asia: The United Nations Economic commission for Asia and the Far East. - Bibliography: p. 383-388. - New Haven, Yale university press, 1963. - xii, 400 p.
"Published for the Carnegie endowment for international peace."

97. **Winton, H. N. M.** Man and the environment: a bibliography of selected publications of the United Nations system, 1946-1971. - Comp. and edited by Harry N. M. Winton. - New York, Unipub. inc. R.R. Bowker, 1972. - xxi, 305 p.
Annotated bibliography of over 1,200 monographs, manuals, bulletins, papers, proceedings published by the United Nations and related agencies that deal with problems of global environment.
Classified under 59 subject areas in the environmental sciences and listed chronologically by publication date. Among the areas covered are: environmental pollution, population growth, protein sources, food additives, animal resources, plant resources, soil science, water resources, hydrometeorology and hydrology.
Four indexes: Author index, Series and serial index, Title index, Subject index.

98. **Woltz, C. G.** Bloc voting in the United Nations, 1946-1951. - Bibliography: p. 351-354. - New York, 1956.
Microfilm copy of typewritten manuscript. Positive.
Collation of the original: 354 p.
Diss. - New York university.

1399.   **World** eco-crisis: international organizations in response. - Includes
         bibliographies. - Edited by David A. Kay and Eugene B. Skolnikoff.
         Madison, Wis., Univ. of Wisconsin press, 1972. - viii, 324 p.
         Activities of UN and specialized agencies in the field of environment.

1400.   **World health organization.** Bibliography on bilharziasis=Bibliographie
         de la bilharzioze, 1949-1958. - Geneva, 1960. - 158 p.

1401.   -- --- Bibliography on hookworm disease=Bibliographie de
         l'ankylostomiase, 1920-1962. - Geneva, 1965. - 251 p.

1402.   -- --- Bibliography on medical education, 1946-1955. - Geneva,
         1958. - 391 p.

1403.   -- --- Bibliography on the epidemiology of cancer=Bibliographie
         de l'épidémiologie du cancer, 1946-1960. - Geneva, 1963.
         - 168 p.

1404.   -- --- Bibliography on yaws=Bibliographie du pian, 1905-1962.
         - Geneva, 1958. - 391 p. E F

1405.   -- --- Risques pour la santé du fait de l'environnement. - Includes
         bibliographies. - Genève, Organisation mondiale de la santé,
         1972. - 406 p.

1406.   -- **Library.** Bibliographies prepared by the WHO Library. - 1972-
         . - Geneva, 1972-   . -   v.
         Forms Part II of WHO Library acquisitions.

1407.   -- --- Current awareness service.

         (a) This service, designed to replace the conventional indexing system,
         became operational in May 1972.
         (b) The intention is to operate it for two months for headquarters
         staff only before extending it out-posted staff.
         (c) Regional Offices will be supplied with lists of the subject headings for
         which monthly searches are made for headquarters staff, indicating the
         format.
         (d) From these lists, staff can select the searches they would like to receive
         regularly.
         (e) In addition, out-posted staff will be invited to ask for searches on
         subject headings not yet supplied to headquarters staff.
         (f) Regional Office libraries will continue to receive the conventional
         indexing service on cards for those periodicals not covered by MEDLARS.

1408.   -- - -- Geomedical index:

         (a) This is a supplement to WHO Library Acquisitions proposed to start
         in July 1972. It will contain all citations retrieved for the current
         awareness service which also contain a geographical heading. Arrangement
         will be alphabetically by geographical terms, reproduction by offset.
         (b) Regional Offices will be supplied with copies of this index for
         distribution to their out-posted staff.

1409.   -- --- Retrospective bibliographies on specific topics
         (demand searches):

         (a) This service became operational with the receipt of the complete MEDLARS
         data base of nearly 1 500 000 references at the end of January 1972.
         (b) Search requests from out-posted staff were accepted beginning 20 April 1972.
         (c) Supplies of search request forms were made available to Regional Office
         libraries.
         (d) This service will be extended to members of WHO expert advisory panels
         and to national institutions and health administrations with limited or no access
         to computers.

World health organization. Library. (Cont'd)

410.   -- --- The World health organization: a brief guide to publications and documents. - Geneva, 1971. - 10 p.
Prepared for the Orientation Seminar on Documentation of International Organizations in the United Nations System organized by UNITAR, and the Library, Information Service and other services of the UN office and with the Specialized Agencies at Geneva, 8-12 March 1971. - Working Paper no.5.

411.   -- **Regional office for Europe.** Health planning and health economics in countries of Eastern Europe: abstracts of books and articles, 1965-1969. - Copenhagen, 1971.
- iv, 172 p.

412.   **World intellectual property organization. Library.** Études bibliographiques. - no. 1-   . - Genève, 1966-   . -   v.
   1. Catalogue des périodiques de la Bibliothèque de l'OMPI. 3ème ed.
   2. Collection des usuels de la Bibliothèque de l'OMPI.
   3. La licence obligatoire en matière de brevets.
   4. Catalogue des publications et documents d'archives des BIRPI conservés à la Bibliothèque.
   5. Le brevet européen. Le brevet scandinave.
   6. Cessation des marques.
   7. Protection de la correspondance et des lettres missives.
   8. Les marques de service.
   9. La protection de la propriété industrielle en URSS.
  10. Commentaires sur la Convention de Paris.
  11. Etudes consacrées au brevet dans les pays socialistes.
  12. Bibliographie sélective de commentaires sur la Convention de Berne.
  13. Examen préalable.
  14. Bibliographie sélective d'ouvrages en langue anglaise concernant la propriété industrielle.

413.   -- --- Bibliographie des publications officielles d'offices nationaux de proprété industrielle. - Genève, 1967. - 1 v.

14.   **World meteorological organization.** Bibliographie météorologique internationale. - Genève, 1954.

15.   -- --- Catalogue of meteorological data for research. - Geneva, 1965.

16.   -- --- One hundred years of international co-operation in meteorology: 1873-1973; a historical review. - Geneva, 1973. - - 53 p. - (Its: Publications. WMO.no.345.)

17.   -- --- Selected bibliography on urban climate. - Geneva, 1970.

18.   **Zacher, M. W.** Dag Hammarskjold's United Nations. - Bibliography: p. 281-288. - New York, Columbia university press, 1970. - 295 p. - (Columbia university studies in international organization.7)

19.   **Zacklin, R.** The amendment of the constitutive instruments of the United Nations and specialized agencies. - Bibliography: p. 201-208. - Leyden, A.W. Sijthoff, 1968. - xii, 216 p.
Another ed. issued with thesis note.

1420.   **Zahariade, Z.**   Le statut financier des services publics internationaux. -
          Bibliography: p. 177-178. - Paris, Domat-Montchrestien, 1938. -
          181 p.
          Thèse - Univ. de Paris.
          Union postale universelle.

1421.   **Zaorski, R.**   Konwencje genewskie o prawie morza. - Bibliography:
          p. 269-274. - Gdynia, Wydawn. morskie, 1962. - 274 p.
          Summaries in Russian and English: p. 248-268.
          United Nations conference on the law of the sea. 2nd, Geneva, 1960.

1422.   **Zarkovich, S. S.**   Le programme des Nations Unies pour le développe-
          ment; étude critique. - Notes, partly bibliographical. - Paris, Presses
          universitaires de France, 1970. - 246 p. - (Etudes "Tiers monde":
          croissance, développement, progrès. no.24.)
          On cover: Publications de l'I.E.D.E.S.

1423.   **Zinser, R.**   Das GATT und die Meistbegünstigung; das Kernstück des
          GATT und seine Bedeutung für die internationalen Wirtschafts-
          beziehungen. - Bibliography: p. 183-202. - Baden-Baden, A. Lutzeyer,
          1962. - 202 p. - (Handbuch für europäosche Wirtschaft.   Schriften-
          reihe.   Bd. 24.)

1424.   **Zollikofer, P. L.**   Les relations prévues entre les institutions spécialisées
          des Nations Unies et la Cour internationale de justice. - Bibliography:
          p. 87-90. - Leyde, A.W. Sijthoff, 1955. - 94 p.

1425.   **Zyai, A.**   La Banque internationale pour la reconstruction et le
          développement. - Bibliography: p. 373-391. - Paris, 1954.
          Microfilm copy of typewritten manuscript. Negative.
          Collation of the original: 439 p.
          Thèse - Univ. de Paris.

C. WORLD POLITICS, INTERNATIONAL RELATIONS, PEACEKEEPING OPERATIONS, SECURITY, DISARMAMENT

26. **Adams, M.** The search for a settlement in the Middle East. - Bibliographical notes. - London, Political quarterly pub. co., 1968. - p. 417-438.
"Reprinted from 'The political quarterly', v. 39, no. 4. October-December, 1968."

27. **Aïrapetïan, M. E.** Novyĭ tip mezhdunarodnykh otnosheniĭ. - Bibliographical notes. - Moskva, Izd-vo, "Mysl' ", 1964. - 278 p.
At head of title: M.E. Aïrapetïan. V.V. Sukhodeev.

28. **Akademiïa nauk SSSR. Institut Afriki.** Afrika v mezhdunarodnykh otnosheniïakh. - Bibliography at the end of each part. - Moskva, Izd-vo "Nauka", 1970. - 369 p.
"Otvetstvennyĭ redaktor Anat. A. Gromyko."
Africa and international relations.

29. **-- Institut mirovoĭ ėkonomiki i mezhdunarodnykh otnosheniĭ.** Razvivaiùshchiesïa strany v mirovoĭ politike. - Bibliography: p. 242-258. - Moskva, Izd-vo "Nauka", 1970. - 258 p.

30. **Akzin, B.** New states and international organizations; a report prepared on behalf of the International political science association. - Bibliographical notes. - Paris, Unesco, International political science association, 1955. - 200 p.
At head of title: Benjamin Akzin.

31. **Albonetti, A.** Hegemonie oder Partner schaft in der europäischen Aussenpolitik. - Includes bibliographical notes. - Baden-Baden, Nomos Verlagsgesellschaft, 1972. - 125 p. - (Schriftenreihe europäische Wirtschaft. Bd. 47.)
"Die Originalausgabe erschien... unter dem Titel 'Egemonia o parteeipazione?'."
Europe - Foreign relations. Security, International - Europe, Western. North Atlantic treaty organisation. International agencies. Europe, Western - Foreign relations - U.S.

32. **Alker, H.R.** World politics in the General assembly. - Partly bibliographical. - New Haven, Yale university press, 1965. - xxvi, 326 p. - (Yale studies in political science. 15.)
At head of title: Hayward R. Alker and Bruce M. Russett.

33. The **analysis** of international politics: essays in honor of Harold and Margaret Sprout. - Bibliographical notes: p. 388-390. - Edited by James N. Rosenau... and others. - New York, Free press, 1972. - xii, 397 p.
International relations - Research. Foreign policy. World politics. Forecasting. Technology. United Nations. General assembly.

34. **Andemicael, B.** Peaceful settlement among African states: roles of the United Nations and the Organization of African unity. - Bibliography: p. 64-68. - New York, 1972. - vi, 68 p. - (UNITAR PS. no.5.)

35. **Annales** d'études internationales=Annals of international studies.-1970-   . - Includes bibliographies. - Genève, Association des anciens de l'I.U.H.E.I., 1970-   . - v.
Pub. annually.

1436.   **Annuaire** polonais des affaires internationales.-1959/60-   . - Includes
         bibliographies. - Varsovie, Institut polonais des affaires internationales,
         1960-   . -   v.

1437.   **Arbatov, G.A.**   Ideologicheskaïa bor'ba sovremennykh mezhdunarodnykh
         otnosheniïakh; doktrina, metody i organizafsiïa vneshnepoliticheskoï
         propagandy imperializma. - Bibliographical notes. - Moskva, Politizdat,
         1970. - 349 p.

1438.   The **arms** trade with the third world.- Bibliography: p. 884-896. -
         Stockholm, Almqvist & Wicksell, 1971. - xxxi, 910 p. - (Stockholm
         international peace research institute.   SIPRI monographs.)
         Weapons. Arms and armor. Developing countries - Armed forces. Security, International.

1439.   **Aron, R.**   Diversity of worlds; France and the United States look at
         their common problems/ by Raymond Aron and August Heckscher. -
         Bibliographical notes. - New York, Reynal, 1957. - xiii, 178 p.

1440.   -- --- Études politiques. - Bibliography: p. 561-562. - Paris, Gallimard
         1972. - 564 p. - (Bibliothèque des sciences humaines.)
         Political science. Politics, Practical. International relations.

1441.   The **Atlantic** community; an introductory bibliography. - Prepared by the
         Conference on Atlantic community, Bruges. - v.1-   . - Leiden,
         A.W. Sythoff, 1961-   . -   v.

1442.   **el-Ayouty, Y.**   The United Nations and decolonization: the role of Afri
         Asia. - Bibliography: p. 259-264. - The Hague, M. Nijhoff, 1971. -
         xxix, 286 p.

1443.   **Bailey, G.**   The East-West problem; a re-assessment. - Bibliography:
         p. 70-71. - London, Friends East-West relations committee, 1960. -
         71 p.

1444.   **Ball, G. W.**   The discipline of power: essentials of a modern world structu
         Bibliography: p. 359-363. - Boston, Little, Brown, 1968. - 363 p.
         "An Atlantic monthly press book."

1445.   **Ball, M. M.**   International relations/ by M. Margaret Ball and Hugh B.
         Killough. - Bibliography: p. 599-620. - New York, Ronald press, 1956.
         viii, 667 p.

1446.   **Ballaloud, J.**   L'ONU et les opérations de maintien de la paix. -
         Bibliography: p. 233-235. - Paris, A. Pedone, 1971. - 239 p.

1447.   **Banerjee, A. C.**   Revision of Charter of United Nations. - Notes, partly
         bibliographical. - Calcutta, A. Mukherjee, 1961. - 272 p.

1448.   **Barclay, G. St. J.**   20th century nationalism. - Bibliography: p. 215-216.
         Weidenfeld and Nicolson, 1971. - 224 p. - (Revolution of our time.)
         Nationalism. Revolutions. World politics. International relations. World war, 1939-1945.
         United Nations.

1449.   **Barnett, S. N.**   Interpretation of the United Nations Charter by the
         International court of justice. - Bibliography: p. 361-396. - New York,
         1958.
         Collation of the original: 3, 396 p.
         Thesis - Columbia university.

50. **Barraine, R.** La réglementation des rapports internationaux et l'organisation des Nations Unies. - Bibliography: p. 4. - Paris, Libr. générale de droit et de jurisprudence, 1946. - 319 p.

51. **Baskin, ĪU. ĪA.** Mezhdunarodnoe pravo: problemy metodologii, ocherki metodov issledovaniiâ. - Bibliography: p. 159-174. - Moskva, Izd-vo "Mezhdunarodnye otnosheniiâ", 1971. - 174 p.
At head of title: ĪU. ĪA. Baskin, D. I. Fel'dman.
International law. International relations - Sources.

52. **Beaton, L.** The reform of power: a proposal for an international security system. - Notes, partly bibliographical. - London, Chatto & Windus, 1972. - 240 p.
Security, International. Disarmament. Nuclear weapons and disarmament. Nuclear weapons - International control. International organization. International relations. United Nations - Disarmament. North Atlantic treaty organization.

53. **Beckett, Sir W. E.** The North Atlantic treaty, the Brussels treaty and the charter of the United Nations. - Bibliographical notes. - London, Stevens & sons, 1950. - viii, 75 p. - (Library of world affairs. no. 12.)

54. **Beghè Loreti, A.** Il recesso dalle organizzazioni internazionali. - Notes, partly bibliographical. - Milano, A. Giuffrè, 1967. - 230 p. - (Rome. Università. Facoltà di economia e commercio. Pubblicazioni. v. 29.)

55. **Beilenson, L. W.** The treaty trap; a history of the performance of political treaties by the United States and European nations/ by Laurence W. Beilenson, assisted by Bernard M. Dain. - Bibliography: p. 292-313. - Washington, D.C., Public affairs press, 1969. - xii, 344 p.
"A Foreign policy research institute book."

56. **Bell, C.** The convention of crisis: a study in diplomatic management. - Bibliography: p. 125-126. - London, Oxford university press, 1971. - vi, 131 p. - (Oxford paperbacks. 276.)
"Published for the Royal institute of international affairs."

57. -- --- Negotiation from strength; a study in the politics of power. - Bibliography: p. 215-220. - London, Chatto & Windus, 1962. - 223 p.

58. **Bentwich, N. D. M.** A commentary on the charter of the United Nations/ by Norman Bentwich and Andrew Martin. - Bibliography: p. 229-231. - London, Routledge & Kegan, 1950. - xxviii, 239 p.

59. **Bergeron, G.** La guerre froide inachevée: rétrospective: 1945-1962, expectative: 1963-1970, prospective: 1971- . - Notes, partly bibliographical. - Montréal, Presses de l'Université de Montréal, 1971. - xiv. 315 p.
"Cet ouvrage a été publié grâce à une subvention accordée par le Conseil canadien de recherche en sciences sociales et provenant de fonds fournis par le Conseil des arts du Canada."
Cold war.

60. **Best, G. L.** Diplomacy in the United Nations. - Bibliography: leaves 232-241. - Ann Arbor, Mich., University microfilms, 1962. - vi, 263 l.
Photostat reproduction (positive) of microfilm copy.
Diss. - Northwestern university.

1461.   **Bibliografía** general de la literatura latinoamericana. - Paris, UNESCO, 1972.
         187 p.
         Contents: l. Perido colonial.   2. Siglo XIX.   3. Época contemporánea.
         Indice general de nombres.

1462.   **Bibliografie** hlavních československých prací z mezinárodních vztahů
         publikovaných v kniží formě, 1945-1966. - Sest. Ladislav Kučera. Praha,
         Ústav pro mezinárodní politiku a ekonomii, 1967. - 406 p. - (Prameny
         a studie k mezinarodnim vztahům. 1967. sv. 4.)
         Added title-page (with title: Bibliography of the main Czechoslovak studies in the sphere
         of international relations), contents and introduction in English.

1463.   **Bibliographie** Völkerrecht und internationale Beziehungen. - 1.-   Jhg.;
         1972-   . - Potsdam-Babelsberg, Deutsche Akademie für Staats- und
         Rechtswissenschaft "Walter Ulbricht", Informationszentrum Staat und
         Recht, 1972-   . - v.
         Pub. semi-monthly.
         "Verantwortlich für den Inhalt: Institut für internationale Beziehungen - Abteilung wissen-
         schaftliche Dokumentation."
         Superseded: 1972, Referatezeitschrift Völkerrecht und internationale Beziehungen. (1965-1971.)
         International law - Bibliography.   International relations - Bibliography.   International organisation
         Bibliography.

1464.   A **bibliography** for students of politics. - London, Oxford university press,
         1971. - 113 p.

1465.   **Birnbaum, K. E.**   Frieden in Europa: Voraussetzungen, Chancen, Versuche
         Bibliography: p. 141-146. - Opladen, C.W. Leske, 1970. - 146 p. -
         (Deutsche Gesellschaft für auswärtige Politik.   Forschungsinstitut.
         Aktuelle Aussenpolitik.)
         "Originalausgabe: 'Peace in Europe' ... Ubersetzer: Karl Römer."

1466.   -- --- Peace in Europe; East-West relations, 1966-1968 and the prospects
         for a European settlement. - Bibliography: p. 148-151. - London, Oxfor
         university press, 1970. - xii, 159 p.
         "Written under the auspices of the Harvard Center for international affairs and published in
         co-operation with the Royal institute of international affairs."

1467.   **Bloch, R.**   La fonction publique internationale et européenne. - Bibliograpl
         p. 213-214, - Paris, Libr. générale de droit et de jurisprudence, 1963. -
         219 p. - (Économie et législation européennes. 1.)

1468.   **Bloomfield, L. P.**   Controlling small wars; a strategy for the 1970s/ by
         Lincoln P. Bloomfield and Amelia C. Leiss. - Bibliographical notes. -
         London, A. Lane, The Penguin press, 1970. - 313 p.

1469.   -- --- Evolution or revolution?   The United Nations and the problem o
         peaceful territorial change. - Bibliographical notes: p. 195-213. - Cambri
         Mass., Harvard university press, 1957. - 220 p.

1470.   **Blühdorn, R.**   Internationale Beziehungen; Einführung in die Grundlagen
         der Aussenpolitik. - Bibliography: p. 339-346. - Wien, Springer, 1956. -
         xii, 391 p. - (Rechts- und Staatswissenschaften. 14.)

1471.   **Boasson, C.**   Approaches to the study of international relations. -
         Bibliographical notes. - 2nd ed. - Assen, Van Gorcum, 1972. - 126 p. -
         (Groningen.   Rijksuniversiteit.   Polemologisch instituut.   Polemological
         studies. 2.)

472. **Bobrow, D. B.** Computers and the policy-making community: applications to international relations/ by Davis B. Bobrow and Judah L. Schwartz. - Bibliographies at the end of most chapters. - Englewood Cliffs, N.J., Prentice Hall, 1968. - viii, 374 p. - (Prentice -Hall series in automatic computation.)

473. **Bonnemaison, A.** L'Armée internationale et le Comité d'état-major (articles 43 et 47 de la Charte). - Bibliography: v. 2, p. 293-302. - Paris, 1952. - 3 v.
Thèse - Paris.

474. **Bosc, R.** La société internationale et l'église. - t. 1-   . - Includes bibliographies. - Paris, Spes, 1961-   . -   v. - (Bibliothèque de la recherche sociale.)
At head of title: Institut catholique de Paris.

475. -- --- Le tiers monde dans la politique internationale. - Bibliography: p. 123-124. - Paris, Aubier-Montaigne, 1968. - 126 p. - (Tiers monde et développement.)

476. **Bothe, M.** Streitkräfte internationaler Organisationen, zugleich ein Beitrag zu völkerrechtlichen Grundfragen der Anwesenheit fremder Truppen. - Bibliography: p. 179-192. - Köln, C. Heymann, 1968. - xii, 192 p. - (Max-Planck-Institut für ausländisches öffentliches Recht und Völkerrecht. Beiträge zum ausländischen öffentlichen Recht und Völkerrecht. 47.)

477. **Bottenberg, P.** Die politischen Leitungsfunktionen der Generalsekretäre internationaler Organisationen. - Bibliography: leaves viii-xvii. - Göttingen, 1959. - xvii, 169 l.
Diss. - Georg-August-Universität in Göttingen.

478. **Bourquin, M.** Stabilité et mouvement dans l'ordre juridique international. - Bibliography: p. 473. - (In Academy of international law, The Hague. Recueil des cours, 1938, II. Paris, 1938. v. 64, p. 347-477.)

479. **Bowett, D. W.** The search for peace. - Bibliography at the end of each chapter. - London, Routledge & K. Paul, 1972. - xiii, 236 p. - (World studies series.)
Pacific settlement of international disputes.

480. **Boyd, J. M.** United Nations peace-keeping operations: a military and political appraisal. - Bibliography: p. 243-252. - New York, Praeger, 1971. - xv, 261 p. - (Praeger special studies in international politics and public affairs.)

481. **Bozeman, A. (Brummer).** The future of law in a multicultural world. - Bibliography: p. 195-217. - Princeton, N.J. Princeton university press, 1971. - xvii, 229 p.

482. -- --- Politics and culture in international history. - Bibliography: p. 523-537. - Princeton, N.J., Princeton university press, 1960. - xiii, 560 p.
"Publication of this book has been aided by the Ford foundation program."

1483. **Brainard, A. P.** The United Nations and the question of disarmament, 1950-1955. - Bibliography: leaves 282-310. - Ann Arbor, Mich., Univers. microfilms, 1962. - 301 l.
Thesis - Univ. of Washington.

1484. **Bretton, P.** La coexistence pacifique/ par Philippe Bretton et Jean-Pierre Chaudet. - Includes bibliographies. - Paris, A. Colin, 1971. - 327 p. - (Collection U. sér.: "Relations et institutions internationales".)
World politics. International relations. Peace. U.S. - Foreign relations - U.S.S.R. Nuclear weapons - International control.

1485. **Brzezinski, Z. K.** Alternative to partition; for a broader conception of America's role in Europe. - Bibliographical notes: p. 177-183. - New Y McGraw-Hill, 1965. - xi, 208 p. - (Council on foreign relations. Atlan policy studies.)

1486. -- --- Between two ages: America's role in the technetronic era. - Bibliographical notes: p. 311-324. - New York, Viking press, 1970. - xvii, 334 p.

1487. **Buchmann, J.** A la recherche d'un ordre international. - Bibliographical notes. - Louvain, E. Nauwelaerts, 1957. - 215 p. - (Léopoldville. Université lovanium. Publications. 3.)

1488. **Bulletin** bibliographique de documentation internationale contemporaine, pub. par la Bibliothèque de documentation internationale contemporaine et par le Centre européen de la Dotation Carnegie pour la paix internationale=Bibliographical bulletin on international affairs... - 1re série etc. 1re/3me année, 1926/1928. - Paris, Les Presses universitaires de France, 1926- . - v.
Pub. monthly.
Supersedes the Bulletin de l'Office de documentation internationale contemporaien. 1926-1928, pub. par l'Office de documentation internationale contemporaine et par l'Institut international de coopération intellectuelle.
General index pub. every three years.

1489. **Burton, J. W.** International relations; a general theory. - Bibliography: p. 275-280. - Cambridge, University press, 1965. - viii, 288 p.

1490. -- --- Peace theory; preconditions of disarmament. - Notes, partly bibliographical. - New York, A.A. Knopf, 1962. - xi, 200 p.

1491. **Butterfield, H.** Diplomatic investigations; essays in the theory of international politics/ edited by Herbert Butterfield and Martin Wight. - Notes, partly bibliographical. - London, G. Allen & Unwin, 1966. - 27?

1492. **Byrd, R. O.** Quaker ways in foreign policy. - Bibliographical notes: p. 211-224. - Toronto, Univ. of Toronto press, 1960. - xxi, 230 p.

1493. **Bystrický, R.** Mezinárodní obchodní úmluvy a instituce. - Notes, partly bibliographical. - Praha, Státní nakl. politické lit-ry, 1955. - 286 p.

1494. **Cable, J.** Gunboat diplomacy; political applications of limited naval force. - Bibliography: p. 231-242. - London, Chatto & Windus, 1971. - 251 p. - (Institute for strategic studies. Studies in international security. 16.)
Navies. War-ships. Naval art and science. Diplomacy. Security, International.

495. **Campagnolo, U.** La plus grande révolution: une paix qui n'a pas pour alternative la guerre. - Notes, partly bibliographical. - Neuchâtel, Éd. de la Baconnière, 1971. - 258 p. - (L'évolution du monde et des idées.)

496. **Cantori, L. J.** The international politics of regions: a comparative approach/ by Louis J. Cantori and Steven L. Spiegel. - Bibliography at the end of each part. - Englewood Cliffs, N.J., Prentice Hall, 1970. - xi, 432 p.

497. **Cardis, F.** Fédéralisme et intégration européenne. - Bibliography: p. 263-267. - Lausanne, Centre de recherches européennes, École des H.E.C., Univ. de Lausanne, 1964. - 269 p.

498. **Cardon, R. L.** Las Naciones Unidas y la conservación de la paz. - Bibliography: p. 195-198. - Rosario, Impr. de la Univ. nacional, 1952. - 198 p.

499. **Carey, J.** UN protection of civil and political rights. - Bibliographical notes. - Syracuse, N.Y., Syracuse university press, 1970. - xii, 205 p. - (Procedural aspects of international law series. v.8.)

500. **Carnegie endowment for international peace.** Current research in international affairs: a selected bibliography of work in progress by private research agencies in the United States, United Kingdom, Canada... and others. - 1st-5th; 1947/49-1952. - New York, 1948-1952. - v. - (International conciliation. no. 437.)
Subtitle varies slightly.
Issued separately from "International conciliation", 1952- .
Discontinued with issue of 1952.

501. -- --- **Library.** Brief reference list.-no. 1- ; 1934- . - Washington, D.C., Carnegie endowment for international peace, 1934- . - v.

502. **Carrión Simbrelo, M. H.** Delimitación de competencias entre la ONU y los organismos regionales; en materia relativa al mantenimiento de la paz y seguridad internacionales/ por María Elena Carrión Simbrelo. - Bibliography: p. 189-190. - México, D.F., 1964. - 191 p.
At head of title: Universidad nacional autónoma de México. Escuela nacional de ciencias politicas y sociales.

503. **Castrén, E. J. S.** Kansainvälinen oikeus. - "Yhdistyneiden Kansakuntien peruskirja": p. 379-410. - Helsinki, W. Söderström, 1947. - 410 p. - (Suomalainen lakimiesyhdistys. Helsingfors. Julkaisuja. B-sarja. n:o 14.)

504. **Catholic association for international peace.** The role of the Christian in the world for peace; a symposium based on the Silver jubilee conference of the Catholic association... November 7-9, 1952. - Bibliography: p. 148-156. - Washington, 1953. - 156 p.

505. -- --- **Post-war world committee.** The United Nations charter/ by Thomas H. Mahony and the Post-war world committee. A report. - Bibliography: p. 24. - Washington, 1945. - 24 p. - (Its: Pamphlet no. 36.)

1506.   **Cavaré, L.**   Les sanctions dans le cadre de l'O.N.U. - Bibliography: p. 28
         (In Academy of international law, The Hague.   Recueil des cours, 195
         Paris, 1953.   v. 80, p. 191-291.)

1507.   **Chakravarti, R.**   Human rights & the United Nations. - Bibliography:
         p. 205-213. - Calcutta, Progressive publishers, 1958. - xv, 218 p.

1508.   **Chambour, R.**   La responsabilité de l'Occident devant le danger de guerre
         Bibliographical notes. - n.p. Ed. méditerranéennes, 1970. - 276 p.

1509.   The **changing** environment of international relations/ by Grayson Kirt... a
         others. - Notes, partly bibliographical. - Washington, D.C., Brookings
         institution, 1956. - ix, 158 p. - (Brookings lectures.   1956.)

1510.   **Charrière, J. A.**   Problèmes de la ville internationale; actualité et perspec-
         tives à l'aide de deux modèles: Genève et Vienne. - Bibliography:
         l leaf following leaf 73. - Vienne, 1969.   73 l.
         Diplomarbeit - Diplomatische Akademie, Wien.

1511.   Die **Charta** der Vereinten Nationen=The Charter of the United Nations=La
         Charte des Nations Unies. - (In: Hüfner, Klaus.   Zwanzig Jahre Verein
         Nationen; internationale Bibliographie, international bibliography, biblio-
         graphie internationale, 1945-1965.   Berlin, W. de Gruyter, 1968. p. 25-

1512.   **Chaumont, C. M.**   Nations Unies et neutralité. - Bibliography: p. 57-58.
         (In Academy of international law, The Hague.   Recueil des cours,
         1956, I.   Leyde (Pays-Bas), A. W. Sijthoff, 1957.   v. 89, p. 1-59.)

1513.   **Cheever, D. S.**   Organizing for peace; international organization in world
         affairs. - Bibliography at the end of each chapter. - London, Stevens &
         sons, 1954. - x, 917, iv p. - (Library of world affairs, no. 27.)
         At head of title: Daniel S. Cheever.   H. Field Haviland, jr.

1514.   **Chichvarin, V. A.**   Okhrana prirody i mezhdunarodnye otnosheniiã. -
         Bibliographical notes: p. 259-285. - Moskva, Izd-vo "Mezhdunarodnye
         otnosheniiã", 1970. - 286 p.

1515.   **Claude, I. L.**   European organization in the global context. - Bibliographi
         notes. - Bruxelles, 1965. - 34 p. - (Brussels.   Université libre.   Institut
         d'études européennes.   Enseignement complémentaire.   t.12.)
         "Lectures given on March 15-16-17, 1965.'

1516.   **Clemens, D. S.**   Yalta. - Bibliography: p. 331-341. - New York, Oxford
         university press, 1970. - x, 356 p.

1517.   **Colard, D.**   Le désarmement. - Bibliography: p. 121-124. - Paris,
         A. Colin, 1972. - 125 p. - (Collection U2.   196.)

1518.   **Colloque sur la paix par la recherche scientifique, Brussels, 1969.**   La
         paix par la recherche scientifique. - Notes partly bibliographical. -
         Bruxelles, 1970. - 321 p. - (Brussels.   Université libre.   Institut de
         sociologie.   Centre de sociologie de la guerre.   Études de sociologie de
         la guerre.)

519.   **Columbia** essays in international affairs: the dean's papers. - Includes
        bibliographies. - 1st-   ; 1965-   . - New York, Columbia university
        press, 1966-   . -   v.
        Pub. annually.
        "By students of the Faculty of international affairs, Columbia university."
        Editor: 1965-   , Andrew W. Cordier.

520.   **Columbia university. School of international affairs.** The School of
        international affairs and the regional institutes; reports on publications. -
        1st-   ; 1963/64-   . - New York, 1965-   . -   v.
        Pub. biennially.
        Editor: 1964/65-   , Andrew W. Cordier.

521.   **Commission to study the organization of peace, New York.** Charter review
        conference; ninth report and papers presented to the Commission. -
        Notes, partly bibliographical. - New York, 1955. - 226 p.

522.   -- --- Organizing peace in the nuclear age; report. - Notes, partly biblio-
        graphical: p. 225-233. - New York, New York university press, 1959. -
        xvii, 245 p.
        "Arthur N. Holcombe, chairman."
        "This eleventh report of the Commission... is the third in a series dealing with the general
        problem of strengthening the United Nations." - Foreword.

523.   -- --- Peaceful coexistence: a new challenge to the United Nations:
        twelfth report. - Notes, partly bibliographical. - New York, 1960. -
        47 p.
        "Arthur N. Holcombe, chairman."

524.   -- --- Regional arrangements for security and the United Nations;
        eighth report and papers presented to the Commission. - Notes, partly
        bibliographical. - New York, 1953. - 144 p. - (Its: Publications.
        no. 23.)

525.   -- --- The United Nations and human rights; eighteenth report. -
        Bibliographical notes. - Dobbs Ferry, N.Y., Oceana publications, 1968. -
        xi, 239 p.
        "Clark M. Eichelberger, chairman."

526.   **La concurrence** sur les marchés extérieurs, les firmes et les organisations
        internationales. - Notes, partly bibliographical. - Genève, Libr. Droz,
        1971. - p. 937-1138. - (Institut de science économique appliquée,
        Paris. Economies et sociétés; cahiers de l'I.S.E.A. t. 5, no. 6.)

527.   **Conférence des hautes études internationales.** Travaux en cours dans le
        domaine des relations internationales. - Paris, Carnegie endowment for
        international peace, Centre européen, 1952. - 59 p.
        "La Conférence des hatues études internationales a préparé la présente bibliographie, éditée par
        les soins de la Dotation Carnegie." - p. 3.

528.   **Conference on a design for international relations research: scoep,
        theory, methods, and relevance, Philadelphia, 1969.** A design for
        international relations research: scope, theory, methods, and relevance. -
        Notes, partly bibliographical. - Edited/ by Norman D. Palmer. - Phila-
        delphia, 1970. - ix, 307 p. - (American academy of political and social
        sciences, Philadelphia. Monograph. 10.)

1529.   **Conference on international organizations in Europe and the changing European system, Geneva, 1970.** International organizations in Europ and the changing European system. - Bibliographical notes. - Geneva, 1970. - 56 p.
"Conference sponsored by the European centre of the Carnegie endowment for international peace."

1530.   -- **2nd, Geneva, 1971.** International organizations in Europe and the changing European system. - Notes, partly bibliographical. - Geneva, 1972. - 119 p.
"Conference sponsored by the European centre of the Carnegie endowment for international peace."

1531.   **Conflict** in world politics. - Edited by Steven L. Spiegel and Kenneth Waltz. - Bibliographical notes. - Cambridge, Mass., Wintrhop, 1971. -

1532.   **Constantin, F.** L'Organisation des Nations Unies et les territoires non-autonomes: contribution à l'histoire de la décolonisation et à l'étude du processus décisionnel dans les organisations internationales. - t.1-3. Bibliography: 11 leaves, t. 3. - Bordeaux, Centre universitarie de po copiage de l'A.G.E.B., 1970. - 3v.
Paged continuously. (661 1.)
Reproduced from typewritten copy.
Thèse - Univ. de Bordeaux.

1533.   **Contemporary** international relations. - 1949/1950-   . - Includes bibliographies. - Cambridge, Mass., Harvard university press, 1949-
        v.
Pub. annually.
Editor: 1949-   , Norman J. Padelford.

1534.   **Coordinating committee on documentation in the social sciences.** International repertory of social science documentation centres. - Prepared for the Department of social sciences, Unesco. - Paris, United Nations educational, scientific and cultural organisation, 1952. 42 p. E F
At head of cover-title: Documentation in the social sciences.

1535.   **Copeland, M.** The game of nations; the amorality of power politics. - Bibliography: p. 257-261. - London, Weidenfeld and Nicolson, 1970. - 272 p.

1536.   **Corbett, P. E.** The individual and world society. - Notes, partly bibliographical. - Princeton, N.H., Princeton university, 1953. - 59 p. - (Center for research on world political institutions, Princeton universit Publications. no.2.)

1537.   -- --- Law in diplomacy. - Bibliographical notes. - Princeton, N.J., Princeton university press, 1959. - xii, 290 p.
"Published by the Center of international studies, Princeton university."

1538.   **Corkran, H.** Patterns of international cooperation in the Caribbean, 1942-1969. - Bibliographical notes: p.267-277. - Dallas, Southern Methodist university press, 1970. - xviii, 285 p.
"A Jno. E. Owens memorial foundation publication."
Caribbean area - Foreign relations.

539. **Courlander, H.** Shaping our times: what the United Nations is and does. - Bibliography: p. 235-237. - New York, Oceana publications, 1960. - 242 p.

540. **Cox, A. M.** Prospects for peacekeeping. - Bibliography: p. 167-169. - Washington, D.C., Brookings institution, 1967. - xii, 178 p.

541. **Cox, R. W.** International organisation: world politics; studies in economic and social agencies. - Edited/ by Robert W. Cox. - Notes, partly bibliographical. - London, Macmillan, 1969. - 319 p.
"Papers prepared under the auspices of the International political science association."

542. **Crespo, J. B.** La conferencia de San Francisco y la seguridad de los pueblos. - Bibliography: p. 347. - Buenos Aires, El Ateneo, 1946. - 347. p.

543. **Current** thought on peace and war. - v.1-   ; 1960-   . - New York, 1960-   . -   v.
Pub. irregularly.
Issued by; 1960, Institute for international order; 1961-1968, Current thought.
Publication suspended 1969-1971.
A world affairs digest of literature and research on achieving peace.
Bibliographies on peace, international relations, international organisation, United Nations, peacekeeping operations, international security, disarmament.

544. **Degerman, A.** Samarbete över gränserna; studie-handbok til radioserien "För en enad värld" våren 1950. - Bibliography: p. 171-172. - Stockholm, Radiotjänst, 1950. - 172 p.

545. **Delmas, C.** Armements nucléaires et guerre froide. - Bibliography: p.175-179. - Paris, Flammarion, 1971. - 183 p. - (Questions d'histoire. 25.)

546. **Denver, Colo. University. Social science foundation.** Monograph series in world affairs.- v.1, no.1-   ; 1963/64-   . - Includes bibliographies. - Denver, Colo., Univ. of Denver, 1964-   . -   v.

547. **Derpa, R. M.** Das Gewaltverbot der Satzung der Vereinten Nationen und die Anwendung nichtmilitärishcer Gewalt. - Bibliography: p. 137-149. - Bad Homburg, Athenäum Verlag, 1970. - 149 p. - (Völkerrecht und Aussenpolitik. 8.)

548. **Deutsch, K. W.** The analysis of international relations. - Bibliography: p. 210-211. - Englewood Cliffs, N.J., Prentice Hall, 1968. - x, 214 p. - (Foundations of modern political science series.)

549. **Dimitrov, T. D.** Simulation in social sciences with special regard to international relations; selective bibliography. - Geneva, 1969. - 31 p.
At head of title: United Nations. Library, Geneva. Catalogue Department.

550. The **Diplomat's** annual. - 6th-   ; 1951-   . - London, Diplomatic press and publishing co., 1951-   . -   v.
Annual edition of the "Diplomatic bulletin." (1951-65.)
Monthly supplement: "Diplomatic and consular list". (1966- Ja. 1968.)   From Mar. 1968, replaced by section in "Diplomatic bookshelf".

551. **Discord** and harmony: readings in international politics. - Bibliographical notes. - Edited by Ivo D. Duchacek. - New York, Holt, Rinehart and Winston, 1972. - xiv, 397 p.

· M

1552.   **Documents** on international relations in the Caribbean. Edited by Roy Preiswerk. - Bibliographical notes: p. 836-842. - Rio Piedras, Institute of Caribbean studies, University of Puerto Rico, 1970. - 853 p. - (University of the West Indies, St. Augustine, Trinidad. Institute of international relations. Document and monograph series.

1553.   **Dossier** de l'Europe des six du plan Schuman à la commission Rey: où en est la Communauté?   où va-t-elle? - Bibliography: p. 320-32 Verviers (Belgique), Gérard, 1969. - 336 p. - (Marabout université. v. 176.)
"Dossier établie par Maryse Charpentier, avec la collaboration de H. Brugmans... et d'autres.

1554.   **Dossiers** de la guerre froide. - Bibliography: 4 p. following p. 386. - Verviers (Belgique), Gérard, 1969. - 386 p. - (Marabout université. v. 177.)
At head of title: J. Mordal. G.A. Chevallaz. R. Gheysens. J. de Launay.

1555.   **Douglas, W. O.** International dissent: six steps toward world peace. - Bibliographical notes. - New York, Random house, 1971. - 155 p.

1556.   **Draper, T.** Israel and world politics; roots of the third Arab-Israeli wa Bibliographical notes: p. 266-270. - New York, Viking press, 1968. x, 278 p. - (Viking compass books. C 233.)

1557.   **Duchacek, I. D.** Nations and men: an introduction to international politics. - Bibliographical notes. - 2nd ed. - New York, Holt, Rineha and Winston, 1971. - xv, 560 p.

1558.   **Dulles, E. L.** Détente: cold war strategies in transition. - Edited by Eleanor Lansing Dulles and Robert Dickson Crane, with the assistance of Mary Catherine McCarthy. - Notes, partly bibliographica New York, F.A. Praeger, 1965. - x, 307 p.
"Published for the Center for strategic studies, Georgetown university."

1559.   **Dunn, F. S.** War and the minds of men. - Bibliographical notes. - Ne York, Council on foreign relations, 1950. - xvi, 115 p.

1560.   **Durdenevskiĭ, V. N.** Piât' prinfsipov mirnogo sosushchestvovaniâ. - Bibliography: p. 117. - Moskva, Gos. izd-vo îurid. lit-ry, 1957. - 117
At head of title: V.N. Durdenevskiĭ, M.I. Lazarev.
Peaceful coexistence.

1561.   **Duroselle, J. B.** Politiques nationales envers les jeunes états, sous la direction de Jean-Baptiste Duroselle et Jean Meyriat. - Notes, partly bibliographical. - Paris, A. Colin, 1964. - 347. p. - (Foundation natic des sciences politiques. Cahiers. 131.)
At head of title: Centre d'étude des relations internationales.

1562.   **Dworkis, M. B.** An analytical survey of concepts and plans of world government. - Bibliography: p. 672-815. - New York, 1952.
Microfilm copy of typewritten manuscript. Positive.
Collation of the original: vi, 815 p.
Diss. - New York university.

1563.   **Dzélépy, E. N.** Le secret de Churchill: vers la troisième guerre mond 1945-   . - Notes, partly bibliographical. - Paris, Le Pavillon, R. M 1972. - 294 p.
World war, 1939-1945.

564. **East-West** contacts; a bimonthly review. - v.4- ; 1970- . - The Hague, International documentation and information centre (Interdoc), 1970- . - v.
Pub. bi-monthly, 1970; monthly, 1971- .

565. **Edwards, D. V.** International political analysis. - Bibliographical notes. - New York, Holt, Rinehart and Winston, 1969. - xiii, 366 p.

566. **Egorov, V. N.** Mezhdunarodnye otnosheniĩa: bibliograficheskiĩ spravochnik, 1945-1960 gg. - Moskva, Izd-vo Instituta mezhdunarodnykh otnosheniĩ, 1961. - 405 p.

567. -- --- Mirnoe sosushchestvovanie i revoliûtsionnyĩ profsess. - Bibliography: p. 200-222. - Moskva, Izd-vo "Mezhdunarodnye otnosheniĩa", 1971. - 222 p.
U.S.S.R. - Foreign policy. International relations. Revolutions.

568. -- --- Vneshniâiâ politika i mezhdunarodnye otnosheniĩa: bibliograficheskiĩ spravochnik, 1961. - iĩun' 1964 g. - Moskva, Izd-vo "Mezhdunarodnye otnosheniĩa", 1965. - 279 p.

569. **Eisler, R.** Winning the peace; a comprehensive policy, outlined by Robert Eisler and Eric George Hart. - Notes, partly bibliographical: p. 223-269. - London, F. Muller, 1948. - ix, 269 p.

570. **Ėkonomicheskoe** planirovanie i diplomatiĩa; rol'mezhdunarodnykh otnosheniĩ, vneshneĩ politiki i diplomatii v planirovanii razvitiĩa molodykh natsional'nykh gosudarstv. - Bibliographical notes: p. p. 272-278. - Pod red. V.D. Shchetinina. - Moskva, Izd-vo "Mezhdunarodnye otnosheniĩa", 1970. - 279 p.

571. **Elkordy, A. H. M.** Crisis of diplomacy: the three wars... and after... - Bibliography: p. 245-260. - San Antonio, Tex., 1971. - xii, 296 p.
Jewish-Arab relations. United Nations - Middle East. Middle East - Politics. Israel (State) - Foreign relations - Arab states.

572. **Emeny, B.** Mainsprings of world politics. - Bibliography: p. 58-62. - New York, 1956. - 62 p. - (Foreign policy association. Department of popular education. Headline series. no. 118.)

573. **Engers, J. F.** Hoofdstuk XI van het Handvest van de Verenigde Naties. - Bibliography: p. 243-248. - Amsterdam, N.V. Noord-hollandsche uitgevers maatschappij, 1956. 0 xvi, 248 p.

574. **Ereli, E.** United Nations supervision of provisional measures for the cessation of hostilities. - Bibliography: p. 308-319. - Medford, Mass., 1956.
Microfilm copy of typewritten manuscript. Negative.
Collation of the original: vi, 319 p.
Thesis - Fletcher school of law and diplomacy.
With this on same reel: Moser, Leo John. The human rights program of the United Nañ tion Nations, 1945-1955.

575. **Études** internationales. v.1- ; 1970- . - Includes bibliographies. - Québec, Institut canadien des affaires internationales, 1970- . - v.
Pub. quarterly.

1576. **Europas** Zukunft zwischen Ost und West, mit einer Einführung von
Curt Gasteyger und Beiträgen von James F. Brown... u.a. - Bibliographica
notes. - Baden-Baden, Nomos Verlagsgesellschaft, 1971. - 158 p. -
(Schriftenreihe europäische Wirtschaft. Bd. 42.)
Original ed. pub. under title: Europe between East and West.

1577. The **European** community in the 1970's. - Edited by Steven Joshua
Warnecke. - Includes bibliographies. - New York, F. A. Praeger, 1972. -
xxii, 228 p. - (Praeger special studies in international politics and
public affairs.)
"Published for the European studies committee, Graduate division, City university of New York."

1578. The **evolving** United Nations: a prospect for peace? - Edited by
Kenneth J. Twitchett. - Bibliography: p. 229-239. - London, Europa
publications, 1971. - xv, 239 p.
"Published for the David Davies memorial institute of international studies."

1579. **Fabian, L. L.** Soldiers without enemies: preparing the United Nations
for peace-keeping. - Bibliography: p. 269-270. - Washington, D.C.,
Brookings institution, 1971. - viii, 315 p.

1580. **Falk, R. A.** Toward a theory of war prevention. - Notes, partly
bibliographical. - Edited by Richard A. Falk and Saul H.
Mendlovitz. - New York, World law fund, 1966. - xx, 394 p. -
(Strategy of world order. v.1.)

1581. **Fanshawe, M.** The Charter explained. - Bibliography: on p. 39. - London,
United Nations association, 1945. - 39 p.

1582. **Farnie, D. A.** East and West of Suez: the Suez Canal in history,
1854-1956. - Bibliography: p. 759-798. - Oxford, Clarendon
press, 1969. - ix, 860 p.

1583. **Feis, H.** From trust to terror; the onset of the cold war, 1945-1950. -
Bibliography: p. 413-418. - New York, W.W. Norton, 1970. - xx, 428

1584. **Fischer, P.** Europarat und parlamentarische Aussenpolitik. - Bibliography:
p. 131-134. - München, R. Oldenbourg, 1962. - 134 p. - (Deutsche
Gesellschaft für auswärtige Politik. Forschungsinstitut. Dokumente und
Berichte. Bd. 16.)

1585. **Fleming, D. F.** The cold war and its origins, 1917-1960. - v. 1-2. -
Notes, partly bibliographical. - London, G. Allen and Unwin, 1961. -
2 v.

1586. **Flynn, A. H.** World understanding: a selected bibliography. -
Dobbs Ferry, N.Y. - Published for the United Nations
association of the United States of America by Oceana
publications, 1965. - xv, 263 p.

1587. **Fondation nationale des sciences politiques.** Eléments de
bibliographie sur l'histoire des idées et des faits politiques
économiques et sociaux depuis le milieu du XVIIIe siècle. -
Paris, Ed. Domat Montchrestien, 1946. - 135 p.

588. **For** peace and the dignity of man. - Bibliography: p. 91-94. - Dobbs Ferry, N.Y., Oceana publications, 1964. - 118 p. - (The Oceana library on the United Nations. Study guide series. 5.)
"The material was assembled by the UNESCO youth institute, under the auspices of UNESCO and in co-operation with the United Nations and the other organizations covered in the series."

589. **Foreign** affairs bibliography: a selected and annotated list of books on international relations, 1919-   . - New York, Harper, 1933-   . -   v. in   v.
Pub. by the Council on foreign relations.

590. **Foreign** policy. - 1970/71-   . - Includes bibliographies. - New York, National affairs, inc., 1970-   . -   v.
Pub. quarterly.

591. **Foreign** policy and the developing nation. - Richard Butwell, editor. - Bibliographical notes at the end of each chapter. - Lexington, Univ. of Kentucky press, 1969. - 236 p.
Contributors: Henry Bienen... and others.

592. **Forndran, E.** Probleme der internationalen Abrüstung die internationalen Bemühungen um Abrüstung und kooperative Rüstungssteuerung, 1962-1968. - Bibliographical notes: p. 301-338. - Frankfurt/M., A. Metzner, 1970. - xxviii, 450 p. - (Rüstungsbeschränkung und Sicherheit. Bd. 8.)

593. **Forsythe, D. P.** United Nations peacemaking: the Conciliation commission for Palestine. - Bibliography: p. 187-195. - Baltimore, The Johns Hopkins university press, 1971. - xvii, 201 p.

594. **Forward, N.** The field of nations: an account of some new approaches to international relations. - Bibliography: p. 194-200. - London, Macmillan, 1971. - vii, 207 p. - (New studies in international relations.)

595. **Fox, W. T.** The super-powers. The United States, Britain, and the Soviet Union, their responsibility for peace. - Bibliography notes: p. 165-172. - New York, Harcourt, Brace and co., 1944. - 184 p.
Institute of international studies, Yale university.

596. **Frank, L. A.** The arms trade in international relations. - Bibliography: p. 259-266. - New York, F.A. Praeger, 1969. - xviii, 266 p. - (Praeger special studies in international politics and public affairs.)
Bibliographical notes at the end of each chapter.

597. **Frankel, J.** International relations. - Bibliography: p. 170-172. - 2nd. ed., - London, Oxford university press, 1969. - xv, 175 p. - (Opus. 44.)
Oxford paperbacks university series.

598. **Friedmann, W. G.** De l'efficacité des institutions internationales. - Texte inédit tr. de l'anglais et adapté par Simone Dreyfus. - Bibliography: p. 184-185. - Paris, A. Colin, 1970. - 199 p. - (Collection U. sér: "Relations et institutions internationales".)

1599.   **Friis, F. T. B.** Förenta Nationerna: mål, medel och verksamhet. -
         Bibliography: p. 297-300. - Stockholm, Aldus/Bonniers, 1965. - 313 p.
         (Aldusböckerna. A. 125.)
         "Danska originalets titel: 'De Forente Nationer: mål, midler og virke' (1963). Översättning
         av Lars Erik Blomqvist."

1600.   **Fulbright, J. W.** The arrogance of power. - Bibliographical notes:
         p. 259-264. - New York, Random house, 1966. - xv, 264 p.
         Expanded version of the Christian A. Herter Lecture series delivered at the Johns Hopkins
         School of advanced international studies.

1601.   -- - -- - Old myths and new realities, and other commentaries. - Biblio-
         graphical notes. - New York, Random house, 1964. - viii, 147 p. -
         (Vintage books. V-264.)

1602.   -- - -- - Prospects for the West. - Bibliography: p. 123-127. - Cambridge,
         Mass., Harvard university press, 1963. - ix, 132 p. - (William L. Clayton
         lectures on international economic affairs and foreign policy.)

1603.   **Furniss, E. S.** American military policy; strategic aspects of world
         political geography. - Bibliography: p. 475-484. - New York, Rinehart,
         1957. - xiii, 494 p.

1604.   **Gange, J.** University research on international affairs. - Bibliography:
         p. 134-141. - Washington, D.C., American council on education,
         1958. - xvii, 147 p. - (Studies in universities and world affairs.)
         "Prepared for the Carnegie endowment for international peace."

1605.   **Geneva research centre.** Tentative list of studies in the fields of inter-
         national relations now in preparation. - Geneva, 1938. - 51 l.

1606.   **Gibson, J. S.** The development of mutual security arrangements and the
         impact upon the functioning of the United Nations in the maintenanc
         international peace and security. - Bibliography: p. 279-287. - New Yc
         1956.
         Microfilm copy of typewritten manuscript. Positive.
         Collation of the original: 3, ix, 287 p.
         Thesis - Columbia university.

1607.   **Giles, R. S.** The development of a United Nations' military policy, with
         emphasis on the United States. - Bibliography: p. 418-420. - Chicago,
         1952.
         Collation of the original: vii, 420 p.
         Diss. - Univ. of Chicago (thesis no. 1627.)

1608.   **Giraud, É.** L'interdiction du recours à la force; la théorie et la pratique
         des Nations Unies. - Notes, partly bibliographical. - Paris, A. Pedone,
         1963. - 44 p.
         At head of title: A propos de l'affaire cubaine. La "Quarantaine".
         "Extrait de la 'Revue générale de droit international public', juillet-septembre 1963, no.3."

1609.   **Glick, E. B.** The policies of the Latin American governments toward
         Israel in the United Nations. - Bibliography: p. 297-321. - Gainesville,
         Fla., 1955.
         Microfilm copy of typewritten manuscript. Made in 1955 by University microfilms (Publica-
         tion no. 12, 772). Positive.
         Collation of the original: ix, 321 p. tables.
         Diss. - Univ. of Florida.

10.   **Golay, P. W.**   La Charte des Nations-Unies et ses antécédents. - Biblio-
        graphy: p. 203-209. - Bâle, 1945.
        Collation of the original: 215 p.
        Thèse - Univ. de Bâle.

11.   **Goodrich, L. M.**   Charter of the United Nations.   Commentary and
        documents/ by Leland M. Goodrich and Edvard Hambro. - Bibliography:
        p. 387-400. - Boston, World peace foundation, 1946. - xiii, 400 p.

12.   -- - -- Commentaire de la charte des Nations Unies.   Éd. française établie
        par André-Marie Guynat et revue par Edvard Hambro. - Bibliographical
        notes. - Neuchâtel, Éd. de la Baconnière, 1946. - 429 p. - (Histoire et
        société d'aujourd'hui.)
        At head of title: Leland M. Goodrich et Edvard Hambro.

13.   -- - -- The United Nations and the maintenance of international peace
        and security/ by Leland M. Goodrich and Anne P. Simons. - Bibliog-
        raphical notes. - Washington, Brookings institution, 1955. - xiii, 709 p.

14.   **Gordenker, L.**   The United Nations in international politics. - Edited by
        Leon Gordenker. - Bibliographical notes. - Princeton, N.J., Princeton
        University press, 1971. - 241 p.
        "Written under the auspices of the Center of international studies, Princeton university."

15.   **Government** and opposition. - v.1-   ; 1965-   . - Includes bibliographies. -
        London, 1965-   . -   v.
        Pub. quarterly.
        "A quarterly journal of comparative politics, published by Government and opposition, with the
        assistance of the London school of economics and political science."
        Political science research.   World politics.

16.   **Grandin, A.**   Bibliographie générale des sciences juridiques, politiques,
        économiques et sociales de 1800 à 1925-1926. - Publiée par la
        Société anonyme du Recueil Sirey. - Paris, Société anonyme du
        Receuil Sirey, L. Tenin, directeur, 1926. - 3 v.
        At head of title: Société anonyme du Recueil Sirey.
        Vol.3, Tables: 1.Table alphabétique par ordre de matières.   2. Table alphabétique par
        noms d'auteurs, des anonymes et des publications périodiques.
        Supplément. 1er-19e; 1926/27-1950. Paris, Recueil Sirey, 1928-1951. 18 v.
        Ceased pub. with v.19 (1950).

17.   **Greber, A.**   Die dauernde Neutralität und das kollektive Sicherheitssystem
        der Vereinten Nationen. - Bibliography: p. 7-11. - Zürich, Juris-Verlag,
        1967. - 127 p.
        Diss. - Univ. Freiburg in der Schweiz.

18.   **Green, J. F.**   The United Nations and human rights. - Notes, partly
        bibliographical. - Washington, D.C., Brookings institution, 1956. - viii,
        194 p.
        "The present publication... will comprise part three of the volume on 'The United Nations and
        promotion of the general welfare'... and is published in advance of the rest of the volume." -p.v.

19.   **Grimal, H.**   La décolonisation, 1919-1963. - 3e éd. - Bibliography:
        p. 399-401. - Paris, A. Colin, 1970. - 407 p. - (Collection U.
        sér.: "Histoire contemporaine".)

1620.   **Gross, E. A.**   The United Nations: structure for peace. - Notes, partly
         bibliographical. - New York, Harper, 1962. - ix, 132 p.
         "Published for the Council on foreign relations."

1621.   **Gross, F.**   World politics and tension areas. - Notes, partly biblio-
         graphical: p. 335-365. - New York, New York university press,
         1966. - xvii, 377 p.

1622.   **Haas, E. B.**   Collective security and the future international system. -
         Notes, partly bibliographical: p. 99-117. - Denver, Colo., 1968. -
         117 p. - (Denver, Colo. University. Social science foundation.
         Monograph series in world affairs. v.5, no.1, 1967/68.)
         At head of title: The Social science foundation and Graduate school of international
         studies. University of Denver.

1623.   -- --- Human rights and international action: the case of freedom of
         association. - Bibliographical notes: p. 161-175. - Stanford, Calif.,
         Standford university press, 1970. - xiii, 184 p.

1624.   **Hadawi, S.**   The Arab-Israeli conflict (cause and effect). - Bibliographical
         notes. - Beirut, 1967. - v, v, 58 p.

1625.   **Hadwen, J. G.**   How United Nations decisions are made/ by John G.
         Hadwen and Johan Kaufmann. - Notes, partly bibliographical: p.139-144
         Leyden, A.W. Sijthoff, 1960. 144 p.

1626.   **Hagemann, M.**   Der provisorische Frieden;   die Bauprinzipien der inter-
         nationalen Ordnung seit 1945. - Bibliography: p. 729-735. - Erlenbach-
         Zürich, E. Rentsch, 1964. - 744 p.

1627.   **Hague. Peace palace. Library.**   Catalogue/ par P.C. Molhuysen et
         E.R. Oppenheim. - Leyde, A.W. Sijthoff, 1916. - xlv p., 1576 col.
         At head of title: Bibliothèque du Palais de la paix.

1628.   -- --- 1er-3me suppl. - Leyde, A.W. Sijthoff, 1922-37. 3 v.

1629.   -- --- Index alphabétique par noms d'auteurs ou mots d'ordre du
         Catalogue 1916 et des suppléments 1922 et 1929. - Leyde,
         A.W. Sijthoff, 1932. - 1466 col.

1630.   -- --- Index sommaire par ordre alphabétique des matières du Catalogue
         1916 et des suppléments 1922 et 1929. - Leyde, A.W. Sijthoff, 1933.
         2 v. in 1.

1631.   -- --- Index alphabétique par noms propres du 3me suppl. 1937. -
         Leyde, A.W. Sijthoff, 1937. - 79 p.

1632.   -- --- Classement du catalogue systématique. - 1954. - 20 p.

1633.   -- --- Selective bibliographies. - 1-   . - Leyden, A.W. Sijthoff,
         1953-   . -   v.

34. **Hahn, C. H.** Der Schuman-Plan; eine Untersuchung im besonderen Hinblick auf die deutsch-französische Stahlindustrie. - Bibliography: p. 155-158. - München, R. Pflaum, 1953. - 158 p.

35. **Haile, M.** United Nations consideration of domestic questions and their international effects. - Bibliography: p. 177-180. - New York, 1961.
Microfilm copy of typewritten manuscript. Positive.
Collation of the original: iii, 180 p.
Diss. - Columbia university.

36. **Halderman, J. W.** The United Nations and the rule of law; Charter development through the handling of international disputes and situations. - Bibliography: p. iii-iv. - Dobbs Ferry, N.Y., Oceana publications, 1966. - v,248 p.

37. **Halle, L. J.** The cold war as history. - Bibliography: p. 419-421. - London, Chatto & Windus, 1967. - xiv, 434 p.

38. **Hamilton, T. J.** The United Nations in crisis. - Bibliography: p. 59-62. - New York, 1961. - 62 p. - (Foreign policy association. Headline series. no. 146.)

39. **Hammarskjöld forum. 13th, New York, 1968.** The Middle East: prospects for peace; background papers and proceedings. - Quincy Wright, author of the working paper, Isaac Shapiro, editor. - Bibliography: p. 85-107. - Dobbs Ferry, N.Y., Oceana publications, 1969. - x, 113 p.
"Published for the Association of the bar of the city of New York."

40. **Harbottle, M.** The blue berets. - Bibliography: p. 129-145. - London, L. Cooper, 1971. - 157 p.

41. **Harley, J. E.** Documentary textbook on the United Nations; humanity's march towards peace: a volume emphasizing official co-operation for world peace, especially the United Nations and related specialized agencies. - Bibliography: p. 853-912. - Los Angeles, Calif., Center for international understanding, 1947. - xx, 952 p.

542. **Harrington, C. W.** The problem of disarmament in the United Nations. - Bibliography: p. 174-179. - Genève, Impr. centrale, 1950. - 179 p.
Thèse - Genève.

543. **Hartmann, F. H.** The relations of nations. - Bibliography: p. 613-637. - New York, Macmillan, 1957. - xv, 637, xi p.

544. **Hastings, P.** The cold war, 1945-1969. - Bibliography: 1 p. preceding p.6. - London, Benn, 1969. - (20th century histories.) - 127 p.

545. **Hero, A. O.** Americans in world affairs. - Notes, partly bibliographical: p. 114-165. - Boston, Mass., 1959. - iii, 165 p. - (Studies in citizen participation in international relations. v.1.)
"Sponsored by the World peace foundation."

646. **Hill, N. L.** International administration. - Bibliography: p. 247-250. - New York, McGraw-Hill book company, 1931. - xi, 292 p.

1647.   **Hilmi, A.**   Die Unvollkommenheit der Satzung der Vereinten Nationen. - Bibliography: p. v-vii. - Bonn, 1952.
Collation of the original: vii, 74 p.
"Abhandlung zur Erlangung des Grades eines Doktors der Rechte..." - Rheinische Friedrich-Wilhelm Universität zu Bonn.

1648.   **Histoire** des relations internationales/ pub. sous la direction de Pierre Renouvin. - Bibliography at the end of each chapter. - t. 1er-   . - Paris, Hachette, 1953-   . -   v.

1649.   **Hoffman, A. S.**   International communication and the new diplomacy. - Notes, partly bibliographical: p. 199-206. - Bloomington, Indiana university press, 1968. - viii, 206 p. - (Indiana. University. International studies.)

1650.   **Hoffmann, S.**   Contemporary theory in international relations. - Bibliography: p. 286-287. - Englewood Fliffs, N.J. Prentice Hall, 1960. - x, 293 p.

1651.   -- ---   Influence des organisations internationales sur les compétences de Etats en matière politique, 1815-1952. - Bibliography: p. 532-547. - Paris, 1953.
Microfilm copy of typewritten manuscript. Negative.
Collation of the original: 557 p.
Thèse - Univ. de Paris.

1652.   -- ---   Organisations internationales et pouvoirs politiques des états. - Bibliography: p. 419-427. - Paris, A. Colin, 1954. - 427 p. - (Foundation nationale des sciences plitiques. Cahiers. 52.)

1653.   **Holcombe, A. N.**   A strategy of peace in a changing world. - Notes, partly bibliographical. - Cambriges, Mass., Harvard university press, 1967. - 332 p.

1654.   **Hovey, J. A.**   The superparliaments: inter-parliamentary consultation and Atlantic cooperation. - Bibliography: p. 187-197. - New York, F.A. Praeger, 1966. - xiv, 202 p. - (Praeger special studies in international politics and public affairs.)

1655.   **Howe, J. T.**   Multicrises: sea power and global politics in the missile age. - Bibliography: p. 368-399. - Cambridge, Mass., M.I.T. press, Massachusetts institute of technology, 1971. - xii, 412 p.

1656.   **Hoyt, A. J.**   Regionalism and the United Nations. - Bibliography: p. 303-328. - Los Angeles, Calif., 1954.
Collation of the original: vii, 522 p. tables.
Diss. - Univ. of Southern California.

1657.   **Hudson, G. F.**   The hard and bitter peace; world politics since 1945. - Bibliography: p. 301-307. - London, Pall Mall press, 1966. - 319 p.
Bibliographical notes: p. 297-299.

1658.   **Hugo, G.**   Appearance and reality in international relations. - Bibliography: p. 197-200. - London, Chatto & Windus, 1970. - 207 p.

1659.   Das **198** (hundertachtundneuzigste) Jahrzehnt: eine Team-Prognose für 1970 bis 1980; 26 Original-Beiträge, hrsg. ... von Claus Grossner. - Bibliography: p. 535-540. - Hamburg, C. Wegner, 1969. - 551 p.

1660.   **IÂnchenko, S. E.** Razdel mira mezhdu soiûzami kapitalistov. - Notes, partly bibliographical. - Minsk, Izd-vo "Vysshaiâ shkola", 1965. - 93 p.

1661.   **Institut français de polémologie.** Études polémologiques.-no.1-   . - Includes bibliographies. - Paris, 1971-   . -   v.

1662.   **Institut für internationale Politik und Wirtschaft, Berlin.** IPW-Berichte. - 1.-   Jhg.; 1972-   . - Includes bibliographies. - Berlin, 1972. -   v.
Pub. monthly.
Superseded: Apr. 1972, Its: DWI-Berichte. (1950-1972.)

1663.   **Institut mezhdunarodnykh otnoshenii, Moscow.** Uchenye zapiski. - Includes bibliographies. - vyp. 1-   . - Moskva, 1958-   . -   v.
International relations.

1664.   **Integration;** Vierteljahreshefte zur Europaforschung. - v.1, no.1-   ; 1969-   . - Includes bibliographies. - Brussels, 1969-   . -   v.
Pub. quarterly.
"Herausgeber: Kommission der Europäischen Gemeinschaften."

1665.   **International** affairs: an annotated and intensively indexed compilation of significant books, pamphlets, and articles/ by the Universial reference system. - 2nd ed. - Oxford, Pergamon press, 1969. - xx, 1206 p. - (Political science, government, and public policy series. v.1.)
"Prepared under the direction of Alfred de Grazia, general editor.. and others."

1666.   **International conference on humanitarian law, San Remo, 1970.** Atti del Convegno internazionale di diritto humanitario=Actes du Congrès international de droit humanitarie=Proceedings of the International conference on humanitarian law. - Notes, partly bibliographical. - Lugano, Grassi, 1971. - 385 p.
Text partly Italian, partly French, partly English.
Civil rights. United Nations. General assembly. Universal declaration of human rights.

1667.   **International institute of intellectual co-operation.** Annuaires et périodiques servant à l'étude scientifique des relations internationales. - Paris, 1931. - 77 p. - (C. 114.1931.)

1668.   **International law association. Committee on the Charter of the United Nations.** Preliminary report on self-defence under the Charter of the United Nations and the use of prohibited weapons/ by Georg Schwarzenberger, rapporteur. - Notes, partly bibliographical. - n.p. 1961. - 25 l. - (International law association. Miscellaneous preparatory and interim documents and committee reports. no.3.)
At head of title: International law association. Brussels conference (1962).

1669.   -- --- Report on self-defence under the Charter of the United Nations and the use of prohibited weapons/ by Georg Schwarzenberger, rapporteur. - Bibliography: p. 44-46. - n.p., 1962. - 46 p. - (International law association. Miscellaneous preparatory and interim documents and committee reports. no.5.)
At head of title: International law association. Brussels conference (1962).

1670.　International law association. Committee on the Charter of the United Nations. Report on some aspects of the principle of self-defence in the Charter of the United Nations and the topics covered by the Dubrovnic resolution/ by Georg Schwarzenberger. - Bibliography: p.73-79. - London, 1958. - 79 p.

1671.　-- Committee on the review of the Charter of the United Nations. Rep by Georg Schwarzenberger. - Bibliography: p. 94-98. - London, 1954. - 98 p.
　　　Submitted to the 46th Conference of the Association at Edinburgh, August 8th-14th, 1954.

1672.　International organisation and integration; a collection of the texts of documents relating to the United Nations, its related agencies and regional international organisations, with annotations. - Editors in chief: H.F. van Panhuys, L.J. Brinkhorst, and H.H. Maas. Co-ordinating editor: M. van Leeuwen Boomkamp. - Deventer, Æ.El Kluwer, 1968. - xxvi, 1141 p.
　　　"Published under the auspices of the Cornelis von Vollenhoven foundation, Leyden and the Europe institute, Leyden."
　　　Earlier ed. issued with the title:　United Nations textbook.

1673.　International peace research association. Conference. (Inaugural), Groningen, 1965. Proceedings. - Bibliography at the end of some chapters. - Assen, van Gorcum, 1966. - vi, 372 p. - (IPRA studies in peace research. 1.)

1674.　-- Conference. 2nd, Tällberg (Sweden), 1967. Proceedings. - v.1-2. - Bibliography at the end of some chapters. - Assen, van Gorcum, 1968. 2 v. - (IPRA studies in peace research. 2.)

1675.　-- General conference. 3rd, Karlovy Vary, Czechoslovak Republic, 1969 - Proceedings. - v.1-3. - Bibliographies at the end of some chapters. - Assen, Van Gorcum, 1970. - 3 v. - (International peace research associ tion.　IPRA studies in peace research. 4.)

1676.　International peace research institute, Stockholm. The problem of chemi and biological warfare. pt.1-　. Provisional ed. - Includes bibliographie Stockholm, 1970-　.　v.
　　　At head of title: SIPRI, Stockholm international peace research institute.

1677.　International political science association. World congress. 6th, Geneva, 1964. International organizations=Les organisations internationales. Int.Org/Gén/F, Int. Org/1-8. - Notes, partly bibliographical. - Geneva, 1964. - 1 v.
　　　Texts partly English, partly French.

1678.　International relations:　a selection of current readings. - no.1-2; Februar 1947-　. - Cambridge, Mass., 1947-　. v. - (Massachusetts institu of technology.　Publications in international affairs.)
　　　Prepared by the International relations division, Department of economics and social science, Massachusetts institute of technology.

1679.　International security; reflections on survival and stability. Edited by Kenneth J. Twitchett. - Bibliography at the end of each chapter. - London, Oxford university press, 1971. - ix, 148 p. - (Oxford paperbacks.)

80. An **introduction** to the study of human rights: based on a series of lectures delivered at King's college, London, in the autumn of 1970. - Bibliography: p. 123-127. - London, Europa publications, 1972. - 127 p.

81. **Iredell, V. R.** Procedure for maintaining peace according to the United Nations Charter, 1945-1955. - Bibliography: p. 185-189. - Chicago, Ill., 1958.
Microfilm copy of typewritten manuscript. Positive.
Collation of the original: 189 p. tables.
Diss. - Univ. of Chicago.

82. **Issues** of today; a series of discussion pamphlets by staff writers of the Times newspaper. - Includes bibliographies. - no.1-   . - London, Times' education services, 1969. -   . - v.

83. **Italy. Aeronautica militare. Stato maggiore. Ufficio studi.** ONU ed altre organizzazioni internazionali. - Bibliography: p. 6. - Roma, Tip. G.Bardi, 1953. - 197 p. - (Its: Quaderno di cultura. n.29.)

84. **Jacob, P. E.** The dynamics of international organization; the making of world order/ by Philip E. Jacob and Alexine L. Atherton. - Notes, partly bibliographical. - Homewood, Ill., Dorsey press, 1965. - xvii, 723 p. - (Dorsey series in political science.)

85. **Jaenke, S. F.** Citizen participation in international organizations. - Bibliography: p. 286-298. - Urbana, Ill., 1952.
Microfilm copy of typewritten manuscript. Made in 1953 by University microfilms (Publications no. 4001). Positive.
Collation of the original: iv, ii, 298 p.
Thesis - Univ. of Illinois.

86. **James, A.** The politics of peace-keeping. - Select bibliography: p. 441-444. - London, Chatto & Windus, 1969. - 452 p. - (Institute for strategic studies. Studies in international security. no.12.)
"Study of the UN's peace-keeping operations up to mid-1968."

87. **Jenks, C. W.** The world beyond the charter in historical perspective; a tentative synthesis of four stages of world organization. - Bibliographical notes. - London, G.Allen and Unwin, 1969. - 199 p.

88. **Jiménez de Aréchaga, E.** La coordination des systèmes de l'ONU et de l'Organisation des états américains pour le règlement pacifique des différends et la sécurité collective. - Bibliography: p. 521-523. - (In Academy of international law, The Hague. Recueil des cours, 1964, I. Leyde (Pays-Bas), A.W. Sijthoff, 1964. v. 111, p. 419-526.)

89. **Kaeckenbeeck, G. S. F. C.** La charte de San-Francisco dans ses rapports avec le droit international. - Bibliography: p. 321-328. - (In Academy of international law, The Hague. Recueil des cours, 1947, I. Paris, 1948. v. 70, p. 109-330.)

90. **Kampf** der Friedenskräfte gegen Aggression und Aufrüstung; UNO-Bilanz 1968/69. - Bibliographical notes. - Berlin, Staatsverlag der Deutschen demokratischen Republik. 1969. - 238 p.

1691.   **Kapteyn, P. J. G.**   L'Assemblée commune de la Communauté européenne
        du charbon et de l'acier; un essai de parlementarisme européen. -
        Bibliography: p. 258-263. - Leyde, A.W. Sijthoff, 1962. - 270 p. -
        (Aspects européens. sér. C: Études politiques. no.9.)

1692.   **Karaosmanoğlu, A. L.**   Les actions militaires coercitives et non coercitive
        des Nations Unies. Préface de Georges Perrin. - Bibliography: p. 307-
        Genève, E. Droz, 1970. - 320 p. - (Travaux de droit, d'économie, de
        sociologie et de sciences politiques. no.82.)

1693.   **Kay, D. A.**   The United Nations political system. Edited by David A.
        Kay. - Notes, partly bibliographical. - New York, J. Wiley, 1967. -
        x, 419 p.

1694.   **Keohane, R. W.**   Transnational relations and world politics. - Edited/
        by Robert O. Keohane and Joseph S. Nye. - Bibliography: p. 399-408.
        Cambridge, Mass., Harvard university press, 1972. - xxix, 428 p.
        "Written under the auspices of the Center for international affairs, Harvard university."

1695.   **Khouri, F. J.**   The Arab-Israeli dilemma. - Bibliography: p. 409-424. -
        Syracuse, N.Y., Syracuse university press, 1968. - xi, 436 p.

1696.   **Kim, T.**   Die Vereinten Nationen und ihr kollektives Sicherheitssystem:
        Studie über die UN-Aktion gegen die Intervention der Volksrepublik
        China im Korea-Krieg. - Bibliography: p. 218-246. - München, Verlag
        UNI-Druck, 1968. - vi, 246 p.

1697.   **King, G. E. N.**   World friendship: a bibliography; sources of education:
        material. - Boston, Chapman & Grimes, 1935. - 81 p.

1698.   **Kintner, W. R.**   Eastern Europe and European security/ by William
        R. Kintner and Wolfgang Klaiber. - Bibliography: p. 377-393. -
        New York, Dunellen, 1971. - xix, 393 p.
        "Foreign policy research institute book."

1699.   **Kipp, H.**   UNESCO: Recht, sittliche Grundlage, Aufgabe. - Bibliography:
        p. 9-17. - München, Isar, 1957. - 227 p. - (Institut für Staatslehre
        und Politik, Mainz. Veröffentlichungen. Bd. 8.)

1700.   **Klare, M. T.**   War without end: American planning for the next
        Vietnams. - Bibliography: p. 449-464. - New York, A.A.Knopf,
        1972. - xx, 464 p.

1701.   **Kniâzhinskiĭ, V. B.**   Zapadnaiâ Evropa i problema mirnogo sosushche-
        stvovaniiâ. - Bibliographical notes. - Moskva, Sotsékgiz, 1963. - 285 p.

1702.   **Knorr, K. E.**   Contending approaches to international politics. - Edited
        by Klaus Knorr and James N. Rosenau. - Notes, partly bibliographical.
        Princeton, N.J., Princeton university press, 1969. - 297 p.
        "Published for the Princeton Center of international studies."

1703.   - - - - -   On the uses of military power in the nuclear age. - Biblio-
        graphical notes. - Princeton, N.J., Princeton university press, 1966. -
        x, 185 p.
        "Published for the Princeton Center of international studies."

704. **Kodifikacija** principa miroljubive i aktivne koegzistencije; zbirka radova. - Bibliographical notes. - Strucna redakcija Milan Šahović. - Beograd, Izdanje Instituta za medunarodnu politiku i privredu, 1969. - 426 p.
International relations.

705. **Koexistenz** zwischen Ost und West: Konflikt, Ko-operation, Konvergenz. Mit Beiträgen von Adolf Adam... u.a. Hrsg. von Hans Mayrzedt und Helmut Romé. - Bibliography: p. 323-346. - Wien, Europa Verlag, 1966. - 346 p. - (Europäische Perspektiven.)

706. **Kolko, G.** The limits of power: the world and United States foreign policy, 1945-1954. - Bibliographical notes: p. 719-798. - New York, Harper & Row, 1972. - xii, 820 p.
At head of title: Joyce and Gabriel Kolko.

707. **Kolloquium "25 Jahre Vereinte Nationen und internationale Sicherheit", Vienna, 1970.** Proceedings of the Colloquium: "25th anniversary of the United Nations and international security". - Bibliographical notes. - Vienna, International institute for peace, 1970. - i, 84 p. - (Peace and the sciences. no.2, 1970.)

708. **Koo, W.** Voting procedures in international political organizations. - Bibliography: p. 339-343. - New York, Columbia university press, 1947. - vii, 349 p.

709. **Kopal, V.** Otázka ozbrojených sil OSN. - Bibliography: p. 127-129. - Praha, 1961. - 162 p. - (Československá akademie věd. Rozpravy: Řada spolecenských věd. v. 71, no.7.)
Summary in English with title: The problem of the United Nations armed force: p.130-161.

710. **Krabbe, B.** Contributions to United Nations peacekeeping operations: the policy of some small Western European countries. - Bibliography: leaves 78-83. - Genève, 1971. - 83 p.
Mémoire - Institut universitaire de hatues études internationales.
United Nations - Peacekeeping operations. United Nations - Armed forces. United Nations emergency force. United Nations - Scandinavia. United Nations - Austria. United Nations - Switzerland.

711. **Krieg** und Frieden in der modernen Staatenwelt. - Notes, partly bibliographical. - Gütersloh, C. Bertelsmann, 1966. - 496 p. - (Krieg und Frieden. Bd. 7.)
Beiträge der Sozialwissenschaft. 2. Ausgewählt und eingeleitet von Uwe Nerlich.

712. **Kulski, W. W.** International politics in a revolutionary age. - Bibliography: p. 611-629. - New York, J.B. Lippincott, 1964. - xiv, 650 p.

713. **Kuz'min, E. L.** Mirovoe gosudarstvo: illiuzii ili real'nost'; kritika burzhuaznykh kontseptsii suvereniteta. - Bibliographical notes. - Moskva, Izd-vo "Mezhdunarodnye otnosheniia", 1969. - 198 p.

714. **Lacouture, J.** Le poids du tiers monde; un milliard d'hommes. - Notes, partly bibliographical. - Paris, B. Arthaud, 1962. - 329 p. - (Collection Notre temps. 3.)
At head of title: Jean Lacouture. Jean Baumier.

1715.   **Lafeber, W.** America, Russia, and the cold war, 1945-1966. - Biblio-
         graphy: p. 261-275. - New York, J. Wiley, 1967. - xi, 295 p. -
         (America in crisis.)

1716.   **Lall, A.** Modern international negotiation; principles and practice. -
         Notes, partly bibliographical: p. 355-383. - New York, Columbia
         university press, 1966. - xii, 404 p.
         "Prepared and published as part of the research program of the Columbia university,
         School of international affairs," - Foreword.

1717.   -- --- The UN and the Middle East crisis, 1967. - Notes, partly
         bibliographical. - New York, Columbia university press, 1968. - viii,
         322 p.

1718.   **Langenhove, F. van.** La crise du système de sécurité collective des
         Nations Unies, 1946-1957. - Bibliography: p. 261- 265. - Bruxelles,
         Institut royal des relations internationales, 1958. - 272 p.

1719.   **Langsam, W. C.** The world since 1919/ by Walter Consuelo Langsam
         and Otis C. Mitchell. - Bibliography: p. 689-716. - 8th ed. - New
         York, Macmillan, 1971. - xx, 743 p.

1720.   **Lapidoth, R. (Eschelbacher).** The Security council in the May 1967
         crisis: a study in frustration. - Notes, partly bibliographical. -
         Jerusalem, 1969. - 19 p.
         "Published by the Israel law review association, under the auspices of the Faculty of
         law, Hebrew university of Jerusalem."
         Reprinted from 'Israel law review', v.4, no.4, October 1969.

1721.   **Lee, J.** The diplomatic persuaders: new role of the mass media in
         international relations. - Bibliography: p. 197-199. - New York,
         J. Wiley, 1968. - xviii, 205 p. - (Wiley series on government and
         communication.)
         "In 1967 the Washington journalism center and American university conducted a series of
         seminars on the use of mass media by governments... Sixteen of these talks have been
         included in this book." - Book jacket.

1722.   The **legal** principles governing friendly relations and co-operation
         among states in the spirit of the United Nations charter. - Biblio-
         graphical notes. - Leyden, A.W. Sijthoff, 1966. - 152 p.
         "Lectures delivered during the seminar organized by the World federation of United
         Nations associations, Smolenice castle, Czechoslovakia, April 20-24, 1965, by
         M.K. Nawaz... and others."

1723.   **Lent, E. S.** Supranationale politische Integration durch Stärkung der
         Vereinten Nationen; eine Untersuchung des Programmes der Welt-
         bewegung für einen Weltbundesstaat. - Bibliography: p. 6-11 at the
         end. - Wien, 1954.
         Microfilm copy of typewritten manuscript. Negative.
         Collation of the original: ix, 250, 11 p.
         Diss. - Univ. Wien.

1724.   **Lerche, C. O.** The cold war, and after. - Bibliography: p. 143-145. -
         Englewood Cliffs, N.J., Prentice Hall, 1965. - viii, 150 p. - (Spectrum
         books. S-117.)

25. **L'Huillier, F.** De la Sainte-alliance au Pacte atlantique: histoire des relations internationales à l'époque contemporaine. - Includes bibliographies. - Neuchâtel, Éd. de la Baconnière, 1954-1955. - 2 v. - (Histoire et société d'aujourd'hui.)
Contents: 1. Le dix-neuvième siècle, 1815-1898. 2. Le vingtième siècle, 1898-1954.

26. -- --- Histoire de notre temps; politiques nationales et conflits internationaux, 1945-1962. - Bibliography: p. 397-407. - Paris, Sirey, 1964. - 409 p.
At head of title: F. L'Huillier avec la collaboration de D.W. Brogan... et d'autres.

27. -- --- Les institutions internationales et transnationales/ par Fernand L'Huillier, avec la collaboration de G. Hourdin... et d'autres. - Bibliography: p. 281-289. - Paris, Presses universitaires de France, 1961. - xvi, 295 p. - (Bibliothèque de la science politique. 3e sér.: Les institutions politiques.)

28. **Libbrecht, E.** Entreprises à caractère juridiquement international. - Bibliography: p. 609-638. - Leiden, A.W. Sijthoff, 1972. - 645 p.
Thèse. - Univ. de Genève.

29. **Linkage** politics; essays on the convergence of national and international systems. - Edited by James N. Rosenau. - Notes, partly bibliographical. - New York, Free press. 1969. - xii, 352 p.
"Published for the Princeton Center of international studies."

30. **Liu, L. Y-yun.** China as a nuclear power in world politics. - Bibliography: p. 107-115. - London, Macmillan, 1972. - 125 p.

31. **Lukacs, J. A.** A history of the cold war. - Notes, partly bibliographical. - Garden City, N.Y., Doubleday, 1961. - 288 p.

32. **Lyon, P.** War and peace in South-East Asia. - Bibliography: p. 231-238. - London, Oxford university press, 1969. - xii, 244 p.
"Issued under the auspices of the Royal institute of international affairs."

33. **McAllister, G.** The bomb; challenge and answer/ by Alexander Haddow... and others. - Edited by Gilbert McAllister. - Bibliography: p. 151-153. - London, B. T. Batsford, 1955. - 160 p.

34. **Mach, N. von.** Le Conseil de l'Europe et la Charte des Nations Unies. - Bibliography: p. 193-204. - Bonn, Impr. Köllen, 1955. - 204 p.
Thèse - Genève.

35. **McKay, V.** African diplomacy; studies in the determinants of foreign policy. - Notes, partly bibliographical. - London, Published for the School of advanced international studies, Johns Hopkins university by Pall Mall press, 1966. - xiii, 210 p.

36. **McKnight, A.** Atomic safeguards; a study in international verification. - Bibliography: p. 285-287. - New York, 1971. - xii, 301 p. - (United Nations institute for training and research. UNITAR series. no.5.)

37. **MacLaurin, J.** The United Nations and power politics. - Notes, partly bibliographical: p. 456-462. - London, G. Allen & Unwin, 1951. - xiii, 468 p.
"John MacLaurin is the pen name of an outstanding educationalist." - Book jacket.

N

1738.   **McLellan, D. S.**   The theory and practice of international relations/ by
         David S. McLellan, William C. Olson and Fred A. Sondermann. -
         Notes, partly bibliographical. - Englewood Cliffs, N.J.. Prentice Hall,
         1960. - xv, 542 p.

1739.   **Macridis, R. C.**   Foreign policy in world politics. - Bibliography at the
         end of each chapter. - Englewood Cliffs, N.J., Prentice Hall, 1958. -
         xi, 420 p.

1740.   **McWhinney, Ed.**   Law, foreign policy, and the East-West détente. -
         Bibliography: p. 121-123. - Toronto, Univ. of Toronto press, 1964. -
         viii, 123 p.
         "This volume has its roots in the Conference on law and world affairs, held in the
         Faculty of law of the University of Toronto on January 17 and 18, 1964." - Foreword.

1741.   **Maier, F. L.**   World peace by covenant; the United Nations considered
         as an international organization for securing world peace. - Notes,
         partly bibliographical. - New York, Exposition press, 1955. - 142 p.

1742.   **Malik, C.**   Man in the struggle for peace. - Notes, partly bibliographical.
         New York, Harper & Row, 1963. - xlvi, 242 p.
         "The lectures by Charles Malik at the twentieth annual lecture series of the Claremont
         colleges, Claremont, California.

1743.   **Manell, A. E.**   Sanctions under the charter of the United Nations. -
         Bibliography: p. 245-255. - Berkeley, 1948.
         Microfilm copy of typewritten manuscript. Made by Library photographic service,
         University of California (no. 4591). Positive.
         Collation of the original: x, 255 p.
         Thesis - Univ. of California.

1744.   **Manin, P.**   L'Organisation des Nations Unies et le maintien de la paix;
         le respect du consentement de l'Etat. - Bibliography: p. 329-334. -
         Paris, Libr. générale de droit et de jurisprudence, 1971. - iv, 343 p. -
         (Bibliothèque de droit international. t. 60.)
         "Ouvrage couronné par la Faculté de droit et des sciences économiques de Paris et honoré
         d'une subvention du Ministère de l'éducation nationale."

1745.   **Manly, C.**   The UN record: ten fateful years for America. -
         Bibliographical notes: p. 237-243. - Chicago, H. Regnery, 1955. -
         xi, 256 p.

1746.   **Mao, J. Y.**   The principle of sovereign equality in the United Nations. -
         Bibliography: p. 370-387. - Chicago, Ill., 1956.
         Microfilm copy of typewritten manuscript. Positive.
         Collation of the original: xi, 387 p.
         Thesis. - Univ. of Chicago.

1747.   **Marchand, G.**   1 ou zéro: le monde sera mondialiste our ne sera
         plus. - Includes bibliographies. - Paris, Club humaniste, 1973. -
         179 p.

1748.   **Martin, L. W.**   Neutralism and nonalignment; the new states in world
         affairs. - Notes, partly bibliographical: p. 239-244. - New York,
         F.A. Praeger, 1962. - xxi, 250 p. - (Books that matter.)
         "Published for the Washington center of foreign policy research at the School of advanced
         international studies, the Johns Hopkins university." - Half-title.

1749. **Mates, L.** Nonalignment: theory and current policy. - Bibliographical notes. - Belgrade, Institute of international politics and economics, 1972. - 543 p.
Original ed. pub. under title: Nesvrstanost: teorija i savremena praksa.
Neutrality. Nonaligned nations.

1750. **Mathiot, A.** Les territoires non autonomes et la charte des Nations Unies. - Bibliographical notes. - Paris, Libr. générale de droit et de jurisprudence, 1949. - 76 p.
"Extrait du no.4 de 1948 et du no.1 de 1949 de la Revue juridique et politique de l'Union française.

1751. **Mathisen, T.** Methodology in the study of international relations. - Bibliography: p. 253-256. - New York, Macmillan, 1959. - x, 265 p.

1752. -- - -- Research in international relations. - Bibliography: p. 229-233. - Oslo, Universitetsforlaget, 1963. - vii, 238 p.

1753. **May, M. M.** Strategic arms technology and doctrine under arms limitation agreements. - Bibliographical notes. - Princeton, N.J., 1972. - 31 p.- (Princeton university. Center of international studies. Research monographs. no.37.)

1754. **Mélanges** Pierre Renouvin: études d'histoire des relations internationales. - Notes, partly bibliographical. - Paris, Presses universitaires de France, 1966. - xxvii, 240 p. - (Paris. Université. Faculté des lettres et sciences humaines. Série "Études et méthodes". t. 13.)

1755. **Melchoir de Molènes, C.** L'Europe de Strasbourg: une première expérience de parlementarisme international. - Bibliography: p. 749-751. - Paris, Éd. Roudil, 1971. - 774 p.

1756. **Merle, M.** La vie internationale. - Bibliography: p. 295-297. - Paris, A. Colin, 1963. - 302 p. - (Collection U. sér. "Société politique".)

1757. **Merritt, R. L.** Communication in international politics. - Notes, partly bibliographical. - Urbana, Univ. of Illinois press, 1972. - x, 461 p.
"One of the twenty-seven sets of panels comprising the 66th Annual meeting of the American political science association, held on September 8-12, 1970, in Los Angeles was devoted exclusively to the field of international political communication." - Pref.
Mediation, International.

1758. **Métall, R. A.** "Vereinte Nationen" oder "Vereinigte Nationen"? - Notes, partly bibliographical. - n.p., 1957. - p. 29-34.
"'Die Friedenswarte' ... Separatum vol. 54, Nr. 1 (1957)."

1759. **Mexico. Universidad nacional. Facultad de ciencias políticas y sociales. Centro de relaciones internacionales.** Boletín. - Includes bibliographies. - no. 1- ; 1970- . - México, 1970- . - v.
Pub. monthly.

1760. **Meynaud, J.** Les groupes de pression internationaux. - Bibliographical notes: p. 429-503. - Lausanne, 1961. - 560 p. - (Études de science politique. 3.)

1761. **Mezerik, A. G.** Arab-Israel conflict and the United Nations. - Bibliography: p. 44a-b. - New York, 1962. - 110 p. - (International review service. v.8, no. 73.)
Cover-title.
Reproduced from typewritten copy.

1762. **Mezhdunarodnata, 1971.** - Includes bibliographies. - Sofiiā, Partizdat, 1971. - 120 p. - (Mezhdunarodna politika. 12.)
World politics - 1970-   . International relations.

1763. **Migliazza, A.** Il fenomeno dell'organizzazione e la comunità internazionale. Bibliographical notes. - Milano, A. Giuffrè, 1958. - viii, 288 p. - (Studi di diritto internazionale. 21.)

1764. **Miller, L. B.** World order and local disorder; the United Nations and internal conflicts. - Bibliography: p. 217-227. - Princeton, N.J., Princeton university press, 1967. - 235 p.
"Published for the Center of international studies, Princeton university."

1765. **Miller, R. I.** Dag Hammarskjold and crisis diplomacy. - Notes, partly bibliographical, at the end of each chapter. - n.p., Oceana publications, 1961. - 344 p. - (Oceana library on the United Nations.)

1766. **Milletlerarasi** münasebetler türk yilligi=The Turkish yearbook of internationa: relations. - 1960-   . - Includes bibliographies. - Ankara, Dis Münasebetler enstitüsü, Siyasal bilgiler fakültesi, Ankara Universitesi, Institute of international relations, Faculty of political sciences, Univ. of Ankara, 1961-   . - v.
Pub. annually.

1767. **Mills, L. A.** World politics in transition/ by Lennox A. Mills and Charles H. McLaughlin. - Bibliography at the end of each chapter. - New York, H. Holt, 1957. - x, 757 p.
"Intended as a text for introductory courses in international relations." - Pref.

1768. **Mironov, N. V.** Pravovoe regulirovanie vneshnikh snosheniĭ SSSR, 1917-1970 gg. - Bibliography: p. 267-294. - Moskva, Izd-vo "Mezhdunarodny otnosheniiā", 1971. - 294 p.
International relations.

1769. **Mirskiĭ, Z. ÎA.** U karty mira; kak izmenilsiā mir za 50 let. - Bibliographical notes. - Moskva, Politizdat, 1967. - 237 p.
At head of title: Z. Mirskiĭ. A. Borisov. A. Kufsenkov.

1770. **Moch, J. S.** Destin de la paix / par Jules Moch. - Notes, partly bibliographical. - Paris, Mercure de France, 1969. - 299 p.

1771. **Modelski, G. A.** The international relations of internal war. Notes, partly bibliographical. - Princeton, N.J., Center of international studies, Woodrow Wilson school of public and international affairs, Princeton university, 1961. - 24 p. - (Princeton university. Center of international studies. Research monographs. no. 11.)

1772. **Modern** world; annual review for international relations and political science. - 1960/61-   . - Includes bibliographies. - Köln, Kiepenheuer & Witsch, 1961-   . - v.
Pub. annually.
"Built round articles that first appeared in German in 'Moderne Welt'." - Foreword.
"English translation by Kathleen Szasz."

1773. **Monteil, V.** Le problème du Moyen-Orient. - Includes bibliographies. - Genève, Délégation permanente de la Ligue des Etats arabes, 1968. - 15 p.
"Conférence donnée au Centre culturel Lebret, à Dakar."

1774. **Morgan. R.** West European politics since 1945: the shaping of the European community. - Bibliography: p. 232-233. - London, B.T. Batsford, 1972. - 243 p.

1775. **Morray, J. P.** From Yalta to disarmament; cold war debate. - Bibliographical notes: p. 351-361. - London, Merlin press, 1962. - xii, 368 p.

1776. **Morse, E. L.** A comparative approach to the study of foreign policy: notes on theorizing. - Notes, partly bibliographical. - Princeton, N.J., Center of international studies, Woodrow Wilson school of public and international affairs, Princeton university, 1971. - 42 p. - (Princeton university. Center of international studies. Research monographs. no. 36.)

1777. **Moskowitz, M.** Human rights and world order; the struggle for human rights in the United Nations. - Notes, partly bibliographical: p. 169-197. - New York, Oceana publications, 1958. - 239 p.

1778. **Murav'ev, B.** Le problème de l'autorité superétatique. - Bibliography: p. 125-126. - Neuchâtel, Éd. de la Baconnière, 1950. - 132 p. - (L'Évolution du monde et des idées.)
At head of title: Boris Mouravieff.

1779. **National education association of the United States.** Teaching about the United Nations Charter. - Bibliography: p. 38-39. - Washington, D.C., 1946. - 39 p.

1780. **Niaki, D.** Les sanctions dans le cadre de l'Organisation des Nations Unies. - Bibliography: l. 258-264. - Paris, 1953.
Microfilm copy of typewritten manuscript. Negative.
Collation of the original: 268 l.
Thèse - Univ. de Paris.

1781. **Nicholas, H. G.** The United Nations as a political institution. - Bibliography: p. 181-184. - London, Oxford university press, 1959. - 222 p.

782. -- --- The United Nations as a political institution. - Bibliography: p. 192-195. - 2nd ed. - London, Oxford university press, 1962. - 232 p. - (Oxford paperbacks. no. 57.)

783. **Ninčić, D.** The problem of the sovereignty in the Charter and in the practice of the United Nations. - Bibliography: p. 345-358. - The Hague, M. Nijhoff, 1970. - xiii, 358 p.

784. **Northedge, F. S.** A hundred years of international relations/ by F.S. Northedge and M.J. Grieve. - Bibliography: p. 371-380. - London, Duckworth, 1971. - x, 397 p.

785. **Northrop, F. S. C.** The taming of nations; a study of the cultural bases of international policy. - Bibliographical notes: p. 337-349. - New York, Macmillan, 1952. - xii, 362 p.

1786.   **Notes** et études documentaires. - no. 1-   ; 1945-   . - Paris,
         Documentation française, 1945-   . -   v.
         Pub. bi-weekly.
         At head of title: 1945- 14 Feb. 1946. Ministère de l'information; 15 Feb. 1946-
         17 Jan 1959, Présidence du Conseil. Secrétariat général du gouvernement. Direction de
         la documentation.
         Title varies: 1945-3 Feb. 1949. Notes documentaires et études.

1787.   **Nové** zahranični knihy. - Řada A: Současná politika a mezinárodní
         vztahy. - 1969-   . - Praha, Státni knihovna ČSSR, Universitni
         knihovna, 1969-   . -   v. - (Novinkova služba.)

1788.   **Nye, J. S.** Peace in parts: integration and conflict in regional
         organization. - Bibliographical notes. - Boston, Little, Brown and
         Company, 1971. - xiv, 210 p. - (Perspectives on international
         relations.)
         Written under the auspices of the Center for international affairs, Harvard university.

1789.   **O'Brien, C. C.** The United Nations sacred drama/ by Conor Cruise
         O'Brien and Feliks Topolski. - Bibliography: p. 311-318. - London,
         Hutchinson, 1968. - 320 p.

1790.   **"Obshchii rynok"** i mezhdunarodnye otnosheniiâ v Zapadnoi Evrope. -
         Sbornik statei po materialam zarubezhnoi pressy. - Bibliography:
         p. 255-261. - Moskva, Izd-vo "Progress", 1970. - 262 p.
         "Sostavitel' A.N. Shebanov. Redaktor B.N. Antonovich."
         Common market. Communauté économique européenne. Economic integration - Europe.

1791.   **Ogley, R.** The United Nations and East-West relations. - Select
         bibliography: p. 58. - Brighton, Engl., 1972. - 58 p. - (Institute for
         the study of international organisation. Monographs. 1st series.
         no. 6.)

1792.   The **origins** of the cold war, 1941-1947; a historical problem with
         interpretations and documents. - Edited by Walter LaFeber. -
         Bibliography: p. 171-172. - New York, J. Wiley, 1971. - x, 172 p. -
         (Problems in American history.)

1793.   **Pacaut, M.** Le monde contemporain, 1945-1963. - Bibliography at the
         end of each chapter and p. 277-281. - Paris, A. Colin, 1964. -
         295 p. - (Collection U. sér.: "Histoire contemporaine".)
         At head of title: Marcel Pacaut et Paul M. Bouju, avec la collaboration de Serge Adour...
         et d'autres.

1794.   **Padelford, N. J.** International politics; foundations of international
         relations/ by Norman J. Padelford and George A.Lincoln. - Biblio-
         graphies at the end of some chapters. - New York, Macmillan, 1954. -
         xii, 719 p.

1795.   **Palmer, N. D.** International relations; the world community in transition
         by Norman D. Palmer and Howard C. Perkins. - Bibliography at the
         end of each chapter. - Boston, Houghton Mifflin, 1953. - ix, 1270 p.

1796.   **Pancarci, V.** De la Charte des Nations Unies à une meilleure organisatio
         du monde. - Bibliography: p. 211-213. - Paris, A. Pedone, 1962. -
         213 p. - (Revue générale de droit international public. Publications.
         nouvelle sér. no.4.)

1797.   **Papadopoulos, A. N.** Synchronos diethnēs zōē: apopseis kai problēmata. - Bibliography at the end of each part. - Leukōsia, 1967-1968. - 203 p.
        International relations.

1798.   **Papini, R.** La rupture des relations diplomatiques et ses conséquences. - Bibliography: p. 271-285. - Paris, A. Pedone, 1972. - 299 p.

1799.   **Peace** research reviews. - Includes bibliograhies. - v.1- ; 1967-   . - Oakville, Canadian peace research institute, 1967-   . -   v.
        Pub. irregularly.

1800.   **Peace research society (international).** Papers. - Includes bibliographies. - v.12- . 1969-   . - Philadelphia, 1969-   . -   v.

1801.   **Peaslee, A. J.** United Nations government. - Includes bibliographies. - New York, Justice house, 1945. - xi, l, 183 p.

1802.   **Pechota, V.** The quiet approach: a study of the good offices exercised by the United Nations Secretary-general in the cause of peace; selected bibliography. - New York, 1972. - p. 90-91. - (UNITAR. Monographs on peaceful settlement of disputes. no.6.)

1803.   **Penrose, E. F.** The revolution in international relations; a study in the changing nature and balance of power. - Notes, partly bibliographical. - London, F. Cass, 1965. - xxii, 290 p.

1804.   **Pereira da Silva, F. C.** A carta das Naçoes Unidas; comentário às disposições da carta de S. Francisco, em confronto com o pacto da Sociedade das nações. - Bibliography: p. 279-280. - Lisboa, Livraria popular, 1945. - 287 p.

1805.   **Pesant, L. R.** Les obligations découlant de la Charte des Nations Unies. - Bibliography: p. 185. - Paris, 1948.
        Microfilm copy of typewritten manuscript. Positive.
        Collation of the original: 185 p.
        Thèse - Univ. de Paris.

1806.   **Pfaltzgraff, R. L.** The Atlantic community: a complex imbalance. - Notes, partly bibliographical, at the end of each chapter. - New York, Van Nostrand Reinhold, 1969. - vi, 216 p. - (New perspectives in political science. 22.)

1807.   **Pfeifenberger, W.** Die Vereinten Nationen: ihre politischen Organe in Sicherheitsfragen. - Bibliography: p. 639-662. - Salzburg, A. Pustet, 1971. - 662 p. - (Salzburger Universitätsschriften. Schriften zu Recht und Politik. Bd. 11.)
        United Nations - History. World politics - 1945-   . Security, International.

1808.   **Plano, J. C.** Forging world order; the politics of international organization/ by Jack C. Plano and Robert E. Riggs. - Bibliography at the end of each chapter. - New York, Macmillan, 1967. - viii, 600 p.

1809.   **Pochon, C.** Le processus de satellisation des États dans la société internationale. - Bibliography: p. 235-241. - Fribourg, 1971. - 243 p.
        Thèse - Univ. de Fribourg.
        Sovereignty. International relations. Alliances.

1810.   **Political and economic planning.**   Regional development in the European
         economic community. - Bibliography: p. 86-90. - London, G. Allen
         and Unwin, 1962. - 95 p.

1811.   **Potočný, M.** Legal principles of peaceful co-existence. - Bibliographical
         notes. - Praha, Státní pedagogické nakl., 1968. - 316 p. - (Acta
         Universitatis XVII. Novembris Pragensis. Fakulta spolecenskovedni.
         Vědecký sborník; řada právni.   sv. čis. 1.)
         At head of title: Miroslav Potocný, Stanislav Myslil.
         Translated from Czech by Zdeněk Červenka.

1812.   **Poulantzas, N.** Pouvoir politique et classes sociales. - Includes biblio-
         graphies. - t.1-2. - Paris, F. Maspero, 1971. - 2 v. - (Petite collection
         Maspero. 77-78.)

1813.   **Power** and law: American dilemma in world affairs, papers of the
         conference on peace research in history. - Edited by Charles A. Barke
         Baltimore, Md., Johns Hopkins press, 1971. - xii, 205 p.
         "Papers... of the Conference on peace research in history... Plattsburgh, New York, in early
         September, 1968."

1814.   **Princeton university. Foreign policy analysis project. Organizational
         behavior section.** Foreign policy analysis series. - no.1-5. - Princeton,
         N.J., 1953-54. - 1 v.

1815.   **Problemy** istorii mezhdunarodnykh otnosheniĭ. - Sbornik stateĭ pamiãti
         akademika E.V. Tarle. - Bibliographical notes. - Leningrad, Izd-vo
         "Nauka", 1972. - 426 p.
         At head of title: Akademiiã nauk SSSR. Otdelenie istorii. Leningradskoe otdelenie
         Instituta istorii SSSR.
         International relations.

1816.   **Puchala, D. J.**   International politics today. - Bibliographical notes. -
         New York, Dodd, Mead, 1971. - xiv, 379 p.
         International relations. World politics. Security, International. United Nations. Internationa
         organisation. Disarmament.

1817.   **Puryear, P. L.**   The disposition of political petitions with respect
         to Africa in the United Nation's Trusteeship council. - Bibliography:
         p. 141-142. - Chicago, Ill, 1955.
         Microfilm copy of typewritten manuscript. Made in 1955 by Library Department of
         photographic reproduction, Univ. of Chicago. Positive.
         Collation of the original: vi, 142 p.
         Diss. - Univ. of Chicago.

1818.   **Qual, L. di**   Les effets des résolutions des Nations Unies. - Bibliography:
         p. 275-277. - Paris, Libr. générale de droit et de jurisprudence, 1967. -
         ii, 283 p. - (Bibliothèque de droit international.   t. 37.)
         "Ouvrage publié avec le concours du Centre national de la recherche scientifique."

1819.   **Racine, R.** Vers une Europe nouvelle par le Plan Schuman. - Biblio-
         graphy: 1 p. following p. 242. - Neuchâtel, Éd. de la Baconnière,
         1954. - 242 p. - (L'évolution du monde et des idées.)

1820.   **Rajan, M. S.** United Nations and domestic jurisdiction. - Bibliography:
         p. 637-657. - Bombay, Orient Longmans, 1958. - xiii, 679 p.
         "Published under the auspices of the Indian council of world affairs."

1821.   **Raux, J.** Les relations extérieures de la Communauté économique européenne. - Bibliography: p. 531-540. - Paris, Ed. Cujas, 1966. - 577 p.
Thèse - Univ. de Rennes.

1822.   **Razvivaiūshchaiāsiā** ėkonomika i mezhdunarodnaiā politika. - Pod red. K. Ivanova. - Bibliographical notes. - Moskva, Izd-vo "Mezhdunarodnye otnosheniiā", 1967. - 318 p.

1823.   **Readings** on the international political sestem. - Edited by Naomi Rosenbaum. - Bibliographical notes. - Englewood Cliffs, N.J., Prentice-Hall, 1970. - vi, 442 p. - (Foundations of modern political science series.)
International agencies. International relations. World politics. Security, International. Disarmament. United Nations.

1824.   **Renouvin, P.** Introduction à l'histoire des relations internationales. - Bibliography: p. 457-489. - Paris, A. Colin, 1964. - 520 p.
At head of title: Pierre Renouvin. Jean-Baptiste Duroselle.
"Cet ouvrage est publié sous le patronage de la Fondation nationale des sciences politiques."

825.   **Resources** devoted to military research and development: an international comparison. - Bibliography: p. 94-112. - Stockholm, Almqvist & Wiksell, Stockholm international peace research institute, 1972. - 112 p.

826.   **Reuter, P.** Le droit au secret et les institutions internationales. - Notes, partly bibliographical. - n.p., Centre national de la recherche scientifique, 1956. - p. 46-65.
"Extrait de l'Annuaire français de droit international. II, 1956."

827.   -- --- Le Plan Schuman. - Bibliography: p. 627. - (In Academy of international law, The Hague. Recueil des cours, 1952, II. Paris, 1953. v. 81 p. 519-629.)

828.   **Revision** of the United Nations charter; a symposium edited by Indian council of world affairs. - Notes, partly bibliographical. - Bombay, Oxford university press, 1956. - 144 p.

829.   **Revue** diplomatique=Diplomatic review. - v.1-   ; mars 1936-   . - Genève, 1936-   . - v.
Pub. monthly.
Includes: Oct. 1964, Pour l'Europe, Bulletin périodique de l'Association des amis de Robert Schumann.
1936-67, issued in French only with title: Archives diplomatiques et consulaires:
1968-69, issued in French and English with title: Archives diplomatiques et consulaires.
Diplomatic and consular review; 1972-   , issued in French only with title: Archives diplomatiques et consulaires.

830.   **Revue** roumaine d'études internationales. - v.1, no.1/2-   ;
1967-   . - Includes bibliographies. - Bucarest, 1967-   . - v.
Pub. semi-annually, 1967-1969, quarterly, 1970-   .
At head of title: Association de droit international et de relations internationales de la République socialiste de Roumanie.
Texts partly French, partly English, partly Russian.

1831.   **Riches, C. A.**   Majority rule in international organization; a study of
         the trend from unanimity to majority decision. - Bibliography:
         p. 307-314. - Baltimore, Johns Hopkins press, 1940. - viii, 322 p.-
         (Johns Hopkins university.   Studies in historical and political
         science.   Extra volumes.   New series.   no. 28.)

1832.   **Rienow, R.**   Contemporary international politics. - Bibliography at the
         end of each chapter. - New York, T.Y. Crowell, 1961. - xv, 431 p.

1833.   **Robertson, A. H.**   European institutions; co-operation, integration,
         unification. - Bibliography at the end of each chapter. - London,
         Stevens, 1959. - xix, 372 p. viii p. - (Library of world affairs. no.44.)
         "Published under the auspices of the London institute of world affairs."

1834.   **Robinson, J.**   Human rights and fundamental freedoms in the Charter
         of the United Nations; a commentary. - Bibliographical notes. -
         New York, Institute of Jewish affairs of the American Jewish congress
         and World Jewish congress, 1946. - iv, 166 p. - (Institute of Jewish
         affairs, New York.   From war to peace. no.4.)

1835.   **Rogers, W. C.**   International administration: a bibliography. - Chicago,
         Public administration service, 1945. - vi, 1, 32 p. - (Public administra-
         tion service. no.92.)

1836.   **Rome.   Università.   Istituto di studi giuridici.**   Relazione sull'attivita'
         della cattedra di organizzazione internazionale nel decennio 1956-66. -
         Rome, 1967. - 39 p.
         At head of title: Università degli studi di Roma.   Facoltà di scienze politiche.   Istituto
         di studi giuridici.

1837.   **Rosecrance, R. N.**   Action and reaction in world politics; international
         systems in perspective. - Notes, partly bibliographical. -   Boston,
         Little, Brown, 1963. - xii, 314 p.

1838.   **Rosenau, J. N.**   International politics and foreign policy; a reader in
         research and theory. - Notes, partly bibliographical, at the end of
         some chapters. - New York, Free press of Glenco, 1961. - xii, 511 p.

1839.   -- --- The scientific study of foreign policy. - Notes, partly biblio-
         graphical. - New York, Free press, 1971. - xv, 472 p.

1840.   **Ross, A.**   De Forenede Nationer: fred og fremskridt. - Bibliography
         at the end of each chapter. - Kobenhavn, Nyt nordisk forlag,
         A. Busck, 1963. - 432 p.

1841.   **Rostow, W. W.**   The United States in the world arena; an essay in
         recent history. - Notes, partly bibliographical, at the end of each
         section. - New York, Harper, 1960. - xxii, 568 p. - (Massachusetts
         institute of technology.   Center for international studies.   American
         project series.)

1842.   **Russo, A. L.del**   International protection of human rights. -
         Bibliography: p. 354-361. - Washington, D.C., Lerner law book co.,
         1971. - xi, 361 p.
         With this: Universal declaration of human rights. p. 263-349.

43.   **Ruyssen, T. E. C.**   La société internationale. - Bibliography: p. 224-236. - Paris, Presses universitaires de France, 1950. - 240 p. - (Bibliothèque de philosophie contemporaine.)

44.   **Ruzié, D.**   Organisations internationales et sanctions internationales. - Bibliography: p. 214. - Paris, A. Colin, 1971. - 223 p. - (Collection U. sér.: "Relations et institutions internationales".)
      Sanctions (International law).

45.   **Safran, N.**   From war to war: the Arab-Israeli confrontation, 1948-1967; a study of the conflict from the perspective of coercion in the context of inter-Arab and big power relations. - Notes, partly bibliographical: p. 421-432. - New York, Pegasus, 1969. - 464 p.

46.   **Salini, M. P.**   Dagli organismi pubblici internazionali funzionali alla societè per azioni europea: le singole tecniche e i modelli uniformi di constituzione. - Bibliography: l. 217-228. - Milano, CIRIEC, 1970. - 228 l. - (Centro italiano di ricerche e d'informazione sull'economia delle imprese pubbliche e di pubblico interesse.   Collana di studi e monografie. n. 43.)
      At head of title: Stesura a circolazione privata.

47.   **Salkeld, R.**   War and space. - Bibliography: p. 192-194. - Englewood Cliffs, Prentice-Hall, 1970. - xxiv, 195 p.

48.   **Salomon, A.**   L'O.N.U. et la paix: le Conseil de sécurité et le règlement pacifique des différends (chapitre VI de la Charte des Nations Unies). - Bibliography: p. 193-198. - Paris, Ed. internationales, 1948. - 204 p.

49.   **Samii, C. B.**   The Arab-Asian bloc in the United Nations; a case study: the questions of colonialism, West-Soviet disputes, human rights and fundamental freedoms, and West-Soviet conflicts. - Bibliography: p. 302-322. - Lawrence, Kansas, 1955.
      Collation of the original: iv, ii, 322 p.
      Diss. - Univ. of Kansas.

50.   **Sanakoev, S. P.**   Teoriiā i praktika sofsialisticheskikh mezhdunarodnykh otnosheniĭ. - Bibliographical notes. - Moskva, Politizdat, 1970. - 70 p.
      International relations.

51.   **Saran, V.**   Sino-Soviet schism: a bibliography, 1956-1964. - London, Asia pub. house, 1971. - xv, 162 p.

52.   **Sathyamurthy, T. V.**   The politics of international cooperation; contrasting conceptions of U.N.E.S.C.O. - Bibliography: p. 251-265. - Genève, E. Droz, 1964. - 313 p. - (Travaux de droit, d'économie, de sociologie et de sciences politiques. no.20.)

53.   **el-Sayed, R. A.**   The Baghdad pact in world politics. - Bibliography: p. 260-302. - Genève, Ed. Médecine et hygiène, 1971. - 302 p.
      Thèse - Univ. de Genève, Institut universitaire de hatues études internationales.

1854.   **Schenkel, P.** Vom Völkerbund über die Vereinten Nationen zur wahren
Völkergemeinschaft. - Bibliography: 2nd-3rd p. following p. 203. -
Graz, 1953.
Microfilm copy of typewritten manuscript. Negative.
Collation of the original: 203 p.
Inaug. Diss. - Karl-Franzens-Universität (Graz).

1855.   **Schiffer, W.** The legal community of mankind; a critical analysis of the
modern concept of world organization. - Bibliography: p. 357-362. -
New York, Columbia university press, 1954. - x, 367 p.
Notes, partly bibliographical: p. 303-356.

1856.   **Schneider, J. W.** Treaty-making power of international organizations. -
Bibliography: p. 145-150. - Genève, Libr. E. Droz, 1959. - 150 p.

1857.   **Schneider, L. G. C. A. M.** Collectieve veiligheid; een studie over het
handvest der Verenigde Naties, de resolutie "Uniting for peace" en
het Noord atlantisch verdrag. - Bibliography: p. 117-120. - Nimegen,
Drukkerij Gebr. Janssen, 1954. - 120 p.
Proefschrift - Nijmegen.

1858.   **Schümperli, W.** Die Vereinten Nationen und die Dekolonisation. -
Bibliography: p. 147-150. - Bern, H. Lang, 1970. - 158 p.
"Dissertation zur Erlangung der Würde eines Doktors der Philosophie vorgelegt der
Philosophisch-Historischen Fakultät der Universität Basel."

1859.   **Seara Vázquez, M.** Del Congreso de Viena a la paz de Versailles. -
Bibliography: p. 457-473. - Mexico, 1969. - vi, 473 p. - (Mexico.
Universidad nacional. Facultad de ciencias politicas y sociales.
ser.: Documentos. 1.)
International relations - Sources. Treaties - Collections.

1860.   -- - - - Paz y conflicto en la sociedad internacional. - Notes, partly
bibliographical. - Mexico, 1969. - vii, 410 p. - (Mexico. Universidad
nacional. Facultad de ciencias politicas y sociales. ser.: Estudios. 6.)

1861.   -- - - - El problema del espacio cósmico en las Naciones Unidas. -
Bibliography: p. 577-587. - n.p., 1960. - p. 569-587.
"Sobretiro de 'Ciencias politicas y sociales', año VI, núm. 22, octubre-diciembre de 1960,
México, D.F."

1862.   **Seton-Watson, H.** Neither war nor peace; the struggle for power in
the post-war world. - Bibliographical notes: p. 474-486. - London,
Methuen, 1960. - 504 p.

1863.   **al-Shallchy, M.** Les travaux des Nations Unies en vue de la révision
de la Charte; (application des articles 108 et 109 de la Charte). -
Bibliography: p. 150-164. - Tunis, Soc. l'action d'éd. et de press,
1967. - 164 p.

1864.   **Shurshalov, V. M.** Mezhdunarodnye pravootnosheniiā. - Bibliography:
p. 231-238. - Moskva, Izd-vo "Mezhdunarodnye otnosheniiā", 1971. -
238 p.
International relations.

55. **Silverstein, S. S.** Les conventions des Nations-Unies concernant la liberté de l'information. - Bibliography: p. 165-169. - Paris, 1951.
Microfilm copy of typewritten manuscript. Negative.
Collation of the original: 172 p.
Thèse - Paris.
On same reel with: Tsien, Jon-hing. L'individu en droit international public depuis la charte des Nations Unies.

56. **Singer, M. R.** Weak states in a world of powers: the dynamics of international relationships. - Notes, partly bibliographical. - New York, Free press, 1972. - xii, 431 p.

57. **Singh, N.** Human rights and international co-operation. - Notes, partly bibliographical. - New Delhi, S. Chand, 1969. - xvi, 511 p.
"Shri Panch Tribhuban inaugural lectures, delivered at the University of Tribhuban, Nepal (1969)."

58. **Siotis, J.** Social science and the study of international relations. - Bibliographical notes. - London, Stevens, 1970. - 24 p.
"Reprinted from 'The year book of world affairs', 1970, volume 24."
"Published under the auspices of the London institute of world affairs."

59. **Skolnikoff, E. B.** The international imperatives of technology: technological development and the international political system. - Bibliography: p. 187-194. - Berkeley, 1972. - ix, 194 p. - (California, University. Institute of international studies. Research series. no. 16.)

70. **Smith, E. P.** Regionalism within the United Nations. - Bibliography: l. 379-429. - Evanston, Ill., 1951. - iii, 432 l.
Diss. - Northwestern university (Evanston, Ill.)
"Appendix: Tabulation of votes in the United Nations": leaves 430-432.

71. **Smith, G. S.** A selected bibliography on peace-keeping. - Ottawa, 1966. - 35 p. - (Canada. Department of national defence. Operational research division. ORD report. no.66/R14.)

72. **Snell, J. L.** The meaning of Yalta; big three diplomacy and the new balance of power/ by John L. Snell, editor... and others. - Bibliographical notes: p. 218-229. - Baton Rouge, Louisiana state university press, 1956. - xiii, 239 p.

73. **Snyder, R. C.** Foreign policy decision-making; an approach to the study of international politics. - Includes bibliographies. - Edited by Richard C. Snyder, H.W. Bruck and Burton Sapin. - Glencoe, Ill., Free press, 1962. - vii, 274 p.

74. **Sobakin, V. K.** Kollektivnaîa bezopasnost' - garantiîa mirnogo sosushchest-vovaniîa. - Bibliography: p. 495-517. - Moskva, Izd-vo IMO, 1962. - 517 p.
International security and peaceful co-existence.

75. **Société des nations. Bibliothèque.** Répertoire des données publiées regulièrement dans les journaux officiels=Analysis of material published regularly in official gazettes. - Genève, 1935. - 24 p. - (Its: Listes bibliographiques. Miscellaneous bibliographies. no.4.)

1876. **Socini, R.** Gli accordi internazionali delle organizzazioni inter-governativ‹ Notes, partly bibliographical. - Padova, CEDAM, 1962. - xxxii, 295 p (Cagliari. Università. Facoltà di giurisprudenza. Pubblicazioni. ser. 1 (Giuridica). v. 3.)

1877. **Soto, J. de.** Les relations internationales de la Communauté européenne du charbon et de l'acier. - Bibliography: p. 113. - (In Academy of international law, The Hague. Recueil des cours, 1956. II. Leyde (Pays-Bas), A.W. Sijthoff, 1957. v.90, p. 29-116.)

1878. **Sotsiologicheskie** problemy mezhdunarodnykh otnosheniĭ. - Bibliographic‹ notes. - Moskva, Izd-vo "Nauka", 1970. - 326 p.
Half-title: Akademiiа nauk SSSR. Institut filosofii.
International relations.

1879. **La souveraineté** au XXe siècle/ par M. Bettati... et d'autres. - Biblio- graphies at the end of some chapters. - Paris, A. Colin, 1971. - 287 p. - (Collection U. sér.: "Relations et institutions internationales"
Sovereignty. International relations. State succession. Ocean bottom. Pacific settlement of international disputes. Conflict of lwas. Science - International co-operation.

1880. **Spanier, J. W.** World politics in an age of revolution. - Bibliography: p. 417-426. - London, Pall Mall press, 1967. - xii, 434 p.

1881. **Spravochnik** lektora-mezhdunarodnika. - Bibliographical notes. - Moskva, Izd-vo "Mezhdunarodnye otnosheniiâ", 1965. - 185 p.
"V sostavlenii spravochnika priniâli uchastie: Akhtamziân A.A., Voshchenkov K.P. ... i dr."

1882. **Sprout, H. H.** Foundations of international politics/ by Harold and Margaret Sprout. - Notes, partly bibliographical. - Princeton, N.J., D. Van Nostrand, 1962. - vi, 734 p.

1883. -- - - -   Toward a politics of the planet earth. - Bibliography at the end of each chapter. - New York, Van Nostrand Reinhold, 1971. - x, 499 p.
"Written under the auspices of the Center of International studies, Princeton university."

1884. **Sprudzs, A.** Treaty sources in legal and political research: tools, techniques and problems; the conventional and the new. - Biblio- graphical notes. - Tucson, Ariz., Univ. of Arizona press, 1971. - 63 p (Arizona. University. Institute of government research. Internation‹ studies. 3.)
Treaties - Interpretation and construction. Treaty-making power. International organization‹ International relations.

1885. **Stanford** journal of international studies. - Includes bibliographies. - v.1-   ; 196 -   . - Stanford, Calif., Stanford university, School of law, 196 -   . -   v.
Pub. annually.

1886. **Stanley, J.** The international trade in arms/ by John Stanley & Maurice Pearton. - Bibliographical notes. - London, Chatto & Windus 1972. - ix, 244 p.
"For the International institute for strategic studies."

1887. **Stasinopoulos, M. D.** Responsabilité civile de l'état du fait des actes de gouvernement ayant trait aux relations internationales. - Notes, partly bibliographical. - Paris, Recueil Sirey, 1961. - 53 p.

888. **Stefanini, F.** Historique comparé de l'élaboration du Pacte de la S.D.N. et de la Charte des Nations Unies: influence du premier sur la seconde. - Bibliography: 1. 87. - Paris, 1949.
Microfilm copy of typewritten manuscript. Negative.
At head of title: Université de Paris. Faculté de droit.
Collation of the original: 87 l.
Thèse - Paris.

889. **Sternberg, F.** The coming crisis. - Bibliography: p. 267-274. - New York, J. Day, 1947. - viii, 280 p.
Translated from the German by Edward Fitzgerald.

890. **Stillman, E.** The new politics; America and the end of the postwar world/ by Edmund Stillman and William Pfaff. - Bibliographical notes: p. 184-186. - New York, Coward-McCann,, 1961. - 191 p.

891. **Stone, J.** Aggression and world order; a critique of United Nations theories of aggression. - Notes, partly bibliographical. - London, Stevens, 1958. - xiv, 226, viii p. - (Library of world affairs. no. 39.)
"Published under the auspices of the London institute of world affairs."

892. **Strategic** survey, 1970-   . - Includes bibliographies. - London, Institute for strategic studies, 1971. - v.
Pub. annually.

893. The **study** of international affairs: essays in honour of Kenneth Younger. - Bibliographical notes. - Edited by Roger Morgan. - London, Oxford university press, 1972. - x, 309 p.
"Published for the Royal institute of international affairs."
International relations. United Nations. International law. Economic integration. Economic relations. Commonwealth of nations.

894. **Szalai, A.** The future of international organizations. - Bibliographical notes. - n.p., 1970. - 20 p.
"European-American seminar 'Organizations of the future', Noordwijk (Netherlands), August30-September 4, 1970.

895. **Szemenyei, J.** Nemzetközi gazdasági intézmények: GATT, OEEC, EPU, Sterlingterület. - Bibliography: p. 199-200. - Budapest, Közgazdasági és jogi könyvkiadó, 1957. - 211 p.
At head of title: Szemenyei - Halmosy.

896. **Tatarovskaiã, I. M.** Razvivaiũshchiesiã strany v bor'be za mir. - Bibliographical notes: p. 160-166. - Pod red. V. IÃ. Aboltina. - Moskva, Izd-vo, "Mezhdunarodnye otnosheniiã", 1970, - 166 p.
At head of title: Akademiiã nauk SSSR. Institut mirovoĭ ëkonomiki i mezhdunarodnykh otnosheniĭ.

897. **Taylor, P.** International co-operation today; the European and the universal pattern. - Bibliography: p. 158-161. - London, Elek books, 1971. - vii, 165 p. - (International relations series. 3.)

898. **Technology** and international relations/ by Bernard Brodie, William T.R. Fox, Hornell Hart... and others. - Bibliographical notes. - Ed. by William Field Ogburn. - Chicago, Univ. of Chicago press, 1949. - vii, 201 p. - (Harris foundation lectures (University of Chicago) 1948.)

1899.   **Tel** que nous l'avons vécu. - Includes bibliographies. - 1971-   . - Paris, Éd. Réalités, 1972-   . - v.
Pub. annually.
History, Modern - 20th century. World politics. International relations.

1900.   **Ténékidès, G.** Homogénéité et diversité des régimes politiques au sein des organisations internationales. - Notes, partly bibliographical. - Athènes, Impr. A. Klissiounis, 1961. - 683-711 p.
"Extrait des 'Mélanges Sériades', publiés par l'École supérieure de sciences politiques 'Panteios' d'Athènes."

1901.   **Thanassecos, L.** Chronologie des relations internationales, 1914-1971: exposés thématiques. - Paris, Mouton, 1972. - 690 p.
International relations - Chronology. World politics. History, Modern - 20th century.

1902.   The **theory** of international relations; selected texts from Gentili to Treitschke. - Introduced and edited by M.G. Forsyth... and others. - Includes bibliographies. - New York, Atherton press, 1970. - 353 p.

1903.   **Timerbaev, R. M.** Mirnyĭ atom na mezhdunarodnoĭ arene. - Bibliographical notes. - Moskva, Izd-vo "Mezhdunarodnye otnosheniiā", 1969. - 174 p.

1904.   **The Times, London.** Cuttings from The Times. - Originally comp. by The Times Intelligence department. - Oct. 1918-   . - Tylers Green, Buckinghamshire, England, University microfilms, 1971-   . - v.
Photocopy (Xerox). Positive.
On spine: The Times cuttings book; international & Leage of nations, United Nations.

1905.   **Tinbergen, J.** The European economic community: conservative or progressive? - Bibliography: 4th p. following p. 38. - Stockholm, Almqvist & Wicksell, 1963. - 38 p. - (Wicksell lectures. 1963.)

1906.   **To** the point. - v.1-   ; 1972-   . - Johannesburg, 1972-   . - v.
Pub. fortnightly.
World politics - 1970-   . Economic conditions. Africa - Politics. Economic development Africa. Social conditions. Science and technology. Culture.

1907.   **Tomsk, Russia. Universitet.** Voprosy mezhdunarodnykh otnosheniĭ. - Bibliographical notes. - vyp.   . - Tomsk, 1968-   . - v. - (Its: Trudy. Seriiā istoricheskaiā. t. 195.)
At head of title: Trudy Tomskogo ordena trudovogo krasnogo znameni gosudarstvennogo universiteta imeni V.V. Kuĭbysheva. Kafedra novoĭ i noveĭsheĭ istorii.
International relations.

1908.   **Toscano, M.** The history of treaties and international politics. - Notes, partly bibliographical. - v.1-   . - Baltimore, Johns Hopkins press, 1966-   . - v.
Original ed. pub. under title: Storia dei trattati e politica internazionale.

1909.   **Trân-minh-Tiêt.** L'Asie et la paix mondiale. - Notes, partly bibliographic Paris, Nouvelles éd. latines, 1970. - 460 p. - (Collection "Cahiers de l'Asie du sud-est".)

1910.   **Trefousse, H. L.** The cold war; a book of documents. - Edited with ar introduction by H.L. Trefousse. - Bibliography: p. 293-296. - New York, Capricorn books, 1966. - xxi, 296 p.

11. **Truyol Serra, A.** L'expansion de la société internationale aux XIXe et XXe siècles/ par Antonio Truyol y Serra. - Bibliography: p. 173-178. - (In Academy of international law, The Hague. Recueil des cours, 1965, III. Leyde (Pays-Bas), A.W. Sijthoff, 1965. v. 116, p. 89-179.

12. -- --- Genèse et structure de la société internationale. - Bibliography: p. 635-640. - (In Academy of international law, The Hague. Recueil des cours, 1959, I. Leyde (Pays-Bas), A.W. Sijthoff, 1960. v. 96, p. 553-642.)

13. **Tsoutsos, A. G.** Politique et droit dans les relations internationales; études sur l'évolution de l'ordre juridique international. - Bibliographies at the end of some chapters. - Paris, Libr. générale de droit et de jurisprudence, 1967. - 323 p.
Contents: - A. Le problème allemand. - B. Le problème cypriote. - C. La légalité internationale.

14. **Turenhoudt, E. van.** Le bilan de l'O.N.U. en 1947. - Bibliographical notes. - Bruxelles, 1948. - 84 p. - (Belgium. Ministère de la défense nationale. Service d'éducation à l'armée. La vie courante. no.14.)

15. **United Nations.** Protection des minorités: mesures spéciales de protection de caractère international en faveur de groupes ethniques, religieux ou linguistiques. - Notes, partly bibliographical.- New York, 1967. - iv, 56 p. - (Its: Publications. Sales numbers. 1967.XIV.4.) E F R S
Its: Documents. E/CN.4/Sub.2/214/Rev.1, E/CN.4/Sub.2/221/Rev.1.

16. -- **Dag Hammarskjold library, New York.** International terrorism: a select bibliography. - New York, 1972. - 6 p. - (Its: Occasional reading list. no.5/Rev.1)
The recent decision by the General assembly to place the issue of international terrorism on the agenda of its 27th session (Agenda item no.92) has prompted the issue of this selected bibliography. It brings together monographic and periodical literature on various aspects of the subject.

17. -- **Division for public administration.** The central organs of the civil service in the developing countries. - Bibliography: p. 226-229. - New York, 1969. - viii, 229 p. - (United Nations. Publications. Sales numbers. 1968.II.H.3.)
United Nations. Documents. ST/TAO/M/41.
At head of title: Department of economic and social affairs. Division for public administration.

18. -- **Economic and social council.** Bibliography on the protection of human rights of works published after December, 1939. - New York, 1961. - 248 p. - (Its: Documents. E/CN.4/540.)
Section I. General questions: bibliographies, human rights in general; human rights and international relations, peace, world order, regional order, etc.; historical antecedents of the Universal declaration of human rights; United Nations and human rights; international protection of human rights; domestic protection of human rights. - Section II. Tarticular rights: subjects related to the contents of Art. 1-30 of the U.D.

19. -- --- Répertoire des données publiées régulièrement dans les journaux officiels=Analysis of material published regularly in official gazettes. - Genève, 1958. - 39 p. - (Its: Listes bibliographiques-Miscellaneous bibliographies. no.1.)
Analysis by country. Subject index. Inventory of the entire collection of official gazettes.
Analysis of important material published in 199 official gazettes.

o

1920.   **United Nations. Library. New York.** Annotated list of official
         gazettes in the United Nations Headquarters library. - New York,
         1959. - 54 p.
         It is arranged alphabetically by name of country. Each entry contains: title of gazette;
         language; frequency; years held by the Library; library classification symbol; contents;
         indexes.

1921.   -- **Secretary-general, 1961-1971 (Thant).** Portfolio for peace:
         excerpts from the writings and speeches of U Thant, Secretary-
         general of the United Nations, on major world issues, 1961-1971. -
         Includes bibliographies. - New York, 1970. - 140 p. - (United
         Nations. Publications. Sales numbers. 1970.I.24.) E F R S
         At head of title: Office of public information.

1922.   **United Nations association of the United States of America.** Controlli
         conflicts in the 1970s; a report of a National policy panel establishe
         by the United Nations association of the United States of America.
         Bibliography: p. 62. - New York, 1969. - 62 p.

1923.   **United States. Congress. House. Committee on foreign affairs.** The
         Baruch plan: U.S. diplomacy enters the nuclear age/ by Leneice N.
         Notes, partly bibliographical. - Washington, 1972. - vi, 67 p.
         At head of title: Science, technology, and American diplomacy.
         "Prepared for the Subcommittee on national security policy and scientific developments."

1924.   -- --- The cold war: origins and developments. Hearings before the
         Subcommittee on Europe of the Committee... 92nd Congress, 1st.
         sess. - Bibliographical notes. - Washington, D.C., 1971. - iv, 231 p.

1925.   -- --- Sanctions as an instrumentality of the United Nations: Rhode
         as a case study. - Hearings before the Subcommittee on international
         organizations and movements of the Committee. - 92nd Congress,
         2nd sess. - Bibliographical notes. - Washington, D.C., 1972. - iv, 179

1926.   -- **Senate. Committee on foreign relations.** Review of the United
         Nations Charter; a collection of documents, selected and arranged by
         Subcommittee on the United Nations Charter of the Committee on
         foreign relations. - Pursuant to S. Res. 126. - Bibliography: p. 887-8
         Washington, 1954. 0 xii, 895 p. - (83rd Congress, 2nd session. Senat
         Doc. no.87.)

1927.   -- **Department of State.** The Department of State bulletin. - Includes
         bibliographies. - v.1-   ; 1939-   . - Washington, D.C.,
         1939-   . -   v.
         Pub. weekly.
         Supersedes: Its: Press releases, and Its: Treaty information bulletin.

1928.   -- **Information agency.** International relations. - Washington, D.C.,
         United States Information agency, Information center service, 1969. -
         ii, 45 p. - (Its: Subject bibliographies. no.6/69.)

1929.   -- **Library of Congress. Division of bibliography.** List of references
         on Europe and international politics in relation to the present issues,
         comp. under the direction of Hermann H.B. Meyer, chief bibliog-
         rapher. - Washington, Govt. print. off., 1914. - 144 p.
         European war, 1914-1918 - Bibl. Europe - Politics - 19th and 20th cent. - Bibl. Interna-
         tional law and relations - Bibl.

1930. **United States. Library of Congress. European affairs division.** The United States and Europe: a bibliographical examination of thought expressed in American publications during 1948-1952. - Washington, D.C., 1948-1953. - 1 v.

1931. -- **General reference and bibliography division.** A guide to bibliographic tools for research in foregin affairs. - Comp. by Helen F. Conover. - Washington, 1956. - 145 p.

1932. The **United States** and international organization: the changing setting. - Notes, partly bibliographical. - Edited by Lawrence S. Finkelstein. - Cambridge, Mass., M.I.T. press, 1969. - vii, 216 p.

1933. **L'univers** politique; relations internationales. - 1968- . - Includes bibliographies. - Paris, Ed. Richelieur, 1968- . - v.
"Ouvrage annuel établi sous la direction de Jean Meyriat."

1934. **Van Dyke, V.** Human rights, the United States, and world community. - Bibliographical notes: p. 255-284. - New York, Oxford university press, 1970. - ix, 292 p.

1935. -- --- International politics. - Bibliography at the end of each chapter. - New York, Appleton-Century-Crofts, 1957. - ix, 483 p. - (Appleton-Century-Crofts political science series.)

1936. **Van Wagenen, R. W.** Research in the international organization field; some notes on a possible focus. - Notes, partly bibliographical. - Princeton, N.J., 1952. - 78 p. - (Center for research on world political institutions, Princeton university. Publications. no. 1.)

1937. **Venezia, J. C.** Stratégie nucléaire et relations internationales. - Bibliography: p. 171-172. - Paris, A. Colin, 1971. - 175 p. - (Collection U. sér.: "Relations et institutions internationales".)

1938. Die **Vereinten** Nationen und Regionalpakte=The United Nations and regional organizations=Les Nations Unies et les accords régionaux. - (In: Hüfner, Klaus. Zwanzig Jahre Vereinte Nationen; internationale Bibliographie, international bibliography, bibliographie internationale, 1945-1965. Berlin, W. de Gruyter, 1968. p. 313-319)

1939. **Vergleich** zum Völkerbund=Comparison with the League of nations= Comparaison avec la Société des nations. - (In: Hüfner, Klaus. Zwanzig Jahre Vereinte Nationen; internationale Bibliographie, international bibliography, bibliographie internationale, 1945-1965. Berlin, W. de Gruyter, 1968. p. 40-43.)

1940. **Verniers, L.** International cooperation and you. - Notes, partly bibliographical. - Brussels, Union of international associations, 1962. - 82 p. - (Union des associations internationales, Brussels. Publications. no. 177.) E F

1941.   **Villacrés, M. J. W.** Organismos regionales de América, Europa, Asia,
         Africa y Oceania. - Bibliography: 1 leaf following leaf 65. -
         Guayaquil, Ecuador, Escuela de piplomacia, Universidad de
         Guayaquil, 1966. - 65 l.

1942.   **Vysotskiĭ, V. N.** Zapadnyĭ Berlin i ego mesto v sisteme sovremennykh
         mezhdunarodnykh otnosheniĭ. - Bibliography: p. 447-479. - Moskva,
         Izd-vo, "Mysl' ", 1971. - 482 p.
         Berlin (West Berlin.)

1943.   **Walsh, A. E.** The structure and development of the common market/
         by A.E. Walsh and John Paxton. - Bibliography: p. 202. - London,
         Hutchinson, 1968. - viii, 232 p.

1944.   **Waltz, K. N.** Man, the state and war; a theoretical analysis. -
         Bibliography: p. 239-251. - New York, Columbia university press,
         1959. - vii, 263 p.

1945.   **Watkins, J. T.** General international organization; a source book/ by
         James T. Watkins IV, and J. William Robinson. - Notes, partly
         bibliographical. - Princeton, N.J., D. Van Nostrand, 1956. - xi,
         248 p. - (Van Nostrand political science series.)

1946.   **Watson, A.** Europe at risk. - Bibliography at the end of each chapter. -
         London, G.G. Harrap, 1972. - 224 p.
         Europe - Politics - 1965. Europe - Economic policy. Common market. Communauté
         économique européenne. Common market - Great Britain.

1947.   **Wegmann, B.** Die Europäische und Atlantische Gemeinschaft in der
         Ost-West-Spannung. - Bibliography: p. 56. - Hrsg. von der Bundes-
         zentrale für Heimatdienst. - Bonn, 1953. - 56 p.

1948.   Die **Welt:** Daten, Fakten, Informationen. - Includes bibliographies. -
         1968-   . - Berlin, Dietz, 1968-   . -   v.
         Pub. annually.
         Prepared by the Deutsches Institut für Zeitgeschichte, Berlin.

1949.   **Williams, W. L.** Intergovernmental military forces and world public
         order. - Bibliography: p. 643-703. - Leiden, A.W. Sijthoff, 1971. -
         xiii, 703 p.

1950.   **Woo, C. H.** Pacific settlement of international disputes by the
         Security council. - Bibliography: p. 178-187. - Berkeley, 1949.
         Microfilm copy of typewritten manuscript. Made by Library photographic service.
         University of California (no. 4591). Positive.
         Collation of the original: vi, 187 p.
         Thesis - Univ. of California.

1951.   **Wood, J. D.** Building the institutions of peace. - Notes, partly
         bibliographical. - London, G. Allen & Unwin, 1962. - 101 p. -
         (Swarthmore lectures. 1062.)

952. **Woodman, D.** Himalayan frontiers: a political review of British,
      Chinese, Indian and Russian rivalries. - Bibliography: p. 322-348. -
      New York, F.A. Praeger, 1969. - xii, 423 p. - (Books that matter.)

953. **World** polity; a yearbook of studies in international law and organiza-
      tion. - Notes, partly bibliographical. - v.1-   . - Washington, Institute
      of world polity,   Georgetown university, 1957-   . - v.

954. **Worldsociety**; how is an effective and desirable world order possible? -
      a symposium. - Bibliographical notes. - Edited by B. Landheer... and
      others. - The Hague, M. Nijhoff, 1971. - vi, 211 p.

955. **Wright, P. Q.** On predicting international relations, the year 2000. -
      Bibliographical notes: p. 33-42. - Denver, Colo., 1969. - 42 p. -
      (Denver, Colo.   University.   Social science foundation.   Monograph
      series in world affairs. 1969/70. no.1.)
      At head of title: The Social science foundation and Graduate school of international
      studies;   University of Denver.)

956. -- ---- Problems of stability and progress in international relations. -
      Bibliographical notes: p. 333-360. - Berkeley, Univ. of California
      press, 1954. - xiv, 378 p.

957. -- ---- The study of international relations. - Bibliography at the end
      of each chapter. - New York, Appleton-Century-Crofts, 1955. -
      xii, 642 p. - (Century political science series.)

958. **Yost, C.** The insecurity of nations; international relations in the
      twentieth century. - Bibliography: p. 259-264. - New York,
      F.A. Praeger, 1968. - x, 276 p.
      "Published for the Council on foreign relations."

959. **Young, O. R.** The politics of force; bargaining during international
      crises. - Notes, partly bibliographical. - Princeton, N.J., Princeton
      university press, 1968. - xii, 438 p.
      "Published for the Center of international studies, Princeton university."

960. -- ---- A systemic approach to international politics. - Bibliography:
      p. 58-67. - Princeton, N.J., Center of international studies, Woodrow
      Wilson school of public and international affairs, Princeton university,
      1968. - iii, 67 p. - (Princeton university. Center of international
      studies. Research monographs. no.33.)

961. **Yugoslavia.   Institut za medunarodnu politku i privredu.** Godišnjak. -
      Includes bibliographies. - 1963-   . - Beograd, 1964-   . - v.
      International relations.

962. -- ---- International problems. - 1st-   ; 1960-   . - Includes
      bibliographies. - Beograd,   The Institute for international politics
      and economy, 1960-   . - v.
      Pub. annually.
      "Translations of selected articles from Its: 'Medunarodni problemi'."
      1960 has title of original (Medunarodni problemi) and articles selected from 1956-1959 issues.

963. -- ---- Revizija Povelje Ujedinjenih nacija; dokumentacioni materijal. -
      Bibliography: p. 105-118. - Beograd, 1955, 118 p.
      United Nations.   Charter.

1964. **Zacharias, E. M.** Behind closed doors; the secret history of the cold war/ by Ellis M. Zacharias, in collaboration with Ladislas Farago. - Bibliography: p. 333-357. - New York, G.P. Putnam's sons, 1950. - viii, 367 p.

1965. **Zaslawski, E.** Les rapports des organisations internationales, SDN et ONU, avec la théorie de la responsabilité internationale des états. - Notes, partly bibligoraphical. - Paris, n.d.
Microfilm copy of typewritten manuscript. Negative.
Collation of the original: iv, 264 p.
Thèse - Univ. of Paris.

1966. **Zawodny, J. K.** Guide to the study of international relations; selected sources. - San Francisco, Chandler pub. co., 1966. - xii, 151 p. - (Chandler publications in political science.)

1967. **Zellentin, G.** Intersystemare Beziehungen in Europa: Bedingungen der Friedenssicherung. - Bibliography: p. 287-299. - Leiden, A.W. Sijthoff, 1970. - xvi, 307 p. - (European aspects. ser.C; Politics. no.20.)
"Gedruckt mit Unterstützung der Deutschen Forschungsgemeinschaft."

1968. **Zenkner, H.** Le Conseil de sécurité et le règlement pacifique des différends. - Bibliography: p. 134. - Paris, 1952.
Microfilm copy of typewritten manuscript. Negative.
Collation of the original: 136 p.
Thèse - Univ. de Paris.

1969. **Zimmerman, W.** Soviet perspectives on international relations, 1956-1967. - Bibliography: p. 295-327. - Princeton, N.J., Princeton university press, 1969. - 336 p. - (Columbia university. Russian institute. Studies.)

1970. **Zurhellen Nollau, D.** El valor constitucional de la Carta de las Naciones Unidas. - Bibliography: p. 79-83.- Mexico, 1950. - 83 p.
Tesis - Mexico.

D. ACCESSION LISTS, LISTS OF PERIODICALS AND SELECTED ARTICLES PUBLISHED BY INTERNATIONAL LIBRARIES

1971. **Asociación latinoamericana de libre comercio. Biblioteca.** Boletin de la Biblioteca. - v.1-   ; 1963-   . - Montevideo, 1963-   . - v.

1972. **Communautés européennes. Bibliothèque.** Ausgewählte Zeitschriftenaufsätze=Articles sélectionés=Articoli selezionati= Geselacteerde tijdschriftenartikelen. - no.1-   . - Luxembourg, 19 -   . - v.

973. -- --- Neu-Erwerbungen der Bibliothek=Acquisitions récentes de la Bibliothèque. - no.1-74. - Luxembourg, 1966-1972. - v.

974. -- --- Systematischer Katalog der Bücher: allgemeines=Catalogue systématique des ouvrages: géneral=Catalogo sistematico dei libri: generale=Systematische katalogus van de boeken: algemeen. - 196 -   : - Bruxelles, 196 -   - v

975. -- --- Systematischer Katalog der Buecher: Wissenschaften, Technik=Catalogue systématique des ouvrages: sciences, technique=Catalogo sistematico dei libri: scienza, tecnica= Systematische katalogus van de boeken: Wetenschappen, techniek. - 196 -   . - Bruxells, 196 -   . v.

976. -- **Bibliothèque centrale.** Bulletin des acquisitions=Verzeichnis der Neuerwerbungen=Bollettino delle acquisizioni=Lijst van aanwinsten. - 1ère- année. - Luxembourg, 1958-   . - v.

977. **Council of Europe. Bibliothèque et documentation.** Bulletin de bibliographie. - Série: questions sociales. - v.1-9. - Annual subject index.

978. **European organization for nuclear research. Library.** CERN Library accessions list: books and pamphlets. - 1955-   . - v.

979. -- --- CERN Library accessions list: preprints and reports. - 1955-   . - v.

980. **Food and agriculture organization. Library.** Catalogue of annuals currently received by the Library=Catalogue des publications annuelles parvenant régulièrement à la Bibliothèque=Catalogo de publicaciones anuales que se reciben regularmente en la Biblioteca. - Rome, 1968. - xxxviii, 314 p.
Contents: 1. Country index. 2. Subject index. 3. Alphabetical catalogue of annuals currently received. 4. Short-title list of annuals by country of publication. 5. Short-title list of annuals by subject.

981. -- --- List of recent accessions. - 1967-1972. - (S/LI:LRA 72/5, etc.)
Contents: 1. General. 2. Social sciences. 3. Natural sciences. 4. Environment. 5. Applied sciences and technology.

1982.   **General agreement on tariffs and trade. Library.** Monthly
list of publications received in the GATT Library.
- no.4/5   ; 1972-   . - Geneva, 1972-   . -   v.
- (INT(9172) 11 etc.)

1983.   **Institut universitaires de hautes études internationales. Bibliothèque.**
Nouvelles acquisitions. -   . - Genève, 19 . -   v.
Contents:
Généralités. Sciences sociales: sociologie, science politique, philosophie politique,
colonies, politiques coloniales, politique internationale, relations internationales,
coopération internationale, économie, histoire de l'économie travail, syndicats,
socialisme, communisme, histoire sociale, droit, philosophie du droit, droit international, droit international privé, droit diplomatique, droit maritime, droits de
l'homme, droit commercial, organisation internationale, organisations européennes,
guerre, armées, strategie, désarmement. Mathématiques. Sciences naturelles. Géo-
graphie. Histoire.

1984.   **International atomic energy agency.** Film catalogue. - no.1-10;
. - Vienna,   . -   v.
Contents:
1. Information for borrowers. 2. Films by number. 3. Subject index. 4. Alphabetical title index. 5. Series index. 6. Country index. 7. Language index.
The films listed in this catalogue - all 16 mm optical sound, unless otherwise
indicated - are available on free loan for educational, non-commercial, non-profit
showings only, involving no admission charges or appeal for funds. Most of the
films have been donated to the Agency by the governments of member States.

1985.   -- --- IAEA Library catalogue of books: 1968-1970. - Vienna,
1971. - 235 p.
This is the first cumulative volume of the IAEA Library new acquisitions.
Includes author index, title index, corporate entry index.

1986.   -- --- List of periodicals in the field of nuclear energy.
- no.1-   . - Vienna, 1961-   . -   v. - (Its: Documents.
STI/DOC/30. no.1, etc.)

1987.   -- --- New acquisitions in the IAEA and UNIDO libraries. -
September 1971-   . - Vienna, 1971-   . -   v.
A classified computer produced list of new books and serials.

1988.   -- --- Conference proceedings in the IAEA Library.

1989.   -- **Library.** List of new reports in the IAEA Library. - Vienna,
1972. - 40 p.
With the expansion of the INIS system during 1972 to full subject scope, the
Library ceased the monthly announcement of non-convention literature in its
Acquisitions list. Starting in January 1973, all non-conventional literature
received in the Library will be included on a regular basis in the Atomindex.

1990.   -- --- New acquisitions. - v.1-   ; 1958-   . - Vienna, 1958-
. -   v.
Pub. semi-annually, 1958- Aug. 1959; monthly, Sept. 1959-   .
Title varies: 1958-1963, Accessions list; 1964-June/Aug 1967, Recent acquisitions:
Sept. 1967-June 1970, New books in the IAEA library.

1991.   **International civil aviation organization. Library.** Recent
accessions. - v.1-27; 1947-1972. - Montreal, 1947-1972.
-   v.
Quarterly list of books, documents, pamphlets and periodicals.

92.   **International coffee organization. Library.** Accessions bulletin.
       - no.1-   . - London, 1970-   . - v.
       Contains: annuals, new periodicals, books, reports and pamphlets, articles in
       periodicals.

93.   **International institute for labour studies. Library.** Selected
       acquisitions. - List no.1-102; 1963-1972. - (INST/LIB/SA/1-102.)

94.   **International labour office. Central library and documentation
       branch.** International labour documentation: semi-monthly
       abstract bulletin. - no.1-   ; 1965-   . - Geneva, 1965-
       1972. -   v.
       Produced by computer. Each issue is arranged in numerical order by entry
       numbers with index of descriptors. Major ILO documents and publications
       are chosen, abstracted and listed here. Cumulative editions with very detailed
       author, country and subject indexes have been published by G. K. Hall and
       Co. in Boston:
           (a)   1965-1969.   8v.
           (b)   1970-1971

95.   -- --- International labour documentation: supplementary
       list.
       Pub. weekly.
       Lists all new ILO documents and publications.
       Distributed to ILO officials (Headquarters and Field).

96.   -- --- List of additions to the Library. - April/June 1938-1964.

97.   -- --- Register of periodicals currently received (alphabetical and
       country list). - Geneva, 1970. - 201 p. - (Its: LD/NOTES/42.)

98.   **International monetary fund/International bank for reconstruction.
       and development. Joint library.** List of recent additions.
       - no.1-300, - Washington, 1958-1972. -   v.
       Contents: 1. General. 2. Africa. 3. America. 4. Asia. 5. Europe. 6. Oceania.

99.   -- --- List of recent periodical articles. - 1947-1972. -   v.
       Contents: 1. Economic theory. 2. Descriptive economics. 3. International
       monetary fund, International bank for reconstruction and development,
       International finance corporation, International development association.

00.   **International telecommunication union. Central library.**
       Liste des acquisitions récentes=List of recent acquisitions=
       Lista de adquisiciones recientes. - v.1-   ; no.1-   ;
       1952-   . - Genève, 1952-   . -   v.

01.   -- --- Liste des périodiques=List of periodicals=Lista de
       revistas. - 3ème éd. - Genève, 1972. - 107 p.
       Contents: 1. Alphabetical list of periodicals. 2. Keyword index.

02.   -- --- Liste des publications annuelles=List of annuals=
       Lista de publicaciones anuales. - 1ère éd. - Genève, 1972.
       - 26 p.
       Contents: 1. Index by country. 2. Alphabetical list of annuals. 3. List of
       annuals by country.

2003.   **International trade centre.** Annotated directory of regional and
          national trade and economic journals. - Geneva, 1971. - vii, 153 p.
          Financed by a grant from the Swedish international development authority.
          Contents: pt.1. Regional journals. pt. 2. National journals.
          Appendix I: Alphabetical list of journals by titles.
          Appendix II: A. Libraries consulted. B. Documentary sources used.

2004.   - - **Documentation service.** International trade documentation:
          annotated list of publications received by the International trade
          centre. - no. 23-   : April 1971-   . - Geneva, 1971-   .
          -   v. - (ITC/DS/1, etc.)
          Contents: 1. Main-subject index. 2. Annotated list.

2005.   - - - - - International trade documentation: cumulative list of
          statistical publications received from 1st August 1971 to
          30 June 1972=Liste cumulative des publications statistiques
          reçues du 1er août 1971 au 30 juin 1972. - Geneva, 1972. -
          154 l. - (Its: ITC/DS/STST/7.)
          Contents:
          Introductory note. Statistics issued by international organisations. Statistics
          relating to more than one country. Statistics relating to individual countries.

2006.   - - - - - International trade documentation: list of statistics
          received=Liste des statistiques reçues. 1969-   . - Geneva,
          1969-   . - v. - (ITC/DS/STST/5, etc.)
          References are listed by international organisations, followed by countries,
          in alphabetical order.

2007.   **Inter-parliamentary union. International centre for parliamentary
          documentation. Library.** Liste d'ouvrages et articles catalogués=List
          of books and articles catalogued.
          Contents: 1. Sciences politiques: systèmes politiques, élections, vie
          parlementaire, partis politiques. 2. Droit: droit international, institutions
          et organisations internationales, droit public.

2008.   **Organisation for economic co-operation and development.
          Library.** Liste des abonnements aux publications périodiques.
          - 1962-   . - Paris, 1961-   . - v.
          Superseded: 1962, Organisation for European economic co-operation. Library.
          Liste des abonnements aux périodiques. 1955-1961.

2009.   - - - - - Catalogue des périodiques=Catalogue of periodicals.
          - 1969-1970. - Paris, 1970. - 485 p.
          Contents: Annex I: Subjects.
                        Annex II: Code frequency.
                        pt.1: by countries.
                        pt.2: by international organizations.

2010.   - - - - - Ouvrages et périodiques nouveaux=New books and
          periodicals. - 1961-1972. - Paris, 1961-1972.
          Publ. monthly.
          La liste est partagée en deux parties (I. Ouvrages; II. Périodiques), dont
          la première contient les chapitres suivants:

          A. Ouvrages par matières
          B. Ouvrages par auteurs
          C. Ouvrages publiés par des collectivités
          D. Documents imprimés, publiés par des organisations internationales.

11. **Organisation for European economic co-operation. General affairs department.** Bulletin de documentation: list d'articles séléctionnés des périodiques reçus au Service de la documentation...=Research and reference bulletin: list of selected articles extracted from periodicals received by the Research and reference branch... - v.2; février-août 1949. - Paris, 1949. - 1 v.
Pub. monthly.
Ceased publication with issue of August 1949.
1. Economic conditions - Bibliography. 2. Periodicals - Indexes.

12. **Pan American union. Columbus memorial library.** List of books accessioned and periodical articles indexed.
Monthly.
Contains: Documents of the OAS and publications of the Pan American union.

13. **Union of international associations.** Bibliographie des ouvrages et documents reçus par l'UAI. - In: Associations internationales= International associations.

14. -- --- Directory of periodicals published by international organizations. - Brussels, 1969. - 240 p. - (UAI. Publications. no. 212.)

15. **United Nations. Dag Hammarskjold library, New York.** Current bibliographical information=Renseignements bibliographiques d'actualité. - v.1-   ; 1971-   . - New York, 1971-   .   v. - (Its: Documents. ST/LIB/SER.K/1, etc.)
Pub. semi-monthly.
Superseded: 1971, Its: (1) New publications in the Dag Hammarskjold library= Nouvelles publications reçues par la Bibliothèque Dag Hammarskjold. (1949-1970), and (2) Current issues; a selected bibliography on subjects of concern to the United Nations. (Dec. 1965-1970.)

16. -- --- List of periodicals available in the Dag Hammarskjold library. - pt.1: Law. - (ST/LIB/27.)
Contents: 1. List of periodicals. 2. Subject index. 3. Country of publication index.

17. -- --- **Economic commission for Africa. Library.** Check-list of serials currently received in the ECA library=Liste de contrôle des périodiques reçus à la bibliothèque de la CEA. - Addis Ababa, 1968. - 77 p.

18. -- --- List of selected UN documents received in the ECA Library. - v.1-7.

19. -- --- New acquisitions in the UNECA library=Nouvelles acquisitions de la Bibliothèque de la CEA. - v.1-   ; 1962-   . - Addis Ababa, 1962-   . -   v. - (Its: E/CN.14/LIB/SER.B/1, etc.)
Pub. monthly, 1962-68; bi-monthly, 1969-   .

20. -- --- Periodicals received in the UNECA Library. - Addis Ababa, 1961. - v, 113 p. - (Its: Bibliographies. E/CN.14/LIB/ SER.A/1.)
With this: Supplement: New periodicals received. 1962-   .

2021.   **United Nations. Economic commission for Africa. Library.** UN, UN
         specialized and operating agencies serials currently received in the
         ECA Library-Périodiques de l'ONU, des institutions spécialisées et des
         organes d'exécution de l'ONU reçus régulièrement à la Bibliothèque
         de la CEA. - 1970. - 168 p. - (E/CN.14/LIB/SER.A/5.)

2022.   -- **Economic commission for Asia and the Far East. Library.**
         List of selected articles. - v.1-7. - Bangkok, 1966-1972. -   v.
         Contents: 1. Generalities, documentation and organization of material.
         2. Social sciences. 3. Natural sciences. 4. Applied sciences. 5. Arts and
         recreation. 6. History. 7. United Nations and Asia and the Far East.

2023.   -- **Library, Geneva.** League of nations & United Nations
         Monthly list of selected articles: cumulative, 1920-1970.
         - pt.1-   . - Edited by Norman S. Field. - Dobbs Ferry,
         N.Y., Oceana publications, 1971-   . -   v.

2024.   -- ---- Liste mensuelle d'articles sélectionnés=Monthly list of
         selected articles. - v.1-44; 1929-1972.

2025.   -- ---- Liste mensuelle d'ouvrages catalogués=Monthly list of books
         catalogued. - v.1-46; 1928-1973. - Geneva, 1928-1973.

         Contents: 1. Political, historical and geographical questions. 2. Legal
         questions. 3. Social, humanitarian and health questions. 4. Education.
         5. Finance. 6. Communications and transport. 7. Reference works.
         The List includes the major documents of the United Nations and
         specialized agencies as a result of the centralized cataloguing project.

2026.   -- ---- **Processing section.** Catalogue of periodicals, annuals and
         special series currently received at the United Nations Library=
         Catalogue des revues, annuaires et séries spéciales régulièrement
         reçus à la Bibliothèque des Nations Unies=Catàlogo de revistas,
         anuarios y series especiales recibidos corrientemente en la
         Biblioteca de las Naciones Unidas=Katalog periodiki,
         ezhegodnikov i spetsial'nykh serii poluchaemykh Bibliotekoĭ
         OON, Zheneva. - Geneva, 1972. - ix, 463 p.
         Includes 9,063 titles.
         Contents: 1. Alphabetical catalogue of periodicals (national and international).
         2. International annuals. 3. Country list of governmental reports, statistical
         yearbooks, official and non-official annuals. - 4. Official gazettes. 5. Parlia-
         mentary documents. 6. Laws, statutes, laws reports, etc. 7. Newspapers.
         8. Index of corporate authors. 9. Index by country of origin.

2027.   -- **Library, New York.** Current bibliographies of periodical articles
         in the United Nations Library: a subject list. - New York, 1952. -
         47 l.
         First draft.
         Contents: 1. List of abbreviations. 2. General (international). 3. General (by
         country or region). 4. Political matters. 5. Economic matters. 6. Legal matters.
         7. Social matters. 8. Administrative matters. 9. Science and technology.
         10. Trusteeship; non-self-governing territories. 11. Geography. 12. Areas and
         countries. 13. Philosophy. 14. Documentation and librarianship. 15. Linguistics.
         16. Index.

28. **United Nations conference on trade and development. Joint ECE/
     UNCTAD reference unit.** Contents of recent periodicals.

29. -- --- Documents list. no.1-   .

30. -- --- Newspapers and periodicals received by ECE/UNCTAD
     reference unit. - v.1-2. - Geneva, 1972. - 2 v. - (UNCTAD/ADM/
     10/Rev.1, etc.)
     Contents: v.1. Titles in alphabetical order. - v.2. Country list (arranged
     alphabetically by title under country of publication). - v.3. International
     organization list (arranged alphabetically by title under name of international
     organization).

31. **United Nations educational, scientific and cultural organisation.
     Co-operative educational abstracting service.** Educational
     abstracts. - Abstract no.1-   .
     "Published in implementation of resolution 1.14 adopted by the General
     conference of Unesco of its 14th session."

32. -- **Library.** Liste des périodiques reçus au 1er août 1970.
     Supplement. - 1972-   .
     Les périodiques sont classés (1) par sujet, selon la calssification décimale
     universelle, (2) par ordre alphabétique.

33. -- --- New publications in the Unesco library=Nouvelles
     publications acquises par la Bibliothèque de l'Unesco.
     Contents: Communication of ideas. Bibliography. Libraries. Press.
     Film catalogues. Psychology. Religion. Sociology. Population. Family
     planning. Political science. Race questions. Economics. Politics and
     government. Education. Status of women. Philology. Astronautics.
     Applied sciences. Printing. Publishing. Mass communications. Literature.
     Historical sciences. References books.

34. **United Nations industrial development organization. Industrial
     documentation unit.** List of periodicals currently received
     by the UNIDO Library. - Vienna, 1972. - 105 p.
     This computer-produced list of periodicals consists of two sections:
     1. a listing by title for each publication, followed by the name of its
        publisher and place of issue;
     2. a subject classification based on the UNIDO Thesaurus of industrial
        development terms.

35. -- --- Monthly list of accessions: books. - no.1-   . - Vienna,
     1970-   . -   v.

36. **United Nations institute for training and research.** Publications
     available or in preparation. - New York, 1971. - 2 p.
     Contents: 1. UNITAR research reports. 2. Peaceful settlement. 3. UNITAR series.
     4. UNITAR lecture series. 5. UNITAR training manuals.

37. **Universal postal union. Bibliothéque et service de documentation.**
     Catalogue de l'UPU: périodicothèque; répertoire des périodiques
     de la Bibliothèque du Bureau international. - Berne, 1970. -
     54 p.

038. -- --- Liste des nouvelles acquisitions. - no.1-   .
     Contents: 1. Partie postale. 2. Partie générale.

2039.   **World health organization. Library.** WHO Library
         acquisitions=Acquisitions de la bibliothèque de l'OMS.
         - 1947-   , Geneva, 1947-   . -   v.
         Pub. monthly.
         The list is divided into three parts.
         I.   Recent acquisitions.
         II.   Bibliographies prepared by the WHO Library.
         III.   WHO publications.
         Each quarter, a supplementary list of new and discontinued periodicals
         and title changes in the WHO Library is included.

2040.   -- --- List of peridoicals in the WHO Library. - Geneva,
         1971. - 366 p.
         Now produced from computer tapes and is published as a supplement to
         WHO Library Acquisitions. New edition with subject and geographical
         index in press.

2041.   **World intellectual property organization. Library.** Liste
         bibliographique mensuelle=Monthly bibliographical list.
         - 1961-1972. - Genève, 1961-1972. -   v.
         Contents: 1. Books and selected articles. 2. Periodicals.

2042.   -- --- Répertoire des périodiques. - Genève, 1969. - 1 v.

2043.   **World meteorological organization. Library.** Selective list
         of acquisitions=Choix d'acquisitions. - 1965-1972. - Geneva,
         1965-1972. -   v.

E. NATIONAL SURVEYS OF INTERNATIONAL DOCUMENTATION

2044. **Arshinkova, S.** Obzor na sbirkata "Izdaniiã na Organizatsiiâta na Obedinenite Natsii i na spetsializiranite kŭm neiã organizatsii" v Narodnata biblioteka "Kiril i Metodii".
- Izvestiiã na Narodna biblioteka "Kiril i Metodii"=Annales de la Bibliothèque national "Kiril i Metodij". - 11: p.369-405, 1970.
Summaries in Russian and English: p.405.
Survey of the UN collection of documents in the National library "Kiril i Metodi", Bulgaria.

2045. **Bulgaria. Ministerstvo na vunshnite raboti.** Organizatsiia na obedinenite natsii: tematichnopredmeten pokazalets. - In: Vunshna politika na Narodna Republika Bulgariia, t.1, p. 623-629, 1970.

2046. **Cholganskaiã, V. L.** Publikatsii Organizatsii Ob"edinennykh Natsii i ee spetsializirovannykh uchrezhdenii: obzor za 1945-1965 g. - Moskva, Izd-vo "Nauka", 1968.
Commentary and bibliographic presentation of UN and specialized agencies publications in the USSR.

2047. **Copenhagen. Kongelige bibliotek.** FN, 1945-1970.
- Preface: Ninel Kledal. - København, 1970. - 18 p.
"Det kongelige Bibliotek, der er depotbibliotek for FN-publikatiner, har fundet det rimeligt at markere 25-året for verdensorganisationens oprettelse med en udstilling af dokumenter og publikationer udgivet af FN".

2048. Az **ENSZ** 1970 évi titkársági kiadványai az Országgyülési Könyvtárban. - Budapest, 1971. - 68 p.
UN publications in the Hungarian Parliament Library.

2049. **Europa**-Archiv: 1946-1965; Sammelregister, 1.-20. Jahrgang. - Bonn, Deutsche Gesellschaft für auswärtige Politik, 1966. - 32 323 p.
Cumulative index to "Europa-Archiv: Zeitschrift für internationale Politik" edited by Wilhelm Cornides.

2050. **Finland. Riksdagsbiblioteket.** Yhdistyneitä Kansakuntia käsittelevää kirjallisuutta. Litteratur om Förenta Nationerna.
- Luettelon on laatinut Aili Jalava. - Helsinki, Eduskunnan kirjasto - Riksdagsbiblioteket, 1965. - 38 p.
Supplement: 1-   . 1968-   .

2051. **Great Britain. Stationery office.** International organisations publications. - 1955-   . - London, 1956-   . - v.
"Supplement to the Stationery office catalogue."

2052.   **Hüfner, Klaus.** Zwanzig Jahre Vereinte Nationen:
         internationale Bibliographie=international bibliography=
         bibliographie internationale, 1945-1965. - Berlin,
         W. de Gruyter, 1968. - Lv, 519 p. - (Beiträge zur
         auswärtigen und internationalen Politik. Bd.2.)
         At head of title: Klaus Hüfner. Jens Naumann.

2053.   **Hungary, Magyar Unesco bizottsag.** Unesco kiadvanyok,
         1970-   ; valogatott bibliográfia. - Budapest, 1971-   .
         -    v.
         Survey of UNESCO publications in Hungary.

2054.   **Japan. Diet. Library.** Catalogue of the League of Nations
         and the United Nations publications for the period of
         1920-1968 in the National Diet library. - v.1-   . - Tokyo,
         National Diet library, 1971-   . -   v.
         Title in English and Japanese. Text partly English, partly Japanese.

2055.   -- --- Guide to United Nations documents. - Tokyo, 1960.
         - 70 p.
         Title in Japanese. Text in Japanese and English.
         Title romanized: Kokusairengo shiryo riyo no tebiki.

2056.   **Morocco. Centre national de documentation.** Index ONU -
         Maroc: Organisation des Nations Unies. - Rabat, 1972. - 138 p.
         - 435 documents. - (Its: Documentation du CND. 50763-
         51197.)
         At head of title: Royaume du Maroc. Secrétariat d'Etat au plan au
         développement régional et à la formation des cadres.
         Tables des matières
         1. Abréviations: Classes de documents; Langues; Autres termes; Code
             géographique; Abréviations particulières.
         2. Index analytique.
         3. Index auteurs.
         4. Liste bibliographique.

2057.   **National central library, Taipei.** Unesco documents: an annotated
         bibliography with an index to documents related to China. -
         Taipei, 1970. - 130, xxvii, iii p.

2058.   **Norske Nobelinstitutt, Oslo. Biblioteket.** Nordisk litteratur
         om de Forente Nasjoner; et utvalg böker og tidsskrift-
         artikler skrevet i årene 1959-1964/ utarb. ved Nobel-
         instituttets bibliotek av Ågot Brekke. - Oslo, Norsk
         samband for de Forente Nasjoner, 1965. - 43 1.

2059.   **Royal institute of international affairs, London.** Index to
         UN documents. - Dec. 1947, with one suppl. to Sept. 1948
         and Suppl. 2 to March 1949. - 3 v.

2060.   **Seoul, Korea. University. Library.** Catalogue of the United
         Nations depository library. - Seoul, 1970. - 245 p.
         Title-page in English and Korean. Text in English only.

2061.   **Società italiana per l'organizzazione internazionale.** Nota
         bibliografica. no.1-   ; 1959-   . - Roma, 1959-   .
         -    v.

2062.   **Sweden. Riksdagsbiblioteket.** United Nations, 1966-1969.
        - Stockholm, 1970. - xi, 96 p. - (Its: Fŏrteckning
        ŏver Riksdagsbibliotekets nyfŏrvärv. List of accession to
        the Library of the Swedish parliament. 1970: 1.)
        "Fŏrteckning ŏver Fŏrenta Nationernas publikationer utgivna ar 1966 fram
        t.o.m. hŏsten 1969, vilka under denna tidrymd inkommit till och
        katalogiserats i biblioteket". - Fŏrord.

2063.   **Thompson, E. M.** Resources for teaching about the United
        Nations, with annotated bibliography. - Washington, D.C.,
        National education association of the United States, 1962.
        - 90 p.
        "Prepared for the Committee on international relations."

2064.   **United Nations depository library, Kyoto.** United Nations and
        the United Nations specialized agencies publications issued
        in Japanese. - 1965/1966-   . - Kyoto, 1967-   .
        - v.
        Title in Japanese. Text partly Japanese, partly English.

2065.   **United States. Library of Congress.** The National union
        catalog: a cumulative author list representing Library of
        Congress printed cards and titles reported by other
        American libraries. - 1800-1972. - Washington, 1942-1972.
        - v.
        Includes major documents produced by international organizations and gives
        the most comprehensive coverage of international documentation in general.

2066.   -- **Office of education.** The United Nations and related
        organizations: a bibliography/ prepared in the International
        educational relations branch. - Washington, D. C., U.S.
        Department of health, education, and welfare, Office of
        education, 1960. - 17 p.

P

F. JOURNALS REVIEWING INTERNATIONAL DOCUMENTATION

2067.   **Activities**. - Paris, Organisation for economic co-operation and
        development, 19   . EF
        Monthly.
        Contains lists of publications under subjects discussed.

2068.   **American** journal of international law. - v.64, no.4,
        September 1970.
        American society of international law. Annual meeting. 64th, New York,
        1970.
        Proceedings.
        Contents: The United Nations appraisal at 25 years.
        - 1st session: The United Nations and peacekeeping.
        - 2nd session: The United Nations and legal aspects of the search for
                           peace in the Middle East.
        - 3rd session: The United Nations and race: will UN law affect victims
                           of racial discrimination and oppressors; Extraterritorial
                           application of law; the United Nations and science.
        - 4th session: The United Nations and disarmament; the United Nations
                           and environment; Practical aspects of international litigation.
        - Address by the president of the Society, Oscar Schachter: The future
           of United Nations. - p. 277-285.
        - Report on United Nations documents. - p.263-264, 293-314.

2069.   The **American** political science review. - Menasha, Wisconsin,
        American political science association, 1920-   .
        Quarterly.

2070.   **Associations** internationales≃International associations. - 1954-1972.
        - Bruxelles, Union of international associations, 1954-1972.
        Monthly.
        Title varies: 1949-1950, Bulletin mensuel de l'Union des associations
        internationales; 1951-1953, NGO Bulletin≃Bulletin ONG.

2071.   **Bulletin** analytique de documentation politique, économique et
        sociale contemporaine. - Paris, Fondation nationale des
        sciences politiques, 1946-   .
        Monthly.
        Dans le Plan de classement partie II: Relations internationales et études
        comparatives.

2072.   **Centre d'etudes et de documentation africaine, Brussels.**   Cahiers
        du CEDAF. - Bruxelles, 1971-   .
        Monthly.
        Reviews major international publications.

2073.   **Centre de réflexion sur le monde non occidental, Paris.**   Bulletin. -
        1ème-   année; 1963-   . - Paris, Fédération pour le respect
        de l'homme et de l'humanité, 1963-   . - v.
        Pub. bi-monthly.
        Contains references to international documents.

        Comunità internazionale. - Roma, Società italiana per
        l'organizzazione internazionale, 1946-   .
        Quarterly.

175. **Documentation** et information pédagogiques: bulletin du
Bureau international d'éducation. - 1ère-46 année. - Genève,
1927-   .
Quarterly.

176. **FID** News bulletin. - The Hague, 1951-   .
Presents major international publications.

177. **Foreign** affairs. - New York, 1922-   .
Quarterly.
Contains: Source material from UN, ICJ, UNESCO, FAO, ILO, European
communities, OECD.

178. **France. Secrétariat d'Etat aux affaires étrangères. Centre de
documentation.** Bulletin bibliotraphique. - 1968-   . -
Paris, 1968-   . -   v.

179. **General agreement on tariffs and trade.** International trade
news bulletin; a monthly record of news reports on items
related to the operation of the General agreement.
- v.1-9; 1950-1959. - Geneva, 1950-1959. - 10 v.
Pub. monthly.
Title varies: Jan-Mar. 1950, Trade news bulletin.
French ed. has title: Bulletin du commerce international.
Superseded in part by: 1960, Its: Developments in commercial policy.

180. **India** quarterly. - New Delhi, 1945-   .
Contains bibliographic information for major international publications.

181. **Intergovernmental maritime consultative organization.** Bulletin,
- no.1-   ; 1962-   . - London, 1962-   .   E/F
Twice a year.
Contains: List of IMCO publications available.

182. **International** associations=Associations internationales.
see: Associations internationales=International associations

183. **International council of scientific unions.** Publications of the
ICSU family. - In: The year book of the International
council of scientific unions, 1972. - Rome, 1972.

184. **International institute for labour studies.** Bulletin. - no.1-9;
1962-1972. - Geneva, 1962-1967. -   v.
Each issue contains a List of IILS publications.

185. **International** labour review. - Geneva, International labour
office, 1921-1972.
Monthly.

Contains bibliographies, reviews and notes on new publications in the field of
economic and social life of concern to International labour organisation.

2086.   **International** organization. - Boston, World peace foundation,
         1947-   .
         Quarterly.
         Contains: Selected bibliography:
         I.   General.
         II.   United Nations: General; Political and security questions;
                 Administrative and budgetary matters; Legal questions; International
                 atomic energy agency.
         III.   Specialized agencies: Food and agriculture organization; Inter-
                 governmental maritime consultative organization; International bank
                 for reconstruction and development; International civil aviation
                 organization; International labour organisation; International monetary
                 fund; United Nations educational, scientific and cultural organisation;
                 World health organization.
         IV.   Regional matters: Africa; American States; Organization of American
                 States; Latin American free trade association; Atlantic community;
                 North Atlantic treaty organization; British commonwealth of nations;
                 the Caribbean; Eastern Europe; Council for mutual economic
                 assistance; Warsaw treaty organization; Far East; Southeast Asia
                 treaty organization; Arab league; Central treaty organization; Non-
                 aligned nations; Western Europe; Benelux economic union; Council of
                 Europe; European commission of human rights; European atomic
                 energy community; European coal and steel community; European
                 economic community; European free trade association; European
                 organization for nuclear research; Nordic council; Western european union.
         V.   Other functional organizations: Bank for reconstruction and
                 development; General agreement on tariffs and trade; International
                 sugar council; Interparliamentary union.

2087.   **International** social science journal. - Paris, UNESCO, 1949-   .
         Quarterly.
         In each issue:
         Documents and publications of the United Nations and specialized agencies.

2088.   **International** studies quarterly. - Detroit, 1966-   .
         Quarterly.

2089.   **International telecommunication union.**   Telecommunication
         journal. - Geneva, 1962-   .   E F
         Monthly.
         Contains: List of recent and forthcoming publications.

2090.   **Journal** of voluntary action research. - Boston, Association of
         voluntary action scholars, 1965-   .
         Quarterly.

2091.   Le **Monde** diplomatique. - 1ère-19 année. - Paris, 1954-   .
         Monthly.
         Contains: L'activité des organisations internationales.

2092.   **NATO** review. - Brussels, 1954-   .
         Monthly.
         Contains: NATO publications.

2093.   **Nature** and resources: newsletter about scientific research
         on environment, resources and conservation of nature.
         - v.1-8. - Paris, UNESCO, 1965-1972. -   v.
         Contains: New Unesco publications.

2094.   **Nouvelles** de l'UNITAR. - v.1-   . - New York, 1970-   .
         v. E F
         Contains: Publications de l'UNITAR, ouvrages déjà parus ou à paraître sous peu.

95. **Organisation for economic co-operation and development. Development centre.** Liaison bulletin between development research and training institutes. - 1964-   . - Paris, 1964-   . -   v.
Pub. irregularly, 1964-1966; quarterly, 1967-   .
Issued also in French.
Contents: I. Training and research news. II. Research and documentation in the institutes. III. Notebook of co-operation. IV. Books, specialized bibliographies and new periodicals.
Tool of easy reference in the field of economic and social development.

96. **Peace** research abstracts journal. - Clarkson, Ontario, 1964-
Monthly.
Published with assistance from UNESCO.
An official publication of the International peace research association.

97. **Résumés** analytiques des pêches mondiales: compte rendu trimestriel des travauz techniques paraissant sur les pêches et les industries connexes. - v.1-23. - Rome, FAO, 1950-1972.
Contains: Un index des noms d'auteurs, un index des matières et un index des références croisées aux numéros des résumés, au noms des auteurs et aux codes FWS et CDU.

98. **Revista** Interamericana de bibliografía=Inter-American review of bibliography. - Washington, D.C., 1951-   .
Quarterly.
Contains: Publications of the OAS and its specialized organizations.

99. **Revue** française de science politique. - Paris, 1951-   .
Bi-monthly.
Contains: Informations bibliographiques.

00. **RQ** Magazine: official quarterly journal of the Reference services division, American library association.
Contains: Selected UN publications: brief annotations/ by Milton Mittelman.

01. **Social** science information=Information sur les sciences sociales. - Paris, Conseil international des sciences sociales, 1954-   .

02. **Social** sciences. - Moscow, USSR Academy of sciences, 1970-   .
Contains major international publications.

03. **Social** sciences and humanities index. - New York, 1920/1923-

Quarterly with annual cumulations.

04. **Town** planning review. - Liverpool, 1949-   .
Quarterly.
Contains a chapter for books and documents received.

05. **UNESCO** chronicle. - v.1-18. - Paris, 19 -   .   E F
Monthly.
Contains: List of works in English or French published by Unesco during the last month.
News of the Secretariat, permanent missions and national commissions.

2106.   **UN** monthly chronicle. - New York, 1967-   .   E F
         Monthly.
         Contains: Documents - selected list:
         I.   Political and security: Apartheid; Communications; Cyprus; Disarmament;
                   Implementation of the Declaration on the granting of independence
                   to colonial countries and peoples; Implementation of Declaration on
                   strengthening international security; Humanitarian problems on Sub-
                   continent; India-Pakistan; Indo-China; Middle East; Namibia; Palestine
                   refugees; Peace-keeping operation; Peaceful uses of the sea-bed;
                   Portuguese territories; Southern Rhodesia.
         II.   Economic and social.
         III.   Human rights.
         IV.   Publications. Official records.

2107.   **UNIDO** Newsletter. - no.1-   . - Vienna, 19   .
         New major publications.

2108.   **World health organization.** Bulletin. - Geneva, 1947-1972. E/F
         Monthly.

2109.   -- --- WHO chronicle. - 1947-1972.   EFRSC
         Monthly.

2110.   **World meteorological organization.** Bulletin. - Geneva, 1952-1972.
         EF
         Quarterly.
         Contains: Recent WMO publications.

G. LIBRARY JOURNALS CONCERNED WITH INTERNATIONAL DOCUMENTATION

11.   **ALA** bulletin. - v.17-63; mars 1923-1969. - Chicago, American
      library association, 1923-1969. - 45 v.
      Pub. bi-monthly, 1923-25; monthly (except bi-monthly July-August), 1926-69.
      Absorbed: 1931, Adult education and the library.
      Proceedings of the association's annual conference issued as a regular number of the
      bulletin, 1923-69.
      Superseded by: 1970, American libraries.

12.   **American** libraries; bulletin of the American library association. -
      v.1-   ; 1970-   . - Chicago, 1970-   . -   v.
      Pub. monthly (except bi-monthly July-August).
      Superseded: 1970, ALA bulletin. (mars 1923-1969).

13.   **Association des bibliothécaires français.** Bulletin d'informations. -
      nouv. sér., no.13-   ; 1954-   . - Paris, 1954-   . -   v.
      Three issues per year, 1954-64; quarterly, 1965-   .
      Includes bibliographies.

14.   **Bibliotekovedenie** i bibliografiia za rubezhom. - vyp.1-   . -
      Moskva, Izd-vo "Kniga", 19   . -   v.
      At head of title: Gosudarstvennaia ordena Lenina biblioteka SSSR imeni V.I. Lenina.
      Librarianship and bibliography abroad.

15.   **Biblos:** österreichische Zeitschrift für Buch- und Bibliothekswesen,
      Dokumantation, Bibliographie und Bibliophilie. - Jhg. 1-   ; 1952-
         . - Wien, 1952-   . -   v.
      Pub. quarterly.
      Editor: J. Stummvoll.
      Includes bibliographies.

16.   **Bulletin** des bibliothèques de France. - 1e-   année; 1956-   . -
      Paris, Direction des bibliothèques et de la lecture publique, 1956-
         . -   v.
      Pub. monthly.
      Superseded: 1956, (1) France. Bibliothèque nationale. Bulletin de documentation
      bibliographique. (1937-1955), and (2) France. Direction des bibliothèques de France.
      Bulletin d'informations.
      Issued by: 1956-63, Direction des Bibliothèques.

17.   **Centre national de la recherche scientifique, Paris.** Science de
      l'information, documentation. - no.   -   ; 1973-   . - Paris,
      1973-   . - v. - (Its: Bulletin signlétique. 101.)

18.   **Fénix.** - no.1-   ; 1945-   . - Lima, Biblioteca nacional, 1945-   . -
      v.
      Pub. irregularly; 1945-52; annually, 1953-   .

19.   **FID** news bulletin. - v.1-   . - The Hague, 19   . -   v.
      Monthly publication of the General secretariat of the International federation for
      documentation.
      Contains: Calendar, conferences announced, organization of information,
      standardization, automation, training, terminology, revision of the UDC, FID
      publications, documentation literature, journals, book notices, reports,
      directories, abstracting/indexing services, bibliographices.

2120.   **Herald** of library science. - v.1-   ; 1962-   . - Varanasi, 1962-   .
          - v.
          Pub. quarterly.
          "Sponsored by the Sarada Ranganathan endowment for library science."

2121.   **IFLA** news. - no.1-   ; 19   . - The Hague, 19   . -   v.   E F

2122.   **Information**: news, sources, profiles. - v.1-   ; 1970-   . - New
          York, Science associates/International, Inc., 1970-   . -   v.
          Journal for information specialists, librarians, documentalists, computer scientists,
          research and administrative personnel concerned with any aspect of the development,
          acquisition, storage, use and transfer of scientific information.

2123.   **Information** storage and retrieval: theory and practice. - v.8-   ;
          1972-   . - Oxford, 1972-   . -   v.
          Pub. bi-monthly.
          Title in English only. Texts partly English, partly French, partly German.
          Includes bibliographies.

2124.   **International** library review. - v.1-   ; 1969-   . - London, 1969-   .
          - v.
          Pub. quarterly.
          Includes bibliographies.

2125.   **Libri:**   international library review and IFLA communications. -
          v.1-   ; 1950-   . - Copenhagen, 1950-   . -   v.
          Pub. quarterly.
          Texts partly English, partly German, partly French.
          Includes bibliographies.

2126.   **Journal** of documentation. - v.1-   ; 1945-   . - London, Aslib,
          1945-   . -   v.
          Pub. quarterly.
          "Devoted to the recording, organization, and dissemination of specialized knowledge."
          Includes bibliographies.

2127.   **Library** & information science abstracts. - 1969-   . - London,
          Library association and Aslib, 1969-   . -   v.
          Pub. bi-monthly.
          Superseded: 1969, Library science abstracts.

2128.   **Library** association record. - new ser., v.3-   ; March-December,
          1925-   . - London, Library association, 1925-   . -   v.
          Pub. quarterly, 1925-30; monthly, 1931-   .
          Supplement: Liaison. 1957-   .

2129.   **Library** journal. - v.45-   ; 1920-   . - New York, 1920-   . -
          v.
          Pub. semi-monthly (monthly, July-Aug.).
          Includes bibliographies.
          Supplement: (1) Junior libraries (1954-1961), (2) School library journal, 1961-   .

2130.   The **library** quarterly. - v.6-   ; 1936-   . - Chicago, 1936-   .
          - v.
          Pub. quarterly.

2131.   **Library** resources & technical services. - v.1-   ; 1957-   . -
          Fulton, Resources & technical services division, American library
          association, 1957-   .   v.
          Pub. quarterly.
          Supersedes: 1951-1956, Journal of cataloging and classification.

32.   **Library** trends. - v.1-   ; 1952-   . - Urbana, University of Illinois
       Graduate school of library science, 1952-   . -   v.
       Pub. quarterly.
       Includes bibliographies.

33.   **Program:** news of computers in libraries. - v.1-   ; 1970-
       London, Aslib, 1972-   . -   v.
       Pub. quarterly.
       "School of library and information studies, the Queen's university of Belfast."
       Includes bibliographies.

34.   **Revue** internationale de la documentation. - v.5-32; 1938-
       1965. - La Haye, 1938-1965. - 14 v.
       Pub. quarterly.
       At head of title: Fédération internationale de documentation.
       Title varies: 1938, I.I.D. communicationes; 1939-45, F.I.D. communicationes;
       1947-61, Revue de la documentation. Review of documentation.
       Texts partly English, partly French, partly German.
       Includes bibliographies.
       Absorbed by: 1966, Fédération internationale de documentation. FID news
       bulletin.

35.   **Sovetskaia** bibliografiia. - vyp. 40-   ; 1955-   . - Moskva,
       Vsesoiuznaia kniznaia palata, 1955-   . -   v.
       Pub. irregularly, 1955-1958; bi-monthly, 1959-   .

36.   **Special** libraries. - v.35-   ; 1944-   . - New York, Special libraries
       association, 1944-   . -   v.
       Ten issues per year, 1944-70; monthly, 1971-   .
       Includes bibliographies.

37.   **United States. Library of Congress.** Information bulletin. - 1945-   . -
       Washington, D.C., 1945-   . -   v.
       Pub. weekly.

38.   **United Nations educational, scientific and cultural organisation.**
       Bibliography, documentation, terminology. - v.1-   ; 1961-   . -
       Paris, 1961-   . -   v.
       Pub. bi-monthly.
       French ed. has title: Bibliographie, documentation, terminologie.
       Superseded: Mar. 1961, Its: (1) Monthly bulletin on scientific documentation and
       terminology. (1956-1960), and (2) Bibliographical news.
       Title varies: Mar. 1961, Bulletin on bibliography, documentation and terminology.

39.   -- --- Unesco bulletin for libraries. - v.1-   ; 1947-   . - Paris,
       1947-   . -   v. E F R S
       Pub. monthly, 1947-59; bi-monthly, 1960-

40.   **Veringung schweizerischer Bibliothekare.** Nachrichten=Nouvelles=Notizie. -
       Jhg.8-   ; Mai 1932-   . - Bern, 1932-   . -   v.
       Pub. irregularly, 1932-46; bi-monthly, 1947-   .
       Texts partly German, partly French, partly Italian.

41.   **Zentralblatt** für Bibliothekswesen. - 44. -   Jhg.; 1927-   . -
       Leipzig, 1927-   . -   v.
       Pub. monthly.

V. ACTIVITIES OF INTERNATIONAL LIBRARIES

2142.   **Aubrac, R.** Le Centre de documentation de la FAO: essai de diffusion des informations rassemblées par une organisation internationale. - Associations internationales=International associations 19: 587-595, septembre 1967.

2143.   **Breycha-Vauthier, A. C.** La Bibliothèque des Nations Unies de Genève. - Bulletin de l'Unesco à l'intention des bibliothèques 5: 81-89, mars 1951.

2144.   -- --- La Bibliothèque des Nations Unies de Genève, centre international de documentation en sciences sociales. - Revue de la documentation=Review of documentation 24: 66-69, mai 1957.

2145.   -- --- Les lectures pour les prisonniers de guerre. - F.I.D. Communications X: 21-23, fasc. 2, 1943.

2146.   -- --- Le rôle des bibliothèques des Nations Unies dans le monde. - Libri 12: 122-126, no.2, 1962.

2147.   -- --- Survey of the FAO library. - Rome, 1959. - 18 p. - (Food and agriculture organization. Conference. 10th, Rome, 1959. Documents. C59/11, 25 July, 1959.)

2148.   -- --- Vital problems of international libraries. - Journal of documentation 21: 248-251, December 1965.

2149.   **Buntrock, H.** Survey of the world agricultural documentation services. - Luxembourg, Centre for information and documentation, European communities, 1971. - 55 p. - (EUR 4680e.)
Prepared on behalf of the FAO Panel of experts on "AGRIS", International information system for the agricultural sciences and technology.

2150.   **Cain, J.** Structure and functions of the Unesco department of documentation, libraries and archives. - Unesco bulletin for libraries 25: 311-317, no.6, 1971.

2151.   **Carter, E. J.** Unesco's library programs and work. - Library quarterly 18: 235-244, October 1948.

2152.   **Clapp, V. W.** United Nations Library. - Library of Congress information bulletin 8: 14-15, 1949.

2153.   -- --- United Nations Library, 1945-1961. - Libri 12: 111-121, 1962.

2154.   -- --- The United Nations Library: organization, work, utilization of staff: report of a review conducted April 28-May 3, 1952. - New York, 1952. - 80 p. - (United Nations. Documents. A/C.5/L.177.)

155. **Coblans, H.** Unesco Library. - Unesco bulletin for libraries 4:
      641-675, 1950.

156. **Dag** Hammarskjold library. - Library of Congress information
      bulletin 20: 714-718, 1961.

157. **Dag** Hammarskjold library: gift of the Ford foundation. - New York,
      United Nations, 1962. - 165 p. - (Proceedings of the dedication
      ceremony and the Symposium.)

158. **Dale, D. C.** An American in Geneva: Florence Wilson and the
      League of nations Library. - In: The journal of library history.
      v.7, no.2, 1972, p. 109-129.
      The only woman library director in Europe in 1919, founder of the League of
      nations Library.
      Bibliographical notes: p. 126-129.

159. -- --- The United Nations Library, its origin and development. -
      Chicago, American library association, 1970. - xvi, 236 p.
      Bibliography: p. 179-223.

160. **Davidica, M.** United Nations Headquarters library. - St. Paul,
      Minn., 1962. - 10 p.

161. **Dimitrov, T. D.** Cooperation, coordination and mutual assistance
      of international libraries. - Luxembourg, 1967. - 3 1.
      "Statement made to the 2nd AIL Symposium, 23 June 1967."

162. **Donne, R.** Activities of the OECD and its Development centre in
      the field of documentation. - Paris, 1970. - 3 p.
      Document presented at the Meeting of the General assembly, International federation
      for documentation, Buenos Aires, 17-18 September, 1970.

163. **European** law libraries=Guide européen des bibliothèques de
      droit. - London, Morgan-Grampian, 1971. - 678 p.
      "Prepared by the International association of law libraries under the auspices of
      the Council of Europe."

164. **Fiebert, E. E.** Dag Hammarskjold library. - Philadelphia, Pa.,
      Drexel institute of technology, 1963. - 26 p.

165. **Field, N. S.** La Bibliothèque de l'Organisation des Nations Unies
      à Genève. - Bulletin de l'Unesco à l'intention des bibliothèques
      23: 355-357, 374; novembre-décembre 1969.

166. **Food and agriculture organization. Publication division. Terminology
      and reference section.**FAO Terminology and reference section:
      services and collections, a guide. - Rome, 1969. - 14 p. - (Its:
      Publications. PU:TRS/69/1.)

167. **Garde, P. K.** The United Nations family of libraries. - New
      York, Asia pub. house, 1970. - 252 p. - (Sarada Ranganathan
      lectures. 1966.)
      "Ranganathan series in library science. 22."
      Bibliography: p.231-242.

2168.   **Gomez de Silva, G.**   Library services of the United Nations.
- Library journal 74: 1297-1299, September 15, 1949.

2169.   **Groesbeck, J.**   The United Nations headquarters library. -
Revue de la documentation 25: 33-36, mai 1958.

2170.   **Haden, J. W.**   I.L.O. library. - Revue de la documentation=
Review of documentation 24: 70-72, mai 1957.

2171.   **Heaps, W. A.**   Library aids plans of Unesco. - Library journal 74:
1066-1068,1949.

2172.   -- --- Unesco's reference service. - Library journal 74:
1278-1280, 1949.

2173.   -- --- Unesco's references books. - Library journal 74:
1163-1165, 1949.

2174.   **Henderson, S.**   La bibliothèque du Bureau international du travail. -
Genève, 1936.

2175.   **Hoppes, M.**   The Library of the League of Nations at Geneva.
- Library quarterly 31: 257-268, July 1961.

2176.   **Hubbard, U. P.**   La Bibliothèque de la Société des Nations.
- Conciliation internationale, bulletin: 819-821, nos. 7-8-9, 1937.

2177.   **International atomic energy agency.**   IAEA Library facilities and
services. - Vienna, 1972. - 14 p.
Loan regulations. The collection and services. Reference services. Technical reports.
United Nations and IAEA documents. Film library. Photocopying services.
Acquisitions. Regular library publications.

2178.   **Izant, H. A.**   Documentation activities of the WHO library.-
Revue de la documentation=Review of documentation 24:
73-74, mai 1957.

2179.   -- --- World health organization and medical librarianship.
- In: International congress of medical librarianship. Proceedings.
London, 1953, p.9-16.

2180.   **Kent, F. L.**   The UNESCO library. - Library quarterly 26:
31-40, January 1956.

2181.   **Kepple, R. R.**   The library of the International atomic energy
agency. - Revue internationale de la documentation 32:
16-18 février 1965.

2182.   -- --- Missions for an international library. - Special libraries 60:
521-526, October 1969.
The International atomic energy agency library, Vienna.

2183.   -- --- Serving readers in a special international library: International
atomic energy agency library, Vienna. - College and research
libraries 28:   203-207, 1967.

4.   **Koekebakker, F. A.**   De bibliotheek van de Voedsel en
      Landbouworganisatie van de Verenigde Naties te Rome.
      - Bibliotheekleven 45: 410-421, 1960.
      FAO library, Rome.

35.   **Kujath, K.**   Les bibliothèques économiques des Communautés
      européennes. - Luxembourg, 1972. - 22 1.
      At head of title: Fédération international des associations de bibliothécaires. Sous-
      section des bibliothéques de sciences sociales. Congrès FIAB, Budapest 1972.

36.   **Lake, H. A.**   The Library of the International labour office. -
      Library association record. v,23., p. 356-364, November 1921.

37.   -- --- Libraries and documentation centres. - Association of
      international libraries. Newsletter. no.11, August, 1967. Annex I:
      6 1.
      Statement made to the 2nd AIL Symposium, June 1967

38.   **Landheer, B.**   De bibliotheek van de Verenigde Naties en andere
      internationale bibliotheken. - Bibliotheekleven 47: 505-513, 1962.
      Library of the United Nations and other international libraries.

39.   **League of nations.**   The League of nations library. - Geneva,
      Information section, 1938. - 45 p. - (Its: League of nations
      questions. no.10.)
      Contents:
      Role and purpose of the Library; the Library as an information centre; a brief
      historical retrospect; the Library premises; the collection of the Library; the
      various categories of printed matter received and sorted by the Library; catalogues;
      the Library staff.

90.   -- --- Libraries of the Secretariat and the International labour
      office: report by the Commission of experts. - Geneva, 1923. -
      (Its: Documents. C.204.M.120.1923.)

91.   -- **Library.**   Dispositions concernant l'usage de la Bibliothèque par
      les personnes n'appartenant pas aux organisations de la Société
      des nations. - Genève, 1932. - 4 p.   E F

92.   **Libraries** of the United Nations: a descriptive guide. - New York,
      1966. - 126 p. - (United Nations. Publications. Sales no.
      1966.I.6.)
      UN Documents. ST/LIB/17.

93.   **Library** of the United Nations. - Special libraries 43: 127-128,
      April 1952.

94.   **Maday, A. de.**   La bibliothèque du Bureau international du travail. -
      Genève, Meyer, 1937. - 1 v.

95.   **Milam, C. H.**   The United Nations library. - Library quarterly 23:
      267-280, October 1953.

96.   **Monk, R. C.**   United Nations library: gift of the Ford
      foundation. - External affairs (Canada) 12: 626-628, May 1960.

2197.   **Most** vital special library in the world: Dag Hammarskjold
        library. - Special libraries 53: 13-14, 1962.

2198.   **Neet, H. E.** Bibliothèques et centres de documentation à Genève
        dans le domaine des sciences sociales. - Répertoire établi par
        Hanna Elisabeth Neet. - Genève, 1972. - xiii, 162 p.
        At head of title: Institut universitaire de hautes études internationales. Bibliothèque.
        Enquête sur cinquant-trois bibliothèques et centres de documentation à Genève.

2199.   Le **nouveau** bâtiment de la Bibliothèque des Nations Unies.
        - Bulletin de l'Unesco à l'intention des bibliothèques 14:
        78-81, mars-avril, 1960.
        New York; avec plans.

2200.   **Pan American union. Columbus memorial library.** Fifty years
        of the Library of the Pan American union, 1890-1940.
        - Washington, 1940. - 9 l. - (Its: Bibliographic series. no.23.)

2201.   -- --- Inter-American library relations. - no. 1-   . - Washington,
        D.C., 19   . -   v.
        A quarterly newsletter.

2202.   **Rasmussen, S. H.** League of nations library during the war.
        - College and research libraries 5: 195-202, 1944.

2203.   **Ravage, D.** La bibliothèque des Nations Unies à Lake Success. -
        Revue de la documentation 17: 124-133, septembre 1950.

2204.   **Renseignements** pratiques sur la Bibliothèque de la Société des
        Nations. - Genève, 1936. - 7 p.

2205.   **Rounds, J. B.** Research facilities of the International labour office
        available to libraries. - Geneva, International labour office, 1939. -
        70 p.
        Contents:
        Ch. 1. The International labour office. Ch. 2. The Library. Ch. 3. The archives and
        general information section. Ch.4. Publications.
        Appendices: 1. Libraries having global subscriptions to all I.L.O. publications.
        Short bibliography.

2206.   **Rózsa, G.** La spécialisation et l'intégration: quelques aspects du
        travail d'information des bibliothèques internationales. - Genève,
        1970. - 9, ii l.
        At head of title: Symposium de l'Association des bibliothèques internationales
        (AIL), Vienne.

2207.   -- --- Történeti gyüjtemények és nemzetközi információs központ:
        az ENSZ genfi könyvtára. - Tudományos és müszaki tájékoztatás
        10: 745-761, 1971.
        Summaries in English, Russian and German: p.759-761.
        UN Library, Geneva as a research centre.

2208.   **Salute** to the United Nations. - ALA (American library association)
        bulletin 49: 489-507, 538; October 1955.
        Series of articles.

2209.   **Sevensma, T. P.** La bibliothèque de la Société des nations.
        - Paris, 1929. - 13 p.
        At head of title: Association des bibliothécaires français.

2210.   **Simari, A.** International trade documentation and the Documentation
service of the International trade centre UNCTAD/GATT. - Geneva,
1971. - 11 p. - (ITC/INF/28/Rev.1.)

2211.   **Stern, A.** Woodrow Wilson collection in the United Nations
library. - New York, 1954. - 33 p.
Thesis - Columbia university.

2212.   **Stummvoll, J.** Als Bibliotheksdirektor bei den Vereinten
Nationen. Biblos 8: 53-59, Heft 2, 1959.
As director of the United Nations Library: notes from a diary.

2213.   -- - -- Die "Dag Hammarskjöld Bibliothek" der Vereinten
Nationen in New York. - Libri 12: 97-110, no.2, 1962.

2214.   -- - -- Der Neubau der Bibliothek der Vereinten Nationen.
- Biblos 9: 57-76, Heft 2, 1960.

2215.   A **summary** of Unesco's activities in the field of libraries,
documentation and archives, 1967-71. - Unesco bulletin for
libraries 25: 318-331, no.6, November-December 1971.

2216.   **United Nations.** Annual report of the Headquarters Library, the
Geneva Library, and the libraries of the economic commissions.
- 1946-1971. - New York, 1946-1971.   v. - (Its: ST/LIB/1-29.)

2217.   **United Nations. Dag Hammarskjold library, New York.**
Reports. - 1948-1971. - New York, 1948-1971. -   v.
Pub. annually.
Series includes also miscellaneous reports and surveys on the Library.
Issued by: 1948-1949, United Nations. Department of public information.
Library services.

2218.   -- - -- Story of the development of the Dag Hammarskjold library,
including a record of the dedication ceremonies. - New York,
United Nations, 1962. - 165 p.
"The Dag Hammarskjold library, gift of the Ford foundation."
Bibliography: p. 61-62.

2219.   -- **General assembly. 4th session, New York, 1949.**
Library policy and organization: report of the 5th Committee.
- New York, 1949. - (A/C.5/298, 21 September 1949.)

2220.   -- **Library, Geneva.** Reports on the Library. - 1936/37-1971.
- Geneva, 1937-1971. -   v.
Pub. annually.
Issued by: 1937-45, League of nations. Secretariat. Library.
Reports for 1936/37-1945, detached from: League of nations.   Reports on the
work of the League, 1936/37-1945.

2221.   The **United Nations** library: gift of the Ford foundation.
- United Nations review 6:   22-23, November 1959.

2222.   **Vladimirov. L.I.** The libraries of the United Nations: their
goals, activities and problems. - New York, 1966. - p.209-219.
"Reprinted from 'Journal of library history', vol.1, no.4 (October, 1966)."
Bibliography: p.219.

2223.   -- - -- Sistema bibliotek Organizatsii Ob"edinennykh Natsiĭ. -
Informatsiia o bibliotechnom dele i bibliografii za rubezhom. -
vyp.1(24): 8-12, 1968.

VI. MODERN TRENDS. OPERATIONAL INFORMATION SYSTEMS:

AGRIS	-	International information system for the agricultural sciences and technology (FAO, Rome)
CAIP	-	Computer assisted indexing programme (UN, Dag Hammarskjold Library, New York)
CARIS	-	Computerized agricultural research information system (FAO, Rome)
CDS	-	Computerized documentation service (UNESCO, Paris)
CLADES	-	Latin American centre for economic and social documentation (ECLA, Santiago de Chile)
INDIS	-	Industrial information system (UNIDO, Vienna)
INIS	-	Integrated nuclear information system (IAEA, Vienna
ISIS	-	Integrated set of information systems (ILO, Geneva)
PRIS	-	Pilot project reports information subsystem (UN, New York)
SIRIUS	-	Système integré de recherche d'information utilisant des symboles (UNCTAD, Geneva)
UNISIST	-	World science information system (UNESCO, Paris)

Note: Limited largely to documentation based systems oriented to documents produced by or used by intergovernmental organizations of the UN system.

2224. **Advisory committee for INIS, Vienna, 1971.** Summary discussions and recommendations: final report. - Vienna, 1971. - 7 1. - (PL-476/5.)
At head of title: International atomic energy agency.

2225. **Aines, A. A.**   Fashioning a global environmental quality information and data network. - Revista dell'informazione= Information review 1: 107-114, no.6, 1970.

2226. **Alger, C. F.**   Research on research: a decade of quantative and field research on international organizations. - International organization 24:   414-450, no.3, 1970.
Bibliography: p.445-447.

2227. **Auburn, F. M.**   The United Nations international law abstracting and print-out service (UNAPROS). - 7 U.G.L.R. (1970) 156.

2228. **El-Ayouty, Y.**   United Nations documentation as a research undertaking: issues and approaches. - New York, 1971. - 23 p.
At head of title: United Nations institute for training and research.

2229. **Barrett, D. D.**   ISIS: processing system: acquisitions, cataloguing module, analysis module. - Geneva, 1972. - 1 v.
At head of title: International labour office. Central library and documentation branch.

0. **Beer, S.** Managing modern complexity. - In: Panel on science and technology. 11th meeting, Washington, D.C., 1970. - The management of information and knowledge. p. 41-62.
    Contents:
    1. Threat systems. 2. Bases of argument. 3. Elucidation of systematic character-istics. 4. Metasystem management.

1. **Berggren, G. A.** Report on visit to Santiago, Chile, 8-30 April 1970. - Santiago, United Nations documentation centre, 1970.

2. **Beyerly, H.** Industrial information system (INDIS): internal report number 2 on computerized processing of UNIDO publications and documents for information storage, retrieval and dissemination/ by Harold Beyerly, Marianne Vespry and Violet Vince. - Vienna, United Nations industrial development organization, 1970. - 16 p. 14 l.

3. **Boisier, S.** Case studies on information systems for regional development. - Geneva, 1970. - 78 p. - (United Nations research institute for social development. Report. no. 70.9.)

34. **Brack, W. A.** General programme for ECE/UNCTAD reference unit: description of data. - Geneva, UNCTAD, 1971. - 37 l.
    At head of title: UNCTAD IBM programme.

35. **Buntrock, H.** Draft survey of the world agricultural documentation services. - Rome, Food and agriculture organization, Documentation centre, 1970. - 55 p. - (FAO/DC/AGRIS.1.)
    Prepared on behalf of the FAO panel of experts on "AGRIS".

36. **Canada. Auditor general.** Electronic data processing in the United Nations family of organizations. - v.1-2. - Ottawa, 1970. - 2 v.

37. **Chernysh, V. I.** Informatsionye protsessy v obshchestve. - Moskva, Izd-vo "Nauka", 1968. - 101 p.
    At head of title: Akademiia nauk SSSR. Nauchnyĭ sovet po kibernetike. Sektsiia filosofskikh voprosov kibernetiki.
    Bibliography: p. 97-101.
    Information process in society.

38. **Clark, J. W.** Development of trans-disciplinary conceptual aids: simple techniques for education, research, pre-crisis management, and program administration highlighting patterns of information transaction and sub-system interdependence/ project proposed by Jere W. Clark and Anthony J. N. Judge. - Brussels, 1970. - 13 p. - (Union of international associations. Study papers: INF/6.)

39. **Coblans, H.** Use of mechanised methods in documentation work. - London, Aslib, 1966. - 89 p.
    Bibliography: p.61-73.

Q

2240.   **Computer**-assisted indexing project: procedural charts.
          - New York, 1968.
          Instructions for work in Dag Hammarskjold library, New York.

2241.   **Conferencia especializada sobre la aplicación de la ciencia y la tecnologia
          al desarrollo de América Latina, Brasilia, 1972.** Informe final. - In
          Planeamiento nacional de servicios bibliotecarios. v.1, p. 132-136. -
          Washington, D.C., 1972. - OAS.   Estudios bibliotecarios. no. 8.

2242.   **Crane, D.** Transnational networks in basic science.
          - In: Transnational relations and world politics,
          Harvard university,   Center for international affairs,
          p.235-251, 1972.

2243.   **Curnow, R. G.** Étude des systèmes d'information scientifique
          et technique en Europe plus particulièrement des systèmes
          à ordinateurs et du rôle que pourrait avoir la CEE dans
          ces systèmes. - Genève, 1969. - 25 p. - (SC.TECH.1969/12.)
          At head of title: Commission économique pour l'Europe.   Réunion d'experts
          gouvernementaux de la coopération scientifique et technique (20-24 janvier 1969)

2244.   **Dalenius, T. S.** Control of classification/   by T. E. Dalenius
          and O. Frank. - Review of the International statistical
          institute 36: no.3, 1968.

2245.   **Data** bases, computers, and the social sciences/ edited by
          Ralph L. Bisco. - New York, J. Wiley, 1970. - xiii, 291 p.
          - (Information sciences series.)
          "Based on the papers presented at the fourth annual conference of the
          Council of social science data archives, held at the University of California
          in Los Angeles in June, 1967."
          Bibliography at the end of each chapter.

2246.   **Delgado, R. R.** Centro regional de información y
          documentación económica para America Latina.
          - 1o-3o informe. - Santiago, 1969-1970.

2247.   A **dictionary** of computers. - Anthony Chandor with John Graham,
          Robin Williamson. - Harmondsworth, Mddx, Penguin books, 1970. -
          406 p. - (Penguin reference books.)

2248.   **Dubois, G.** The FAO Documentation centre: an experiment
          in the service of developing countries. - Rome, 1970.
          - 10 p. - (FAO.GIL:DC/INF/1.)
          Report presented to the 4th World congress of IAALD (International
          association of agricultural librarians and documentalists), Paris, 20-25 April 1970.

2249.   **Evans, L. H.** Documents and publications of contemporary
          international governmental organizations/ by Luther Harris
          Evans and J. T. Vambery. - Law library journal (Chicago) 64:
          338-362, August 1971.

2250.   -- --- Special classification scheme of international
          governmental organizations materials/   by Luther Harris
          Evans and J. T. Vambery. - Law library journal (Chicago) 64:
          356-359, August 1971.

2251. **Foskett, A. C.** The subject approach to information. - 2nd ed.
rev. and enl. - London, Clive Bingley, 1971. - 429 p.
Pt. 1. Theory of information retrieval systems. Pt. 2. Pre-coordinate indexing
languages. Pt. 3. Post-coordinate systems. Pt. 4. Future prospects.
Bibliography at the end of each chapter.

2252. **Harrod, L. M.** The librarians' glossary of terms used in librarianship
and the book crafts and reference book. - London, Andre Deutsch,
1971. - 784 p.
It is primarily a glossary of library terms but includes such subjects as printing,
paper-making, publishing, binding and illustrating.

2253. **Henderson, A. M.** Electronic data processing in the United
Nations family of organizations: a concept for effective
growth and utilization. - New York, 1970. - 2 v.
- (United Nations. General assembly. 25th session.
Documents. A/8072.)
Contents:
v.1:   1.   Introduction.
        2.   The emerging role of the computer.
        3.   Preparing for the future.
        4.   EDP resources within the United Nations family.
        5.   The need for co-ordinated development of computer applications.
        6.   UNDP information system requirements.
        7.   Implementation of the recommended concept.

Annexe: Note on a study of electronic data processing facilities and needs of
         the United Nations and the specilized agencies and IAEA.

v.2:   comprises individual reports on the organizations participating in the study.

2254. **Information** retrieval & library automation letter. - v.1-   ; 1970-
. - Mt. Airy, Maryland, 1970-   . -   v.
Pub. monthly.
New techniques, new equipment, new software, events, meetings, case experience,
federal policy, international developments, networks, communications, media innovation,
new publications, technology transfer, organization for information services - public
and private.

2255. **Information systems for regional development - a seminar,
Lund, 1969.** General papers / edited by Torsten Hägerstrand
and Antoni R. Kuklinski. - Lund, 1971. - xiv, 266 p.
- (Lund. Universitet. Geografiska institutet. Lund studies in
geography. Ser. B. Human geography. no.37.)
At head of title: United Nations research institute for social development.
University of Lund, Dept. of social and economic geography.
Includes bibliographies.

2256. **Intergovernmental conference for the establishment of a world
science information system, Paris, 1971.** Final report.
- Paris, Unesco, 1971. - 60 p. EFSR.
At head of title: UNISIST.

2257. **International atomic energy agency.** The design and
implementation of an international nuclear information system/
by J. E. Woolston and others. - Vienna, 1970. - p.607-619.
Reprint from "Handling of nuclear information".

2258. -- **Library.** IAEA specifications for microfiche copies of
periodicals. - Vienna, 1968. - 12 p.

2259.   **International business machines corporation.** Introduction to data management: student text. - New York, 1970. - 53 p.
Data management and information. Fields and records. Data storage devices. Data organization. Functions of data management. Data base systems concepts. Index.

2260.   -- --- Introduction to IBM system/360: direct access storage devices and organization methods; student text. - White Plains, N.Y., 1969. - 70 p.
This text discusses the physical characteristics and capacities of the following direct access storage devices available for system/360 models 25, 30, 44, 50, 65, 67, 75 and 85.

2261.   -- --- Searching normal text for information retrieval. - White Plains, N.Y., 1969. - 18 p.
Data processing application: how data enters the systems, current information selection, tetrospective searching, computer-prepared publications, system operation, programs.

2262.   -- --- Selective dissemination of information. - White Plains, N.Y., 1962. - 11 p.
Data processing application.   The SDI system. The mechanized SDI system. Expanding SDI.

2263.   **International computing centre, Geneva.** Progress report. - Geneva, 1972. - 7 1. - (United Nations. Documents. CO-ORDINATION/R.933.)
At head of title: Administrative committee on co-ordination. 56 session. Preparatory committee. 17th session.

2264.   **The international** directory of computer and information system services. - 1969-   . - London, Europa pub., 1969-   . - v.
"Published for the Intergovernmental bureau for information technology, Rome, Italy."

2265.   **International federation for documentation. Meeting of the study committee "Research on the theoretical basis of information", Moscow, 1970.** Proceedings. - Moscow, 1970. - 143 p.
At head of title: Vsesoiūznyĭ institut nauchnoĭ i tekhnicheskoĭ informafsii.

2266.   **International federation for information processing. Administrative data processing group.** IAG communications. - 1971-   . - Amsterdam, 1971-   . - v.

2267.   **International labour office.** L'introduction des ordinateurs dans les organismes de sécurité sociale: généralités et études préliminaires. - Genève, 1972. - iv,   76 p.

2268.   **Inter-organization board for information systems and related activities meeting, Geneva, 1971.** An IOB task force to design a computer-based information system to handle documents and other literature related to development. - Geneva, 1971. - 10 p.
"Submitted as a joint UNDP/ILO proposal."

2269.   **Inter-organization board for information systems and related activities. 3rd session, Geneva, 1972.** Report. - Geneva, 1972. - 1 v. - (United Nations. Documents. CO-ORDINATION/R.924.)
At head of title: Administrative committee on co-ordination. Fifty-sixth session.   Preparatory committee. Seventieth session.   Item 21 of the provisional agenda.

2270.   **Introduction** to information science. - Compiled and
        edited by Tefko Saracevic. - New York, R. R. Bowker,
        1970. - xxiv, 751 p.
        Bibliographical notes at the end of each chapter.

2271.   **Jackson, R. G. A.**   A study of the capacity of the United
        Nations development system. - v.1-2. - Geneva, 1969.
        - 2 v. - (United Nations. Documents. DP/5.)
        U.N. Publications. Sales no.1970.I.10.
        Bibliography: p.483-485 (v.2.)
        Chapter VI: Information systems concept.
          I. Study background and information policies.
         II. Synopsis of information system concept:
              (a) Introduction;
              (b) Foundation for the information system concept; contents of
                  UN development co-operation; UNDCC; existing organizational
                  structure; recommended organizational structure.
              (c) Types of supporting information required;
              (d) Concepts of information flow;
              (e) Components of information system;
              (f) Responsibilities for information systems;
              (g) Categorization or classification of data.
        III. Technical and scientific information sub-system:
              (a) Introduction;
              (b) Technical and scientific information requirements;
              (c) Problems in existing T & S information systems; lack of structure;
                  growing volume; failure to publish some information; wide
                  geographical distribution; reliance on individual recall; current
                  improvement efforts.
              (d) Technical and scientific information sub-system concept; providing
                  access through agency facilities; designating a UNDP information
                  facility; building a network of national documentation centres:
              (e) Procedures for operating the system; documentation
                  co-ordinating centres; specialized agency activities;   Dag
                  Hammarskjold library activities; national documentation
                  centre activities; information request activities;
              (f) Recommendations for system implementation.
         IV. Economic and social information sub-system:
              (a) Introduction;
              (b) Economic and social information requirements; requirements of the
                  country programming team;   Headquarters requirements;
                  requirements of specialized agencies and others;
              (c) Problems in existing information systems; illustrative problems;
                  current improvement efforts;
              (d) Economic and social information sub-system concept; reliance on
                  historical statistical series; provision of country framework; central
                  analysis and interpretation capability.
              (e) Procedures for operating the proposed system;
              (f) Recommendations for system implementation; providing an
                  organizational framework; providing analysis and interpretation
                  capability; modifying agency systems; building an updating
                  capability in the country; developing arrangements for financing
                  E & S requirements.
          V. Operational and administrative information sub-system:
              (a) Introduction;
              (b) Operational and administrative information requirements;
                  programme and project operations; programme or
                  administrative support;
              (c) Problems in existing O & A systems; current O & A
                  information problems; improvement efforts;
              (d) Operational and administrative sub-system concept; concept and
                  procedures for operational activity control; concept for
                  administrative support processes; concept for operational
                  activity planning;
              (e) Recommendations for sub-system implementation; establishing MISS
                  at UNDP Headquarters; developing project classification codes;
                  building a system for operational activity control; strengthening
                  operational activity planning information; improving administrative
                  support information.
         VI. Principles and guidelines for system implementation.
              (a) Introduction;
              (b) Principles for systems implementation; assigning management
                  responsibility; installing controls for implementation;
              (c) Management responsibilities; operational information;   E & S and
                  T & S information; administrative information;
              (d) Mechanisms for systems implementation.

2272.   **Janco, M.** Informatique et capitalisme/ par Manuel Janco et Daniel
         Furjot. - Paris, F. Maspero, 1972. - 272 p. - (Economie et
         socialisme. no.18.)
         Bibliographie sommaire: p. 265-266.
         Aspects économiques, politiques, idéologiques de l'informatique. Introduction aux
         techniques de l'informatique.

2273.   **Jordain, P. B.** Condensed computer encyclopedia. - New York,
         McGraw-Hill book company, 1969. - 605 p.

2274.   The **journal** of micrographics. - v.1-   ; 1967-   . - Silver Spring,
         Md., National microfilm association, 1967-   . -   v.
         Pub. bi-monthly.
         A bi-monthly devoted to the science, technology, art and applications of microphotography.
         Includes bibliographies.
         1. Microphotography. 2. Microfilms. 3. Information storage and retrieval systems -
         Engineering.

2275.   **Judge, A. J. N.** The impact of the computer/communication/
         information revolution of non-governmental organizations and
         their members during the second U.N. development decade
         (1970-1980) and the foreseeable future: an attempt of
         computers and communication devices on local, national
         and international associations involved in the development
         process. - Geneva, 1969. - 15 p. - (11/GC/21.)
         Paper submitted for the 11th Conference of non-governmental organizations
         in consultative status with the United Nations Economic and social council,
         9-11 July 1969.

2276.   -- --- The improvement of communication within the
         world-system: research uses, applications and possibilities
         of a computer-based information centre on national and
         international organizations and related entities. - Brussels,
         1969. - 1 v. - (UAI. Study papers: INF/2.)

2277.   -- --- Information systems and inter-organization space.
         - The Annals of the American academy of political and
         social science 393: 47-64, January 1971.

2278.   -- --- Inter-contact - un centre d'information et une
         technique: description d'un projet de centre d'information
         sur les organisations internationales et nationales et les
         organismes connexes, basé sur ordinateur. - Bruxelles,
         Union des associations internationales, 1969. - 40 p.
         - (UAI. Study paper: INF/3.)

2279.   -- --- International organizations and the generation of the will to
         change: the information systems required. - Brussels, 1970. - 1 v.
         - (UAI. Study papers: INF/5.)

2280.   -- --- Inter-organizational data and data bank design.
         - Puerto Rico, 1971. - 20 p.
         Paper presented to the Workshop on international organization data,
         jointly sponsored by International studies association, Union of
         international associations, and United Nations Institute for training
         and research.

Judge, A.J.N. (Cont'd)

281. -- --- Organizational apartheid - United Nations, U.N.
      agencies, intergovernmental organizations, multinational
      business enterprises, international nonprofit associations:
      who needs whom in the second United Nations develop-
      ment decade (1970-1980)? - Brussels, 1971. - 16 p.
      - (UAI. Study papers: INF/1)

282. -- --- Relationship between elements of knowledge: use of
      computer to facilitate construction, comprehension and
      comparison of the concept thesauri of different schools of
      thought. - Honolulu, Social science research institute,
      University of Hawaii, 1972.
      At head of title: COCTA. Committee on conceptual and terminological
      analyses. International political science association.

283. -- --- La visualisation du réseau d'organisation: l'U.A.I.,
      banque de données internationales. - Belgium. Ministère
      des affaires étrangères et du commerce extérieur. Textes
      et documents. - Bruxelles, 1970.

284. -- --- World problems and human development: outline
      proposals for a computerized data collection project
      leading to publication of a Yearbook of world problems and
      human development. - Brussels, 1972. - 1 v. - (UAI. Study
      paper: PROB/2.)

285. **Kawalec, W.** Statistical information systems for regional
      development and planning in Poland. - Geneva, 1969.
      - 161 p.
      "Programme IV - Regional development."

286. **Kenney, L.** Information needs of the users of the library
      of a large international organisation: implications for the
      design of a catalogue. - Geneva, 1965. - 56 p. - (ILO.
      Central library and documentation branch. DOC/NOTES/10.)

287. **Klaus, G.** Kibernetika i obshchestvo. - Perevod s nemetskogo. -
      Moskva, Izd-vo "Progress", 1967. - 431 p.
      Original ed. pub. under title: Kybernetik und Gesellschaft.
      Cybernetics.

288. **LIST:** library and information science today. 1971-   ;
      an international registry of research and innovation.
      - New York, Science associates-international. - 1971-   .
      - v.

289. **Mantz, M. R.** Need for and viability of a United Nations
      computation centre in Santiago. - Santiago, 1970. - 33 p.

290. **Marthaler, M. P.** ISIS: progrès après cinq ans. - Geneva,
      1969. - p. 351-360.
      "Reprinted from: NT A6/1969."

2291.   **Martin, M. D.**   Reference manual for the preparation of
        machine-readable bibliographic descriptions. - First draft,
        December 1971. - Paris, International council of scientific
        unions, Abstracting board, 1971. - 1 v.
        Prepared by the UNISIST/ICSU-AB Working group on bibliographic
        descriptions, with the financial assistance of UNESCO.

2292.   **Martini, G. S.**   The Computer-assisted indexing programme of
        the United Nations: a brief description. - Geneva, 1972.
        - 14 p. and annexes. - (UNITAR/EUR/SEM.1/WP.II/7.)
        Working paper submitted to the International symposium on documentation of
        the United Nations and other intergovernmental organizations, Geneva, 1972.

2293.   **Mashinnye** metody analiza informat͡sii ob opyte nauchno-tekhnicheskogo
        razvitii͡a. - Moskva, Izd-vo "Nauka", 1972. - 310 p.
        Half-title: Akademii͡a nauk SSSR. Nauchnyĭ sovet po kibernetike. Sekt͡sii͡a filosofskikh
        voprosov kibernetiki.
        Analysis of information storage and retrieval systems in science and technology, use of
        electronic calculating machines in technological forecasting.
        Includes bibliographies.

2294.   **Mondini, A.**   Trends in teleprocessing. - Rivista dell'
        informazione=Information review 3: 98-103, no.1, 1972.

2295.   **Morrill, C.**   Computers and data processing: a guide to information
        sources. - Detroit, Mich., 1969. - 275 p.

2296.   **National academy of sciences.**   Libraries and information technology:
        a national system challenge, a report to the Council on library
        resources, Inc.,/ by the Information systems panel, Computer
        science and engineering board. - Washington, D.C., 1972. - xi, 84 p.
        Contents:
        1. Observations and recommendations.   2. Discussion of problems and issues.
        Annex A: Dimensions of cost and usage.
        Annex B: Site visits to key activities and institutions.
        Annex C: Information technology: key characteristics and development trends.

2297.   -- --- Inventory of major information systems and services in science
        and technology. - Paris, 1971. - 340 p.

2298.   **Organisation for economic co-operation and development.**
        Computerised data banks in public administration: trends
        and policies issues/ by Uwe Thomas. - Paris, 1971.
        - 69 p. - (Its: OECD information studies. 1.)
        Bibliography: p.67-69.

2299.   -- --- Macrothesaurus: a basic list of economic and social development
        terms. - English ed. - Paris, 1972. - 244 p.
        "The development of this macrothesaurus in 1971-1972 was carried out with the financial
        support of the International development research center, Ottawa, Canada."
        Foot-notes, partly bibliographical.

2300.   -- --- **Development centre.**   Liste d'ouvrages de référence
        sur les institutions utilisées par le service "Question-
        réponse-développement"=List of reference books on
        institutions used by the "Development enquiry service".
        - Paris, 1970. - 151 p.

2301.   **Panel on improvement or alterations in the general development
        patterns of INIS, Vienna, 1970.**   Papers. - no.1-7. - Vienna,
        1970. - (PL-423/INF.1-7.)
        At head of title: International atomic energy agency.

02. **Panel on science and technology. 11th meeting, Washington, D.C.,**
     1970. The management of information and knowledge: a compilation
     of papers. - Washington, D.C., Committee on science and astronautics,
     U.S. House of representatives, 1970. - vii, 130 p.
     Papers:
     1. Kahn, H. The "emergent United States"... post-industrial society.
     2. Beer, S. Managing modern complexity.
     3. Boorstin, D.J. Self-liquidating ideals.
     4. Amer, P. The individual: his privacy, self-image, and obsolescence.
     5. Wiio, O.A. Technology, mass communication and values.
     6. Kozmetsky, G. Education as an information system.
     7. Green, T.F. Education and schooling in post-industrial America: some directions for
        policy.

03. **Panel on system for the acquisitions, transmission and processing**
     of hydrological data (SAPHYDATA). Hydrologic information
     systems. - Edited by G.W. Whetstone. - Paris, Geneva, Unesco-
     WMO, 1972. - 72 p. - (UNESCO. Studies and reports in hydrology.
     no.14.)
     References. Selected USSR references. Selected WMO references. Studies and reports
     in hydrology. p.71-72.
     A contribution to the International hydrological decade.

04. **Panel on the preparation of the final proposal for INIS,**
     Vienna, 1968. Report of the INIS study team, Vienna,
     4 March - 28 June 1968. - Vienna, 1968. - 107 p.
     - (PL-308).
     At head of title: International atomic energy agency.

05. **Pelzer, C. W.** International information networks: the
     International nuclear information system. - ASLIB
     proceedings 24: 38-55, no.1, 1971.
     Paper presented at the ASLIB annual conference, Darmstadt, West
     Germany, 10th-14th October 1971.

06. **Pilot project reports information subsystem (PRIS).**
     Bibliography of technical co-operation project report:
     demonstration project issue. - (ST/OTC/SER.   ).

307. -- --- Country index: demonstration project issue.
      - (ST/OTC/SER.D/1.)

308. -- --- Digest of technical co-operation project reports:
      demonstration project issue. - (ST/OTC/SER.A/1.)

309. -- --- Numerical list demonstration project issue. -
      (ST/OTC/SER.B/1.)

310. -- --- Questionnaire for evaluation of PRIS outputs.
      - New York, 1971. - 5 p.

311. -- --- Subject index to technical co-operation project
      reports: demonstration project issue. - (ST/OTC/SER.C/1.)

312. -- --- Summary list of technical co-operation project
      reports: demonstration project issue. - (ST/OTC/SER.A/1.)

2313.   **Pritchard, A.**   A guide to comptuer literature: an introductory survey
of the sources of information. - London, Clive Bingley, 1969. -
130 p.
Contents:
Comptuer literature, academic periodicals, commercial periodicals, miscellaneous periodicals,
control of periodicals, research reports and government publications, trade literature,
theses, patents, conferences, translations, abstracts and indexes, books, annual reviews,
bibliographies, glossaries and dictionaries, handbooks, standards, looseleaf services:
journal-type and data compilations, data compilations - hardware, directories, biographical
data, libraries and the organisation of information, library and union catalogues.

2314.   **Rothman, M. H.**   Citation rules and forms for United
Nations documents and publications. - Brooklyn, N.Y.,
1971. - 64 p.

2315.   **Rózsa, G.**   Information need of social science. - Geneva,
1971. - 6 p.
Paper submitted to the International conference on training for
information work, Rome, 1971.

2316.   **Russell, M.**   Analysis of questionnaires for evaluation of
PRIS outputs.
At head of title: Inter-office demonstration project (IODP) for
storage and retrieval of technical and scientific information project
reports information subsystem (PRIS).

2317.   **Selected** mechanized scientific and technical information systems. -
Edited by Lynn Ockerman, Anna E. Cacciapaglia, Melvin Weinstock. -
Washington, D.C., 1968. - iii, 143 p.
At head of title: COSATI.
Prepared for the Panel on operational techniques and systems committee on scientific
and technical information, Federal council for science and technology by Herner and
Company, under contract no. OEC 1-7-070895-3777.
Contents:
Defense documentation center; Highway research board; National aeronautics and space
administration; National library of medicine; U.S. Department of agriculture; U.S. Depart-
ment of commerce; U.S. Department of health, education and welfare, ERIC; U.S.
Department of the interior; U.S. Patent office, ICIREPAT; U.S. Air force, foreign
technology division; List of acronyms; Index of individuals; Subject index.

2318.   **Seymour, H.**   The United Nations and modern documentation
retrieval. - Geneva, 1972. - 8 p. - (UNITAR/EUR/SEM.1/
WP.II/4.)
Paper submitted to the International symposium on documentation of the
United Nations and other intergovernmental organizations, Geneva, 1972.

2319.   **Shepard, M. D.**   La infrastictura bibliotecologica de los sistemas
nacionales de información. - Washington, D.C., Organización de
los estados americanos, 1972. - vii, 136 p. - (lPlaneamiento
nacional de servicions bibliotecarios. v.1.)
OAS.   Estudios bibliotecarios. no.8.
La información y su naturaleza. Mecanismos de la información. La biblioteca como
mecanismo institucional de información. Sistemas de información y su creación.
Planeamiento y cooperación en le diseño de sistemas de información locales,
regionales y mundiales. Identificación de los problemas especiales de América Latina.
Demanda de información. Factores positivos en el desarrollo de servicios de información científica y tecnológica. Apuntes para el diseño de un sistema o de sistemas de
información para América Latina con referencia especial a la infrasstructura biblio-
tecológica.

2320.   **Simari, A.**   Information and its technologies and the
responsibility of the managerial class in the development of
modern society. - Rivista dell'informazione=Information
review 1: 157-160, no.3/4, 1970.

21. **Skjelsbaek, K.** The growth of international nongovernmental organization in the twentieth century. - In: Transnational relations and world politics, Harvard university, Center for international affairs, p.70-92, 1972.

22. **Slovar'** terminov po informatike na russkom i angliĭskom iâzykakh. - Moskva, Izd-vo "Nauka", 1971. - 359 p.
    At head of title: G.S. ZHdanova, E.S. Kolobrodova, V.A. Polushkin, A.I. Chernyĭ.
    3035 terms of informatics under 48 subject classes. Alphabetical arrangement of terms in Russian and English. List of acronyms.
    Bibliography: p. 356-357.

23. **Symposium on new techniques in library and documentation work, Genève, ILO Building, 1963.** Documents and reports. - Geneva, 1963. - 1 v.

24. **System development corporation, Falls Church, Va.** Microfiche storage: final report, August 1970. - Washington, D.C., U.S. Dept. of commerce, 1970. - 1 v.
    "Prepared for Defense documentation center, Defence supply agency by System development corporation, Falls Church, Va."
    "Reproduced by National technical information service".
    Bibliography: p.D-1-D-8.

25. **Szalai, A.** The future of international organizations. - 20 p.
    European-American seminar "Organizations of the future", Noordwijk (Netherlands), 1970.

26. -- --- The United Nations and the social and behavioral science. - American journal of international law 64: no.4, 1970.

27. **Taube, M.** Information storage and retrieval; theory, systems, and devices/ edited by Mortimer Taube and Harold Wooster. - New York, Columbia university press, 1958. - xi, 228 p. - (Columbia university studies in library service. no.10.)
    Contains working papers and a condensed record of a Symposium on information storage and retrieval theory, systems, and devices, held in Washington, D. C.,   March 17-18, 1958. - Introd.

28. **Tell, B. V.** Scandinavian collaboration in documentation: an organisational study. - Rivista dell'informazione= Information review 1:   115-120, no.6, 1970.

29. **Terminologicheskiĭ** slovar' po informatŝionnoĭ teorii i praktike na russkom i ispanskom iâzyke=Diccionario terminologico de la teoria y la practica de la información en ruso y español. - Moskva, La Habana, 1969. - 190. p.
    At head of title: Gosudarstvennyĭ komitet Soveta ministrov SSSR po nauke i tekhnike. Akademiiâ nauk SSSR. Vsesoiûznyĭ institut nauchnoĭ i tekhnicheskoĭ informatŝii. Academia de ciencias de Cuba. Instituto de documentación e información científica y tecnica.
    Consejo de radacción: A.I. Mijailov, Jorge Valdés Miranda.
    Bibliography: 1 p. following p. 190.

30. **Thompson, G. K.** Computerized information systems and development assistance/ by G. K. Thompson and W. D. Schieber. - Industrial research and development news 5: 2-5, no.3, 1970.

2331.   **Thompson, G. K.** Information retrieval in the computer age. -
         Associations internationales=International associations 5: 295-297, 1971.

2332.   -- --- Instrumentos de trabajo necasarios para permitir el
         establesimiento de una red latinoamericana de documentación
         económica y social. - Santiago, Chile, 1971. - 10 p.
         At head of title: Comisión económica para América latina (CEPAL). Centro latino-
         americano de documentación económica y social (CLADES). Reunión sobre tecnicas
         modernas de documentación, Santiago, Chile, 27 al 30 de septiembre de 1971.
         Summary: arrangements for avoiding duplication of effort among participating centres;
         standards for bibliographic description; systems of content analysis; mechanism for
         merging and repackaging the various inputs submitted by the cooperating centres;
         provision for links between the proposed network and other computer-assisted systems
         in operation or planned, in particular within the family of international organisations.
         Bibliography: 1 p. following p.10.

2333.   **Tocatlian, J. J.** UNISIST; a world science system; joint project
         of the United Nations educational, scientific and cultural
         organisation (UNESCO) and the International council of
         scientific unions (ICSU). - Rivista dell' informazione=
         Information review 1: 121-125, no.6, 1970.

2334.   **Toute** la profession de l'informatique: description des postes et
         profils-type. - Paris, Ed. Test, 1971. - 141 p. - (Bibliothèque
         Promotion informatique.)

2335.   **Unesco/ICSU central committee on the feasibility of a
         world science information system.** UNISIST; abrégé de
         l'étude sur la réalisation d'un système mondial
         d'information scientifique effectué par...le Comité central
         Unesco/CIUS chargé d'étudier la possibilité de créer un
         système mondial d'information scientifique. - Paris,
         Unesco, 1971. - 95 p.   FESR

2336.   **Unesco-ICSU central committee to study the feasibility of a
         world science information system (UNISIST). 4th session,
         Paris, 1969.** Report. - Paris, 1969. - 6, 4 p. - (UNESCO-
         ICSU/CSI/5.15.)
         At head of title: United Nations educational, scientific and cultural
         organization.   International council of scientific unions.   Joint project
         on the communication of scientific information.

2337.   **UNISIST;** a forum. - ASLIB proceedings 24: 111-122,
         February 1972.

2338.   **UNISIST/ICSU-AB working group on bibliographic descrip-
         tions.** Reference manual. - pt.1-3. - Paris, UNESCO, 1972.

2339.   **United Nations. Administrative committee on co-ordination.**
         Development and co-ordination of the activities of the
         organizations within the United Nations system: reports...
         on recent development in the use of computers and common
         information needs in the U.N. system. - New York, 1971.
         - 1 v. - (United Nations. Documents. E/5013.)
         At head of title: United Nations. Economic and social council.
         51st session.   Concerns creation and functions of the International computing
         centre.

). **United Nations. Administrative committee on co-ordination.**
Special report. - New York, 1970. - 7 p.
- (U.N. Documents. E/4893.)
United Nations. Economic and social council. 49th session. Agenda item 26 (b).

1. -- --- Report on recent developments in the use of
computers and common information needs in the United
Nations system. - New York, 1971. - 10 p. - (United
Nations. Economic and social council. Documents. E/5013.)

2. -- **Computer users' committee. Sessions.** Reports and
summary of proceedings.
Includes documents of Working party on standardization, Working party on
computer needs and ways of meeting them, and Technical study group.
Recommendations submitted to CCAQ: CCAQ/SEC/10, etc.

3. -- **Department of economic and social affairs.** The
application of computer technology for development.
- New York, 1971. - 122 p. - (United Nations. Publications.
Sales numbers. 1971.II.A.1.).   EFS

4. -- **Development programme.** Continuation of the
consideration of the improvement of the capacity of the
United Nations development system: management
information systems. - New York, 1970. - 50,8,7 p.
- (Its: Documents. DP/L.162/Add.1.)
At head of title: United Nations. Development programme. Governing
council. 11th session 1971. Agenda item 5(b) (iii).

5. -- **Economic and social council.** Resolutions adopted...
on the interagency co-operation relating to computers.
Symbols: E/RES/593(VI)   E/RES/1551(XLIX)
            E/RES/1455(XLVII)
Re: Creation and functions of the International computing centre.
Other documents:
     E/1090, E/1623 (LI), E/4341, E/4486, E/4668, E/4893, E/5133.

6. -- **Economic commission for Europe.** Inventory of major
information systems and services in science and technology=
Répertoire des principaux systèmes et services d'information
en science et technologie=Osnovnye sistemy u sluzhby
nauchno-tekhnicheskoĭ informatsii. - Geneva, 1971. - 340 p.
- (United Nations. Documents. ME/PPD/71/D.8.)

7. -- --- **Committee on the development of trade.** Report
of the Group of experts on the simplification and
standardization of external trade document working papers.
- Geneva, 1970.
This group of experts is responsible for studying the application of the
automatic data processing and coding systems to the international trade
documentation service.

8. -- --- **Meeting of senior governmental advisers on environment.
Geneva, 1970.** Identification of information needed to
promote strong and workable environmental action on
national and international scales. - Geneva, 1970. - 54 p.
- (Its: ENV/Working paper no.4.)

2349.   United Nations. Economic and social council. Enlarged committee for
         programme and co-ordination. 2nd session. Documents. E/AC.51/
         GR/L.9, etc. General review of the programmes and activities of
         the United Nations family in the economic, social, technical co-
         operation and related fields, development of modern management
         techniques and use of computers.

2350.   -- Economic commission for Latin America. Background,
         organization and programmes for the Latin American centre
         for economic and social documentation. - Santiago de Chile,
         1971.
         14th session, 27 April to 8 May 1971.

2351.   -- --- Public administration unit. Consideration on the installation
         of the computer centre in ECLA. - Santiago de Chile, 1970.

2352.   -- General assembly. 22nd session, 1968. Publications and
         documentation of the United Nations: note by the
         Secretary-general. - New York, 1968. - 14 p. - (Its:
         Documents.A/INF/124.)

2353.   -- --- 25th session, 1970. Review and reappraisal of
         United Nations information policies and activities:
         report of the Secretary-general. - New York, 1970.
         - 85 p. - (Its: Documents. A/C.5/1320.)
         At head of title: 25th session. 5th committee. Agenda item 73.

2354.   -- --- 26th session, 1971. Electronic data processing in
         the United Nations family of organizations: report of the
         Secretary-general. - New York, 1971. - 37 p. - (Its:
         Documents. A/C.5/1378.)
         At head of title: 5th committee. Agenda item 76.

2355.   -- --- 27th session, 1972. Publications et documentation de
         l'Organisation des Nations Unies: programme de publications
         périodiques. - Rapport du Secrétaire général. - New York, 1972. -
         12 p. - (Its: Documents. A/8851.)
         Point 80 de l'ordre du jour.
         Contents: I. Publications juridiques. II. Publications relatives aux questions économiques
         et sociales et aux droits de l'homme.

2356.   -- Joint inspection unit on U.N. documentation and on the
         organization of the proceedings of the General assembly and
         its main bodies. Pattern of conferences: report. - New York,
         1971. - ii, 120 p. - (United Nations. Documents. A/8319.)
         At head of title: United Nations. General assembly.   26th session.

2357.   -- Office of technical co-operation. Information on, and
         evaluation of, Pilot project reports information subsystem
         (PRIS).
         Results of evaluation of PRIS outputs.

48.   -- **Secretary-general.** Budget estimates for the financial year
1972: electronic data processing in the United Nations
family of organizations. - New York, 1971. - 37 p.
- (United Nations. Documents. A/C.5/1378.)
At head of title: United Nations. General assembly. 26th session.
Fifth committee. Agenda item 76.

49.   -- --- Inter-agency co-operation relating to computers.
- New York, 1970. - 4 p. - (United Nations. Documents.
E/4933.)
At head of title: United Nations. Economic and social council.
Resumed 49th session. Agenda item 6.
Creation and functions of the International computing centre.

50.   -- --- Transport development: establishment of a United
Nations transport economics and technology documentation
centre. - New York, 1971. - 6 p. - (United Nations.
Documents. E/4964.)
At head of title: United Nations. Economic and social council.
50th session. Agenda item 9(a).

51.   **United Nations educational. scientific and cultural organisation.**
The computerized documentation service of UNESCO.
- Paris, 1972. - 4 p.
Contents: 1. Historical background. 2. Activities in 1970-1972. 3. Projected
activities and development in 1973-1974.

52.   -- --- L'information à l'ère spatiale: le rôle des satellites de
communication. - Paris, 1968. - 219 p. E F
Transformation de la vie sociale à l'âge spatial. La diffusion des informations par
satellites. Les satellites au service de l'éducation. Communications spatiales et échanges
culturels. Problèmes posés par les communications spatiales dans le domaine de la
radio et de la télévision. Perspective ouvertes aux pays en voie de développement.
Problèmes techniques concernant les satellites. Problèmes juridiques et coopération
internationale en matière de communications spatiales. Suggestions en vue de
l'établissement d'un programme de l'Unesco dans le domaine des communications
spatiales.

53.   -- --- UNISIST: study report on the feasibility of a world science
information system/ by the United Nations educational, scientific
and cultural organisation and the International council of scientific
unions. - Paris, Unesco, 1971. - 161 p. E F R S
Includes bibliographies.

54.   -- --- World guide to science information and documentation
services=Guide mondial des centres de documentation et
d'information scientifique. - Paris, Unesco, 1965. - 211 p.
- (Its: Documentation and terminology of science=Documentation
et terminologie scientifique.)

55.   -- --- World guide to technical information and documentation
services=Guide mondial des centres de documentation et
d'information techniques. - Paris, Unesco, 1969. - 287 p.
- (Its: Documentation and terminology of science=
Documentation et terminologie scientifiques. no.10.)

2366. **United States. Library of Congress. Information systems office.**
The MARC pilot project: final report on a project sponsored
by the Council on library resources, inc. - Prepared by
Henriette D. Avram. - Washington, D.C., 1968. - 183 p.
Contents:
Background and history of the MARC pilot project; objectives and constraints;
MARC tape formats; system description; support programs for the participating
libraries; codes developed for language, publisher, and place of publication;
character sets; cost models; evaluation of MARC I and comparison with MARC II;
potential uses of machine-readable data; bibliography.

2367. -- **National science foundation.** Nonconventional scientific and
technical information systems in current use. - no.1- -
Washington, D.C., 1964- . - v.
Contents:
Guide to organizations; the system description questionnaire; manual, uniterm, edge-
punched and interior punched card systems; tabulating card systems; peek-a-boo
systems; photographic systems; index of individuals and authors; classified equipment
index; alphabetical equipment index; system size index; list of acronyms; index of
geographical locations; alphabetic subject index.

2368. **Ursul, A. D.** Priroda informat͡sii: filosofskiĭ ocherk. - Moskva,
Politizdat, 1968. - 285 p.
Nature of information; philosophical approach.

2369. **Vásárhelyi, P.** DARE: Unesco computerized data retrieval system
for documentation in the social and human sciences: including
an analysis of the present system. - Paris, UNESCO, 1972. -
43 p. - (United Nations educationa, scientific and cultural
organisation. Reports and papers in the social sciences. no.27.)
Contents:
1. Existing system. 2. Improvements needed. ¡. DARE: data retrieval system for
documentation in the social and human sciences. 4. Maintaining the data base.
5. Answering questions. 6. Preparing indexes. 7. Launching DARE.

2370. **Verhoeven, F. R. J.** Feasibility study for the establishment
of a regional information, documentation and research
centre. - Santiago, United Nations documentation centre,
1970. - 55 p.

2371. **Vickery, B. C.** Techniques modernes de documentation: analyses
des systèmes de recherche de documents. - Traduit per J. Céron
et d'autres. - Paris, Dunod, 1962. - xi, 178 p. E F
Table des matières:
1. But de l'étude. 2. Analyse des systèmes de recherche documentaire. 3. La
description des documents. 4. Langages descripteurs. 5. Modèles de structures.
6. Organisation de fichiers et codification. 7. Méthodes de recherche. 8. Automatisation de l'enregistrement et de la recherche documentaire. 9. But, paramètres
et performances. 10. La terminologie en recherche documentaire.

2372. **Viet, J.** An international documentation network: UN cooperation
with the OECD Development enquiry service. - Industrial research
and development news, UNIDO, v.6, no.2, p. 6-10, 25-29, 1972.

2373. **Vsesoi͡uznyĭ institut nauchnoĭ i tekhnicheskoĭ informat͡sii.** Teorii͡a
i praktika nauchno-tekhnicheskoĭ informat͡sii: sbornik lekt͡siĭ. -
Moskva, 1969. - 731 p.
Kursy povyshenii͡a kvalifikat͡sii rukovodi͡ashchikh, inzhenerno-tekhnicheskikh i nauchnykh
organov nauchno-tekhnicheskoĭ informat͡sii.
Theory on informatics and information practice in science and technology.

74. **Wasser, N.** The use of the computer in the Joint ECE/UNCTAD reference unit. - Geneva, 1972. - 5 p.
A description of a programme for ECE/UNCTAD reference unit written into SIRIUS (Système integré de recherche d'information utilisant des symboles) which is a general data based management system developed by UNCTAD in 1969. The programme automated the work with journals received in the Reference unit.

75. **Wersig, G.** Terminology of documentation: English-French-German. - Preliminary version prepared by/ Gernot Wersig and Ulrich Neveling. - Paris, UNESCO, 1971. - 257 p.

76. **World meteorological organization.** Further planning of the storage and retrieval service. - Geneva, 1970. - (Its: Planning report. no. 32.)

77. -- --- Means of acquisitions and communications of ocean data. - v.1- . - Geneva, 1972- . - v. - (Its: Marine science affairs.)
Proceedings of the WMO technical conference, Tokyo, 1972.

78. -- --- World weather watch: collection, storage and retrieval of meteorological data. - Geneva, 1969. - 17 p. - (Its: Planning report. no.28.)

79. **Wysocki, A.** Conférence intergouvernementale pour l'UNISIST/ par A. Wysocki et J. Tocatlian. - Bulletin de l'Unesco à l'intention des bibliothèques 26: 62-67, no.2, mars-avril 1972.

80. **Zagari, M.** A commitment at national and international level for the development of information science. - Rivista dell' informazione=Information review 2: 61-64, no.4/5, 1971.
Comments on UNISIST.

81. **ZHukov, N. I.** Informatsiia: filosofskii analiz tsentral'nogo poniatiia kibernetiki. - Izd. 2. - Minsk, 1971. - 275 p.
Basic analysis of information in nature, social life and technology.

R

DIRECTORY OF INTERNATIONAL GOVERNMENTAL ORGANISATIONS - HOW TO OBTAIN THEIR PUBLICATIONS AND DOCUMENTS

A standard official distribution of publications and documents is done by mail to various categories of recipients: Depository libraries (DL); Parliamentary libraries (PL); International study centres (INT); Complete exchanges (CEX); Non-governmental organisations (NGOs); Special library exchanges (EX); Information centres (INF); Ministries, embassies, etc., (GOV); UN branch offices, regional commissions (BR), and Specialized agencies (SA). A direct official distribution is done to Delegations, Secretariat, Press. Orders for publications for which there is a charge should be remitted to sales sections or sales agents, where they exist, as indicated in the present directory.

AFRICAN POSTAL AND TELECOMMUNICATIONS UNION

P.O.Box 593
Pretoria
REPUBLIC OF SOUTH AFRICA

AFRICAN POSTAL UNION

5, 26th July Street
Cairo
ARAB REPUBLIC OF EGYPT

AFRICAN SOCIETY FOR THE DEVELOPMENT OF THE MILLET- AND SORGHUM-
BASED FOOD INDUSTRY

Niamey
NIGER

AFRICAN TRAINING AND RESEARCH CENTRE IN ADMINISTRATION AND
DEVELOPMENT

P.O.Box 310
Tangiers
MOROCCO

AFRO-ASIAN RURAL RECONSTRUCTION ORGANISATION

C/117-118 Defence colony
New Delhi 3
INDIA

AGENCE POUR LA SECURITE DE LA NAVIGATION AERIENNE EN AFRIQUE ET A
MADAGASCAR

Dakar
SENEGAL

AGENCY FOR THE PROHIBITION OF NUCLEAR WEAPONS IN LATIN AMERICA

Avenida Morelos 110
desp 506
Mexico 6 DF
P.O.Box 32-929
MEXICO 1, DF

AIR AFRIQUE

P.O.Box 21017
Abidjan
IVORY COAST

ANZUS COUNCIL

Department of external affairs
Canberra
ACT 2600
AUSTRALIA

ARAB LABOUR ORGANIZATION

c/o   League of Arab States
Midan Al Tahrir
Cairo
ARAB REPUBLIC OF EGYPT

ARAB ORGANIZATION FOR STANDARDIZATION AND METROLOGY

> 11, Mohamed Marashly street
> Zamalek
> POB 690
> Cairo
> ARAB REPUBLIC OF EGYPT

ADMINISTRATIVE CENTRE OF SOCIAL SECURITY FOR RHINE BOATMEN

> Palais du Rhin
> 67-Strasbourg
> FRANCE

AFRICAN AND MALAGASY COFFEE ORGANISATION

> 27 Quai Anatole France
> Paris 7e
> FRANCE

AFRICAN AND MALAGASY HIGHER EDUCATION COUNCIL

> P.O.Box 134
> Ouagadougou
> UPPER VOLTA

AFRICAN AND MALAGASY INDUSTRIAL PROPERTY OFFICE

> BP 887
> Yaounde
> CAMEROON

AFRICAN AND MALAGASY POSTAL TELECOMMUNICATIONS UNION

> av. Patrice Lumumba
> BP 44
> Brazzaville
> PEOPLE'S REPUBLIC OF THE CONGO

AFRICAN AND MALAGASY SUGAR AGREEMENT

> P.O.Box 763
> Fort Lamy
> CHAD

AFRICAN AND MALAGASY UNION OF DEVELOPMENT BANKS

> Palais de l'OCAM
> BP 814
> Yaounde
> CAMEROON

AFRICAN CIVIL AVIATION COMMISSION

> 15, Boulevard de la République
> P.O.Box 2356
> Dakar
> SENEGAL

AFRICAN DEVELOPMENT BANK

> B.P. 1387
> Abidjan
> IVORY COAST

AFRICAN GROUNDNUT COUNCIL

> No. 18B Keffi Street
> Ikoyi
> P.O.Box 3025
> Lagos
> NIGERIA

AFRICAN, MALAGASY AND MAURITIAN COMMON ORGANISATION

> P.O.Box 437
> Yaounde
> CAMEROON

AFRICAN NATIONAL TELEVISION AND BROADCASTING UNION

> 101 rue Carbot
> P.O.Box 3237
> Dakar
> SENEGAL

ARAB POSTAL UNION

> 28, Adly street
> Cairo
> ARAB REPUBLIC OF EGYPT

ARAB STATES BROADCASTING UNION

> 23, Kasr el Nil
> Cairo
> ARAB REPUBLIC OF EGYPT

ARAB TOURISM UNION

> P.O.Box 2354
> Amman
> JORDAN

ASIA-PACIFIC FORESTRY COMMISSION

> c/o   FAO Regional Office
>   Maliwan Mansion
>   Phra Atit Road
>   Bangkok
>   THAILAND

ASIAN-AFRICAN LEGAL CONSULTATIVE COMMITTEE

> 20 Ring Road
> Lajpat Nagar-IV
> New Delhi 14
> INDIA

ASIAN AND PACIFIC COUNCIL

> National Secretariat of Thailand
> Economic Department
> Ministry of Foreign Affairs
> Saranrom Palace
> Bangkok
> THAILAND

ASIAN DEVELOPMENT BANK

> Commercial Center,
> P.O.B. 126
> Makati
> Rizal
> D-708
> PHILIPPINES

ASIAN HIGHWAY CO-ORDINATING COMMITTEE

> Asian highway transport technical bureau
> ECAFE
> Sala Santitham
> Bangkok 2
> THAILAND

ASIAN INDUSTRIAL DEVELOPMENT COUNCIL

>ECAFE Secretariat
>Sala Santitham
>Bangkok 2
>THAILAND

ASIAN-OCEANIC POSTAL UNION

>Post office building
>Plaza Bonifacio
>Manila D-406
>PHILIPPINES

ASIAN PRODUCTIVITY ORGANISATION

>4-14 Akasaka 8-chome
>Minato-ku
>Tokyo 17
>JAPAN

ASSOCIATION BETWEEN THE EUROPEAN ECONOMIC COMMUNITY AND THE PARTNER STATES OF THE EAST AFRICAN COMMUNITY

>Council of the European communities
>rue de la Loi 170
>1040 Brussels
>BELGIUM

ASSOCIATION OF AFRICAN AIRLINES

>Nairobi
>KENYA

ASSOCIATION OF AFRICAN CENTRAL BANKS

>ECA acts as the Secretariat of the Association.
>Addis Ababa
>ETHIOPIA

ASSOCIATION OF AFRICAN UNIVERSITIES

>P.O.Box 5744
>Accra North
>GHANA

ASSOCIATION OF SOUTHEAST ASIAN NATIONS

>c/o Ministry for Foreign Affairs
>Singapore 6
>SINGAPORE

ASSOCIATION OF THE EUROPEAN ECONOMIC COMMUNITY AND THE AFRICAN AND MALAGASY STATES

>Council of European communities
>rue de la Loi 170
>1040 Brussels
>BELGIUM

BANK FOR INTERNATIONAL SETTLEMENTS

>7 Centralbahnstrasse
>CH 4002 Basel
>SWITZERLAND

BENELUX ECONOMIC AND SOCIAL CONSULTATIVE COUNCIL

>21, av. de la Joyeuse Entrée
>1040 Brussels
>BELGIUM

BENELUX ECONOMIC UNION

> 39 rue de la Régence
> 1000 Brussels
> BELGIUM

CARIBBEAN FOOD AND NUTRITION INSTITUTE

> P.O.Box 140
> Kingston 7
> JAMAICA

CATTLE AND MEAT ECONOMIC COMMUNITY OF THE COUNCIL OF THE ENTENTE STATES

> Ouagadougou
> UPPER VOLTA

CENTRAL AFRICAN CUSTOMS AND ECONOMIC UNION

> P.O.Box 946
> Bangui
> CENTRAL AFRICAN REPUBLIC

CENTRAL AMERICAN AIR SAFETY SERVICES CORPORATION

> Aeropuerto de Toncontin
> Apartado postal 660
> Tegucigalpa
> HONDURAS

CENTRAL AMERICAN COMMON MARKET

Permanent Secretariat: (Secretaría Permanente de Integración Económica Centroamericana - SIECA)

> 4a Avenida 10-25 Zona 14
> Guatemala City
> Guatemala

CENTRAL AMERICAN INSTITUTE OF PUBLIC ADMINISTRATION

> Edificio Schyfter 5 y 6 piso
> Avenida Central y Calle 2a-32N
> San José
> COSTA RICA

CENTRAL AMERICAN RESEARCH INSTITUTE FOR INDUSTRY

> Avenida La Reforma, 4-47
> Zona 10 (Apartado postal 1552)
> Guatemala
> GUATEMALA

CENTRAL BANK OF THE STATES OF EQUATORIAL AFRICA AND CAMEROON

> 29 rue de Colisée
> Paris 8ème
> FRANCE

CENTRAL BANK OF THE WEST AFRICAN STATES

> 28 rue du Colisée
> Paris 8ème
> FRANCE

CENTRAL COMMISSION FOR THE NAVIGATION OF THE RHINE

> Palais du Rhin
> 67-Strasbourg
> FRANCE

CENTRAL OFFICE FOR INTERNATIONAL RAILWAY TRANSPORT

>30, Gryphenhübeliweg
>3006 Berne
>SWITZERLAND

CENTRAL TREATY ORGANIZATION

>Old Grand National Assembly Building
>Ankara
>TURKEY

CENTRE FOR INDUSTRIAL STUDIES OF THE MAGHREB

>Tangiers
>MOROCCO

CENTRE FOR LATIN AMERICAN MONETARY STUDIES

>Durango no. 54
>MEXICO 7, DF

COCOA PRODUCERS ALLIANCE

>Western House
>8-10 Broad Street
>B.P. 1718
>Lagos
>NIGERIA

COLOMBO PLAN FOR CO-OPERATIVE ECONOMIC DEVELOPMENT IN SOUTH AND
SOUTHEAST ASIA

>12 Melbourne Avenue
>P.O.Box 596
>Colombo 4
>SRI LANKA

COLUMBIA RIVER TREATY

Canadian Entity: c/o British Columbia Hydro and Power Authority
970 Burrard Street
Vancouver 1
British Columbia, CANADA

United States Entity: c/o Bonneville Power Administration
P.O.B. 3621
Portland
Oregon 97208
UNITED STATES OF AMERICA

COMMISSION OF THE CARTAGENA AGREEMENT

>Avenida 2 de Mayo 1675
>Casilla 3237
>Lima
>PERU

COMMITTEE FOR CO-ORDINATION OF JOINT PROSPECTING FOR MINERAL RESOURCES
IN ASIAN OFFSHORE AREAS (Co-ORDINATING COMMITTEE OFFSHORE PROSPECTING
CCOP).

>ECAFE Secretariat
>Sala Santitham
>Bangkok 2
>THAILAND

COMMONWEALTH ADVISORY AERONAUTICAL RESEARCH COUNCIL

National physical laboratory
Teddington
Middlesex
GREAT BRITAIN

COMMONWEALTH AGRICULTURAL BUREAUX

Farnham House
Farnham Royal
Slough, SL2 3BN
GREAT BRITAIN

COMMONWEALTH COMMITTEE ON MINERAL RESOURCES AND GEOLOGY

Africa House
Kingsway
London, WC2B   6BD
GREAT BRITAIN

COMMONWEALTH FOUNDATION

Marlborough House
Pall Mall
London SW1Y 5HU
GREAT BRITAIN

COMMONWEALTH FUND FOR TECHNICAL CO-OPERATION

Marlborough House
Pall Mall
London SW1Y 5HU
GREAT BRITAIN

COMMONWEALTH OF NATIONS

Commonwealth Secretariat
Marlborough House
Pall Mall
London SW1Y 5HU
GREAT BRITAIN
Also for publications of:
Commonwealth economic consultative council, Commonwealth education
liaison committee

COMMONWEALTH SCIENTIFIC COMMITTEE

Africa House
Kingsway
London WC2B 6BD
GREAT BRITAIN

COMMONWEALTH TELECOMMUNICATIONS ORGANISATION

28 Pall Mall
London SW1Y 5HU
GREAT BRITAIN

COMMONWEALTH WAR GRAVES COMMISSION

32 Grosvenor Gardens
London SW1
GREAT BRITAIN

CONFERENCE OF EAST AND CENTRAL AFRICAN STATES

The Conference has no permanent secretariat

CONFERENCE OF HEADS OF STATE OF EQUATORIAL AFRICA

Ministry of foreign affairs
Bangui
CENTRAL AFRICAN REPUBLIC

CONSULTATIVE COMMITTEE (of the European coal and steel community)

3 bd Joseph II
Luxembourg
LUXEMBOURG

COUNCIL FOR INTERNATIONAL ORGANIZATIONS OF MEDICAL SCIENCES

Unesco House
1 rue Miollis
Paris 15e
FRANCE

COUNCIL FOR MUTUAL ECONOMIC ASSISTANCE
Sovet ekonomicheskoi vzaimopomoshchi

Prospekt Kalinina 56
Moscow
UNION OF SOVIET SOCIALIST REPUBLICS

COUNCIL OF ARAB ECONOMIC UNITY - - ARAB ECONOMIC UNITY AGREEMENT

20 Shania Aisha El Tatmouria
Garden City
Cairo
ARAB REPUBLIC OF EGYPT

COUNCIL OF EUROPE:

Maison de l'Europe
67-Strasbourg
FRANCE

Sales agents for publications of the Council of Europe:

Austria/Autriche
Gerold & Co
Graben 31
Vienna 1

Canada/Canada
Information Canada
Ottawa

Denmark/Danemark
Ejnar Munksgaard
Nörregade 6
Copenhagen

France/France
Librairie Générale de Droit et
 de Jruisprudence
R. Pichon et R. Durand-Auzias
20 rue Soufflot
Paris Ve

Federal Republic of Germany/
République fédérale d'Allemagne
Verlag Dr. Hans Heger
Goethestrasse 54, Postfach 821
D-53 Bonn-Bad Godesburg

Greece/Grèce
Librairie Kauffmann
20 rue Stadiou
Athens

Iceland/Islande
Snaebjörn Jonsson & Co. A.F.
The English Bookshop
Hafnarstroeti 9
Reykjavik

Ireland/Irlande
Stationery Office
Dublin

COUNCIL OF EUROPE (CONT'D)
Sales agents (cont'd)

Italy/Italie
Libreria Commissionaria Sansoni
Via Lamarmora 45
Casella Post 552
Florence

Netherlands/Pays-Bas
N.V. Martinus Nijhoff
Lange Voorhout, 9
The Hague

New Zealand/Nouvelle-Zélande
Government Printing office
20 Molesworth Street
Wellington

Sweden/Suède
Aktiebolaget C.E. Fritze
Kungl. Hovbokhandel
Fredsgatan 2
Stockholm

Switzerland/Suisse
Buchhandl. Hans Raunhardt
Kirchgasse 17
8000 Zürich 1

Librairie Payot
6 rue Grenus
1211 Geneva 11

Turkey/Turquie
Librairie Hachette
469 Istiklal Caddesi
Beyoglu
Istanbul

United Kingdom/Royaume-Uni
H.M. Stationery Office
P.O. Box 569
London

United States/Etats-Unis
Manhattan Publishing Company
225 Lafayette Street
New York 10012
N.Y.

STRASBOURG
Librairie Berger-Levrault
Place Broglie

COUNCIL OF EUROPE RESETTLEMENT FUND FOR NATIONAL REFUGEES AND
    OVER-POPULATION IN EUROPE

            55 avenue Kléber
            75-Paris 16e
            FRANCE

COUNCIL OF THE ENTENTE

            B.P. 1878
            Abidjan
            IVORY COAST

COURT OF JUSTICE (OF THE EUROPEAN COMMUNITIES)

            12 rue de la Côte d'Eich
            Luxembourg
            LUXEMBOURG

CUSTOMS CO-OPERATION COUNCIL

            40 rue Washington
            B-1050 Brussels
            BELGIUM

CUSTOMS UNION BETWEEN SWAZILAND, BOTSWANA, LESOTHO AND SOUTH AFRICA

            Headquarters: none

DANUBE COMMISSION

            Benczúr utca 25
            Budapest
            HUNGARY

DESERT LOCUST CONTROL ORGANISATION FOR EASTERN AFRICA

P.O.Box 4255
Addis Ababa
ETHIOPIA

DIPLOMATIC CONFERENCE OF INTERNATIONAL MARITIME LAW

c/o   Ministère des affaires étrangères et du commerce extérieur
2 rue Quatre Bras
1000 Brussels
BELGIUM

EAST AFRICAN AGRICULTURE AND FORESTRY RESEARCH ORGANIZATION

P.O.Box 30148
Nairobi
KENYA

EAST AFRICAN AIRWAYS CORPORATION

P.O.Box 41010
Nairobi
KENYA

EAST AFRICAN CARGO HANDLING SERVICES LTD

P.O.Box 5187
Mombasa
KENYA

EAST AFRICAN COMMUNITY

Central Secretariat: P.O.Box 1001
Arusha
TANZANIA

EAST AFRICAN DEVELOPMENT BANK

13 Portal Avenue
P.O.Box 7128
Kampala
UGANDA

EAST AFRICAN EXAMINATION COUNCIL

P.O.Box 7066
Kampala
UGANDA

EAST AFRICAN EXTERNAL TELECOMMUNICATIONS COMPANY LTD

P.O.Box 30488
Nairobi
KENYA

EAST AFRICAN HARBOURS CORPORATION

P.O.Box 9184
Dar-es-Salaam
TANZANIA

EAST AFRICAN POSTS AND TELECOMMUNICATIONS CORPORATION

Hannington Road
P.O.Box 7107
Kampala
UGANDA

EAST AFRICAN RAILWAYS CORPORATION

P.O.Box 30121
Nairobi
KENYA

EAST CARIBBEAN CURRENCY AUTHORITY

Treasury Building
P.O.Box 620 C
Bridgetown
BARBADOS

EASTERN AFRICAN NATIONAL SHIPPING LINE

Dar-es-Salaam
TANZANIA

ECONOMIC AND SOCIAL COMMITTEE (EUROPEAN COMMUNITIES)

3 bd. de l'Empereur
1000 Brussels
BELGIUM

EUROPEAN AND MEDITERRANEAN PLANT PROTECTION ORGANISATION

1 rue Le Nôtre
75 Paris 16e
FRANCE

EUROPEAN ASSOCIATION OF MUSIC FESTIVALS

122 rue de Lausanne
Geneva
SWITZERLAND

EUROPEAN ATOMIC ENERGY COMMUNITY

200 rue de la Loi
1040 Brussels
BELGIUM

EUROPEAN BROADCASTING UNION

1 rue de Varembé
CH-1211 Geneva 20
SWITZERLAND

EUROPEAN CIVIL AVIATION CONFERENCE

3 bis Villa Emile-Bergerat
92 Neuilly-sur-Seine
FRANCE

EUROPEAN COAL AND STEEL COMMUNITY

200 rue de la Loi
1040 Brussels
BELGIUM

EUROPEAN COMMISSION FOR THE CONTROL OF FOOT-AND-MOUTH DISEASE

c/o   FAO
Viale delle Terme di Caracalla
0100 Rome
ITALY

EUROPEAN COMMUNITIES;

rue de la Loi 170
1040 Brussels
BELGIUM

Includes publications of:

Commission of the European communities. Council of the European communities, Economic and social committee of the European communities, European parliament, Information service of the European communities, Statistical office of the European communities

For publications of the three European communities (European atomic energy community, European coal and steel community, European economic community) see under their names.

Information offices:

Belgium
Official Spokesman of the Commission of
the European Communities
Rue de la Loi 200, Brussels 1040
Tel: 35.00.40/35.80.40.

France
Bureau d'information des Communautés
européennes
61 rue des Belles Feuilles, Paris 16
Tel: KLEber 53.26

German Federal Republic
Presse und Informationstelle der
Europäischen Gemeinschaften
Bonn, Zitelmannstrasse 11
Tel: 22.60.41/42/43
Berlin, Kurfürstendamm 102
Tel: 886.40.28

Italy
Ufficio Stampa e Informazione delle
Comunità Europea
Via Poli 29, Rome
Tel: 68.97.22

Luxembourg
Bureau dInformation des Commu-
nautés Européennes
Centre Kirchberg, Luxembourg
Tel: 479.41

Netherlands
Voorlichtingsdienst van de Europese
Gemeenschappen
Alexander Gogdweg 22, 's-Gravenhage
Tel: 33.41.23

Switzerland
Bureau d'Information des Communautés
Européennes
72 rue de Lausanne, Geneva
Tel: 31.87.30

United Kingdom
European Community Information Office
23 Chesham Street, London S.W.1
Tel: 01-235.4904

United States
European Community Information Office
Suite 707, 2100 M Street N.W.
Washington, D.C., 20037
Tel: (202) 296-5131
2207 Commerce Building, 155 East 44th st.
New York 10017
Tel: 212 MU 20458

Chile
Avda Providencia 1072, Santiago de Chile
Tel: 25055

Argentina
Calle Bartoleme Mitré 1337, Montevideo
Tel: 984242

Sales agents:

France
Service de vente en France des
publications des Communautés
européennes
26 rue Desaix, 75 Paris 15e
Tel: (1) 306.51.00
CCP Paris 23-96

Belgium
Moniteur belge-Belgisch Staatsblad
40-42 rue de Louvain-Leuvenseweg 40-42
1000 Bruxelles - 1000 Brussel
Tel: 12.00.26
CCP 50-80

Librairie européenne-Europese Boekhandel
244 rue de la Loi-Wetstraat 244
1040 Bruxelles-1040Brussel

Luxembourg
Office des publications officielles des
Communautés européennes
Case postale 1003 - Luxembourg 1
et 29 rue Aldringen, Bibliothèque
CCP 191-90 - Tel: 47941

Bank account: BIL 6-109/6003/200

Federal Republic of Germany
Verlag Bundesanzeiger
5000 Köln 1 - Postfach 108006
(Fernschreiber: Anzeiger Bonn 08 882 595)
Postscheckkonto 834 00 Köln
Tel: (0221) 210348

EUROPEAN COMMUNITIES (CONT'D)

Italy
Libreria della Stato
Piazza G. Verdi 10
00198 Roma
CCP 1/2640
Tel: (6) 8509

Agencies:
00187 Roma   - Via del Tritone 61A et
               61B
00187 Roma   - Via XX Settembre
               (Palazzo Ministero delle
               finanze)
20121 Milano - Galleria Vittorio Emanuele 3
80121 Napoli - Via Chiaia 5
50129 Firenze - Via Cavour 46/R
16121 Genova - Via XII Ottobre 172
40125 Bologna - Strada Maggiore 23/A

Netherlands
Staatsdrukkerij- en uitgeverijbedrijf
Christoffel Plantijnstraat
's-Gravenhage
Giro 425 300
Tel: (070) 814511ç

Great Britain and the Commonwealth
H.M. Stationery Office
P.O.Box 569
London S.E.1

United States
European Community Information Service
2100 M Street, N.W.
Suite 707
Washington D.C. 20037

Ireland
Stationery Office
Begger's Bush
Dublin 4

Switzerland
Librairie Payot
6 rue Grenus
1211 Genève
CCP 12-236 Genève

Sweden
Librairie C.E. Fritze
2, Fredsgatan
Stockholm 16
Post Giro 193, Bank Giro 73/4015

Spain
Libreria Mundi-Prensa
Castello 37
Madrid 1

Other countries:

Office des publications officielles
   des Communautés européennes
Case postale 1003
Luxembourg 1
CCP 191-90
Tel: 47941
Bank account: BIL 8-109/6003/200

EUROPEAN COMPANY FOR THE CHEMICAL PROCESSING OF IRRADIATED FUELS

2400, Mol-Donk
BELGIUM

EUROPEAN COMPANY FOR THE FINANCING OF RAILWAY ROLLING STOCK

Rittergasse, 20
4001 Basel
SWITZERLAND

EUROPEAN CONFERENCE OF INSURANCE SUPERVISORS SERVICES

Ministero dell'industria e dei commercio
Via Veneto 56
Rome
ITALY

EUROPEAN CONFERENCE OF MINISTERS OF TRANSPORT

33 rue de Franqueville
75-Paris 16e
FRANCE

EUROPEAN CONFERENCE OF POSTAL AND TELECOMMUNICATIONS ADMINISTRATIONS

Netherlands PTT Administration
Kortenaerkade 12
The Hague
NETHERLANDS

EUROPEAN CONFERENCE ON SATELLITE COMMUNICATIONS

c/o   European space conference
114 av. de Neuilly
92 Neuilly-sur-Seine
FRANCE

EUROPEAN ECONOMIC COMMUNITY

200 rue de la Loi
1040 Brussels
BELGIUM

EUROPEAN FREE TRADE ASSOCIATION

9-11 rue de Varembé
1211 Geneva 20
SWITZERLAND

EUROPEAN INFORMATION CENTRE FOR NATURE CONSERVATION

Council of Europe
67-Strasbourg
FRANCE

EUROPEAN INVESTMENT BANK

2 place de Metz
Luxembourg
LUXEMBOURG

EUROPEAN MOLECULAR BIOLOGY CONFERENCE

Hills Road
Cambridge CB2 2QH
GREAT BRITAIN

EUROPEAN ORGANIZATION FOR NUCLEAR RESEARCH

Meyrin
1211 Genève 23
SWITZERLAND

EUROPEAN ORGANIZATION FOR THE SAFETY OF AIR NAVIGATION

72 rue de la Loi
1040 Brussels
BELGIUM

EUROPEAN PARLIAMENT

Centre European
Paltaue du Kirchberg
Luxembourg
LUXEMBOURG

EUROPEAN SPACE RESEARCH ORGANIZATION

114 av. Charles de Gaulle
92 Neuilly-sur-Seine
FRANCE

EUROPEAN SPACE VEHICLE LAUNCHER DEVELOPMENT ORGANISATION

114 av. Charles de Gaulle
92 Neuilly-sur-Seine
FRANCE

FEDERATION OF ARAB REPUBLICS

The President
Arab Republic of Egypt
Cairo
ARAB REPUBLIC OF EGYPT

FOOD AND AGRICULTURE ORGANIZATION

Viale delle Terme di Caracalla
00100 Rome
ITALY

Sales agents of the Food and agriculture organization:

Algeria	Société nationale d'édition et de diffusion (SNED), Algiers
Argentina	Librería de las Naciones, Cooperativa Ltda., Alsina 500, Buenos Aires
Australia	Hunter Publications, 58A Gipps Street, Collingwood, Vic. 3066; The Assistant Director, Sales and Distribution, Government Printing Office, P.O.Box 84, Canberra, A.C.T. 2600, and outlets in each state capital city.
Austria	Wilhelm Frick Buchhandlung, Graben 27, Vienna 1
Bangladesh	Shilpa Niketan, 29 D.I.T. Super Market, Mymensingh Road, Dacca 2
Belgium	Agence et Messageries de la Presse, 1 rue de la Petite-Ile, Brussels 7
Bolivia	Librería y Editorial "Juventud", Plaza Murillo 519, La Paz; Librería Alfonso Tejerina, Comercio 1073, La Paz
Brazil	Livraria Mestre Jou, Rua Guaipá 518, Sao Paulo 10; Rua Senador Dantas 19-S205/206, Rio de Janeiro
Bulgaria	Hèmus, 11 place Slaveikov, Sofia
Canada	Information Canada, Ottawa
Chile	Biblioteca, FAO Oficina Regional para América Latina, Av. Providencia 871, Casilla 10095, Santiago; Editorial y Distribuidora Orbe Ltda., Galería Imperio 256, Santiago; Cámera Latinoamericana del Libro, Casilla Postal 14502, Correo 21, Santiago
Colombia	"Agricultura Tropical", Calle 17 no. 4-67, Piso 2, Bogotá; Librería Central, Calle 14 No.6-88, Bogotá
Costa Rica	Imprenta y Libreria Trejos S.A., Apartado 1313, San José
Cuba	Instituto del Libro, Calle 19 y 10 No.1002, Vedado
Cyprus	MAM, P.O.Box 1722, Nicosia
Denmark	Ejnar Munksgaard, Norregade 6, Copenhagen S
Ecuador	Librería Universitaria, Carcía Moreno 739, Quito; Su Librería, Plaza de Independencia, Quito
Egypt	Al Ahram, El Galaa St., Cairo
El Salvador	Librería Cultural Salvadoreña S.A., 6a Calle Oriente 118, Edificio San Martin, San Salvador
Finland	Akateeminen Kiejakauppa, 2 Keskuskatu, Helsinki
France	Editions A. Pedone, 13 rue Soufflot, Paris 5e
Germany	Paul Parey, Lindenstrasse 44-47, Berlin SW 61
Ghana	Ghana Publishing Corporation, P.O.Box 3632, Accra
Greece	"Eleftheroudakis", 4 Nikis Street, Athens
Guatemala	Sociedad Económico Financiera, Edificio "El Cielito", Despacho 222, Zona 1, Guatemala
Haiti	Max Bouchereau, Librairie "A la Caravelle", B.P. 111B, Port-au-Prince
Hong Kong	Swindon Book Co., 13-15 Lock Road, Kowloon
Iceland	Snaebjörn Jónsson and Co. h.f., Hafnarstraeti 9, P.O.Box 1131, Reykjavik
India	Oxford Book and Stationery Co., Scindia House, New Delhi; 17 Park Street, Calcutta
Indonesia	P.T. Gunung Agung, 6 Kwitang, Djakarta
Iran	Economist Tehran, 99 Sevom Esfand Avenue, Tehran
Iraq	Mackenzie's Bookshop, Baghdad
Ireland	The Controller, Stationery Office, Dublin
Israel	Emanuel Brown, formerly Blumstein's Bookstores Ltd., P.O.Box 4101, 35 Allenby Road, and Nachlat Benyamin Street, Tel Aviv; 9 Sblomzion Hamlka Street, Jerusalem
Italy	Libreria Internazionale Rizzoli, Largo Chigi, Rome; A.E.I.O.U., Via Meravigli 16, Milan; Libreria Commissionaria Sansoni, S.p.A., Via Lamarmora 45, Florence; Libreria Macchiaroli, Via Carducci 55/59, 80121 Naples
Japan	Maruzen Company Ltd., P.O.Box 605, Tokyo Central 100-91
Kenya	The E.S.A. Bookshop, P.O.Box 30167, Nairobi; University Bookshop, University College, P.O.Box 30197, Nairobi
Korea	The Eul-Yoo Publishing Co. Ltd., 5 2-Ka, Chong-ro, Seoul
Kuwait	All Prints Distributors and Publishers, P.O.Box 1719, Kuwait
Lebanon	Dar Al-Maaref Liban S.A.L., place Riad El-Solh, B.P. 2320, Beirut
Malaysia	Caxton Stationers Ltd., 13-15 Leboh Pasar Besar, Kuala Lumpur
Mauritius	Nalanda Company Limited, 30 Bourbon Street, Port Louis
Mexico	Manuel Gómez Pezuela e Hijo, Donceles 12, México, D.F.; Editorial Iztaccihuatl S.A., Miguel Schultz 21, México 4, D.F.; Av. Morelos Ote 437, Monterrey, N.L.; Colón 175, Guadalajara, Jal.
Morocco	Librairie "Aux Belles Images", 281 avenue Mohammed V, Rabat
Netherlands	N.V. Martinus Nijhoff, Lange Voorhout 9, The Hague

FOOD AND AGRICULTURAL ORGANIZATION (CONT.'D)

Sales agents (cont'd)

New Zealand	Government Printing Office: Government Bookshops at Rutland Street, P.O.Box 5344, Auckland; Mulgrave Street, Private Bag, Wellington; 130 Oxford Terrace, P.O.Box 1721, Christchurch; Princes Street, P.O.Box P.O.Box 1104, Dunedin; Alma Street, P.O.Box 857, Hamilton
Nicaragua	Librería Universal, 15 de Septiembre 301, Managua
Nigeria	University Bookshop Nigeria Ltd., University College, Ibadan
Norway	Johan Grundt Tanum Forlag, Karl Johansgt. 43, Oslo
Pakistan	Mirza Book Agency, 65 The Mall, Lahore 3
Panama	Agencia Internacional de Publicaciones J. Menéndez, Apartado 2052, Panama
Paraguay	Agencia de Librerías de Salvador Nizza, Calle Pte. Franco No. 39-43, Asunción
Peru	Librería La Universidad, Av.Nicolás de Piérola 639, Lima; Librería Studium, Amargura 939, Lima; Distribuidora Inca, Emilio Althaus 470, Lince, Lima
Philippines	The Modern Book Company, 928 Rizal Avenue, Manila
Poland	Ars Polona-Ruch, Krakowskie Przedmiescie 7, Warsaw
Portugal	Livraria Bertrand, S.A.R.L., Apartado 37, Amadora
Romania	Cartimex, P.O.Box 134-135, Bucharest
Saudi Arabia	Khazindar Establishment, King Faysal Street, Riyadh
Spain	Librería Mundi-Prensa, Castelló 37, Madrid; Librería Agricola, Fernando VI 2, Madrid 4; José Bosch Librero, Ronda Universidad 11, Barcelona; "Adlha", Av. General Mitre 100, Barcelona
Sri Lanka	M.D. Gunasena and Co. Ltd., 217 Norris Road, Colombo 11
Sweden	C.E. Fritze, Fredsgatan 2, 103 27 Stockholm 16; Universitetsbokhandel, Sveavägen 166, Stockholm Va.; Gumperts A.B., Göteborg
Switzerland	Librairie Payot S.A., Lausanne and Geneva; Hans Raunhardt, Kirchgasse 17, Zurich 1
Syria	Librairie Internationale, B.P. 2456, Damascus
Tanzania	Dar es Salaam Bookshop, P.O.Box 9030, Dar es Salaam
Thailand	FAO Regional Office for Asia and the Far East, Maliwan Mansion, Bangkok; Suksapan Panit, Mansion 9, Rajadamnern Avenue, Bangkok
Togo	Librairie du Bon Pasteur, B.P. 1164, Lomé
Turkey	Librairie Hachette, 469 Istiklal Caddesi, Beyoglu, Istanbul
Uganda	The E.S.A. Bookshop, P.O.Box 2615, Kampala
United Kingdom	Her Majesty's Stationery Office, 49 High Holborn, London, W.C.1; P.O.Box 569, London, S.E.1 (Trade and London area mail orders); 13a Castle Street, Edinburgh EH2 3AR; 109 St. Mary Street, Cardiff CF1 1JW; 7 Linenhall Street, Belfast BT2 8AY; Brazennose Street, Manchester M60 8AS; 258 Broad Street, Birmingham 1; 50 Fairfax Street, Bristol BS1 3DE
United States of America	UNIPUB, Inc., 650 First Avenue, P.O.Box 433, New York, N.Y. 10016
Uruguay	Barreiro y Ramos, 25 de Mayo esq. J.C. Gómez, Montevideo; Librería Albe, Soc. Com., Cerrito 566, Montevideo
Venezuela	Suma S.A., Calle Real de Sabana Grande, Caracas; Librería Politécnica, Apartado 50738, Sabana Grande, Caracas; Librería del Este, Pericás S.A., Av.Fco. de Miranda 52, Edificio Galipán, Caracas; Librería Técnica Vega, Plaza Las Tres Gracias, Edificio Odeón, Los Chaguaramos, Caracas
Yugoslavia	Jugoslovenska Knjiga, Terazije 27/11, Belgrade; Prosveta Export-Import Agency, Terazije 16, Belgrade; Cankarjeva Zalozba, P.O.Box 201 - IV, Ljubljana
Other Countries	Requests from countries where sales agents have not yet been appointed may be sent to: Distribution and Sales Section, Food and Agriculture Organization of the United Nations, Via delle Terme di Caracalla, 00100 Rome, Italy

GENERAL AGREEMENT ON TARIFFS AND TRADE

Villa le Bocage
Palais des nations
1211 Geneva 10
SWITZERLAND

GENERAL FISHERIES COUNCIL FOR THE MEDITERRANEAN

c/o   FAO
Viale delle Terme di Caracalla
00100 Rome
ITALY

GENERAL TRADE AND COMMODITIES DIVISION

>10-11 Carlton House Terrace
>London SW1Y 5HX
>GREAT BRITAIN

GENERAL TREATY ON CENTRAL AMERICAN ECONOMIC ECONOMIC INTEGRATION

>4a avenida 10-25
>Zona 14
>Guatemala City
>GUATEMALA

GROUP OF TEN (PARIS CLUB)

>General arrangement to borrow, decided by International Monetary Fund

HAGUE CONFERENCE ON PRIVATE INTERNATIONAL LAW

>2C Javastraat
>The Hague
>NETHERLANDS

IBERO-AMERICAN BUREAU OF EDUCATION

>Avenida de Los Reys Católicos
>Ciudad Universitaria
>Madrid 3
>SPAIN

IBERO-AMERICAN SOCIAL SECURITY ORGANIZATION

>Avenida de Los Reys Católicos
>Ciudad Universitaria
>Madrid 3
>SPAIN

INDO-PACIFIC FISHERIES COUNCIL

>FAO Regional Office
>Maliwan Mansion
>Phra Atit Road
>Bangkok
>THAILAND

INDUSTRIAL DEVELOPMENT CENTRE FOR ARAB STATES

>P.O.Box 1297
>Cairo
>ARAB REPUBLIC OF EGYPT

INSTITUTE FOR ECONOMIC DEVELOPMENT AND PLANNING

>P.O.Box 3186
>Dakar
>SENEGAL

INSTITUTE FOR LATIN AMERICAN INTEGRATION

>Cerrito 253
>2 Piso
>Casilla de Correo, 39
>Sucursal 1
>Buenos Aires
>ARGENTINA

INSTITUTE OF NUTRITION OF CENTRAL AMERICA AND PANAMA

>Carretera Roosevelt
>Zona 11
>Aptdo Postal 11-88
>Guatemala City
>GUATEMALA

INTER-AFRICAN COFFEE ORGANISATION

>24 rue Madeleine-Michelis
>92 Neuilly-sur-Seine
>FRANCE

INTER-AFRICAN COMMITTEE FOR HYDRAULIC STUDIES

>P.O.Box 369
>Ouagoudou
>UPPER VOLTA

INTER-AMERICAN CHILDREN'S INSTITUTE

>Avenida 8 de octubre 2904
>Montevideo
>URUGUAY

INTER-AMERICAN COMMISSION OF WOMEN

>Pan American Union
>Washington, D.C. 20006
>UNITED STATES OF AMERICA

INTER-AMERICAN COMMITTEE FOR AGRICULTURAL DEVELOPMENT

>1725 Eye Street N.W.
>Room 414
>Washington, D.C. 20006
>UNITED STATES OF AMERICA

INTER-AMERICAN COMMITTEE ON THE ALLIANCE FOR PROGRESS

>1725 Eye Street N.W.
>Room 1101
>Washington, D.C. 20006
>UNITED STATES OF AMERICA

INTER-AMERICAN CONFERENCE ON SOCIAL SECURITY

>Comité Permanente Interamericano de Seguridad Social
>Unidad Independencia
>San Jeronimo Lidice
>Apartado 20532
>México 20 DF
>MEXICO

INTER-AMERICAN COUNCIL FOR EDUCATION, SCIENCE, AND CULTURE

>see   Organization of American States

INTER-AMERICAN DEFENSE BOARD

>2600 Sixteenth St N.W.
>Washington D.C., 20441
>UNITED STATES OF AMERICA

INTER-AMERICAN DEVELOPMENT BANK

>808 17th Street N.W.
>Washington, D.C. 20577
>UNITED STATES OF AMERICA

INTER-AMERICAN ECONOMIC AND SOCIAL COUNCIL

>see   Organization of American States

INTER-AMERICAN EXPORT PROMOTION CENTRE

>Carrera 10 no. 14-33
>Pisos 10 y 11
>Aptdo Aéreo 5609
>Bogotá DE 1
>COLOMBIA

INTER-AMERICAN INDIAN INSTITUTE

> Calle de Niños Héroes 139
> México 7 DF
> MEXICO

INTER-AMERICAN INSTITUTE OF AGRICULTURAL SCIENCES

> Executive Headquarters
> Apartado 10281
> San José
> COSTA RICA

INTER-AMERICAN MUSIC COUNCIL

> Department of cultural affairs,
> OAS
> Washington, D.C. 20006
> UNITED STATES OF AMERICA

INTER-AMERICAN NUCLEAR ENERGY COMMISSION

c/o   General secretariat of the OAS
> Washington, D.C. 20006
> UNITED STATES OF AMERICA

INTER-AMERICAN RESEARCH AND DOCUMENTATION CENTRE ON VOCATIONAL TRAINING

> Colonia 993
> Piso 9
> Casilla 1761
> Montevideo
> URUGUAY

INTER-AMERICAN STATISTICAL INSTITUTE

> Pan America Union
> Washington, D.C. 20006
> UNITED STATES OF AMERICA

INTER-AMERICAN TRAVEL CONGRESSES

> General secretariat of the OAS
> Washington, D.C. 20006
> UNITED STATES OF AMERICA

INTER-AMERICAN TROPICAL TUNA COMMISSION

c/o   Scripps Institution of Oceanography
> La Jolla
> Calif. 92037
> UNITED STATES OF AMERICA

INTERGOVERNMENTAL COMMITTEE FOR EUROPEAN MIGRATION (ICEM)

> 9 rue du Valais
> 1211 Genève 14
> SWITZERLAND

INTERGOVERNMENTAL COMMITTEE OF THE INTERNATIONAL CONVENTION OF ROME FOR THE PROTECTION OF PERFORMERS, PRODUCERS OF PHONOGRAMS AND BROADCASTING ORGANIZATIONS

c/o   World intellectual property organization
> 32 chemin des Colombettes
> Case postale 18
> 1211 Genève 20
> SWITZERLAND

INTERGOVERNMENTAL COPYRIGHT COMMITTEE

Place de Fontenoy
75 Paris 7e
FRANCE

INTERGOVERNMENTAL COUNCIL OF COPPER EXPORTING COUNTRIES

3 av. dù Général de Gaulle
92 - Puteaux
FRANCE

INTER-GOVERNMENTAL MARITIME CONSULTATIVE ORGANIZATION

101-104 Piccadilly
London W 1
GREAT BRITAIN

INTERGOVERNMENTAL OCEANOGRAPHIC COMMISSION

Unesco Headquarters
Place de Fontenoy
75 Paris 7e
FRANCE

INTERNATIONAL AFRICAN MIGRATORY LOCUST ORGANISATION

BP 136
Bamako
MALI

INTERNATIONAL AGENCY FOR RESEARCH ON CANCER

16 av. Maréchal Foch
69 Lyon 6e
FRANCE

INTERNATIONAL ATOMIC ENERGY AGENCY

Kaerner Ring 11
A-1010 Vienna 1
AUSTRIA

Sales agents of the International Atomic Energy Agency

Argentina	Comisión Nacional de Energía Atómica, Avenida del Libertador 8250, Buenos Aires
Australia	Hunter Publications, 58A Gipps Street, Collingwood, Victoria 3066
Belgium	Office International de Librairie, 30, avenue Marnix, Brussels 5
Canada	Information Canada, 171 Slater Street, Ottawa, Ont. K1A OS9
C.S.S.R.	S.N.T.L. Spálená 51, Prague 1; Alfa, Publishers, Hurbanovo námestie 6, Bratislava
France	Office International de Documentation et Librairie, 48 rue Gay-Lussac F-75 Paris 5e
Hungary	Kultura, Hungarian Trading Company for Books and Newspapers, P.O.Box 149, Budapest 62
India	Oxford Book and Stationery Comp., 17, Park Street, Calcutta 16
Israel	Heiliger and Co., 3, Nathan Strauss St., Jerusalem
Italy	Agenzia Editoriale Commissionaria, A.E.I.O.U., Via Meravigli 16 I-20123 Milan
Japan	Maruzen Company Ltd., P.O.Box 5050, 100-31 Tokyo International
Netherlands	Martinus Nijhoff N.V., Lange Voorhout 9-11, P.O.Box 269, The Hague
Pakistan	Mirza Book Agency, 65 The Mall, P.O.Box 729, Lahore 3
Poland	Ars Polona, Centrala Handlu Zagranicznego, Krakowskie Przedmiescie 7, Warsaw

INTERNATIONAL ATOMIC ENERGY AGENCY (CONT'D)

Sales agents (cont'd)

Romania	Cartimex, 3-5 13 Decembrie Street, P.O.Box 134-135, Bucarest
South Africa	Van Schaik's Bookstore, P.O.Box 724. Pretoria
Sweden	C.E. Fritzes Kungl. Hovbokhandel, Fredsgatan 2, Stockholm 16
United Kingdom	Her Majesty's Stationery Office, P.O.Box 569, London SE 1
United States of America	UNIPUB Inc., P.O.Box 433, New York, N.Y. 10016
U.S.S.R.	Mezhdunarodnaya Kniga, Smolenskaya-Sennaya 32-34, Moscow G-200
Yugoslavia	Jugoslovenska Knjiga, Terazije 27, Belgrade
Other Countries	Publishing Section, International Atomic Energy Agency, Kärntner Ring 11, P.O.Box 590, A-1011 Vienna,Austria

INTERNATIONAL BANK FOR ECONOMIC CO-OPERATION

15 Kuznetskii most
Moscow K-31
UNION OF SOVIET SOCIALIST REPUBLICS

INTERNATIONAL BANK FOR RECONSTRUCTION AND DEVELOPMENT

1818 H Street, N.W.
Washington, D.C. 20433
UNITED STATES OF AMERICA

INTERNATIONAL BUREAU OF EDUCATION

Palais Wilson
1211 Genève
SWITZERLAND

INTERNATIONAL BUREAU OF WEIGHTS AND MEASURES

Pavillon de Breteuil
92 - Sevres
FRANCE

INTERNATIONAL CENTRE FOR ADVANCED TECHNICAL AND VOCATIONAL TRAINING

140 Corso Unità d'Italia
10127 Torino
ITALY

INTERNATIONAL CENTRE FOR SETTLEMENT OF INVESTMENT DISPUTES

1818 H Street, N.W.
Washington, D.C., 20433
UNITED STATES OF AMERICA

INTERNATIONAL CENTRE FOR THE STUDY OF THE PRESERVATION AND THE RESTORATION OF CULTURAL PROPERTY

Via Cavour 256
Rome 00184
ITALY

INTERNATIONAL CHILDREN'S CENTRE

Château de Longchamp
Bois de Boulogne
75-Paris 16e
FRANCE

INTERNATIONAL CIVIL AVIATION ORGANIZATION

>1080 University Street
>Montreal 101
>CANADA

INTERNATIONAL COFFEE ORGANIZATION

>22 Berners Street
>London W1P 4DD
>GREAT BRITAIN

INTERNATIONAL COMMISSION FOR AGRICULTURAL AND FOOD INDUSTRIES

>24 rue de Téhéran
>75-Paris 8e
>FRANCE

INTERNATIONAL COMMISSION FOR THE CONSERVATION OF ATLANTIC TUNAS

>Calle General Mola 17
>7 Dcha
>Madrid 1
>SPAIN

INTERNATIONAL COMMISSION FOR THE NORTHWEST ATLANTIC FISHERIES

>c/o Bedford Institute
>P.O.Box 638
>Dartmouth
>Nova Scotia
>CANADA

INTERNATIONAL COMMISSION FOR THE PROTECTION OF THE MOSELLE AGAINST POLLUTION

>Ministère des affaires étrangères
>Direction des affaires économiques et financières
>37 quai d'Orsay
>75-Paris 7e
>FRANCE

INTERNATIONAL COMMISSION FOR THE PROTECTION OF THE RHINE AGAINST POLLUTION

>15 Postfach
>54 Koblenz
>FEDERAL REPUBLIC OF GERMANY

INTERNATIONAL COMMISSION FOR THE SCIENTIFIC EXPLORATION OF THE MEDITERRANEAN SEA

>16 bd de Suisse
>Monte Carlo
>MONACO

INTERNATIONAL COMMISSION ON CIVIL STATUS

>Senckenberganlage 31
>6 Frankfurt/Main
>FEDERAL REPUBLIC OF GERMANY

INTERNATIONAL COMMITTEE OF MILITARY MEDICINE AND PHARMACY

Hôpital Militaire
79 rue Saint-Laurent
4000 Liège
BELGIUM

INTERNATIONAL COMPUTATION CENTRE

23 Viale della Civilità del Lavoro
Rome
ITALY

INTERNATIONAL CONFERENCE OF AFRICAN, FRENCH AND MALAGASY STATES
ON INSURANCE SUPERVISION

73 bd Haussmann
75-Paris 8e
FRANCE

INTERNATIONAL COTTON ADVISORY COMMITTEE

South agriculture building
Washington, D.C. 20250
UNITED STATES OF AMERICA

INTERNATIONAL COUNCIL FOR THE EXPLORATION OF THE SEA

Charlottenlund Slot
2920 Charlottenlund
DENMARK

INTERNATIONAL COURT OF JUSTICE

Palais de la Paix
The Hague
NETHERLANDS

INTERNATIONAL DEVELOPMENT ASSOCIATION

1818 H Street N.W.
Washington, D.C. 20433
UNITED STATES OF AMERICA

INTERNATIONAL DIPLOMATIC ACADEMY

4 bis avenue Hoche
75-Paris 8e
FRANCE

INTERNATIONAL EXHIBITION BUREAU

56 av. Victor-Hugo
75-Paris 16e
FRANCE

INTERNATIONAL FINANCE CORPORATION

1818 H Street N.W.
Washington, D.C. 20433
UNITED STATES OF AMERICA

INTERNATIONAL FREQUENCY REGISTRATION BOARD

Place des Nations
1211 Geneva 20
SWITZERLAND

INTERNATIONAL HYDROGRAPHIC ORGANIZATION

Av. Président J.F. Kennedy
Monte Carlo
MONACO

INTERNATIONAL INSTITUTE FOR COTTON

> Room 203
> Solar Building
> 1000, Sixteenth Street N.W.
> Washington D.C. 20036
> UNITED STATES OF AMERICA

INTERNATIONAL INSTITUTE FOR EDUCATIONAL PLANNING

> rue Eugène Delacroix
> 75-Paris 16e
> FRANCE

INTERNATIONAL INSTITUTE FOR LABOUR STUDIES

> Headquarters:
> 154 rue de Lausanne
> CH-1211 Geneva 22
> SWITZERLAND

INTERNATIONAL INSTITUTE FOR THE UNIFICATION OF PRIVATE LAW

> 28, Via Panisperna
> 00184 Rome
> ITALY

INTERNATIONAL INSTITUTE OF REFRIGERATION

> 177 bd. Malesherbes
> 75-Paris 17e
> FRANCE

INTERNATIONAL INVESTMENT BANK

> 17 Presnenskii val
> Moscow
> UNION OF SOVIET SOCIALIST REPUBLICS

INTERNATIONAL LABOUR ORGANISATION

> 154 rue de Lausanne
> 1211 Genève 22
> SWITZERLAND

Sales agents of the International labour organisation

Algeria	Bureau de l'OIT, 19 avenue Claude-Debussy, BP 226, Alger-gare
Argentina	Oficina de la OIT, avenida Julio A. Roca 710, 3° Piso, Buenos Aires
Belgium	Correspondant du BIT (M.J. Fafchamps), 51-53 rue Belliard, B-1040 Bruxelles
Brazil	Organizaçao Internacional do Trabalho, Escritório Brasil, rua da Glória 190, apt. 201, Caixa Postal 607-ZC-00, Rio de Janeiro, Estado da Guanabara
Bulgaria	Correspondant du BIT (M. Alexandre Mintcheff), boulevard Evlogui Guéorguiev 136, Sofia-C
Cameroon	Bureau du l'OIT, Immeuble de l'OAMPI, 2e étage, BP 13, Yaoundé
Canada	ILO Branch Office, 3rd Floor, Room 307, 178 Queen Street, Ottawa 4 Ontario
Chile	Oficina de Enlace de la OIT con CEPAL, Concepción 351, Casilla 2353 Santiago de Chile
China	ILO Branch Office, 84-3, Roosevelt Road, Section 4, PO Box 4200 Taipei 107, Taiwan (Formosa)
Costa Rica	Oficina de la OIT, avenida Central y 6a Calle, edificio Raventos, 7o piso, Apartado postal 10170, San José
Czechoslovakia	Correspondant du BIT (M. Jiri Fischer), UTEIN, Konviktská 5, Prague 1
Ethiopia	ILO Regional Office for Africa, Africa Avenue, PO Box 2788, Addis Ababa
France	Bureau de correspondance du BIT, 205 boulevard Saint-Germain, F-75 Paris 7e
Germany Federal Rep.	Internationales Arbeitsamt, Zweigamt Bonn, Hohenzollernstrasse 21, D-53 Bonn-Bad Godesberg
Hungary	Correspondant du BIT (I. Uranovicz), Bem rakpart 47, Budapest II
India	ILO Area Office, 7 Sardar Patel Marg, Chanakyapuri, New Delhi-21
Indonesia	ILO Country Representative, PO Box 75, Djakarta
Iran	ILO Country Representative, c/o The Resident Representative of the United Nations Development Programme in Iran, PO Box 1555, Teheran

INTERNATIONAL LABOUR ORGANISATION (CONT'D)

Sales agents (cont'd)

Italy	Ufficio internazionale del Lavoro, Ufficio di Corrispondenza, Villa Aldobrandini, via Panisperna 28, I-00184 Rome
Japan	ILO Branch Office, Rm. no. 0503, 5th floor, World Trade Centre Bldg., 5 Shiba-Hamamatsuchô 3-Chôme, Minato-Ku, Tokyo
Kuwait	ILO Country Representative, Shawaik Camp, PO Box 20275, Kuwait
Lebanon	Bureau de l'OIT, Rock and Marble Building, Ramlet-el-Baida, apartments 1B, 2A and 2B, BP 4656, Beyrouth
Luxembourg	See under Belrium
Mexico	Oficina de la OIT, Edificio B, 10o piso, avenida Juárez 42, Apartado Postal 8636, Mexico 1, DF
Nigeria	ILO Area Office, 11 Okotie-Eboh Street, PO Box 2331, Lagos
Pakistan (West)	ILO Area Office, Street 398-E, Sector No. G.6/4, PO Box 1047, Islamabad
Peru	Oficina Regional de la OIT para las Américas, Las Flores 295, San Isidro, Apartado Postal 3638, Lima
Philippines	ILO Area Office, Ramon Magsaysay Centre, PO Box 2695, Manila
Poland	Correspondant du BIT (M. Zdislaw Wierzbicki), U1, Szopena 1, Varsovie 61
Senegal	Bureau de l'OIT, 22 rue Thiers, BP 414, Dakar
Switzerland	International Labour Office, CH-1211 Geneva 22
Tanzania	ILO Area Office, Independence Avenue at corner of Mkwepu Street, PO Box 9212, Dar-es-Salaam
Thailand	ILO Regional Office for Asia, 302 Silom Road, Bangkok Insurance Building, PO Box 1759, Bangkok
Trinidad and Tobago	ILO Area Office, 19 Keate Street, PO Box 1201, Port-of-Spain Bureau de l'OIT, Gümüssuyu caddesi 96, Ayazpasa, Istanbul
Turkey	Bureau de l'OIT, Gümüssuyu caddesi 96, Ayazpasa, Istanbul
USSR	Bureau de correspondance du BIT, Petrovka 15, Apt. 23, Moscou -K9
United Arab Republic	ILO Area Office, 9 Sh. Willcocks, Zamalek, Cairo
United Kingdom	ILO Branch Office, Sackville House, 40 Piccadilly, London W1V 9PA
United States	ILO Branch Office, 666 Eleventh Street, NW, Washington DC 20001
Uruguay	Inter-American Research and Documentation Centre on Vocational Training, Calle Colonia 993, 7oPiso, Casilla de Correo 1761, Montevideo
Yugoslavia	Correspondant du BIT (M. Ratko Pesić), Fruskogorski put 23, Novi Sad (Vojvodine)
Zaire	Réprentant du BIT pour le Congo (Kinshasa), le Burundi et le Rwanda (M.D. Mavrogiannis), BP 7248, Kinshasa
Zambia	ILO Area Office, PO Box 2181, Design House Ltd., Third Floor, Dar-es-Salaam Place, Cairo Road, Lusaka

INTERNATIONAL LEAD AND ZINC STUDY GROUP

Room 901
UN Building
New York
N.Y. 10017
UNITED STATES OF AMERICA

INTERNATIONAL MONETARY FUND

The Secretary
19th & H Streets, N.W.
Washington, D.C. 20431
UNITED STATES OF AMERICA

Sales agents of the International monetary fund

Afghanistan	Da Afghanistan Bank, Kabul
Australia	Reserve Bank of Australia, Box 3947, G.P.O. Sydney 2001
Austria	Austrian National Bank, A-1011 Vienna
Bolivia	Banco Central de Bolivia, La Paz
Brazil	Banco Central do Brasil, Rio de Janeiro
Burma	People's Bank of the Union of Burma, Rangoon
Burundi	Banque de la République du Burundi, B.P. 705, Bujumbura
Ceylon	Central Bank of Ceylon, Colombo 1
Chile	Banco Central de Chile, Santiago
Colombia	Banco de la República, Bogotá
Costa Rica	Banco Central de Costa Rica, San José
Cyprus	Central Bank of Cyprus, P.O.B. 1087, Nicosia
Denmark	Danmarks Nationalbank, DK-1093, Copenhagen
Ecuador	Banco Central del Ecuador, Quito
Egypt	Central Bank of Egypt, Head Office, Cairo
El Salvador	Banco Central deReserva de El Salvador, San Salvador
Ethiopia	National Bank of Ethiopia, P.O.B. 2048 Addis Ababa

INTERNATIONAL MONETARY FUND (CONT'D)

Sales agents (cont'd)

Finland	Bank of Finland, P.O.Box 10160, Helsinki 10
France	Banque de France, 75 Paris 1er
Germany	Deutsche Bundesbank, 6 Frankfurt/Main 1
Greece	Bank of Greece, P.O.B. 105, Athens
Guatemala	Banco de Guatemala, Ciudad de Guatemala
Guyana	Bank of Guyana, P.O.Box 658, Georgetown
Haiti	Banque Nationale de la République d'Haiti, Port-au-Prince
Iceland	The Central Bank of Iceland, Reykjavik
India	Economic Department, Reserve Bank of India, Bombay 1
Iran	Bank Markazi Iran, Teheran
Iraq	Central Bank of Iraq, Baghdad
Ireland	The Central Bank of Ireland, Dublin 2
Israel	Bank of Israel, P.O. Box 780, Jerusalem
Italy	Banca d'Italia, 00184 Rome
Jamaica	Bank of Jamaica, P.O.Box 621, Kingston
Japan	Foreign Department, The Bank of Japan, Tokyo
Jordan	Central Bank of Jordan, P.O.Box 37, Amman
Kenya	Central Bank of Kenya, P.O.Box 30463, Nairobi
Kuwait	Central Bank of Kuwait, P.O.Box 526, Kuwait
Lebanon	Banque du Liban, B.P. No. 5544, Beirut
Liberia	Bank of Monrovia, Monrovia
Libyan Arab Republic	Central Bank of Libya, P.O.Box 1103, Tripoli
Malawi	Reserve Bank of Malawi, P.O.Box 565, Blantyre
Malaysia	Central Bank of Malaysia, P.O.Box 992, Kuala Lumpur
Malta	Central Bank of Malta, Valletta
Mexico	Banco de Mexico, S.A., Mexico 1, DF
Morocco	Banque du Maroc, B.P.445, Rabat
Netherlands	Kas-Associatie, N.V., Amsterdam
New Zealand	Reserve Bank of New Zealand, Box 2498, Wellington
Nicaragua	Banco Central de Nicaragua, Managua, D.N.
Nigeria	Central Bank of Nigeria, Private Mail Bad 12194, Lagos
Norway	Norges Bank, Postboks 336, Ozlo 1
Pakistan	State Bank of Pakistan, Karachi
Peru	Banco Central de Reserva del Peru, Lima
Philippines	Central Bank of the Philippines, Manila
Rwanda	Banque Nationale du Rwanda, B.P. 531, Freetown
Sierra Leone	Bank of Sierra Leone, P.O.Box 30, Freetown
Somalia	Banca Nazionale Somala, P.O.Box 11, Mogadiscio
South Africa	South African Reserve Bank, Box 427, Pretoria
Spain	Banco de España, Madrid 14
Sudan	Bank of Sudan, Foreign Dept., P.O.Box 313, Khartoum
Sweden	Sveriges Riksbank, 103 13 Stockholm 2
Tanzania	Bank of Tanzania, P.O.Box 2939, Dar-es-Salaam
Thailand	Bank of Thailand, G.P.O. 154, Bangkok
Trinidad and Tobago	Central Bank of Trinidad and Tobago, P.O.Box 1250, Port of Spain
Tunisia	Banque Centrale de Tunisie, Tunis
Turkey	Banque Centrale de la République de Turquie, Ankara
Uganda	Bank of Uganda, P.O.Box 7120, Kampala
United Kingdom	Her Majesty's Stationery Office (PTD 3), P.O.Box 569, London, S.E.1
Venezuela	Banco Central de Venezuela, Caracas
Yugoslavia	Banque Nationale de Yougoslavie, P.O.Box 1010, Belgrade
Zambia	Bank of Zambia, P.O.Box 80, Lusaka
United States & countries not listed	The Secretary, International Monetary Fund, 19th & H Streets, N.W., Washington, D.C. 20431, U.S.A.

INTERNATIONAL MOSELLE COMPANY

Franz-Ludwig-Strasse, 21
Postfach 2246
55 Trier
FEDERAL REPUBLIC OF GERMANY

INTERNATIONAL NARCOTICS CONTROL BOARD

Palais des Nations
1211 Geneva 10
SWITZERLAND

INTERNATIONAL NORTH PACIFIC FISHERIES COMMISSION

6640 Northwest Marine Drive
Vancouver 8
British Colombia
CANADA

INTERNATIONAL OCCUPATIONAL SAFETY AND HEALTH INFORMATION CENTRE

route de Lausanne 154
1211 Geneva 22
SWITZERLAND

INTERNATIONAL OFFICE OF EPIZOOTICS

12 rue de Prony
75-Paris 17e
FRANCE

INTERNATIONAL OLIVE OIL COUNCIL

Juan Bravo 102
Madrid 6
SPAIN

INTERNATIONAL ORGANISATION OF LEGAL METROLOGY

11 rue Turgot
75-Paris 9e
FRANCE

INTERNATIONAL PATENT INSTITUTE

97 Nieuwe Parklaan
The Hague
NETHERLANDS

INTERNATIONAL POPLAR COMMISSION

c/o   Forestry department of FAO
             Viale delle Terme di Caracalla
             00153
             ITALY

INTERNATIONAL RADIO CONSULTATIVE COMMITTEE

Place des Nations
1211 Geneva 20
SWITZERLAND

INTERNATIONAL RED LOCUST CONTROL ORGANISATION FOR CENTRAL AND
SOUTHERN AFRICA

P.O.Box 37 and 38
Mbala
Northern Province
ZAMBIA

INTERNATIONAL RELIEF UNION

12 Chemin de Malombré
Geneva
SWITZERLAND

INTERNATIONAL RICE COMMISSION

FAO Regional office
Maliwan Mansion
Phra Atit Road
Bangkok
THAILAND

INTERNATIONAL RUBBER STUDY GROUP

>Brettenham House
>5-6 Lancaster Place
>London WC2 E
>GREAT BRITAIN

INTERNATIONAL SECRETARIAT FOR VOLUNTEER SERVICE

>10-12 Chemin de Surville
>1213 Geneva-Petit Lancy
>SWITZERLAND

INTERNATIONAL SERICULTURAL COMMISSION

>Station de Recherches Séricicoles
>28 quai Boissier de Sauvages
>30-Alès (Gard)
>FRANCE

INTERNATIONAL SUGAR ORGANIZATION

>28 Haymarket
>London SW1Y 4SP
>GREAT BRITAIN

INTERNATIONAL TEA COMMITTEE

>5 High Timber Street
>Upper Thames Street
>London EC4V
>GREAT BRITAIN

INTERNATIONAL TELECOMMUNICATION SATELLITE CONSORTIUM

>950 L'Enfant Plaza South S.W.
>Washington, D.C. 20024
>UNITED STATES OF AMERICA

INTERNATIONAL TELECOMMUNICATION UNION

>Place des Nations
>1211 Genève 20
>SWITZERLAND

INTERNATIONAL TELEGRAPH AND TELEPHONE CONSULTATIVE COMMITTEE

>2 rue de Varembé
>1211 Geneva 20
>SWITZERLAND

INTERNATIONAL TIN COUNCIL

>Haymarket House
>28 Haymarket
>London SW1Y 4ST
>GREAT BRITAIN

INTERNATIONAL TRADE CENTRE UNCTAD/GATT

>Palais des Nations
>1211 Geneva 10
>SWITZERLAND

INTERNATIONAL TSUNAMI INFORMATION CENTER

>National oceanic and atmospheric administration
>2525 Correa Road
>Honolulu
>Hawaii 96822
>UNITED STATES OF AMERICA

INTERNATIONAL UNION FOR THE PROTECTION OF INDUSTRIAL PROPERTY

32 Chemin des Colombettes
Place des Nations
Case Postale 18
1211 Geneva 20
SWITZERLAND

INTERNATIONAL UNION FOR THE PROTECTION OF LITERARY AND ARTISTIC WORKS

32 Chemin des Colombettes
Place des Nations
Cast Postale 18
1211 Geneva 20
SWITZERLAND

INTERNATIONAL UNION FOR THE PROTECTION OF NEW VARIETIES OF PLANTS

32 Chemin des Colombettes
Place des Nations
Case Postale 18
1211 Geneva 20
SWITZERLAND

INTERNATIONAL UNION FOR THE PUBLICATION OF CUSTOMS TARIFFS

38 rue de l'Association
1000 Brussels
BELGIUM

INTERNATIONAL UNION OF OFFICIAL TRAVEL ORGANISATIONS

Centre international
Place des Nations
Case postale 7
1211 Geneva 20
SWITZERLAND

INTERNATIONAL VINE AND WINE OFFICE

11 rue Roquépine
75-Paris 8e
FRANCE

INTERNATIONAL WHALING COMMISSION

Room 276
Great Westminister House
Horseferry Road
London SW1P 2AE
GREAT BRITAIN

INTERNATIONAL WHEAT COUNCIL

Haymarket House
28 Haymarket
London, SW1Y 4SS
GREAT BRITAIN

INTERNATIONAL WOOL STUDY GROUP

Department of trade and industry
Millbank Tower
London SW1
GREAT BRITAIN

INTERPARLIAMENTARY CONSULTATIVE COUNCIL OF BENELUX

Sénat
Palais de la Nation
1000 Brussels
BELGIUM

INTER-STATES SCHOOL FOR RURAL ENGINEERING

P.O.Box 139
Ouagadougou
UPPER VOLTA

INTER-UNIVERSITY COMMITTEE FOR EAST AFRICA

>P.O.Box 16002
>Kampala
>UGANDA

ITALIAN-LATIN AMERICAN INSTITUTE

>Piazza Guglielmo Marconi
>00144 Rome
>ITALY

JOINT INSTITUTE FOR NUCLEAR RESEARCH, DUBNA

>Head Post Office Box no.79
>Moscow
>UNION OF SOVIET SOCIALIST REPUBLICS

LAKE CHAD BASIN COMMISSION

>P.O.Box 727
>Fort Lamy
>CHAD

LATIN AMERICAN CENTER OF PHYSICS

>av. Wenceslau Braz 71
>Rio de Janeiro
>BRAZIL

LATIN AMERICAN EDUCATIONAL COMMUNICATION INSTITUTE

>Auditorio nacional
>Paseo de la reforma
>México 5, DF
>Apartado postal 18-862
>MEXICO 18 DF

LATIN AMERICAN FREE TRADE ASSOCIATION

>Cebollatí 1461
>Casilla de correo 577
>Montevideo
>URUGUAY

LATIN AMERICAN INSTITUTE FOR ECONOMIC AND SOCIAL PLANNING

>Edificio Naciones Unidas
>Avda Dag Hammarskjöld
>Casilla 1567
>Santiago de Chile
>CHILE

LEAGUE OF ARAB STATES

>Midan Al Tahrir
>Cairo
>ARAB REPUBLIC OF EGYPT

LIPTAKO-GOURMA REGION INTEGRATED DEVELOPMENT AUTHORITY

>Route de Fada N'Gourma
>P.O.Box 619
>Ouagadougou
>UPPER VOLTA

MAGHREB ESPARTO BUREAU

>Algiers
>ALGERIA

MAGHREB PERMANENT CONSULTATIVE COMMITTEE

>47 avenue Habib Bourguiba
>Tunis
>TUNISIA

MUTUAL AID AND LOAN GUARANTY FUND OF THE COUNCIL OF THE ENTENTE STATES

> P.O.Box 20824
> Abidjan
> IVORY COAST

MUTUAL ASSISTANCE OF THE LATIN AMERICAN GOVERNMENT OIL COMPANIES

> Casilla correos 1006
> Montevideo
> URUGUAY

NORDIC COUNCIL

> Secretariat of the Presidium
> Nordisk Rad
> Fack
> 103 10 Stockholm 2
> SWEDEN

NORTH ATLANTIC TREATY ORGANIZATION

> Brussels 1110
> BELGIUM

NORTH-EAST ATLANTIC FISHERIES COMMISSION

> Great Westminster House
> Horseferry Road
> London SW 1
> GREAT BRITAIN

NORTH PACIFIC FUR SEAL COMMISSION

c/o
> National Marine Fisheries Service
> Interior Building
> 18th and C St., N.W.
> Washington, D.C. 20240
> UNITED STATES OF AMERICA

ORGANISATION COMMUNE DAHOMEY-NIGER DES CHEMINS DE FER ET DES TRANSPORT

> P.O.Box 16
> Cotonou
> DAHOMEY

ORGANISATION COMMUNE DE LUTTE ANTIACRIDIENNE ET DE LUTTE ANTIAVIAIRE

> P.O.Box 1066
> Dakar
> SENEGAL

ORGANISATION FOR THE COLLABORATION OF RAILWAYS

> Hoza 63/67
> Warsaw
> POLAND

ORGANISATION FOR THE DEVELOPMENT OF AFRICAN TOURISM

> 6 rue Mesnil   BP 322
> 75-Paris 16e   or   Yaounde
> FRANCE   CAMEROON

ORGANISATION FOR THE DEVELOPMENT OF THE SENEGAL RIVER

> 5, Place de l'Indépendence
> Dakar
> SENEGAL

ORGANISATION OF SENEGAL RIPARIAN STATES

> BP 3152
> Dakar
> SENEGAL

ORGANIZATION FOR CO-ORDINATION AND CO-OPERATION IN THE CONTROL OF
MAJOR ENDEMIC DISEASES

>   BP 153
>   Bobo-Dioulasso
>   UPPER VOLTA

ORGANIZATION FOR CO-ORDINATION IN CONTROL OF ENDEMIC DISEASES IN
CENTRAL AFRICA

>   BP 288
>   Yaounde
>   CAMEROON

ORGANIZATION FOR ECONOMIC CO-OPERATION AND DEVELOPMENT

>   2 rue André-Pascal
>   Paris 16e
>   FRANCE

OECD has set up a Development enquiry service designed to provide, free of charge, information upon request, in various areas of economic development. This assistance is available to public and semi-public bodies as ministries, national banks, productivity agencies, training and research institutes, etc. It is not available to private firms. The service consists of:

- supplying documentation, bibliographies, copies of articles and other relevant material to further the decision-making process in economic development;
- indicating specialised institutions and experts;
- supplying information on conferences, meetings, courses and seminars.

Address:

>   Development enquiry service
>   OCED Development centre
>   91 Boulevard Exelmans
>   75-Paris 16e
>   FRANCE

Sales agents of the Organization for economic co-operation and development

Argentina	Libreria de la Naciones, Aisina 500, Buenos Aires
Australia	B.C.N. Agencies Pty, Ltd., 178 Collins Street, Melbourne 3000
Austria	Gerold and Co., Graben 31, Vienna 1
	Sub-agent: GRAZ, Buchhandlung Jos. A. Kienreich, Sackstrasse 6
Belgium	Librairie des Sciences, Coudenberg 76-78, B 1000 Bruxelles 1
Brazil	Mestre Jou S.A., Rua Guaipá 518, Caiza Postal 24090, 05000 Sao Paulo 10; Rua Senador Dantas 19 s/205-6, Rio de Janeiro GB
Canada	Information Canada, Ottawa
Denmark	Munksgaard Boghandel, Ltd., Nörregade 6, Copenhagen
Finland	Akateeminen Kirjakauppa, Keskuskatu 2, Helsinki
Formosa	Books and Scientific Supplies Services Ltd., P.O.B. 83, Taipei, Taiwan
France	Bureau des Publications de l'OCDE, 2 rue André Pascal, F 75 Paris 16
	Sub-agents:
	75 Paris: Presses Universitaires de France, 49 bd. Saint-Michel 5e
	Sciences Politiques (Lih) 30 rue Saint Guillaume, 7e
	13 Aix-en-Provence: Librairie de l'Université
	38 Grenoble: Arthaud
	67 Strasbourg: Berger-Levrault
	31 Toulouse: Privat
Germany	Deutscher Bundes-Verlag G.m.b.H., Postfach 9380, 53 Bonn
	Sub-agents:
	Berlin 62: Elwert & Meurer
	Hamburg: Reuter-Klöckner
Greece	Librairie Kauffmann, 28 rue du State, Athens 132; Librairie Internationale Jean Mihalopoulos et Fils, 75 rue Hermou, B.P. 73, Thessalonika
Iceland	Snaebjorn Jömsson and Co., h.f., Hafnarstraeti 9, P.O.B. 1131, Reykjavik
India	Oxford Book and Stationery Co. New Delhi, Seindia House, Calcutta, 17 Park Street
Ireland	Eason and Son, 40 Lower O'Connell Street, P.O.B. 42, Dublin 1
Israel	Emanuel Brown: 9, Shlomzion Hamalka Street, Jerusalem, 35 Allenby Road and 48 Nahlath Benjamin Street, Tel Aviv
Italy	Libreria Commissionaria Sansoni, Via Lamarmora 45, 50 121 Florence, Via Roncaglia 14, 2) 146 Milan.
	Sub-agents:
	Editrice e Libreria Herder, Piazza Montecitorio 120, 00 186 Rome
	Libreria Rizzoli, Largo Chigi 15, 00 187 Rome
	Librer ia Hoepli, Via Hoepli 5, 20 121 Milan
	Libreria Lattes, Via Garibaldi 3, 10 122 Turin

T

ORGANIZATION FOR ECONOMIC CO-OPERATION AND DEVELOPMENT (CONT'D)
Sales agents (cont'd)

Japan	Maruzen Company Ltd., 6 Tori-Nichome Nihonbashi, Tokyo 103
Lebanon	Redico, Immeuble Edison, Rue Bliss, B.P. 5641, Beyrouth
Netherlands	W.P. Van Stockum, Buitenhof 36, The Hague
	Sub-Agents:
	Amsterdam C: Scheltema and Holkema N.V. Rokin 74-76
	Rotterdam: De Wester Boekhandel, Nieuwe Binnenweg 331
New Zealand	Government Printing Office, Mulgrave Street (Private Bag), Wellington and Government bookshops at Auckland (P.O.B. 5344); Christchurch (P.O.B. 1721); Hamilton (P.O.B. 857); Dunedin (P.O.B. 1104)
Norway	Johan Grundt Tanums Bokhandel, Karl Johansgate 41/43, Oslo 1
Pakistan	Mirza Book Agency, 65 Shahrah Quaid-E-Azam, Lahore 3
Portugal	Livraria Portugal, Rua do Carmo 70, Lisbon
Spain	Mundi Prensa, Castelló 37, Madrid 1; Libreria Bastinos de José Bosch, Pelayo 52, Barcelona 1
Sweden	Fritzes, Kungl, Hovbokhandel, Fredsgatan 2, Stockholm 16
Switzerland	Librairie Payot, 6 rue Grenus, 1211 Geneve 11 and at Lausanne, Neuchatel, Vevey, Montreux, Berne, Bale, Zurich
Turkey	Librairie Hachette, 469 Istiklal Caddesi, Beyoglu, Istanbul and 12 Ziya Gókalp Caddesi, Ankara
United Kingdom	H.M. Stationery Office, P.O.B. 569, London, SE1 9NH
	Branches at:
	Edinburgh, Birmingham, Bristol, Manchester, Cardiff, Belfast
United States of America	OECD Publications Center, Suite 1207, 1750 Pennsylvania Ave., N.W. Washington, D.C. 20006
Venezuela	Libreria del Este, Avda F. Miranda 52, Edificio Galipan, Caracas
Yugoslavia	Jugoslovenska Knjiga, Terzije 27, P.O.B. 36, Belgrade
Other Countries	OECD Publications Office, 2 rue André-Pascal, 75-Paris 16e

ORGANIZATION OF AFRICAN UNITY

P.O.Box 3243
Addis Ababa
ETHIOPIA

ORGANIZATION OF AFRICAN UNITY.   SCIENTIFIC TECHNICAL AND RESEARCH COMMISSION

Private Mail Bag 2359
Lagos
NIGERIA

ORGANIZATION OF AMERICAN STATES

General Secretariat,
Washington, D.C. 20006
UNITED STATES OF AMERICA

ORGANIZATION OF ARAB PETROLEUM EXPORTING COUNTRIES

P.O.B. 20501
Al-Soor Street
KUWAIT

ORGANIZATION OF CENTRAL AMERICAN STATES

Officina Centroamericana
Pino Alto
Paseo Escalón
San Salvador
EL SALVADOR

ORGANIZATION OF THE PETROLEUM EXPORTING COUNTRIES

Dr. Karl Lueger-Ring 10
1010 Vienna
AUSTRIA

PAN AMERICAN HEALTH ORGANIZATION

525 Twenty-third Street N.W.
Washington D.C. 20037
UNITED STATES OF AMERICA

PAN AMERICAN HIGHWAY CONGRESSES

>Pan American union
>Washington D.C.
>UNITED STATES OF AMERICA

PAN AMERICAN INSTITUTE OF GEOGRAPHY AND HISTORY

>Ex-Arzobispado 29
>Mexico 18 DF
>MEXICO

PERMANENT COUNCIL OF THE INTERNATIONAL CONVENTION FOR THE USE OF
APPELLATIONS OF ORIGIN AND DENOMINATIONS OF CHEESES

>c/o   Ministry of Agriculture
>URI
>18 via XX Settembre
>00100 Rome
>ITALY

PERMANENT COURT OF ARBITRATION

>Palais de la Paix
>The Hague
>NETHERLANDS

PERMANENT INTERNATIONAL ASSOCIATION OF ROAD CONGRESSES

>43 avenue du Président Wilson
>75-Paris 16e
>FRANCE

PERMANENT INTERNATIONAL BUREAU OF ANALYTICAL CHEMISTRY OF HUMAN AND
ANIMAL FOOD

>24 rue de Téhéran
>75-Paris 8e
>FRANCE

PICTURE AND SOUND WORLD ORGANISATION

>BP 449
>6600 Locarno
>SWITZERLAND

PLANT PROTECTION COMMITTEE FOR THE SOUTH EAST ASIA AND PACIFIC REGION

>FAO Regional office
>Maliwan Mansion
>Phra Atit Road
>Bangkok
>THAILAND

POSTAL UNION OF THE AMERICAS AND SPAIN

>Calle Buenos Aires 495
>Montevideo
>URUGUAY

REGIONAL CO-OPERATION FOR DEVELOPMENT

>5 Vassal Shirazi
>North of Boulevard
>P.O.B. 3273
>Teheran
>IRAN

REGIONAL INTERNATIONAL ORGANISATION OF PLANT PROTECTION AND ANIMAL
HEALTH

>63 Avenida Norte 130
>Apdo Postal 1654
>San Salvador
>EL SALVADOR

THE RIVER NIGER COMMISSION

P.O.Box 729
Niamey
NIGER

SENEGAMBIA PERMANENT SECRETARIAT

4 Marina Street
Bathurst
GAMBIA

SOCIETE DE DEVELOPPEMENT HOTELIER ET TOURISTIQUE DE L'AFRIQUE DE L'OUEST

P.O.Box 1545
Abidjan
IVORY COAST

SOUTH-EAST ASIA TREATY ORGANIZATION

P.O.Box 517
Bangkok
THAILAND

SOUTH-EAST ASIAN MINISTERS OF EDUCATION SECRETARIAT

Darakarn Bldg
920 Sukhumwit Road
Bangkok 11
THAILAND

SOUTH PACIFIC AIR TRANSPORT COUNCIL

c/o   Ministry for civil aviation
Melbourne
Victoria 3000
AUSTRALIA

SOUTH PACIFIC COMMISSION

Post Box 9
Nouméa
NEW CALEDONIA

SOUTH WEST ATLANTIC FISHERIES ADVISORY COMMISSION

Rua do Jardim Botanico 1008
Rio de Janeiro
BRAZIL

SPECIAL CONSULTATIVE COMMITTEE ON SECURITY

see   Organization of American States

SPECIALIZED CONFERENCE ON THE APPLICATION OF SCIENCE AND TECHNOLOGY TO LATIN AMERICAN DEVELOPMENT

see   Organization of American States

STANDING TECHNICAL SECRETARIAT FOR THE CONFERENCES OF MINISTERS OF NATIONAL EDUCATION IN FRENCH-SPEAKING AFRICAN AND MALAGASY STATES

B.P. 4025
Dakar
SENEGAL

STATISTICAL OFFICE OF THE EUROPEAN COMMUNITIES

Centre Louvigny   Bâtiment Berlaymont (Liaison office)
P.O.Box 130   or   rue de la Loi 200
LUXEMBOURG   1040 Brussels
                           BELGIUM

TANZANIA-ZAMBIA RAILWAY AUTHORITY

>Dar-es-Salaam
>TANZANIA

TAZAMA PIPELINE LTD

>Tazama House
>Buteko avenue
>P.O.Box 1651
>Ndola
>ZAMBIA

TRANS-AFRICAN HIGHWAY CO-ORDINATION COMMITTEE

>ECA
>P.O.Box 3001
>Addis Ababa
>ETHIOPIA

TRANS-SAHARA ROAD COMMITTEE

>Ministry of public works
>135 rue Didouche Mourade
>Algiers
>ALGERIA

TRIPARTITE COMMISSION FOR THE RESTITUTION OF MONETARY GOLD

>9 rue de la Science
>Brussels
>BELGIUM

TRIPARTITE COMMISSION ON THE WORKING CONDITIONS OF RHINE BOATMEN

>Palais du Rhin
>67-Strasbourg
>FRANCE

UNION DOUANIERE ET ECONOMIQUE DE L'AFRIQUE CENTRALE

>P.O.Box 946
>Bangui
>CENTRAL AFRICAN REPUBLIC

UNION OF CENTRAL AFRICAN STATES

>BP 873
>Bangui
>CENTRAL AFRICAN REPUBLIC

UNITED NATIONS

UNITED NATIONS. SECRETARIAT (HEADQUARTERS)

>New York
>N.Y. 10017
>UNITED STATES OF AMERICA

UNITED NATIONS OFFICE AT GENEVA

>Palais des Nations
>1211 Geneva 10
>SWITZERLAND

MAIN ORGANS:

General assembly	H.Q. New York
Economic and social council	H.Q. New York
Security council	H.Q. New York
Trusteeship council	H.Q. New York

UNITED NATIONS

REGIONAL ECONOMIC COMMISSIONS

Economic commission for Africa
Addis Ababa
ETHIOPIA

Economic commission for Asia and the Far East
Santitham Hall
Rajadamnern Avenue
Bangkok
THAILAND

Economic commission for Europe
UN Office at Geneva

Economic commission for Latin America
Edificio Naciones Unidas
Avenida Dag Hammarskjold
Santiago de Chile
CHILE

OTHER UNITED NATIONS ADDRESSES

Administrative committee on co-ordination	H.Q. New York
Advisory committee on administrative and budgetary questions	H.Q. New York
Centre for development planning, projections and policies	H.Q. New York
Centre for economic and social information	UN Office at Geneva
Dag Hammarskjold library	H.Q. New York
Disarmament commission, Headquarters	H.Q. New York
Federation of international civil servants associations	H.Q. New York
Interim commission for the International trade organization	see GATT
International bureau for declarations of death	UN Office at Geneva
International law commission	H.Q. New York
International narcotics control board	UN Office at Geneva
Inter-organization board for information systems and related activities	UN Office at Geneva
Israel-Syria mixed armistice commission	H.Q. New York
Military staff committee secretariat	H.Q. New York

Office of the Special representative of the Secretary-general in Amman

UN Mission in Amman
P.O.Box 1298
General Post Office
Amman
JORDAN

Oficina para la America Latina del alto comisionado de las Naciones Unidas para los refugiados

Carrera 13
No. 45-67
Bogotá
COLOMBIA

OTHER UNITED NATIONS ADDRESSES (CONT'D)

Security council committee on the admission of new members	H.Q. New York
Special committee on peace-keeping operations	H.Q. New York
United Nations capital development fund	see UNDP
United Nations cartographic office (former: Central bureau of the international map of the world on the millionth scale.)	H.Q. New York

United Nations commission for the unification and rehabilitation of Korea

APO San Francisco 96301
California 96301
UNITED STATES OF AMERICA

United Nations commission on international trade law	H.Q. New York
United Nations conciliation commission for Palestine	H.Q. New York
United Nations development programme	H.Q. New York
United Nations disaster relief office	UN Office at Geneva
United Nations environment programme	UN Office at Geneva
United Nations fund for drug abuse control	UN Office at Geneva
United Nations High Commissioner for refugees	UN Office at Geneva
United Nations Library, Geneva	UN Office at Geneva

United Nations Middle East mission

UNMEM
P.O.Box 2324
Nicosia
CYPRUS

United Nations military observer group in India and Pakistan
and Pakist

Faridkot House Lytton Road New Delhi or INDIA	Ayub Mansion Ayub Hill Jellum Road Rawalpandi PAKISTAN

United Nations office for science and technology H.Q. New York or UN Office at Geneva

United Nations peace-keeping force in Cyprus

P.O.Box 1642
Nicosia
CYPRUS

United Nations relief and works agency for Palestine refugees in the Near East

Museitbeh Quarter
Beirut
LEBANON

United Nations truce supervision organization in Palestine

P.O.Box 490
Jerusalem
ISRAEL

United Nations volunteers programme	UN Office at Geneva

UNITED NATIONS INFORMATION CENTRES

Accra — United Nations Information Centre, Liberia and Maxwell Roads, (P.O. Box 2339) Accra Ghana

Addis Ababa — Information Service, United Nations Economic Commission for Africa, (P.O.Box 3001), Addis Ababa, Ethiopia

Algiers — United Nations Information Centre, 19 avenue Claude Debussy, (P.O.Box 803), Algiers, Algeria

Asuncion — Centro de Información de las Naciones Unidas, Calle Coronel Bogado 871, (Casilla de Correo 1107), Asunción, Paraguay.

Athens — United Nations Information Centre, 36 Amalia Avenue, Athens 119, Greece

Baghdad — United Nations Information Centre, 27J.2/1 Abu Nouwas Street, Bataween (P.O.Box 2048 Alwiyah), Baghdad, Iraq

Bangkok — Information Service, United Nations Economic Commission for Asia and the Far East, Sala Santitham, Bangkok, Thailand

Beirut — United Nations Information Centre, United Nations Building (ex Grand Traveaux), Bir Hassan, (P.O.Box 4656), Beirut, Lebanon

Belgrade — United Nations Information Centre, Svetozara Markovica 58, (P.O.Box 157), Belgrade, Yugoslavia

Bogotá — Centro de Información de las Naciones Unidas, Calle 19, Número 7-30 (Séptimo Piso), (Apartado Postal 6567), Bogotá, Colombia

Bucharest — United Nations Information Centre, 16 rue Aurel Vlaicu, Bucharest, Romania

Buenos Aires — Centro de Información de las Naciones Unidas, Charcas 684 (Tercer Piso), Buenos Aires, Argentina

Bujumbura — Centre d'Information des Nations Unies, Avenue de la Poste et Place Jungers, (Boîte Postale 1490), Bujumbura, Burundi

Cairo — United Nations Information Centre, Sh. Osoris, Tagher Building (Garden City), (Boîte Postale 262), Cairo, United Arab Republic

Colombo — United Nations Information Centre, 204 Buller's Road, (P.O.Box 1505), Colombo 7, Ceylon

Copenhagen — United Nations Information Centre, 37 H.C. Andersen's Boulevard, DK-1553 Copenhagen V, Denmark

Dakar — Centre d'Information des Nations Unies, 2 avenue Roume, (Boîte Postale 154), Dakar, Senegal

Dar es Salaam — United Nations Information Centre, Matasalamat Building (P.O.Box 9224), Dar es Salaam, United Republic of Tanzania

Geneva — Information Service, United Nations Office at Geneva, Palais des Nations, 1211 Geneva 10, Switzerland

Kabul — United Nations Information Centre, Shah Mahmoud Ghazi Watt (P.O.Box 5), Kabul, Afghanistan

Karachi — United Nations Information Centre, Havelock Road, (P.O.Box 349 G.P.O.), Karachi 1, Pakistan

Kathmandu — United Nations Information Centre, Lainchaur, Lazimpat, (P.O.Box 107), Kathmandu, Nepal

Khartoum — United Nations Information Centre, House No, 9, Block 6.5.D.E., Nejumi Street, (P.O.Box 1992), Khartoum, Sudan

Kinshasa — Centre d'Information des Nations Unies, Le Royal, Boulevard du 30 Juin, (Boîte Postale 7248), Zaire

Lagos — United Nations Information Centre, 17 Kingsway Road, Ikoyi, (P.O.Box 1068), Lagos, Nigeria

La Paz — Centro de Información de las Naciones Unidas, Avenida Arce No. 2419, (Apartado Postal 686), La Paz, Bolivia

Lima — Centro de Información de las Naciones Unidas, Avenida Arequipa 3330, San Isidro, (Apartado Postal 4480), Lima, Peru

Lomé — Centre d'Information des Nations Unies, Rue Albert Sarraut, Coin Avenue de Gaulle, (Boîte Postale 911), Lomé, Togo

London — United Nations Information Centre, 14/15, Stratford Place, London W1N 9AF, Great Britain

Manila — United Nations Information Centre, WHO Building, United Nations Avenue at Taft Avenue, (P.O.Box 2149), Manila, Philippines

Mexico City — Centro de Información de las Naciones Unidas, Hamburgo 63 (Tercer Piso), Mexico 6, D.F., Mexico

Monrovia — United Nations Information Centre, ULRC Building, (P.O.Box 274), Monrovia, Liberia

Moscow — United Nations Information Centre, No.4/16 Ulitsa Lunacharskogo 1, Moscow, USSR

New Delhi — United Nations Information Centre, 1 Barakhamba Road, New Delhi, India

Paris — Centre d'Information des Nations Unies, 1 rue Miollis, 75 Paris 15e, France

Port Moresby — United Nations Information Centre, Hunter Street, Port Moresby, Papua and New Guinea

Port of Spain — United Nations Information Centre, 19 Keate Street, (P.O.Box 812), Port of Spain, Trinidad and Tobago

UNITED NATIONS INFORMATION CENTRES (CONT'D)

Prague	United Nations Information Centre, Panska 5, Praha 1, Czechoslovakia
Rabat	Centre d'Information des Nations Unies, Angle Avenue Urbain Blanc et rue de Nimes, (Boîte Postale 524), Rabat, Morocco
Rangoon	United Nations Information Centre, 132 University Avenue, Rangoon, Burma
Rio de Janeiro	United Nations Information Centre, Apt. 201, Cruz Lima Street, No. 19, Rio de Janeiro, Brazil
Rome	United Nations Information Centre, Palazzetto Venezia, Piazza San Marco 50, Rome, Italy
San Salvador	Centro de Información de las Naciones Unidas, Avenida Roosevelt 2818, (Apartado Postal 1114), San Salvador, El Salvador
Santiago	Information Service, United Nations Economic Commission for Latin America, Edificio Naciones Unidas, Avenida Dag Hammarskjold, Santiago, Chile
Sydney	United Nations Information Centre, London Assurance Building, 20 Bridge Street, (P.O.Box R 226), Royal Exchange, Sydney 2000, Australia
Tananarive	Centre d'Information des Nations Unies, 26 rue de Liège, (Boîte Postale 1348), Tananarive, Madagascar
Teheran	United Nations Information Centre, Off Takhte Jamshid, 12 Kh. Bandar Pahlavi, (P.O.Box 1555), Teheran, Iran
Tokyo	United Nations Information Centre, Room 411/412, New Ohtemachi Building, 2-1, Ohtemachi 2-chome, Chiyoda-ku, Tokyo, Japan
Tunis	Centre d'Information des Nations Unies, 61 Boulevard Bab Benat, (Boîte Postale 863), Tunis, Tunisia
Washington	United Nations Information Centre, Suite 714, 1028 Connecticut Avenue, N.W. Washington, D.C. 20006, U.S.A.
Yaounde	Centre d'Information des Nations Unies, (Boîte Postale 836), Yaoundé, Cameroon

Sales agents of the United Nations and the International Court of Justice

AFRICA

Algérie	Société nationale d'édition et de diffusion, 3 Bd. Zirout Youcef, Alger
Congo (Rép. démocratique)	Institut national d'études politiques, 39 av. Ch.-de-Gaulle, B.P. 2307, Kinshasa
Ethiopie	Menno Bookstore, P.O.Box 1236, Addis-Ababa
Ghana	University Bookshop, P.O.Box 1, Legon, Accra
Kenya	E.S.A. Bookshop, P.O.Box 30167, Nairobi
Maroc	Editions Laporte "Aux Belles Images", 281 av. Mohammed-V, Rabat
Mozambique	Livraria Academia, Rua Joaquim Lapa, 47, Lourenço Marques
Nigeria	University Bookshop, Nigeria Ltd., University College, Ibadan C.S.S. Bookshops, 50 Yakubu Gowom Street, P.O.Box 174, Lagos Modern University Bookshop Ltd., Private Mail Bag 12003, Lagos University of Lagos Bookshop, University of Lagos, AKOKA-YABA
Ouganda	Uganda Bookshop, P.O.Box 145, Kampala; E.S.A. Bookshop, P.O.Box 2615, Kampala
République arabe unie	Saladine Publications Inc. 28 Talat Harb St., Le Caire
République sud-africaine	Van Schaik's Bookstore (Pty) Ltd., Church Street, P.O.Box 724, Pretoria WM. Dawson and Sons S.A. (Pty) Ltd., P.O.Box 87, Cape Town Universitas Periodicals (Pty) Ltd., P.O.Box 775, Pretoria
République-Unie de Tanzanie	Dar-es-Salaam Bookshop, P.O.Box 9030, Dar-es-Salaam
Rhodésie du Sud	The Book Center, Gordon Ave., Salisbury; Textbook Sales Pty, Ltd., Box 3799, Salisbury
Sénégal	La Maison du Livre, 13 av. Roume, B.P. 2060, Dakar; Librairie universitaire, 26 av. William-Ponty, B.P. 390, Dakar
Soudan	Abdelmoneim Publishing Company, Abdelmoneim Bldg., UN Square, Khartoum

ASIA

Cambodge	Entreprise Khmère de Librairie, Imprimerie & Papeterie Sarl., Phnom-Penh
Ceylan	Lake House Bookshop, Assoc. Newspapers of Ceylon, P.O.Box 244, Colombo
Chine	The World Book Company, Ltd., 99 Chung King Road, 1st Section, Taipeh, Taiwan; The Commercial Press, Ltd., 211 Honan Road, Shanghai
Corée (Rép de)	Eul-Yoo Publishing Co., Ltd., 5, 2-KA, Chongno, Seoul
Hong-kong	The Swindon Book Company, 25 Nathan Road, Kowloon
Inde	Orient Longmans, Calcutta, Bombay, Madras, New Delhi, Hyderabad; Oxford Book & Stationery Company, New Delhi and Calcutta
Japon	Maruzen Company, Ltd., 6 Tori-Nichome Nihonbashi, Tokyo
Pakistan	The Pakistan Co-operative Book Society, Dacca, East Pakistan; Publishers United, Ltd., Lahore

UNITED NATIONS (CONT'D)
Sales agents (cont'd)

Philippines   Philippine Education Company, Inc., 1104 Castillejos, P.O.Box 620,
              Quiapo, Manilla; Popular Bookstore, 1573 Doroteo Jose, Manilla
Singapour   The City Book Store, Ltd., Collyer Quay
Thailand   Nibondh and Co. Ltd., New Road, Sikak Phya Sri, Bangkok;
              Suksapan Panit, Mansion 9, Rajadamnern Avenue, Bangkok
Viet-nam   Librairie-Papeterie Xuan Thu, 185 rue Tu-do, B.P. 283, Saigon
(Rép. du)

EUROPE

Allemagne   Alexander Horn, Spiegelgasse 9, 6200 Wiesbaden; R. Eisenschmidt,
(Rép. Féd.)   Postfach 700306, 6 Frankfurt Main 70; Elwert und Meurer, Haupt-
              strasse 101, D-1000 Berlin 62; W.E. Saarbach, GmbH, Föllerstrasse 2, Koeln
Allemagne   Deutscher Buch Export und Import, GmbH, Leninstrasse 16, Leipzig C 1
(Rép. Dém)
Autriche   Gerold & Co., Graben 31, Vienne; Osterreichische Kommissionsbuch-
              hundlung, Maximilianstrasse 17, Innsbruck; Alpenverlag-Buchhandlung,
              Rudolfskai, 2, 5020 Salzburg-Rathaus.
Belgique   Vander éditeur, 10 Muntstraat, Louvain; Agence et Messageries de la
              Presse S.A., 1 rue de la Petite-Ile, Bruxelles 7; Smith and Son, English
              Bookshop, 71 bd. Adolphe-Max, Bruxelles; Office international de librairie,
              30 av. Marnix, Bruxelles
Chypre   Pan Publishing House, P.O.Box 1209, Strovolos, Nicosia
Danemark   Ejnar Munksgaard Ltd., 6 Nöregarde, Copenhague K
Espagne   Librería José Bosch, 11 Ronda Universidad, Barcelone 7; Librería Mundi
              Prensa, Castelló 27, Madrid 1; Librería La Enseñanza Católica, Avda
              de las Universidades, Aptdo 1, Bilbao
Finlande   Akaateeminen Kirjakauppa 2, Keskuskatu, Helsinki
France   Editions A. Pedone, 13 rue Soufflot, 75 Paris Ve; Librairie de l'Université,
              12a rue Nazareth, Aix-en-Provence; Librairie René Giard, 2 rue Royale, Lille;
              Office international de documentation et de librairie, 48 rue Gay-Lussac,
              75-Paris Ve.
Grande-   H.M. Stationery Office, 49 High Holborn, London W.C.1. (London post
Bretagne   orders: P.O.Box 569, London S.E. 1.); Blackwell's, Broad Street, Oxford
Grèce   Librairie Kauffmann, 28 rue du Stade, Athènes; G.C. Eleftheroudakis Int.,
              4 Nikis Street, Athènes
Hongrie   Kultura, P.O.Box 149, Budapest 62
Islande   Bokaverzlun Sigfusar, Eymondssonar, Reykjavik; Snaebjor Jonsson, English
              Bookshop, Reykjavik
Italie   Libreria Commissionaria Sansoni, Via Lamarmora 45, 50121 Florence;
              Piazza Montecitoria 121, 00186 Rome; A.E.I.O.U., Book Trade Co., Via
              Meravigli 16, Milan; D.E.A. Diffusione, Edizione Anglo-Americane, Via Lima 28,
              Rome; Libreria Int. Di Stefano S.p.a., Via R. Ceccardi, Gênes.
Luxembourg   Librairie du Centre, 49 bd. Royal, "Royal Center", Luxembourg
Norway   Johan Grundt Tanum, Karl Johansgt, 43, Oslo
Pays-Bas   N.V. Martinus Nijhoff, Lange Voorhout 9, La Haye; Meulenhoff-Bruna N.V.,
              Box 197, Beulingstraat 2, Amsterdam; Swetz und Zeitlinger, Keizersgracht 487,
              Rotterdam
Pologne   Ars Polona, Krakowskie, Przedmiescie 7, Varsovie
Portugal   Livraria Rodrigues, Rua Aurea 186, Lisbonne; Teixeira A.M. Co. Livraria
              Classica Editora, Praça dos Restauradores 17, Lisbonne; Livraria Buchholz Lda.,
              Rua Duque de Palmela 4, Lisbonne
Roumanie   Cartimex, P.O.Box 134/135, 126 Calea Victoriei, Bucarest
Suède   C.E. Fritzes Kungl. Hovbokhandel, Fredsgatan 2, Stockholm
Suisse   Librairie Payot 6 rue Grenus, 1211 Genève; Librairie Hans Raunhardt,
              17 Kirchgasse 8000 Zurich; Schweizer Buchzentrum (Centre suisse du livre,
              Coopérative des Libraires suisses), 4600 Olten; Buchhandlung R. Blum,
              Totentanz 10, 4000 Basel
Tchécoslovaquie Artia Ltd., 30 Ve Smeckack, Prague 2
Turquie   Librairie Hachette, 469 Istiklal Caddesi, Istanbul; V. Vecibi Görk Librairie,
              P.O.Box 227-Beyoglu, Istanbul
URSS   Mezhdunarodnaya Knyiga, Smolenskaya Ploshchad, Moscou
Yougoslavie   Cankarjeva Zalozba, P.O.Box 201 Ljubljana; Mladost, Illica 30m, Zagreb;
              Jugoslovenska Knjiga, Terazije 27/11, Belgrade; Prosveta Export Import
              Agency, 16 Terazije, Belgrade

UNITED NATIONS (CONT'D)

Sales agents (cont'd)

LATIN AMERICA

Argentine	Editorial Sudamericana, S.A. Alsina 500, Buenos Aires
Bolivie	Liberia Selecciones, Casilla 972, La Paz; Los Amigos del Libro, Calle Perú esq. España, Casilla 450, Cochabamba
Brésil	Livraria Agir, Rua Mexico 98-B, Caixa Postal 3291, Rio de Janeiro; Livraria Freitas Bastos, S.A., Caixa Postal 899, Rio de Janeiro; Livraria Kosmos Editora, Rua Rosario 135/137, Rio de Janeiro
Chili	Editoral del Pacifico, Ahumada 57, Santiago
Colombie	Libreria America, Calle 51, Núm. 49-58, Medellin; Libreria Buchholz, Av. Jiménez de Quesada 8-40, Bogotá
Costa Rica	Imprenta y Libreria Trejos, Apartado 1313, San José
Cuba	Cubartimpex, Apartado Postal 6540, La Habana

MIDDLE EAST

Iran	Irania A. Distr. Agency, 151 Khiaban Soraya, Téhéran
Iraq	Mackenzie's Bookshop, Al Rashid Str. Baghdad
Israël	Emanuel Brown, 35 Allenby Road, P.O.Box 4101, Tel Aviv
Jordanie	Jordan International Publishing and Distributing Co., P.O.Box 2126, Amman
Koweit	Khayat Kuwait Printing Publishing and Distributing Co. Koweit
Liban	Dar al Maaref S.a.L., Lufti at Alla, place Riad-el-Solh, Beirut
Syrie	Librairie Atlas, Salhieh Street, Damas; Librarie Sayegh, Immeuble Diad, rue du Parlement, Damas

NORTH AMERICA

Canada	The Queen's Printer/L'Imprimerie de la Reine, Ottawa, Ontario
Etas-Unis d'Amérique	Sales section, United Nations, New York UNIPUB, Inc., P.O.Box 433, New York, N.Y. 10016
Porto Rico	Pan American Book Co., P.O.Box 3511, San Juan 17; Bookstore, University of Puerto Rico, Rio Piedras

OCEANIA

Australie	UN Association of Australia, McEwan House, 343 Little Collins St., Melbourne, C.1, Vic; Wea Bookroom, University, Adelaide, S.A., University Bookshop, St. Lucia, Brisbane, Qld.; The Educational and Technical Book Agency, Parap Shopping Centre, Darwin, N.T.; Collins Book Depot Pty. Ltd., Monash University, Wellington Road, Clayton, Vic.; Collins Book Depot Pty. Ltd., 363 Swanston Street, Melbourne; Vic.; The University Bookshop, Nedlands, W.A., University Bookroom, University of Melbourne, Parville N.2, Vic.; University Co-operative Bookshop Limited, Manning Road, University of Sydney, N.S.W.
Nouvelle-Zélande	Government Printing Office, Private Bag, Wellington (and Government Bookshops in Auckland, Christchurch and Dunedin)

United Nations publications may be obtained from bookstores and distributors throughout the world. Consult your bookstore or write to United Nations, Sales Section New York or Geneva

WEST INDIES

Bermudes	Bermuda Book Stores, Reid and Burnaby Streets, Hamilton
Curaçao	Boekhandel Salas, P.O.Box 33
Guyane britannique	Bookers Stores Ltd., 20-23 Church Street, Georgetown
Jamaïque	Sangsters Book Room, 91 Harbour Street, Kingston
Trinité-et-Tobago	Cambell Booker Ltd., Port of Spain

UNITED NATIONS CHILDREN'S FUND

UN Office at Geneva

UNITED NATIONS CONFERENCE ON TRADE AND DEVELOPMENT

UN Office at Geneva or H.Q. New York

UNITED NATIONS EDUCATIONAL, SCIENTIFIC AND CULTURAL ORGANISATION

9 Place de Fontenoy
75 Paris 7e
FRANCE

Sales agents for the United Nations educational, scientific and cultural organisation

Argentina	Editorial Losada, S.A., Alsina 1131, Buenos Aires
Australia	Publications: Educational Supplies Pty., Ltd., Box 33, Post Office, Brookvale 2100, N.S.W.; Periodicals: Dominie Pty. Ltd., Box 33, Post Office, Brookvale 2100, N.S.W. Sub-agent: United Nations Association of Australia, Victorian Division, 4th Floor, Askew House, 364 Lonsdale St., Melbourne (Victoria) 3000.
Austria	Verlag Georg Fromme & Co., Arbeitergasse 1-7, 1051 Wien
Belgium	Jean de Lannoy, 112 rue du Trône, Bruxelles 5
Bolivia	Libreria Universitaria, Universidad San Francisco Xavier, apartado 212, Sucre
Brazil	Fundaçao Getúlio Vargas, Servico de Publicaçoes, caixa postal 21120 Praia de Botafogo 188, Rio de Janeiro, G.B.
Bulgaria	Hemus, Kantora Literatura, bd. Rousky 6, Sofija
Burma	Trade Corporation no.(9), 550-552, Merchant Street, Rangoon
Cameroon	Librairie Richard, B.P. 4017, Yaoundé
Canada	Information Canada, Ottawa (Ont)
Ceylon	Lake House Bookshop, Sir Chittampalam Gardiner Mawata, P.O.Box 244, Colombo 2
Chile	Editorial Universitaria, S.A., casilla 10220, Santiago
Colombia	Liberia Buccholz Galería, avenida Jiménez de Quesada 8-40, apartado aéreo 49-56, Bogotá: Distrilibros Ltd., Pío Alfonso García, carrera 4ª, nos. 36-119 y 36-125, Cartagena; J. Germán Rodríguez N., Calle 17, 6-59, apartado nacional 83, Girardot (Cundinamarca). Editorial Losada Ltd., Calle 18A, no. 7-37, apartado aéreo 5829, apartado nacional 931, Bogotá. Sub-depots: Edificio La Ceiba, Oficina 804, Medellín Calle 37, no. 14-73 Oficina, 305, Bucaramanga; Edificio Zaccour, Oficina 736, Cali.
Congo (People's Rep. of)	Librarie populaire. B.P. 577, Brazzaville
Costa Rica	Librería Trejos S.A., apartado 1313, San José
Cuba	Distribuidora Nacional de Publicaciones, Neptuno 674, La Habana
Cyprus	'MAM', Archbishop Makarios 3rd Avenue, P.O.Box 1722, Nicosia
Czechoslovakia	SNTL, Spalena 51, Praha 1 (Permanent display); Zahranicni literatura, 11 Soukenicka, Praha 1. For Slovakia only: Nakladatelstvo Alfa, Hurbanovo nam 6, Bratislava
Dahomey	Librairie nationale, B.P. 294, Porto Novo
Denmark	Ejnar Munksgaard Ltd., 6 Norregade, 1165 Kobenhavn K
Arab Republic of Egypt	Librairie Kasr El Nil, 38, rue Kasr El Nil, Le Caire. National Centre for Unesco Publications, 1 Tlaaat Harb Street, Tahrir Square, Cairo
Ethiopia	National Commission for Unesco, P.O.Box 2996, Addis Ababa
Finland	Akateeminen Kirjakauppa, 2 Keskuskatu, Helsinki
France	Librairie de l'Unesco, place de Fontenoy, 75 Paris 7e CCP 12508-48
French West Indies	Librairie Félix Conseil, 11 rue Perrinon, Port-de-France (Martinique)
Germany (Fed. Republic)	Verlag Dokumentation, Postfach 148, Jaiserstrasse 13, 8023, München-Pullach. 'The Courier' (German edition only): Bahrenfelder Chausse 160, Hamburg-Bahrenfeld, CCP 27 66 50
Ghana	Presbyterian Bookshop Depot Ltd., P.O.Box 195, Accra; Ghana Book Suppliers Ltd., P.O.Box 7869, Accra; The University Bookshop of Ghana, Accra; The University Bookshop of Cape Coast; The University Bookshop of Legon, P.O.Box 1, Legon
Greece	Librairie H. Kauffmann, 28 rue du Stade, Athenai; Librairie Eleftheroudakis, Nikkis 4, Athenai
Hong Kong	Swindon Book Co., 13-15 Lock Road, Kowloon
Hungary	Akadémiai Könyvesbolt Váci u 22, Budapest V; A.K.V. Könyvtárosok Boltja, Népköztársaság utja 16, Budapest VI
Iceland	Snaebjörn Jonsson & Co., H.F. Hafnarstracti 9, Reykjavik
India	Orient Longmans Ltd., Nicol Road, Ballard Estate, Bombay 1; 17 Chittaranjan Avenue, Calcutta 13; 36a Mount Road, Madras 2; 3/5 Asaf Ali Road, New Delhi 1: Sub-depots: Oxford Book & Stationery Co., 17 Park Street, Calcutta 16 and Scindia House New Delhi: Publications Section, Ministry of Education and Youth Services, 72 Theatre Communication Building, Connaught Place, New Delhi 1

UNESCO (CONT'D)

Sales agents for UNESCO publications: (cont'd)

Indonesia	Indira P.T., Djl. Dr. Sam Ratulangic 37, Djakarta
Iran	Commission nationale iranienne pour l'Unesco, 1/154, avenue Roosevelt, B.P. 1533, Téhéran
Iraq	McKenzie's Bookshop, Al-Rashid Street, Baghdad; University Bookstore, University of Baghdad, P.O.Box 75, Baghdad
Ireland	The National Press, 2 Wellington Road, Ballsbridge, Dublin 4
Israel	Emanuel Brown, formerly Blumstein's Bookstores: 35 Allenby Road and 48 Nachlat Benjamin Street, Tel Aviv; 9 Shlomzion Hamalka Street, Jerusalem
Italy	LICOSA (Libreria Commissionaria Sansoni S.p.A.), via Lamarmora 45, casella postale 552, 50121 Firenze
Jamaica	Sangster's Book Stores Ltd., P.O.Box 366, 101 Water Lane, Kingston
Japan	Maruzen Co. Ltd., P.O.Box 5050, Tokyo International, Tokyo
Kenya	The ESA Ltd., P.O.Box 30167, Nairobi
Khmer Republic	Librarie Albert Portail, 14 avenue Boulloche, Phnom-Penh
Korea	Korean National Commission for Unesco, P.O.Box Central 64, Seoul
Kuwait	The Kuwait Bookshop C. Ltd., P.O.Box 2942, Kuwait
Liberia	Cole & Yancy Bookshops Ltd., P.O.Box 286, Monrovia
Libya	Agency for Development of Publication and Distribution, P.O.Box 34-35, Tripoli
Luxembourg	Librairie Paul Bruck, 22 Grande-Rue, Luxembourg
Malaysia	Federal Publications Sdn. Bhd., Balai Berita, 31 Jalan Riong, Kuala Lumpur
Malta	Sapienza's Library, 26 Kingsway, Valletta
Mauritius	Nalanda Co. Ltd., 30 Bourbon Street, Port Louis
Mexico	CILA (Centro Interamericano de Libros Académicos), Sullivan 31 bis, México 4, DF
Monaco	British Library, 30 boulevard des Moulins, Monte-Carlo
Netherlands	N.V. Martinus Nijhoff, Lange Voorhout 9, 's-Gravenhage
Netherlands Antilles	G.C.T. Van Dorp & Co., (Ned.Ant), N.V. Willemstad (Curaçao, N.A.)
New Caledonia	Reprex S.A.R.L., B.P. 1572, Nouméa
New Zealand	Government Printing Office, Government Bookshops: Rutland Street, P.O.Box 5344, Auckland; 130 Oxford Terrace, P.O.Box 1721, Christchurch; Alma Street, P.O.Box 857, Hamilton; Princes Street, P.O.Box 1104, Dunedin; Mulgrave Street, Private Bag, Wellington
Niger	Librairie Manclert, B.P. 868, Niamey
Nigeria	The University Bookshop of Ife; The University Bookshop of Ibadan, P.O.Box 286 Ibadan; The University of Nsukka; The University Bookshop of Lagos; The Ahmadu Bello University Bookshop of Zaria
Norway	All publications: Johan Grundt Tanum (Booksellers), Karl Johansgate 43, Oslo 1. 'The Courier' only: A/S Narvesens Litteraturjeneste, Box 6125, Oslo 6
Pakistan	The West-Pak Publishing Co. Ltd., Unesco Publications House, P.O.box 374, G.P.O. Lahore: Showrooms: Urdu Bazaar, Lahore and 57-58 Muree Highway, G/6-1, Islamabad. Pakistan Publications Bookshop Sarwar Road, Rawalpindi; Paribagh, Dacca
Peru	'The Courier' only: Editorial Losada Peruana, apartado 472, Lima. Other publications: Distribuidora Inca S.A., Emilio Althaus, 470, Lince, casilla 3115, Lima
Philippines	The Modern Book Co., 926 Rizal Avenue, P.O.Box 632, Manila
Poland	Osrodek Rozpowzechniania Wydawnictw Naukowych PAN, Palac Kultury i Nauki, Warszawa
Portugal	Dias & Andrade Ltd., Libraria Portugal, rua o Carmo 70, Lisboa
Southern Rhodesia	Textbook Sales (PVT) Ltd., 67 Union Avenue, Salisbury
Romania	I.C.E. LIBRI Calea Victoriei, no. 126, P.O.Box 134-135, Bucuresti
Senegal	La Maison du Livre, 13 avenue Roume, B.P. 20-60 Dakar; Librairie Clairafrique, B.P. 2005, Dakar; Librairie 'Le Sénégal', B.P. 1594, Dakar
Singapore	Federal Publications. Sdn Bhd., Times House, River Valley Road, Singapore 9
South Africa	Van Schaik's Bookstore (Pty). Ltd., Libri Building, Church Street, P.O.Box 724, Pretoria
Spain	All publications: Editiones Iberoamericanas, S.A., calle de Oñate 15, Madrid 20; Distribución de Publicaciones del Consejo Superior de Investigaciones Cientificas, Vitrubio 16, Madrid 6; Librería del Consejo Superior de Investigaciones Cientificas, Egipcíacas 15, Barcelona. For 'The Courier' only: Ediciones Liber. apartado 17, Ondárroa (Viscaya)
Sudan	Al Bashir Bookshop, P.O.Box 1118, Khartoum
Sweden	All publications: A/B. C.E. Fritzes Kungl. Hovbokhandel, Fredsgatan 2, Box 16356, 103 27 Stockholm 16. For 'The Courier': Svenska FN-Förbundet, Vasgatan 15, IV, 101 23 Stockholm 1. Postgiro 18 46 92.

UNESCO (CONT'D)

Sales agents for UNESCO Publications: (cont'd)

Switzerland	Europa Verlag, Rämistrasse 5, Zurich; Librairie Payot, 6 rue Grenus, 1211 Genève 11
Tanzania	Dar es Salaam Bookshop, P.O.Box 9030, Dar es Salaam
Thailand	Suksapan Panit, Mansion 9, Rajdamnern Avenue, Bangkok
Togo	Librairie évangélique, B.P. 378, Lomé; Librairie du Bon Pasteur, B.P. 1164; Librairie moderne, B.P. 777, Lomé
Turkey	Librairie Hachette, 469 Istiklal Caddesi, Beyoglu, Istanbul
Uganda	Uganda Bookshop, P.O.Box 145, Kampala
U.S.S.R.	Mezhdunarodnaja Kniga, Moskva, G-200
United Kingdom	H.M. Stationery Office, P.O.Box 569, London SE1 9NH; Government bookshops: London, Belfast, Birmingham, Bristol, Cardiff, Edinburgh, Manchester
United States	Unesco Publications Center, P.O.Box 433, New York, N.Y. 10016
Uper Volta	Librairie Attie, B.P. 64, Ouagadougou, Librairie catholique 'Jeunesse d'Afrique', Ouagadougou
Venezuela	Libreria Historia, Monjas a Padre Sierra, Edificio Oeste 2, no.6 (frente al Capitolio), apartado de correos 7320-101, Caracas
Yugoslavia	Jugoslovenska Knjiga, Terazije 27, Beograd; Drzavna Zaluzba Slovenije Mestni Trg. 26, Ljubliana
Republic of Zaire	La Librairie, Institut politique congolais, B.P. 2307, Kinshasa. Commission nationale de la Republique du Zaire pour l'Unesco, Ministère de l'éducation nationale, Kinshasa

UNITED NATIONS INDUSTRIAL DEVELOPMENT ORGANIZATION

Felderhaus
Rathausplats 2
A91010 Vienna
AUSTRIA

UNITED NATIONS INSTITUTE FOR TRAINING AND RESEARCH

801 United Nations Plaza   or
New York   UN Office at Geneva
UNITED STATES OF AMERICA

UNITED NATIONS RESEARCH INSTITUTE FOR SOCIAL DEVELOPMENT

Palais des Nations
1211 Geneva 10
Switzerland

UNITED NATIONS SOCIAL DEFENCE RESEARCH INSTITUTE

Via Giulia 52
00186 Rome
ITALY

UNIVERSAL POSTAL UNION

Weltpoststrasse 4
CH 3000 Berne 15
SWITZERLAND

UNIVERSITY OF BOTSWANA, LESOTHO AND SWAZILAND

Roma
LESOTHO

WARSAW TREATY ORGANIZATION

c/o   Ministry of defence
Warsaw
POLAND

WEST AFRICAN ECONOMIC COMMUNITY

>P.O.Box 28
>Ouagadoudou
>UPPER VOLTA

WEST AFRICAN EXAMINATION COUNCIL

>7th Avenue Extension
>P.O.box 917
>Accra
>GHANA

WEST AFRICAN MONETARY UNION

>29 rue du Colisée
>75-Paris 8e
>FRANCE

WEST AFRICAN REGIONAL GROUP

>Secretariat provided by the Government of Liberia

WEST AFRICAN RICE DEVELOPMENT ASSOCIATION

>Monrovia
>LIBERIA

WESTERN EUROPEAN UNION

>9 Grosvenor Place
>London S.W.1
>GREAT BRITAIN

WORLD FOOD PROGRAM

>Viale delle Terme di Caracalla
>00100 Rome
>ITALY

WORLD HEALTH ORGANIZATION

>20 Avenue Appia
>1211 Geneve 27
>SWITZERLAND

Sales agents fo WHO:

Algérie	Société nationale d'édition et de diffusion, 3 bd. Zirout Youcef, Alger
Argentina	Librería de las Naciones, Cooperativa Ltda., Alsina 500, Buenos Aires; Editorial Sudamericana S.A., Humberto 1o 545 Buenos Aires
Australia	Australian Government Publishing Service, Sales and Distribution, P.O. Box 84, Canberra, A.C.T. 2600 (mail orders); AGPS Book Centre, 113-115 London Circuit, Canberra City; 347 Swanston St., Melbourne; Commonwealth Centre, 1-3 St. George's Terrace, Perth; Bank House, 315 George St., Sydney; Hunter Publications, 58A Gipps Street, Collingwood, Vic. 3066
Austria	Gerold & Co., I. Graben 31, Wien 1
Belgique	Office international de Librarie, 30 avenue Marnix, Bruxelles
Burma	see India, WHO Regional Office
Canada	Information Canada Bookstore, 171 Slater Street, Ottawa, Ontario KIA OS9; 1735 Barrington Street, Halifax, N.S.; Edifice Aeterna-Vie, 1182 ouest, rue Ste-Catherine, Montréal 110 (Qué.); 221 Yonge Street, Toronto 205, Ontario; 657 Granville Street, Vancouver 2, B.C.,: 393 Portage Avenue, Winnipeg, Manitoba.
Ceylon	see India, WHO Regional Office
Colombia	Distrilibros Ltd., Pío Alfonso Carcía, Carrera 4a, Nos. 36-119, Cartagena
Costa Rica	Imprenta y Librería Trejos S.A., Apartado 1313, San José
Cyprus	MAM, P.O.Box 1674, Nicosia
Denmark	Ejnar Munksgaard Ltd., Norregade 6, Kobenhavn
Ecuador	Librería Científica S.A., P.O.Box 362, Luque 223, Guayaquil
Egypt	Al Ahram Bookshop, 10 Avenue el Horreya, Alexandria
Espagne	Comercial Atheneum S.A., Consejo de Ciento 130-136, Barcelone 15; General Moscardó 29, Madrid 20; Librería Díaz de Santos, Lagasca 95, Madrid 6.

WORLD HEALTH ORGANIZATION (CONT'D)

Sales agents (cont'd)

Federal Republic of Germany	Govi-Verlag GmbH, Beethovenplatz 1-3, Frankfurt a.M.6; W.E. Saarbach, Postfach 1510, Follerstrasse 2, 5 Köln 1; Alex Horn, Spiegelgasse 9, 62 Wiesbaden
Fiji	The WHO Representative, P.O.Box 113, Suva
Finland	Akateeminen Kirjakauppa, Keskuskatu 2, Helsinki
France	Librairie Arnette, 2 rue Casimir-Delavigne, Paris VI
Grèce	G.C. Eleftheroudakis S.A., Librairie internationale, rue Nikis 4, Athènes
Haiti	Max Bouchereau, Librairie "A la Caravelle", Boîte postale 111B, Port-au-Prince
Hungary	Kultura, P.O.Box 149, Budapest 62; Akadémiai Könyvesbolt, Váci utca 22, Budapest V
Iceland	Snaebjörn Jonsson & Co., P.O.Box 1131, Hafnarstraeti 9, Reykjavik
India	WHO Regional Office for South-East Asia, World Health House, Indraprastha Estate, Ring Road, New Delhi 1; Oxford Books & Stationery Co., Scindia House, New Delhi; Sub-agent: 17 Part Street, Calcutta 16
Indonesia	see India, WHO Regional Office
Iran	Mesrob Grigorian, Naderi Avenue (Arbad-Guiv Building), Teheran
Ireland	The Stationery Office, Dublin
Israel	Heiliger & Co., 3 Nathan Strauss Street, Jerusalem
Italie	Edizioni Minerva Medica, Corso Bramante 83-85, Turin; via Lamarmora 3, Milan
Japan	Maruzen Co. Ltd., P.O. Box 5050, Tokyo International, 100-31 Japan
Kenya	The Caxton Press Ltd., Head Office: Gathani House, Huddersfield Road, P.O. Box 1742, Nairobi
Khmer Republic	The WHO Representative, P.O.Box 111, Phnom-Penh
Laos	The WHO Representative, P.O.Box 343, Vientiane
Luxembourg	Librairie Trausch-Schummer, Place du Théâtre, Luxembourg
Malaysia	The WHO Representative, P.O.Box 2550, Kuala Lumpur; Jubilee (Book) Store Ltd., 97 Jalan Tuanku Abdul Rahman, P.O.Box 629, Kuala Lumpur
Maroc	Editions La Porte, 281 avenue Mohammed V, Rabat
Mexico	La Prensa Médica Mexicana, Ediciones Cientificas, Paseo de las Facultades 26, Mexico 20, DF
Mongolia	see India, WHO Regional Office
Nepal	see India, WHO Regional Office
Netherlands	N.V. Maritinus Nijhoff's Boekhandel en Uitgevers Maatschappij, Lange Voorhout 9, 's-Gravenhage
New Zealand	Government Printing Office, Government Bookshops at: Rutland Street, P.O.Box 5344, Auckland; 130 Oxford Terrace, P.O.Box 1721, Christchurch; Alma Street, P.O.Box 857, Hamilton; Princes Street, P.O.Box 1104, Dunedin; Mulgrave Street, Private Bag, Wellington: R. Hill & Son Ltd., Ideal House, Cnr. Gilles Avenue & Eden Street, Newmarket, Auckland, S.E.1.
Nigeria	University Bookshop Nigeria, Ltd., University of Ibadan, Ibadan
Norway	Johan Grundt Tanum Bokhandel, Karl Johansgt, 43, Oslo 1.
Pakistan	Mirza Book Agency, 65 Shahrah Quaid-E. Azam, P.O.Box 729, Lahore 3
Paraguay	Agencia de Librerías Nizza S.A., Estrella No. 721, Asuncion
Pérou	Distribuidora Inca S.A., Apartado 3115, Emilio Althaus 470, Lima
Philippines 1	World Health Organization, Regional Office for the Western Pacific, P.O.Box 2932, Manila; The Modern Book Company Inc., P.O.Box 632, 926 Rizal Avenue, Manila
Poland	Skladnica Ksiegarska, ul. Mazowiecka 9, Warsaw (except periodicals); BKWZ Ruch, ul. Wronia 23, Warsaw (periodicals only)
Portugal	Livraria Rodriguez, 186 Rua Aurea, Lisboa
Replulif of Korea	The WHO Representative, Central P.O.Box 540, Seoul
Republic of Viet-Nam	The WHO Representative, P.O.Box 242, Saigon
Singapore	The WHO Representative, 144 Moulmein Road, G.P.O. Box 3457, Singapore 1
South Africa	Van Schaik's Bookstore (Pty) Ltd., P.O.Box 724, Pretoria
Suisse	Medizinischer Verlag Hans Huber, Länggass Strasse 76, 3000 Berne 9
Sweden	Aktiebolaget C.E. Fritzes Kungl. Hovbokhandel, Fredsgatan 2, Stockholm 16
Thailand	see India, WHO Regional Office
Tunisie	Société Tunisienne de Diffusion, 5 avenue de Carthage, Tunis
Turquie	Librairie Hachette, 469 avenue de l'Indépendance, Istanbul
Uganda	see address under Kenya
United Kingdom	H.M. Stationery Office: 49 High Holborn, London WC1V 6HB; 13a Castle Street, Edinburgh EH2 3AR; 109 St. Mary Street, Cardiff CF1 1JW; 80 Chichester Street, Belfast BT1 4JY; Brazennose Street, Manchester M60 8AS; 258 Broad Street, Brimingham B1 2HE; 50 Fairfax Street, Bristol BS1 3DE. All mail orders should be sent to P.O. Box 569, London SE1 9NH

WORLD HEALTH ORGANIZATION (CONT'D)

Sales agents (cont'd)

United Republic of Tanzania	see address under Kenya
United States of America	The American Public Health Association, Inc., 1015 Eighteenth St. N.W., Washington, D.C. 20036; United Nations Bookshop, New York, N.Y. 10017, (Retail only)
USSR	For readers in the USSR requiring Russian editions: Komsomolskij prospekt 18, Medicinskaja Kniga, Moscow: For readers outside the USSR requiring Russian editions: Kuzneckij most 18, Mezdunarodnaja Kniga, Moscow G-200
Venezuela	Editorial Interamericana de Venezuela C.A., Apartado 50785, Caracas; Librería del Este, A.V. Francisco de Miranda 52, Edificio Galipán, Caracas
Yougoslavie	Jugoslovenska Knjiga, Terazije 27/II, Beograd
Zaïre	Librairie du Zaïre, 12 avenue des Aviateurs, Kinshasa

Orders may also be addressed to the following address, but must be paid for in pounds sterling, US dollars or Swiss francs:

World Health Organization,
Distribution and Sales Service
1211 Geneve 27
SWITZERLAND

WORLD INTELLECTUAL PROPERTY ORGANIZATION

32 chemin des Colombettes
1211 Geneva 20
SWITZERLAND

WORLD METEOROLOGICAL ORGANIZATION

41 avenue Giuseppe Motta
1211 Geneve 20
SWITZERLAND

WORLD TOURISM ORGANIZATION

see   International union of official travel organisations

WORLD WEATHER WATCH

see   World meteorological organization

ZAMBIA-TANZANIA ROAD SERVICES LTD

Kitwe
ZAMBIA

u

LIST OF INTERGOVERNMENTAL ORGANIZATIONS ABBREVIATIONS

AAFRA	-	Association of African airlines
AARRO	-	Afro-Asian rural reconstruction organization
AAU	-	Association of African universities
ACABQ	-	Advisory committee on administrative and budgetary questions (UN)
ACC	-	Administrative committee on co-ordination (UN)
ADB	-	African development bank
ADB	-	Asian development bank
AFCAC	-	African civil aviation commission
AfPU	-	African postal union
AIDC	-	Asian industrial development council
ALO	-	Arab labour organization
ANZUS	-	Anzus council
AOC	-	Associated overseas countries (EC)
AOPU	-	Asian-Oceanic postal union
APEC	-	Asia-Pacific forestry commission
APO	-	Asian productivity organisation
APTU	-	African postal and telecommunications union
APU	-	Arab postal union
ARPEL	-	Asistencia reciproca petrolera estatal latino-americana=Mutual assistance of the Latin American government oil companies
ARUSHA	-	Association agreement EEC/Tanzania, Uganda and Kenya
ASBU	-	Arab States broadcasting union
ASEAN	-	Association of Southeast Asian nations
ASECNA	-	Agence pour la sécurité de la navigation aérienne en Afrique et à Madagascar
ASMO	-	Arab organisation for standardization and metrology
ASPCA	-	Asian and Pacific council
BCEAEC	-	Central bank of the States of Equatorial Africa and Cameroon
BCEAO	-	Central bank of the West African States
BENELUX	-	Benelux economic union
BID	-	Banco interamericano de desarrollo=Inter-American development bank
BIE	-	Bureau international des expositions=International exhibition bureau
BIPM	-	Bureau international des poids et mesures=International bureau of weights and measures
BIS	-	Bank for international settlements
CAARC	-	Commonwealth advisory aeronautical research council
CAB	-	Commonwealth agricultural bureau
CACM	-	Central American common market
CACTAL	-	Conferencia especializada sobre la aplicación de la ciencia y la technologia al desarrollo de America Latina=Specialized conference on the application of science and technology to Latin American development (OAS)
CAFRAD	-	African training and research centre in administration and development
CAMES	-	African and Malagasy higher education council
CARIFTA	-	Caribbean free trade association
CCC	-	Customs co-operation council
CCEAE	-	Conférence des chefs d'Etat de l'Afrique équatoriale= Conference of heads of State of Equatorial Africa
CCES	-	Conseil consultatif économique et social de l'Union économique Benelux=Benelux economic and social consultative council
CCOP	-	Co-ordinating committee off-shore prospecting
CCR	-	Commission centrale pour la navigation du Rhin= Central commission for the navigation of the Rhine
CCTA	-	Commission for technical co-operation in Africa south of the Sahara
CD	-	Commission du Danube=Danube commission
CE	-	Council of Europe
CEAO	-	Communauté économique de l'Afrique de l'Ouest= West African economic community
CEBV	-	Cattle and meat economic community of the Council of the entente States
CEC	-	Commission of European communities
CECAS	-	Conference of East and Central African States
CEIM	-	Centre for industrial studies of the Maghreb
CEMLA	-	Centro de estudios monetarios latinoamericanos= Centre for Latin American monetary studies
CENTO	-	Central treaty organization
CEPT	-	Conférence européenne des administrations des postes et des télécommunications=European conference of postal and telecommunications administrations
CERN	-	European organization for nuclear research
CESI	-	Centre for economic and social information (UN)
CETS	-	Conférence européenne des télécommunications par satellites=European conference on satellite communication
CFNI	-	Caribbean food and nutrition institute
CICA	-	Conférence internationale des contrôles d'assurances des Etats africains, français et malgache=International conference of African, French and Malagasy States on insurance supervision
CIDA	-	Comité interamericano de desarrollo agricola= Inter-American committee for agricultural development
CIDEM	-	Conseil interaméricain de la musique=Inter-American music council

CIEC	-	Commission internationale de l'état civil=International commission on civil status
CIECC	-	Consejo interamericano para la educación, la ciencia y la cultura=Inter-American council for education, science and culture
CIEH	-	Inter-African committee for hydraulic studies
CIES	-	Consejo interamericano economico y social=Inter-American economic and social council (OAS)
CIM	-	Comisión interamericana de mujeres=Inter-American commission of women (OAS)
CIOMS	-	Council for international organizations of medical sciences
CIPEC	-	Inter-governmental council of copper exporting countries
CIS	-	Centre international d'information de sécurité et d'hygiène du travail=International occupational safety and health information centre
CISS	-	Conferencia interamericana de seguridad social=Inter-American conference on social security
CLAF	-	Centro latino-americano de fisica=Latin American centre for physics
CMEA	-	Council for mutual economic assistance
COCESNA	-	Corporación centroamericana de servicios de navegación aerea=Central American air safety services corporation
COMALFA	-	Maghreb esparto bureau
COPAL	-	Cocoa producers' alliance
CPCM	-	Maghreb permanent consultative committee
DLCOEA	-	Desert locust control organisation for Eastern Africa
EAAFRO	-	East African agriculture and forestry research organisation
EAC	-	East African community
EADB	-	East African development bank
EAEC	-	East African examination council
EAEC	-	European atomic energy community
EAMF	-	European association of music festivals
EBU	-	European broadcasting union
EC	-	European communities
ECA	-	Economic commission for Africa (UN)
ECAC	-	European civil aviation conference
ECAFE	-	Economic commission for Asia and the Far East
ECCA	-	Autorité monétaire des Caraïbes orientales=East Caribbean currency authority
ECE	-	Economic commission for Europe (UN)
ECLA	-	Economic commission for Latin America (UN)
ECMT	-	European conference of ministers of transport
ECOSOC	-	Economic and social council (UN)
ECSC	-	European coal and steel community
EDEP	-	Institute for economic development and planning
EEC	-	European economic community
EFTA	-	European free trade association
EIB	-	European investment bank
EIER	-	Inter-States school for rural engineering
ELDO	-	European space vehicle launcher development organisation
EMBO	-	Organisation européenne de biologie moléculaire= European molecular biology organization
EPPO	-	European and Mediterranean plant protection organisation
ESC	-	Economic and social committee (EC)
ESRO	-	European space research organization
EURATOM	-	European atomic energy community
EUROCHEMIC	-	European company for the chemical processing of irradiated fuels
EUROCONTROL-		European organization for the safety of air navigation
EUROFIMA	-	European company for the financing of railway rolling stock
FAO	-	Food and agriculture organization
GA	-	General assembly (UN)
GATT	-	General agreement on tariffs and trade
GFCM	-	General fisheries council for the Mediterranean
Hôtafric	-	Société de développement hôtelier et touristique
IACO	-	Inter-African coffee organisation
IADB	-	Inter-American defense board
IAEA	-	International atomic energy agency
IAIAS	-	Inter-American institute of agricultural sciences
IANEC	-	Inter-American nuclear energy commission
IASI	-	Inter-American statistical institute
IATTC	-	Inter-American tropical tuna commission
IBE	-	International bureau of education
IBEC	-	International bank for economic co-operation
IBRD	-	International bank for reconstruction and development
ICAC	-	International cotton advisory committee
ICAITI	-	Instituto centroamericano de investigación y tecnologia industrial=Central American research institute for industry
ICAO	-	International civil aviation organization
ICAP	-	Instituto centroamericano de administración publica= Central American institute of public administration
ICAP	-	Inter-American committee on the alliance for progress
ICC	-	International children's centre
ICC	-	International computation centre
ICC	-	International computing centre (UN)
ICCAT	-	International commission for the conservation of Atlantic tunas
ICEM	-	Intergovernmental committee for European migration
ICES	-	International council for the exploration of the sea

ICITO	-	Interim commission for the international trade organization (UN)
ICJ	-	International court of justice
ICMMP	-	International committee of military medicine and pharmacy
ICO	-	International coffee organization
ICSID	-	International centre for settlement of investment disputes
IDA	-	International development association
IDB	-	Inter-American development bank
IDCAS	-	Industrial development centre for Arab States
IFC	-	International finance corporation
IFRB	-	International frequency registration board (ITU)
IGC	-	Intergovernmental copyright committee
IGO	-	Inter-governmental organizations
IHB	-	International hydrographic bureau
IIB	-	Institut international des brevets=International patent institute
IIB	-	International investment bank
IIEP	-	International institute for educational planning
III	-	Inter-American Indian institute
IILA	-	Istituto italo-latino americano=Italian-Latin American institute
IIN	-	Instituto interamericano del niño=Inter-American children's institute
IIR	-	International institute of refrigeration
ILC	-	International law commission
ILCE	-	Instituto latinoamericano de la comunicación educativa=Latin American educational communication institute
ILO	-	International labour organisation
ILPES	-	Instituto latinoamericano de planificación economica y social=Latin American institute for economic and social planning
IMCO	-	Inter-governmental maritime consultative organization
IMF	-	International monetary fund
INCAP	-	Institute of nutrition of Central America and Panama
INCB	-	International narcotics control board
INPFC	-	International North Pacific fisheries commission
INTELSAT	-	International telecommunication satellite consortium
IOB	-	Inter-organisation board for information systems and related activities (UN)
IOC	-	Intergovernmental oceanographic commission
IOOC	-	International olive oil council
IPC	-	International poplar commission
IPFC	-	Indo-Pacific fisheries council
IRC	-	International rice commission
IRLSC	-	International red locust control service
IRSG	-	International rubber study group
IRU	-	International relief union
ISC	-	International sericultural commission
ISMAC	-	Israel-Syria mixed armistice commission (UN)
ISVS	-	International secretariat for volunteer service
ITC	-	Inter-American travel congresses
ITC	-	International trade centre (UNCTAD/GATT)
ITIC	-	International Tsunami information center
ITU	-	International telecommunications union
IUOTO	-	International union of official travel organizations
IWC	-	International whaling commission
IWO	-	International vine and wine office
IWSG	-	International wool study group
LAFTA	-	Latin American free trade association
LAS	-	League of Arab States
LCBC	-	Lake Chad basin commission
NATO	-	North Atlantic treaty organization
NGO	-	Non-governmental organizations
OAMCAF	-	African and Malagasy coffee organisation
OAMPI	-	The African and Malagasy industrial property office
OAPEC	-	Organization of Arab petroleum exporting countries
OAS	-	Organization of American States
OAU	-	Organization of African unity
OCAM	-	Organisation commune africaine, malgache et mauritienne=African, Malagasy and Mauritian common organisation
OCCGE	-	Organisation de coordination et de coopération pour la lutte contre les grandes endémies
OCDN	-	Organisation commune Dahomey-Niger des chemins de fer
OCLALAV	-	Organisation commune de lutte anti-acridienne et de lutte antiaviaire
OCTI	-	Office central des transports internationaux par chemins de fer=Central office for international railway transport
ODECA	-	Organization of Central American States
ODTA	-	Organisation pour le développement du tourisme africain=Organisation for the development of African tourism
OECD	-	Organisation for economic cooperation and development
OEI	-	Oficina de educación Ibero-americana=Ibero-American bureau of education
OERS	-	Organisation des Etats riverains du fleuve Sénégal=Organization of Senegal Riparian States
OICMA	-	Organisation internationale contre le criquet migrateur africain=International African migratory locust organisation
OIE	-	Office international des épizooties=International office of epizootics
OIML	-	Organisation internationale de métrologie légale=International organization of legal metrology
OIRSA	-	Organismo internacional regional de sanidad agropecuaria=Regional international organisation of plant protection and animal health
OMVS	-	Organisation for the development of the Senegal river
OPANAL	-	Agência para a proscricào de armas nucleares na América Latina=Agency for the prohibition of nuclear weapons in Latin America
OPEC	-	Organization of the petroleum exporting countries
OSShD	-	Organisation for the collaboration of railways
PAC	-	Pan American highway congresses
PAHO	-	Pan American health organisation
PAIGH	-	Pan American institute of geography and history
PIARC	-	Permanent international association of road congresses
PIBAC	-	Permanent international bureau of analytical chemistry of human and animal food
PSWO	-	Picture and sound world organisation
PUAS	-	Postal union of the Americas and Spain
RCD	-	Regional co-operation for development
SADIAMIL	-	African society for the development of the millet- and sorghum-based food industry
SC	-	Security Council (UN)
SEAMES	-	Southeast Asian ministers of education secretariat
SEATO	-	South-East Asia treaty organisation
SIECA	-	Secretaria permanente del Tratado general de integración económica centroamericana=General treaty on Central American economic integration
SPATC	-	South Pacific air transport council
SPC	-	South Pacific commission
SPF	-	South Pacific forum
STPCM	-	Secrétariat technique permanent de la Conférence des ministres de l'éducation nationale des états d'expression française d'Afrique et de Madagascar=Standing technical secretariat for the conferences of ministers of national education in French-speaking African and Malagasy States
SWAFAC	-	South West Atlantic fisheries advisory commission
TC	-	Trusteeship council (UN)
UAMBD	-	Union africaine et malgache de banques pour le développement=African and Malagasy union of development banks
UAMPT	-	Union africaine et malgache des postes et télécommunications=African and Malagasy postal telecommunications union
UDEAC	-	Union douanière et économique de l'Afrique centrale=Central African customs and economic union
UEAC	-	Union of Central African States
UMOA	-	Union monétaire ouest africain=West African monetary union
UN	-	United Nations
UNACAST	-	United Nations advisory committee on the application of science and technology to development: regional group for Africa
UNAT	-	United Nations administrative tribunal
UNCA	-	United Nations correspondents association
UNCACK	-	United Nations civil assistance command, Korea
UNCCP	-	United Nations conciliation commission for Palestine
UNCIO	-	United Nations conference on international organization, San Francisco
UNCIP	-	United Nations commission for India and Pakistan
UNCITRAL	-	United Nations commission on international trade law
UNCK	-	United Nations commission on Korea
UNCOPUOS	-	United Nations committee on the peaceful uses of outer space
UNCP	-	United Nations conference of plenipotentiaries
UNCSAT	-	United Nations conference on science application and technology for the benefit of the less developed areas
UNCTAD	-	United Nations conference on trade and development
UNCURK	-	United Nations commission for the unification and rehabilitation of Korea
UNDC	-	United Nations disarmament commission
UNDP	-	United Nations development programme
UNDPI	-	United Nations department of public information
UNEF	-	United Nations emergency force
UNEP	-	United Nations environment programme
UNESCO	-	United Nations educational, scientific and cultural organisation
UNETAP	-	United Nations expanded technical assistance programme
UNFICYP	-	United Nations peace-keeping force in Cyprus
UNHCR	-	United Nations. High commissioner for refugees
UNICEF	-	United Nations children's fund
UNIDO	-	United Nations industrial development organization
UNIDROIT	-	International institute for the unification of private law
UNIO	-	United Nations information office
UNITAR	-	United Nations institute for training and research
UNMEM	-	United Nations Middle East mission
UNMOCIP	-	United Nations military observer group in India and Pakistan
UNRISD	-	United Nations research institute for social development

UNSDRI	-	United Nations social defence research institute	URTNA	-	African national television and broadcasting union
UNTSO	-	United Nations truce supervision organization in Palestine	WAEC	-	West African examination council
UNRWA	-	United Nations relief and works agency for Palestine refugees in the Near East	WARDA	-	West African rice development association
			Warsaw pact	-	Warsaw treaty organization
			WEU	-	Western European union
UNVP	-	United Nations volunteers programme	WFP	-	World food program
UPOV-	-	Union internationale pour la protection des obtentions végétales-International union for the protection of new varieties of plants	WHO	-	World health organization
			WIPO	-	World intellectual property organization
			WMO	-	World meteorological organization
UPU	-	Universal postal union	WTO	-	World tourism organization
			WWW	-	World weather watch

The text of this book
was keyboarded in Geneva, Switzerland
under the supervision of the author Mr Th. D. Dimitrov
and the edition was printed in Great Britain by offset lithography, and bound,
at The University Press, Glasgow, by Robert MacLehose & Co. Ltd
for the publishers
International University Publications: London, England
who reserve all rights in the book
including the right to reproduce the book or parts thereof in any form
or by any means.
The paper used for the text is
Dalmore Antique Laid, 85 gsm
and the cloth used for the binding is
Winchester Buckram
The book was published simultaneously
in the United States of America by the American Library Association
for the North American market.